Contents

ETHNIC
BARGAINING

ETHNIC
BARGAINING

THE PARADOX OF
MINORITY EMPOWERMENT

Erin K. Jenne

Cornell University Press

ITHACA AND LONDON

First published 2007 by Cornell University Press

Printed in the United States of America

Library of Congress Cataloging-in-Publication Data
Jenne, Erin K.
    Ethnic bargaining : the paradox of minority empowerment / Erin K.
Jenne.
        p. cm.
    Includes bibliographical references and index.
    ISBN–13: 978-0-8014-4498-2 (cloth : alk. paper)
    ISBN–10: 0-8014-4498-5 (cloth : alk. paper)
    1. Ethnic conflict—Europe, Eastern—History—20th century.
2. Ethnic conflict—Europe, Central—History—20th century.   3. Minor-
ities—Europe, Eastern—Political activity.   4. Minorities—Europe,
Central—Political activity.   5. Europe, Eastern—Ethnic relations
—History—20th century.   6. Europe, Central—Ethnic relations—History
—20th century.   I. Title.
    DJK26.J46 2006
    305.8009437—dc22
                                            2006023304

Cornell University Press strives to use environmentally responsible suppliers and materials to the fullest extent possible in the publishing of its books. Such materials include vegetable-based, low-VOC inks and acid-free papers that are recycled, totally chlorine-free, or partly composed of nonwood fibers. For further information, visit our website at www.cornellpress.cornell.edu.

Cloth printing   10 9 8 7 6 5 4 3 2 1

To the memory

of my Grandparents

Acknowledgments

his book is the culmination of nearly a decade of research and thinking about the politics of group claim making. A great many people have guided me along my path, which at times has been anything but linear. Despite this, I will endeavor to impose a kind of order upon the thanks I am about to dispense.

To begin with, I thank the Belfer Center for Science and International Affairs at Harvard University, and specifically the International Security Program, which generously provided me with two years of postdoctoral funding. My years at Belfer afforded me the opportunity to exchange my ideas with outstanding scholars of security studies, who greatly assisted me in refining my theoretical framework and research design. I thank in particular Sean Lynn-Jones, Steven Miller, and Stephen Walt—each of whom pushed me to extend my arguments, particularly with regard to "the big idea" underlying the project. Fiona Adamson, Samina Ahmed, Ivan Arreguín-Toft, David Edelstein, Monica Duffy Toft, and James Walsh each read and commented on portions of my early draft chapters. Barry Posen gave me very useful feedback on the Sudeten German chapter. I especially wish to express my gratitude to Gregory Mitrovich, who read an early draft of the manuscript, offered ideas for further development, and gave me excellent advice with respect to publication. Mark Kramer, too, read the manuscript in its raw form and gave me useful pointers for revision, particularly concerning my Slovak and Moravian cases.

The World Peace Foundation at Harvard University co-sponsored my fellowship, providing me with office space and unlimited cups of coffee as well as exposure to first-rate scholars from various disciplines, both junior and established. I thank Robert Rotberg for pushing me to contextualize and historicize my analysis and for including me in his many projects. David Carment, another WPF fellow, helped me situate my work in the broader literature on third-party intervention, and Maria Koinova offered me insights into the ways in which ethnic politics have played out in the lives of people in the Balkans.

I am greatly indebted to the institutions that funded my doctoral training and subsequent research. The Department of Political Science at Stanford University supported my first several years of graduate study, which taught me to think like a social scientist. The American Council of Learned Societies, the Stanford Center for Russian and East European Studies, the Deutscher Akademischer Austauschdienst, and the Foreign Language and Area Studies program underwrote three summers of language training in Czech and German—so critical for interviewing and conducting archival work in the field. A grant from the Institute for the Study of World Politics afforded me the resources to spend over a year in Prague doing field research. The Institute for International Studies, the Center for International Security and Cooperation (CISAC), and the MacArthur Foundation later provided me with a predoctoral fellowship and office space for writing up the manuscript. I am especially grateful to Lynn Eden and Scott Sagan and to many others who made my stay at CISAC both fun and productive. I remember it as one of my very best academic experiences.

During fourteen months of fieldwork in the Czech Republic, Slovakia, and Romania, I obtained vital assistance from colleagues and friends at the Institute of Sociology at the Czech Academy of Sciences in Prague. Michal Illner, head of the Sociology Institute, and research fellow Alena Nedomová helped set up meetings with various cabinet officials and parliamentary deputies in the Czech Republic and gave me my initial contacts in Slovakia and Romania. Without their generous assistance, I would not have obtained interviews with numerous politicians, ethnic party leaders, minority activists, scholars, and journalists in each of the three countries. I owe many thanks to Varujan Pambuccian—my key contact in Bucharest. Besides being wonderfully entertaining, he took considerable time out of his busy schedule as a deputy in parliament to help arrange interviews with minority representatives, Romanian cabinet officials, activists, and leaders of Romanian nationalist and ethnic Hungarian parties—sometimes acting as interpreter. Several regional scholars and writers gave me direction for my work. Robert Keprt, Tomáš Kostelecký, Milan Pospíšil, and Jonathan Stein each contributed to my project and offered me friendship while I was abroad. Eagle Glassheim, Ari Shapiro, and Marci Shore, fellow doctoral students in the Czech Republic, helpfully advised me on the ins and outs of archival work in Prague.

Many people have contributed to the theory development and composition, sometimes in ways they might not have predicted. David Abernethy, David Baron, James Fearon, Stephen Krasner, David Laitin, James Morrow, Kenneth Shepsle, and Philippe Schmitter all read drafts of my earlier work and offered invaluable feedback. I especially thank Barry O'Neill for giving me excellent pointers on my game theoretic model and for being a good and entertaining friend—not necessarily in that order. David Primo, too, assisted me greatly with respect to the formal model. My colleagues at Stanford— Louis Ayala, Ian Bremmer, Elizabeth Beaumont, Kathleen Collins, Jennifer Daniels, Robert D'Onofrio, Tanisha Fazal, Tonya Putnam, Carol St. Louis, Jonathan Terra, Svetlana Tsalik, and Marie-Joëlle Zahar—gave me useful advice in the early stages of my dissertation research. Valerie Bunce was kind enough to read the final draft of the manuscript, which greatly helped me to situate the argument in the recent literature on ethnic politics.

I particularly wish to express my gratitude to my advisers. The success of this project is greatly due to the guidance, support, and constructive feedback I received from each of them. Ronald Suny encouraged me think more critically about the politics of identity in Eastern Europe, helping me to contextualize my narrative using insights from nationalism studies. Barry Weingast spent hours helping me develop the formal analysis. He has also given me invaluable professional support and encouragement that continues to this day. Larry Diamond helped me tremendously in the initial formulation and execution of my empirical work. The strength of my comparative framework owes greatly to his careful, incisive remarks. Just as important, Larry could always be relied on for much-needed words of encouragement and advice—from the early research and writing to the final stages of the publication process. Finally, I cannot imagine having a more wonderful graduate adviser than David Holloway. David has always exemplified the highest standards of personal and professional integrity, a model to which I aspire. He has also been a true mentor and has supported my work well after graduate school. I am a great admirer of his, both as a scholar and a person, and feel lucky to have had the opportunity to work with him.

A special thank you to my editor, Roger Haydon, who is the essence of what an editor should be. He steered this project from the beginning and helped me every step of the way. He could always be counted on for thoughtful criticism—on both the theory and the empirics—and has been very supportive in the course of a lengthy review process. Thanks also to three anonymous reviewers who gave me extremely useful advice for revising all parts of the book.

In the final stages of writing, Stephen Saideman read much of the manuscript and provided me with perceptive feedback on the security dimension of my project. Patrick James, too, offered tremendously helpful suggestions, particularly with regard to handling various obstacles in the revisions process. Hurst Hannum, Philip Roeder, Ulrich Sedelmeier, Ivan Szelenyi, Sidney Tarrow, and Milada Anna Vachudova each read portions of my manuscript and gave me useful commentary on my theoretical framework. I also thank my friends and colleagues at Central European University who have made my life in Budapest such a rewarding personal and professional experience. Alexander Astrov, Nitsan Chorev, Karl Hall, Carol Harrington, Elissa Helms, Nicole Lindstrom, Alexander Maxwell, and Tibor Meszmann read drafts of my empirical chapters and offered practical advice for refining my analytical narrative. Thanks also to Stephen Deets, Sherrill Stroschein, Zoltán Alpár Szász at the University of Babeş-Bolyai in Cluj-Napoca and Zoltán Kántor of the László Teleki Institute in Budapest, who assisted me in revising my Hungarian chapter. Thanks to Beáta Huszka, Jana Kolaříková, Robert Safa, and Kateřina Svíčková for excellent research assistance.

My students, particularly those from the region, have helped me connect the theory in the book to the realities of how minority politics affect people in their day-to-day lives—reminding me never to forget the human element of these dramas.

Finally, I thank my family for being solidly behind me through all my crises and triumphs, for loving me for the person I am and not for what I have accomplished. To my mother, Linda Peterson, and to Ed Peterson, for offering me unconditional support and a sympathetic ear. To my sister Julie and cousin Serena, for giving me love and companionship, making me feel closely connected even across a great ocean. Last, but by no means least, to my grandparents, Iva and Carl Jenne, who have been an inspiration to me throughout my life. I dedicate this book to their memory.

Erin K. Jenne

Budapest, Hungary

Abbreviations

CDP	Civic Democratic Party [Czech]
CF	Civic Forum [Czech]
CISAC	Center for International Security and Cooperation
CoE	Council of Europe
CSCE	Commission on Security and Cooperation in Europe
CSEMADOK	Cultural Association of Hungarian Workers of Czechoslovakia [in Slovakia]
DAHR	Democratic Alliance of Hungarians in Romania
DC	Democratic Convention [in Romania]
DCVH	Democratic Community of Vojvodina Hungarians [in Yugoslavia]
DSAP	German Social Democratic Party [Sudeten Germans in Czechoslovakia]
DSK	Democratic Alliance of Kosovo
Fidesz	Fiatal Demokraták Szövetsége (Alliance of Young Democrats); since 1992, Fidesz—Magyar Polgári Szövetség (Fidesz—Hungarian Civic Union) [in Hungary]
GRP	Greater Romania Party
HCNM	High Commissioner on National Minorities
HDCM	Hungarian Christian Democrats [Czechoslovakia/ Slovakia]
HSD-SMS	Movement for Self-Government of Moravia and Silesia [in Czechoslovakia]

IHI	Independent Hungarian Initiative [in Czechoslovakia/Slovakia]
KB	Kameradschaftsbund [Sudeten German in Czechoslovakia]
KLA	Kosovo Liberation Army
MDF	Hungarian Democratic Forum [in Hungary]
MDS	Movement for a Democratic Slovakia [in Czechoslovakia/Slovakia]
MNS	Moravian National Party [in Czechoslovakia]
MOH	Moravian Civic Movement [in Czechoslovakia]
NATO	North Atlantic Treaty Organization
NGOs	nongovernmental organizations
NSF	National Salvation Front [in Romania]
ODA	Občanská Demokratická Aliance (Civic Democratic Alliance) [Czech]
OSCE	Organization for Security and Co-operation in Europe
PAV	Public Against Violence [Slovak]
PDSR	Party of Social Democracy in Romania
PKK	Kurdistan Workers Party
PUNR	National Unity Party of Romanians
SDK	Slovak Democratic Coalition [in Slovakia]
SdP	Sudeten German Party [in Czechoslovakia]
SMK	Hungarian Coalition [in Slovakia]
SMS	Society for Moravia and Silesia [in Czechoslovakia]
SNP	Slovak National Party [in Czechoslovakia/Slovakia]
StB	Státní bezpečnost (the communist secret service) [in Czechoslovakia]
TULF	Tamil United Liberation Front
UNMIK	United Nations Mission in Kosovo
UNPO	Unrepresented Nations and Peoples Organisation
VDA	Verein für Deutschtum im Ausland [in Germany]
VR	Volksdeutscher Rat [in Germany]

Introduction

The vast majority of violent conflicts in the past half-century have taken place at the substate level, including the recent or ongoing wars in Congo, Colombia, Palestine, India, Rwanda, Burundi, Sudan, the Philippines, Indonesia, Myanmar, Yugoslavia, Angola, Nigeria, Azerbaijan, Moldova, Russia, and Georgia.[1] In the 1990s, only 8 of the 110 armed conflicts around the world were between states. Most of the remaining wars were waged between minorities and their governments over demands for national self-determination.[2] In prosecuting these campaigns, the leaders of resistance movements have used terrorism and guerilla warfare to achieve autonomy for the minorities they claim to represent. Cases include the Palestinians in Israel; the Tamils in Sri Lanka; the Chechen separatists in Russia; the Transdniestrians in Moldova; the Kashmiris in India; the Kosovar Albanians in Yugoslavia; the newly independent East Timorese; and the periodically secessionist Acehnese in Indonesia. Lacking established protocols for halting violence at the substate level, such conflicts can drag on for years or even decades, as we have seen in Sudan, Ethiopia, Angola, Northern Ireland, Palestine, and Cyprus.

This book addresses important puzzles that lie at the heart of these struggles. On the macro-level, it investigates why ethnicity[3] is still so politically salient—why so many internal conflicts are waged in the name of self-determination and why tribal conflicts persist in the face of modernization and globalization. I suggest that the discourse of minority rights and self-determination—promulgated by the victors of World War I to serve their geopolitical interests and ensure the stability of the postwar order—effectively constructed both the category of national minorities and the methods they later used to challenge their governments. Today, minority leaders around the world employ this discourse as a means of extracting concessions from their state centers. In some cases, this has improved the status of marginalized groups. In other cases, however, it has worsened and prolonged conflicts at the substate level.

On the micro-level, this book explores why minority leaders vary the intensity of their demands (sometimes rapidly) over time while their grievances remain relatively constant. To illustrate the bargaining logic underlying this behavior, I introduce a model that formalizes the interactions between minority representatives and their host government in the presence of an external lobby actor.[4] The central prediction of the model is that when the minority's external patron credibly signals interventionist intent, minority leaders are likely to radicalize their demands against the center, even when the government has committed itself to moderation. It follows that the successful mediation of triadic conflicts is possible only after relations have been normalized between the minority's host government and lobby actor at the international level. This requires de-triangulating the conflict into separate, and thus more tractable, dyadic disputes between the state government and external lobbyist, on the one hand, and the majority and minority, on the other.[5]

The Puzzle of Minority Radicalization

The literature on minority mobilization is vast, particularly with respect to secessionism and irredentism.[6] Theories of mobilization may be divided broadly into structural and dynamic variants. Structural theories, in turn, fall into three broad subcategories (see table I.1).

Primordialist or essentialist arguments hold that nations today have always existed in one form or other as "proto-nations" or "ethnies" with cultural roots that extend far back in time. Once a group has "awakened" to its identity as a nation in the modern sense, it is only natural that it will seek self-determination—through violence, if necessary. This logic leads us to expect that groups with distinctive national identities will ultimately mobilize around separatist demands in order to achieve the nation-state ideal. Thus, the Chechens sought to secede from the Russian Federation due to profound ethnic differences between the Chechens and Russians. Similarly, the Sudeten Germans in Czechoslovakia rallied around irredentism because they saw themselves as a constituent part of a larger German nation rather than an ethnic German minority in a Slavic state.[7]

More nuanced social psychological accounts acknowledge that ethnic groups are constructed social forms as opposed to organic entities that developed naturally over time.[8] However, because human beings are tribal by

Table I.1. Theories of minority radicalization

Theory	Causal logic			
Structural theories				
Primordialism/essentialism Economic theories/grievances Institutionalist theories	Structural conditions (constant)	+ ? (variable)	→	Minority demands (variable)
Dynamic theories				
Elite-based accounts	Elite incentives (variable)		→	Minority demands (variable)
Ethnic security dilemma/commitment problems	Ethnic fears (variable)		→	Minority demands (variable)
Ethnic bargaining	Bargaining leverage (variable)		→	Minority demands (variable)

nature, their primary loyalties lie with their perceived community—be it an ethnic group, tribe, or nation—for which they are very often willing to fight and die.[9] Roger Petersen advances an explicitly psychological theory of ethnic mobilization, arguing that four human emotions—fear, hatred, resentment, and rage—account for both the nature and intensity of ethnic violence. He allows that these emotions must be triggered by external events, but asserts that "the motivation to participate in or support ethnic violence and discrimination [is] inherent in human nature."[10] Petersen thus provides insights into the psychological bases of ethnic mobilization, while remaining agnostic as to what sets this mechanism into motion.

Stuart Kaufman sheds light on another aspect of ethnic mobilization by unpacking the narratives that transmit human emotions into collective action. He begins by observing that ethnic entrepreneurs could not stir up mass hatred if there was not some preexisting historical understanding to support their racist vitriol. According to his "symbolic politics" theory of ethnic violence, "people respond to ethnic symbols and mobilize for war only if a widely known and accepted ethnic myth-symbol complex justifies hostility to the other group."[11] Thus, it might not have been possible to rally the Serbs against the Croats in 1990s Yugoslavia had there not been a collective memory of crimes committed against them by Croatia's Ustaše regime during World War II.[12]

A related set of theories holds that preexisting group traits such as size, location, and territorial compactness have a direct impact on minority mobilization. Stephen Van Evera argues, for example, that groups that can be easily "rescued" by their homeland states are unlikely to rally around separatism because their very ease of rescue deters their governments from discriminating against them. At the same time, groups for which ethnic rescue is impossible—because they are either too small or sparsely populated—are also unlikely to mobilize for secession due to the infeasibility of such goals. If, however, ethnic rescue is possible but difficult—when the minority is separated from its homeland state by "enemy territory" or when there is significant ethnic intermingling on the local level—there may be incentives for "rescuers to jump through any windows of opportunity that arise."[13] Monica Toft advances a different kind of geographical argument, positing that groups that are concentrated within a "minority region" are more likely to view this territory as their homeland and consequently non-negotiable or "indivisible." If the center or majority also deems this region indivisible from the state, then secessionist conflict may emerge.[14] Whether it is primordial ties, human emotions, collective understandings, or ethnic geography—the above theories all hold that relatively invariant traits play a crucial role in ethnic mobilization.

A second set of structural arguments—*economic theories*—posits that underlying economic disparities between the minority and majority may over time give rise to demands for secession or irredentism. In cases where the region is rich (Slovenia in the former Yugoslavia), its leaders may seek political independence in order to avoid subsidizing a relatively impoverished center. Where the region is poor (Slovakia in the former Czechoslovakia), minority representatives may pursue secession to prevent exploitation by a relatively advanced center.[15] Similarly, *relative deprivation* or grievance theories hold that groups suffering economic discrimination or income disparities will mobilize around collective demands for redress once they have the opportunity or the resources to do so.[16] In this view, minorities will endure significant repression or intergroup inequalities if they are politically weak, as seen in the cases of Jews and Roma in interwar Europe. Mobilization upon economic frustration is only likely when political openings emerge to facilitate collective action. While these accounts have a strong intuitive appeal, recent empirical work casts doubt on the causal influence that either regional disparities or other economic grievances have on group radicalization.[17]

The economic factors that *do* appear to matter are those that directly empower a group to rebel. These include economic incentives for individual members to engage in rebellion (the expected benefits of fighting versus the costs of withdrawing from the normal economy), funding from diasporas, the low cost of recruits, and the existence of primary commodities available for extortion. Thus, economic considerations mainly come into play—at least when it comes to ethnic violence—insofar as they leverage the strategic power of the group.[18]

A third set of structural theories, *institutionalist* or *constructivist* accounts, posits that arrangements for minority autonomy give rise to separatism by creating salient national identities and by providing focal points around which independence movements can take shape.[19] Ronald Suny notes that although the Soviet Nationalities Policies had been implemented to placate and hopefully homogenize the Soviet peoples, they instead created national forms upon which individuals could mobilize for independence as the Soviet empire began to collapse.[20] Dmitry Gorenburg extends this argument by showing exactly *how* these institutions mobilized the masses both "directly, by creating constituencies that support nationalism and providing them with resources, and indirectly, by shaping collective identities and creating social networks that foster the spread of nationalism among the populace."[21] In the Soviet Union and Yugoslavia, minorities with republican status were particularly primed for independence because they already had the trappings of statehood, including banks, national academies, local governments, and communist parties. Groups with republican status therefore had a tendency to pursue secession, whereas most provinces, regions, and oblasts did not.[22] Philip Roeder posits that successful nation-state projects may even *require* preexisting "segmental institutions"—arrangements of minority autonomy at the substate level—that can "align" the various factors necessary to achieve political independence.[23]

The second institutional story has to do with the weakening of the center itself. Given that the mobilizational power of the minority is measured against the repressive power of the state, it follows that when the state center is overstretched or incapacitated, the relative strength of the group is correspondingly enhanced. Valerie Bunce observes that the implosion of Soviet authority was at least as important as the strengthening of the titular minorities in the destruction of the Yugoslav and Soviet states.[24] The same could be said of the nineteenth-century Habsburg and Ottoman Empires, whose constituent nations gained power as their imperial centers went down the path of long, slow decline.

Theories focusing on structural variables such as ethnic geography, social psychological factors, autonomous institutions, and underlying grievances have enriched our understanding as to why some groups engage in separatism and ethnic violence whereas others do not. Although the relative causal weight of these factors varies from case to case, each represents an important piece of the puzzle of minority radicalization. Nonetheless, these arguments tend to overemphasize the impact of domestic or individual-level variables on the process of mobilization. The international scholarship, meanwhile, focuses overly on inanimate features of the *system*—including international norms, global finance, conflict spillover, and demonstration effects.[25] What is missing in the literature is a nuanced analysis of the ways in which *external actors*—and particularly regional players—influence minority behavior at the substate level. The theory of ethnic bargaining aims to address this gap. The theory developed in this book contributes to existing accounts in a second way by demonstrating how bargaining dynamics interact with structural features in the environment to produce radicalization (see table I.2). In doing so, it helps account for the surprising fluctuations in group claims over time. For example, separatist leaders periodically abandon their quest for sovereignty in return for a place in the government or some other side payment (e.g., the Malay-Muslims in Thailand and the Kewris of Mauritania). Others have made 180-degree reversals in their stated aims. The Baluchi leaders in Pakistan, for example, sought statehood when Pakistan gained independence, but later reverted to an integrationist stance. By the mid-1970s, however, they were again calling for sovereignty. Very often minority elites seek independence during a regime change, only to request effective re-annexation a few years (or even months) later. The leadership of Belarus in the former Soviet Union and the Bougainvilleans in Papua New Guinea are examples of the latter pattern.[26]

Two other theoretical approaches claim insight into the timing and intensity of intercommunal conflict. *Elite theories* broadly hold that political leaders mobilize people on an ethnic basis to maintain popular support in the face of international or domestic change.[27] V. P. Gagnon, Jr., for example, argues that ethnic violence "is provoked by elites in order to create a domestic political context where ethnicity is the only politically relevant identity." This strategy enables "endangered elites [to] fend off domestic challengers who seek to mobilize the population against the status quo."[28]

While most of these theories focus on the behavior of state leaders, it may be argued that *minority* leaders too, play the ethnic card for private gain. In his account of the Chechen independence movement, Valery Tishkov notes that secessionism

> is by no means always based on plans for improving the life of the entire population; indeed, it most often promises the contrary. However, for the initiators of independence and a certain part of the population, a "free state" regime can bring quick rewards, including economic ones.[29]

By making temporal predictions, instrumentalist theories would appear to account for the timing of minority radicalization (see table I.1). However, as a causal mechanism, elite interests do not tell us very much. For one thing, there are certainly more opportunistic elites than there are nationalist movements. Why don't self-aggrandizing or threatened leaders everywhere play the ethnic card? Although nationalists dominated the political landscapes of postcommunist Slovakia, Croatia, and Serbia, they were marginalized in Poland, the Czech Republic, and Bulgaria. Second, the fortunes of ethnic entrepreneurs can be seen to wax and wane over time. The Nazi

Table I.2. Triggers of post–World War II secessionist movements

Trigger		Cases
After/anticipation of regime change	Security threat	Afars (Eritrea), Arakanese (Myanmar), Armenians (Azerbaijan), Bagandans (Uganda), Basters (Namibia), Ewes (Ghana), Kachins (Myanmar), Karens (Myanmar), Kashmiris (India), Lozis (Zambia), Lubas (Congo), Lundas/Yekes (Congo), Nagas (India), Palestinians (Israel), Serbs (Croatia), Sikhs (India), Southerners (Sudan), Turkmen (China)
	No security threat	Abkhazis (Georgia—early 1990s), Azeris (Iran), Bakongans (Angola), Basques (France), Bougainvilleans (Papua New Guinea), Buryats (Russia), Cabindans (Angola), Chechens (Russia—early 1990s), Crimean Russians (Ukraine), Croats (Bosnia), East Timorese (Indonesia—post-Suharto period), Ewes (Togo), Kumyks (Russia), Lezgins (Russia), Pashtuns (Pakistan), Serbs (Bosnia), South Ossetians (Georgia), South Tyroleans (Italy), Tatars (Russia), Tuvinians (Russia), Uzbeks (Kyrgyzstan), Transdniestrians (Moldova)
Increased repression		Baluchis (Pakistan), Ibos (Nigeria), Kewris (Mauritania), Kurds (Iraq), Kurds (Turkey), Malay-Muslims (Thailand), Mons (Myanmar), Saharawis (Morocco), Shans (Myanmar), Sri Lankan Tamils, Tibetans (China)
Decreased repression/ weakened state		Afars (Ethiopia), Basques (Spain), Isaaqs (Somalia), Kosovar Albanians (1980s Yugoslavia), Oromo (Ethiopia), Somalis (Ethiopia)

Table I.2—continued

Trigger	Cases
Economic reasons/other	Acehnese (Indonesia), Assamese (India), Casamançais (Senegal), Catholics in Northern Ireland (United Kingdom), Moros (Philippines), Native Hawaiians (United States), Papuans (Indonesia), Quebecois (Canada), Tripuras (India), Tuaregs (Mali)

Sources: Ted Robert Gurr et al., Minorities at Risk (MAR) project files., http://www.cidcm.umd.edu/inscr/mar/; Minority Rights Group, *The World Directory of Minorities* (London, UK: Minority Rights Group International, 1997).

Party in Germany, for example, languished on the political sidelines for decades before gaining widespread support in the 1930s. This suggests that the role of individual leaders is significantly constrained by the environment in which he or she operates.[30] Indeed, the rate at which nationalizing leaders reinvent themselves, or fall out of political favor, casts doubt on the causal impact that elites themselves wield in the process of mobilization. Finally, the notion that opportunistic leaders play the ethnic card to gain or retain popular support simply begs the question as to why this "card" is such a potent populist tool. Because other groups are seen as a threat? Because of rising economic or political instability? In either case, nationalizing elites would then be the by-product of larger environmental conditions rather than the principal force itself.

The *ethnic fears approach* offers yet another dynamic account of minority mobilization. One variant, known as the ethnic security dilemma, holds that groups mobilize in response to the security vacuum brought about by state collapse. The logic follows that, in the context of emerging anarchy, it is difficult to distinguish the offensive from the defensive intentions of other nonstate actors. The resulting uncertainty on both sides, in addition to the considerable advantage of offensive mobilization in civil warfare, creates powerful incentives for each group to strike preemptively or secede, thus increasing the likelihood of ethnic war.[31]

Barry Posen has argued, for example, that the Serbian-Croatian war in 1990s Yugoslavia was the outgrowth of conditions of extreme uncertainty and mutual suspicions concerning what the other would do in the absence of governmental restraint. After the collapse of federal authority, the Croats and Serbs were forced to provide for their own security in an environment conducive to mutual perceptions of threat.[32] This ultimately gave rise to a bloody, secessionist war.

Although persuasive in the abstract, empirical evidence shows that most of the secessionist movements since World War II began when the state was in the process of regime change or transition, not collapse (see table 1-2). To cite a few examples, the Basque and South Tyrolean separatists sought to secede from postwar Spain and Italy, both of which had stable governments; Chechen and Crimean Russian leaders declared their regions' independence from their weakened but stable post-Soviet governments; the Acehnese and East Timorese revived their separatist campaigns against post-Suharto Indonesia—hardly the picture of state failure. Moreover, the ethnic security dilemma cannot account for the many *non*violent secessionist movements. For instance, the Lezgins, Tuvinians, Tatars, and Buryats of post-Soviet Russia; the Basters of newly independent Namibia; the Azeris of postwar Iran; the Bougainvilleans of Papua New Guinea; the Afars of Eritrea; the Papuans of Indonesia; and the Tuaregs of Mali have all undertaken peaceful campaigns for independence. The ethnic security dilemma may explain cases in which a vacuum of state power was followed by separatist violence. However, such cases are extremely rare—most postwar secessionist movements were launched against states whose central governments were still intact, and many of these were prosecuted peacefully or with minimal violence.

A second variant of ethnic fears theories, credible commitment arguments, broadly holds that secessionism emerges during political transition when the state center can no longer guarantee minority protection.[33] James Fearon has argued that ethnic conflict in postcommunist Europe is largely due to the fact that "ethnic majorities are unable to commit themselves not to exploit ethnic minorities in a new state."[34] Fearing future transgressions, such minorities will seek to exit the state while they still can—before a potentially hostile regime consolidates power.

Contrary to the expectations of this approach, however, over half of the secessionist movements in the postwar period emerged in the context of a relatively *benign* regime, which posed little or no threat to the minority. Even more striking, many movements were launched only after authoritarian governments had given way to liberal, pro-minority regimes. For example, the Acehnese and East Timorese campaigns of independence were revived in 1998—after the repressive Suharto government had ceded power to a comparatively moderate administration. Moreover, almost none of the secessionist movements in Eastern Europe emerged until *after* the collapse of their antinational totalitarian regimes.[35] This pattern suggests that secessionism is not always—or even most of the time—driven by fears of future exploitation.

The value of the ethnic fears approach is that it generates clear predictions concerning the *timing* of mobilization, while providing clues as to why the fortunes of nationalist leaders wax and wane over time. The major shortcoming of such theories is that they are extremely thin. Because the *mechanics* of mobilization are poorly specified, they explain neither how political transition generates minority radicalization nor why in most cases this does not occur.[36]

Second, these arguments tend to overemphasize defensive motivations, which is only one factor in the collective action calculus. In competitive games such as politics and even war, players make their decisions on the basis of mixed motives of opportunism *and* fear. As noted earlier, the empirical record reveals that most demands for secession were made when the center was relatively weak and benign, rather than strong and threatening, as predicted by ethnic fears theories.[37] To address this imbalance, I offer a model that integrates defensive and offensive motives in a competitive game between the minority and the center over state resources. By situating this game in the wider context of interstate and trans-state politics, I hope to generate more accurate predictions concerning fluctuations in group claim-making.

Ethnic Bargaining and Power Perceptions

This book develops a theory of ethnic bargaining that challenges much of the conventional wisdom concerning minority mobilization. Rather than being a product of *separate* inputs—preexisting preferences plus group capacity gives rise to mobilization—the perceptions of increased leverage *themselves* create collective desires for more radical demands. Minority leaders then use these demands to bargain for greater concessions from the central government.

This formulation builds on a central insight in the social movements literature that grievances alone cannot generate collective mobilization—there must also be a political opportunity structure to help transmit these grievances into action.[38] Peter Eisinger defines political opportunity structure as "elements in the environment [that] impose certain constraints on political activity or open avenues for it."[39] According to Sidney Tarrow, collective action is enabled by the "expansion" of the political opportunity structure, which may occur when a government liberalizes or when its rulers become preoccupied with foreign engagements.[40] The bargaining theory takes this line of reasoning one step further, arguing that, by leveraging the minority, the opportunity structure is *itself* a potent motive for group radicalization.

This book explores the impact of two types of opportunity structures on ethnic bargaining. The first is the *institutional* opportunity structure—

defined here as a transient political environment that emerges, often unexpectedly, to alter the balance of power between the minority and the center. Examples include the "event generated influences" that Mark Beissinger argues led to the disintegration of the Soviet state. In his account, the "'*glasnost*' tide of nationalism" that emerged in the Baltics provoked similar movements in the less-empowered Caucasian Republics "largely because of their ability to ride the tide of nationalism generated from the actions of others."[41] Consistent with the definition above, these openings were both impermanent and, for the most part, limited to the East Bloc.

Institutional opportunities may produce mobilization even in the absence of salient collective grievances. For instance, the Paris Peace Conference that redrew Europe's political boundaries after World War I served as an opportunity structure galvanizing Sudeten Germans to mobilize around irredentism, despite credible guarantees of protection by the new Czechoslovak government. Another opportunity structure emerged in postcommunist Czechoslovakia in the form of negotiations over the federal constitution. In the course of these talks, Slovak leaders gradually radicalized their demands to extract ever-increasing concessions from the Czechs—despite the fact that the Slovaks were net beneficiaries of the federation. In both cases, it was the opportunity structure, rather than underlying group grievances, that served as the principal catalyst of collective action. Meanwhile, truly beleaguered groups such as the Roma remained quiescent.

Discursive opportunity structures, in contrast, are generally longer-lasting, more malleable, and adaptable to a range of settings. They inform not only the legitimate forms of political organization, but also the means by which these "actors" can pursue their goals. In the contemporary period, ethnic groups are the primary political challengers to national governments, and claim-making is the principal mode by which they bargain with the center over state resources. The ethnic bargaining framework provides these challengers with the "normative toolbox and ideational resource pool that [can] be deployed in pursuit of political objectives."[42]

After tracing the origins of this discursive opportunity structure in chapter 1, the subsequent chapter shows how ethnic bargaining plays out on the *micro*-level to produce shifts in group claims in a single case. In brief, the bargaining model holds that group radicalization is driven by shifting perceptions of relative power against the center. These perceptions are informed both by changes in the institutional opportunity structure and by the actions of the group's external patron (if one exists).[43] For instance, a diplomatic intervention by a homeland state may lead minority representatives to believe that they enjoy leverage against the center. They may respond by escalating their demands to territorial autonomy or secession in an effort to extract side payments from their host government. The Sri

Lankan Tamil Tigers, for example, ratcheted up their demands from affirmative action in the 1970s to secession in the 1980s, largely in reaction to signals of heightened support from neighboring India—particularly their co-ethnics in Tamil Nadu. Conversely, minority leaders are likely to moderate their demands in response to perceptions of diminished outside support. The South Tyroleans of Italy, for example, *de*-escalated their demands from irredentism to cultural autonomy once Austria withdrew its claims on South Tyrol after World War II. In this way, minority representatives continually recalibrate their demands against the center in response to perceived shifts in leverage over time.

Nonstate actors, too, have a major impact on minority behavior. In his work on international activism, Clifford Bob notes that NGOs and transnational activist networks (TAN) can trigger minority mobilization by "[bestowing] legitimacy on challengers who might otherwise have meager recognition," by strengthening challengers with financial support and technical expertise, and by "demonstrating that a movement is not alone, that the world cares, and that an arduous conflict may not be fruitless" (for more on this, see chapter 1).[44]

In the present analysis, external lobby actors and especially kin states (e.g., Serbia in the case of Bosnian Serbs; or Somalia in the case of Ethiopian Somalis) receive special attention.[45] To isolate the effects of power perceptions on minority behavior, I use comparative case analysis to bracket or "control for" many of the structural factors associated with minority mobilization—including historical enmities or "myth complexes," ethnic consciousness, collective grievances, and economic disparities. This allows me to determine the independent influence that the actions of the minority's host government, its external patron (assuming one exists), and changes in the political opportunity structure have on group mobilization.

External patrons also influence political alignments in the host state. Timor Kuran notes that "[f]oreign ethnic activists can heighten a nation's awareness of its divisions, and they can reward expressions of ethnicity."[46] This has important implications for the logic of "ethnic outbidding" in deeply divided societies. According to Alvin Rabushka and Kenneth Shepsle, outbidding occurs when elites compete for the support of their respective ethnic constituencies by attempting to "outflank" one another on ethnic issues.[47] This serves to amplify ethnic cleavages on the ground, increasing the odds of sectarian conflict. Donald Horowitz is also pessimistic about the potential of democratic institutions for inducing inter-ethnic cooperation in severely divided societies.[48] This is because individuals in such societies are predisposed to support parties that represent their own ethnic group to the exclusion of others. Divisions in society thus map onto the political sphere, further exacerbating ethnic tensions on the ground.

Elise Giuliano observes, however, that both theories overpredict ethnic extremism, partly because they wrongly assume that voter preferences in divided societies are intense and polarized along the single dimension of ethnicity. She demonstrates that, by framing issues in nonexclusivist terms, political elites can "generate heterogeneous preferences within groups, common preferences across ethnic groups, and a constituency of political moderates backing certain issues."[49] Kanchan Chandra, too, argues that individuals in patronage-democracies like India will not necessarily vote for ethnic parties if they believe that a nonethnic party is more likely to deliver material benefits.[50] This implies that deeply divided societies do not necessarily lead to ethnically divisive politics. Jóhanna Birner corroborates this thesis, showing that divided democracies yield far more inter-ethnic cooperation than they do conflict.[51]

I build on these insights in chapter 2 by introducing a spatial model that maps the politics of a hypothetical divided society onto a two-dimensional policy space. Following Giuliano, a second dimension has been added to the first dimension of ethnicity to represent the ability of elites to break out of the logic of ethnic outbidding by brokering inter-ethnic compromises along a second issue dimension. Importantly, however, their ability and incentive to do so are greatly circumscribed by the prevailing salience of ethnicity in domestic politics.

Nationalist signals from either the host government or an external lobby actor tend to increase the level of ethnic salience in society. This has the effect of politicizing group differences, leading in extreme cases to sectarian violence. This occurred in Kosovo in the late 1990s, when growing Serbian hostility and partisan intervention by the North Atlantic Treaty Organization (NATO) increased tensions between ethnic Albanians and Serbs on the ground. In the absence of nationalist signals, however, alternative cleavages, such as class, may gain relatively greater salience, inducing inter-ethnic alliances along class lines.[52] Yugoslavia underwent such a transformation after World War II when powerful neighboring states withdrew from their respective zones of interest. This lessened the salience of ethnic markers in postwar Yugoslavia, allowing for the emergence of a pan-ethnic alliance around a common Yugoslav identity.

Ethnic bargaining often has perverse consequences for minorities. This is because the signals that lead groups to challenge their governments may also provoke anti-minority retributions. During the NATO campaign to drive Serbian forces out of Kosovo, for example, an estimated ten thousand ethnic Albanian civilians were killed—mostly by Serbs. This is ten times the number that had been killed in the year leading up to the intervention.[53] U.S.-NATO Commanding General Wesley Clark asserted that the Serbian response to the air strikes was "entirely predictable. . . . The military authorities fully anticipated the vicious approach that Milošević would adopt [once the bombing was under way], as well as the terrible efficiency with which he would carry it out."[54] When a group challenges the center with the expectation of support that never materializes, the backlash can be particularly devastating. Cases of ill-fated minority uprisings include the Kurds in 1990s Iraq, the Tutsis in Rwanda, the Armenians in Nagorno-Karabakh, the Muslims in Bosnia, the Palestinians in the West Bank, and the East Timorese in Indonesia. Alan Kuperman notes that "[i]n most cases of mass killing since World War II—unlike the Holocaust—the victim group has triggered its own demise by violently challenging the authority of the state."[55] The tension between the promise of minority empowerment and what it delivers in practice is a major theme of this book.

Before proceeding further, some definitions are in order.[56] An *ethnic or communal group* is defined here as a community of common descent whose membership is based on one or more shared traits—cultural, linguistic, religious, or otherwise.[57] A *minority* is an ethnic group that is numerically inferior to the politically dominant group in the state or de facto sovereign unit; the term *majority* refers to the group that exercises political dominance in the state, even if it is not in the numerical majority. Examples include the political majorities of apartheid South Africa, Rwanda, Burundi, and other states—groups that are actually minorities in absolute terms.

Ethnic bargaining can now be defined as the modes and practices by which minorities negotiate with the majority over the group's claimant status to state institutions. If successful, the minority may extract concessions from the majority-controlled government, including transfer payments, power-sharing agreements, and/or inclusion in political coalitions. *Majority, host* or *state government, center,* and *dominant group* are used interchangeably throughout the book to refer to the dominant political actor with which the minority bargains at the substate level. An *outside lobby actor,* in turn, denotes any state, organization, or private interest that lobbies directly on behalf of the minority in the course of these negotiations. There are many other external actors (including the European Union; the Organization for Security and Co-operation in Europe, OSCE; and the Council of Europe, CoE) that generally refrain from partisan intervention and instead pressure the minority's host government and/or lobby state to change its policies toward the minority. This distinction is important, for where they do not intervene directly on behalf of the minority, such entities cannot be classified as lobby actors. They are instead exogenous influences on host state and lobby actor preferences, which in turn inform minority calculations as to whether to radicalize.[58]

Finally, a *group demand* or *claim* is defined here as a bid by minority representatives against the center for a degree of control over state institutions. In this context, *minority radicalization* or *mobilization* denotes the collective expression of, or support for, more extreme demands by the minority rank and file. I thus use shifts in the extremity of group demands as a proxy for minority radicalization.[59]

It might be reasonably objected that group demands are a poor measure of radicalization because minority elites have incentives to overstate their preferences in order to win greater concessions from the center. Although this is theoretically possible, in practice group demands are inextricably tied to minority radicalization for at least three reasons. First, claim-making effectively commits a group to collective action—ranging from civil protest to organized violence. Once a recognized minority representative makes an extreme demand, the center can either grant the minority concessions or launch a preventive strike. In either case, the group is locked into mobilization—receiving either a collective reward or, alternatively, a collective punishment.

Second, although the exact distinction between cultural autonomy and territorial autonomy is debatable, it is universally recognized that the latter constitutes a greater challenge than the former. Movement up and down this continuum of claims thus indicates minority radicalization and moderation, respectively. Establishing a demand along this continuum also signals the minority's reservation value—the minimum its leaders will accept in return for peaceful cohabitation with the majority.[60] If they believe they enjoy significant leverage against the center, they may put forward more extreme demands, signaling that the group is prepared to take up arms if the government fails to grant generous concessions. Third, these demands enjoy legitimacy in the international discourse and therefore help mobilize external support for the minority's cause.

In sum, claim-making is central to minority mobilization because it communicates bargaining postures, commits group members to a set of collective behaviors, and attracts outside assistance to the side of the minority. Group demands may even take on a life of their own, leading minority leaders to adopt a more intransigent stance in negotiations with the center because their constituents have internalized these claims.

This book tests the theory of ethnic bargaining using comparative and longitudinal analysis of seven cases of minority mobilization in east central Europe. I have conducted extensive fieldwork on Moravians and Slovaks in postcommunist Czechoslovakia as well as on Hungarian minorities in postcommunist Slovakia and Romania. I have also carried out a detailed historical investigation into the behavior of the Sudeten Germans in interwar Czechoslovakia to determine whether the model travels over time. Finally, I have conducted a plausibility probe into the model's generalizability across space by examining minority behavior in postcommunist Yugoslavia.

There are several potential objections to my case selection. It could be argued, for example, that a model of minority radicalization cannot properly be tested using cases drawn from a relatively peaceful region in Europe. Despite the plausibility of this concern, I have selected these cases partly to correct for what I believe is a bias toward the study of violence in the ethnic conflict literature.[61] Much of this research selects on the dependent variable by focusing on outbreaks of sectarian bloodshed. In doing so, this scholarship places disproportionate emphasis on explaining how or why groups mobilize (sometimes to participate in violence), largely disregarding the question of how groups become *de*-mobilized.

A second problem is that episodes of violence usually feature all or most of the following: nationalizing elites, ethnic outbidding, economic deprivation, institutional breakdown, the presence of arms and/or mercenaries, internal factionalization, and intervention by outside states or organizations. In the midst of this complexity, it is nearly impossible to sort out which factors, if any, are crucial to the escalation of conflict and which are of secondary importance; in such moments, violence is quite simply overdetermined. Finally, a cross-sectional analysis of snapshots of violent conflict cannot be used to satisfactorily separate the causes from the effects of violence. I avoid this problem by tracing minority-majority relations longitudinally through periods of *both* peace and conflict. By examining fluctuations in mobilization over time, it is possible to identify crucial antecedent conditions that are absent in the first state but present in the second.

A second possible objection is that, with an analysis confined to cases from east central Europe, there is no way of knowing whether minority mobilization plays out differently elsewhere. In other words, what we see in Europe may be function of features unique to the region rather than a reflection of universal features of minority politics. Although there is some danger of such a bias, selecting cases from the same region offers significant advantages for hypothesis testing. By examining seven cases of minority-majority relations from the same region, I effectively control for much social, economic, and historical variation in identifying the influence of key factors on minority mobilization. For example, comparing the Slovak and Moravian movements in postcommunist Czechoslovakia helps me challenge the argument that Slovak separatism was a direct outgrowth of its historical experience of autonomy under Austro-Hungary, because the Moravians also had autonomous arrangements under the dual monarchy but failed to advance separatist demands. This case selection also helps control for ethnic variation. East central Europe is home to many minority groups with shared ethnic characteristics; variation in the demands advanced by their leaders therefore cannot be attributed to the ascriptive traits that they have in common. For example, by comparing the behavior of Hungarian minorities in Slovakia and Romania, I control for the unknown effect of being Hungarian in determining the causes of goal differentiation between the two groups. Moreover, the canon of nationalism studies is strongly informed by the history of minority politics in east central Europe.[62] By revisiting these cases, I critically reexamine the prevailing interpretations of these movements. Scholars of elite theories, for example, have cited the negotiated Czechoslovak split in 1993 and the Sudeten German fifth column in interwar Czechoslovakia as decisive evidence that minority rebellion is the result of elite manipulation. These cases therefore constitute tough tests for the theory of ethnic bargaining.

More generally, it may be objected that this theory problematically treats groups as unitary actors in the political arena. I submit that this critique misunderstands the purpose of strategic modeling as it is used here. To yield valid results, the model requires neither that groups behave monolithically nor that they remain unchanged over time, nor even that they have clearly defined boundaries. It merely brackets the prevailing ethnic landscape in any given case to generate predictions concerning how the interactions between the leaders of the minority, majority, and external lobby actor influence ethnic mobilization.

Nor do I assume that groups "speak" with a single voice. Given that there are nearly always multiple voices competing to represent a group, I measure group claims as the *dominant* voice from within this cacophony. This also helps me identify the legitimate leaders of the group. Since extreme positions may be marginalized at some times but dominant at others, it only makes sense to measure group claims *as the most popular (or mainstream) position within the group at every point in time.* Thus, minority or group demands refer to the positions of recognized minority representatives in the same way that government or state claims refer to the positions of recognized state leaders.

Moreover, groups need not be homogeneous to be coherent political players. People very often organize under ethnic banners such as "Bosnian Serbs" or "Abkhazis"—which can serve as stable political identities despite the variety of agendas they usually subsume. Indeed, as Fredrik Barth noted long ago, while the membership and content of ethnicities morph, unite, change, and divide, the *boundaries* that distinguish groups from one another remain remarkably robust over time.[63] Thus, just as policy analysts can speak meaningfully of the behavior of France or Britain in international affairs, one may also speak of the behavior of ethnic groups at the substate level whose political existence is a universally accepted, and therefore consequential, social fact.

This book does not seek to problematize "ancient ethnic hatreds" so widely believed to lie at the heart of sectarian conflict. This has already been accomplished, to my mind, by much of the recent scholarship in ethnic politics. The added value of this project lies instead in problematizing minority claim-making. Rather than taking the claims at face value, I advance and test a theory that group claims serve primarily as bargaining tools by which minority leaders extract concessions from their state centers. Their decision to employ this gambit is informed by their perceptions of relative power, which in turn are driven by perceptions of external support and institutional opportunities. By identifying the proximate triggers for radicalization and moderation, this model has lessons for managing communal conflict. Perhaps the most important implication for policy, however, is that ethnic conflicts are rarely ever completely extinguished, but instead remain a latent—and potentially explosive—schism at the domestic, regional, and global levels.

On the positive side, this also means that groups that pursue secession—even through violence—are rarely destined to adhere to such goals. The cases of the Bosnian Serbs and Croats, the Catholics in Northern Ireland, and the Turks in Cyprus show that separatist organizations may assume a more integrationist stance when the strategic picture changes. Rather than aim for complete cures, peacemakers should therefore attempt to *contain* ethnic disputes at a level that permits constructive dialogue. It must also be remembered that communal cleavages rarely begin and end with the state, but extend to the wider region. It remains for major powers and international organizations to maintain equilibrium at the internal and regional levels as assiduously as that they manage disputes at the interstate level—by paying attention to what they signal to disempowered groups and by creating incentives for governments to de-ethnicize their institutions. Through it all, third party mediators should bear in mind Hippocrates' famous dictum to "make a habit of two things—to help, or at least to do no harm."

CHAPTER ONE

The Origins of Ethnic Bargaining

The contemporary discourse of ethnic bargaining combines Westphalian integrationist rights with a newer brand of segregationist rights born in the age of nationalism.[1] While there is no obvious link between the two discursive traditions, minority leaders can be seen to use them interchangeably in the course of bargaining with their centers. The ethnic bargaining framework thus serves as a kind of master "toolbox" containing all the devices available to minority elites in mobilizing popular challenges against their governments and attracting external support for their cause.[2] These devices have their origins in three distinct, yet overlapping, historical phases: (1) the post-Westphalian period of minority recognition; (2) the League of Nations era of minority protection; and (3) the post–World War II period of minority empowerment.[3] This chapter explores each period in turn, demonstrating how the actions of the leading world powers have contributed to the fitful, nonlinear development of this discourse over time.

Minority Recognition

Integrationist minority rights can be traced back at least as far as the 1648 Treaty of Westphalia.[4] This treaty held, among other things, that the relations between rulers and their subjects could not be determined by outside powers. In return for the right to exercise absolute sovereignty over their territories, European monarchs promised to protect the rights of certain religious minorities in their domains. Reciprocal pledges of noninterference were thus traded for promises to recognize one another's minorities.[5] Although the Treaty of Westphalia is best known as the foundation of the modern state system, it also introduced the principle of minority rights into international law.[6]

Nearly two hundred years later, the Great Powers extended these rights to ethnic minorities. The 1815 Treaty of Vienna, which restored order to the continent in the wake of the Napoleonic Wars, "included for the first time explicit protection for an ethnic as opposed to a religious group."[7] The treaty thus recognized the existence of a Polish nation, granting it a degree of autonomy on the basis of its national distinctiveness. In practice, however, minority recognition continued to take a backseat to realpolitik concerns: over the following decades, Prussia, Russia, and Austria abrogated Poland's autonomous arrangements as soon as they were perceived to threaten their interests.

The European powers gave another nod to minority rights in their treaties with the new states of southeast Europe in the late 1800s. In return for recognition, the agreements mandated that each fledgling state respect the rights of certain minorities within its territory. The 1878 Treaty of Berlin, for example, established explicit rights for the Turkish, Greek, and Romanian minorities residing in Bulgaria.[8] The 1881 International Convention of Constantinople included provisions for Muslims living in areas of Greek control, guaranteeing them the free exercise of Islam and the maintenance of Islamic courts.[9] These protections were driven less by humanitarian concerns than they were by realpolitik considerations—the European Powers wanted to ensure the stability of the Balkans and prevent the out-migration of disgruntled or persecuted minorities to Western Europe. The treaties were also sometimes used as a pretext for Great Power interventions aimed at securing their interests in the region. Where there were no vital interests at stake, a more limited "humanitarian intervention" might be undertaken through diplomatic channels.[10]

The spread of nationalism in the nineteenth century paved the way for grassroots mobilization around the perceived right to national self-determination. This principle—together with the examples of the French and American revolutions—had a particularly galvanizing effect on the Habsburg minorities, which felt themselves doubly oppressed by antinational imperial rule. Unlike earlier movements, the 1848 revolutions in east central Europe were motivated at least as much by nationalist discontent as they were by liberal democratic principles. The discourse of nationalism was also used to justify the unification of the Italian peninsula in 1860 and the German states in 1871.

It is important to note in this respect that Italy and Germany achieved sovereignty not because the international community had recognized their natural rights to statehood but because they were able to seize it through force. Similarly, Hungary was made an equal partner in the Dual Monarchy not because Austria had finally acknowledged the legitimacy of Hungarian claims to independence but because Vienna was desperate for powerful internal allies to counterbalance Prussia's rising power. The Austrians and Hungarians, in turn, granted autonomy to the second-ranking nationalities in their respective domains not out of a shared commitment to minority rights but because of their need for additional internal allies to counter accumulating threats to the empire. Although some European minorities achieved national independence during this period, most continued to endure political, cultural, and/or economic repression—including the Armenians and Jews in the Balkans, the Bretons and Corsicans in France, the Flemish in Belgium, the Alsatians in France, and the Irish in Great Britain.

Minority Protection

The end of World War I inaugurated the second developmental phase of ethnic bargaining. In a series of public speeches, U.S. President Woodrow Wilson popularized the nascent principle of national self-determination, claiming that "no right anywhere exists to hand peoples about from sovereignty to sovereignty as if they were property."[11] This principle combined Enlightenment notions that the people should rule with the nineteenth-century belief that nations were "peoples," concluding that nations therefore had the right to self-government. Out of this admixture came the more controversial *segregationist* strand of rights, which holds that all nations are entitled to political independence.[12]

The idea that "every people has a right to choose the sovereignty under which they shall live" was doubtless part of Wilson's worldview.[13] However, it is important to note that his outlook was also consistent with the widespread contemporary belief that the world was divided into a patchwork of nations and proto-nations that would someday grow up to be nation-states. Interestingly, the antinationalist Lenin also subscribed to this view, writing that "[t]he right of nations to self-determination means only the right to independence in a political sense, the right to free, political secession from the oppressing nation."[14]

Despite this high-flown rhetoric, self-determination was implemented only insofar as it furthered the interests of the victorious Allied Powers. Czechoslovakia and Poland were created in part to establish self-rule for the Czechs, Slovaks, and Poles, but mainly to check the regional ambitions of Germany, Austria, and Hungary. Thus, millions of ethnic Germans were obliged to remain in Poland and Czechoslovakia, two-thirds of Hungary's territory was given to neighboring states, the Germans of Alsace-Lorraine were attached to France, and the German Tyroleans were handed over to Italy—all clear violations of the principle of self-determination. Altogether, the postwar settlement placed almost 100 million people in new states; approximately 25 million were stranded outside their national homelands, including millions of Greeks, Turks, Germans, and Hungarians.[15] Practical exigencies had thus taken precedence over principles in determining the postwar boundaries.[16]

To prevent these inconsistencies from upsetting the peace settlement, the Allies established a system of minority protections under the new League of Nations. The regime consisted of five minorities treaties with the new states of east central Europe, four bilateral treaties with defeated powers, promises by other states to respect minority rights as a condition for gaining membership in the League, and special administrative arrangements for minority regions such as Danzig and Upper Silesia. The minority protections themselves ranged from the right to choose one's citizenship to guarantees of nondiscrimination. There were also provisions for minority schools, subsidies for minority cultural associations, and the right to use one's mother tongue in official business.[17]

Created to stabilize the postwar order, the regime inadvertently served as an early blueprint for today's ethnic bargaining framework. This is because the League system effectively internationalized minority protection. The treaties, for example, were to be taken as fundamental law by the signatory states and could not be contravened without the explicit consent of the League Council. If a government were suspected of violating its commitments under its treaty, council members could bring charges before the Permanent Court of International Justice, which had compulsory jurisdiction over such matters. Most important, the League provided a means by which nationalities could, for the first time, petition for legal redress over the heads of their governments.[18]

Ethnic minorities received a great deal of attention in the early years of the League. The first decade witnessed a rapid growth of minority legislation in the signatory states; monitoring and enforcement of the treaties also underwent significant expansion. As the number of minority petitions to the League mushroomed, a separate Minorities Department was created under the Secretariat to deal with the increased workload. Its staff more than doubled shortly after its inception, and the budget for the Minorities Section increased from 175,000 to over 333,000 Swiss francs over the first ten years.[19] By advocating tirelessly on behalf of group rights, the department also helped legitimize external minority protections in global public opinion.

Minority organizations soon began to use this nascent bargaining frame-work to mobilize against their governments. In the 1920s, they flooded the League Council with petitions for legal redress and assistance.[20] To attract international support for their cause, they also established a number of pan-European alliances. These include the Association of the German Racial Groups in Europe, the Warsaw Congress of Poles Living Abroad, the pan-Russian Congress in Riga, and the minority unions in Hungary. Minor-ity leaders also formed domestic coalitions to leverage their position at the substate level—the association of National Minorities in Germany and the loose minority alliances in Czechoslovakia, Romania, and Poland are ex-amples of the latter arrangements.[21]

By the mid-1920s, minority rights were sufficiently legitimized in the global political discourse that groups began to challenge their governments openly in international fora. At the 1926 Congress of European Nationalities, for example, a representative of the German minority in Hungary proclaimed, "[W]e desire to participate not merely as objects but as subjects. . . . The only question is whether the law of nationalities is of international or of internal concern. Clearly it is a matter of international policy."[22] At the fifth Congress in 1929, a Sudeten German deputy declared ominously that "[t]he character of a minority suits us no longer. We regard ourselves rather as one of the gov-erning people and demand political equality beyond that guaranteed by the Minorities Treaties. . . . It is our unshakeable resolve to bring about a revision of the present constitution."[23]

In the 1930s, the ethnic bargaining framework reverted from the inter-national to the bilateral level, largely due to the declining influence of the League in world politics. From 1929 onward, the League Council devoted its resources to accommodating the intensifying demands of Germany and Hungary on behalf of their co-ethnics in neighboring countries, while ig-noring the plight of truly beleaguered minorities.[24] When the League failed to respond to Poland's decision to withdraw from its treaty in 1934, the minorities system became a virtual dead letter. Observing these develop-ments, minority representatives scaled back their petitions accordingly—the number of appeals submitted to the League Secretariat dropped from 204 in 1930 to 4 in 1938.[25]

A behavioral bifurcation now emerged between the weak and the strong minorities in Europe. Groups with no outside support—such as the Jews and the Roma (gypsies)—grew silent, whereas strong minorities with pow-erful lobby states—the Sudeten Germans and ethnic Hungarians—contin-ued to ratchet up their claims against their hapless governments.[26] Citing national self-determination and the rights of German minorities, the Reich eventually expanded into central Europe, swallowing Austria and annex-ing large chunks of Czechoslovakia and Poland. At the same time, millions of Jews and Roma perished in concentration camps across Europe. Ethnic cleansing continued after the war as the governments of East Central Europe organized reprisals against the very German, Hungarian, and Croatian minorities they had earlier sought to accommodate. Under the Beneš Decrees, which were retroactively ratified by the Czechoslovak Provisional National Assembly in 1946, millions of Germans in Bohemia and Moravia were expelled from the Czech lands on charges of Nazi collaboration—as many as a quarter of a million were killed or executed in the process. In the Czech town of Ústí nad Labem, hundreds and perhaps even thousands of unarmed German civilians were shot or thrown off a bridge into the Elbe river.[27] Overall, at least 12 million ethnic Germans were driven out of the Soviet Union, Poland, Czechoslovakia, and prewar German territory after the war.[28] The Hungarians and Croats were also targeted for reprisals. In 1944, around 40,000 Hungarian civilians were tortured or summarily executed when Serb Partisans recaptured Vojvodina from the occupying Hungarian Army (see chapter 6). In the infamous Bleiburg massacre, tens of thousands of fleeing Croatian soldiers and civilians were slaughtered by the victorious Partisans after Allied forces had turned them back at the Austrian border.[29]

Minority Empowerment

World War II ultimately involved twenty-eight countries and numerous colonies, was fought in two theaters, and resulted in approximately 17 million battleground deaths.[30] Shocked by the unprecedented carnage, the victorious Allied Powers resolved that such a conflict would never be repeated and created the United Nations and other international institutions to consolidate the postwar order. Wary of collectivist ideologies, which Nazi Germany had used to justify territorial expansion, the framers omitted any mention of integrationist minority rights in the founding UN documents.[31]

Segregationist rights suffered a similar fate after the war. Not only did Britain and France renege on promises of independence that they had made to their wartime allies, but they also opposed establishing a general right to self-determination for fear of losing their overseas colonies.[32] In the end, the principle *was* included in the UN Charter; however, it was defined so narrowly as to render it practically meaningless. Article 1(2) of the charter mandated only that states grant as much self-government to their colonies and nationalities "as possible."[33] Achieving independence thus required the consent of the interested state or colonial government, affirming the overriding norm of sovereignty.

Despite these warning signs, a number of groups attempted to cash in on wartime pledges of sovereignty. In 1944, Uighur separatists in China established the Eastern Turkistan Republic, electing a president and designating a national flag.[34] In 1947, the Jurassians in Switzerland launched their own independence movement, appealing to the UN to support their cause. The following is an excerpt from their 1950 national anthem:

> If those who would thwart our independence
> choose to impose their rule in our valleys,
> Then let each of us lunge forward into battle
> and spread dismay among their ranks!
> Our past guides us along the path
> of a free people to the United Nations.[35]

The Nagas of India, too, proclaimed a sovereign Nagaland—on the eve of India's own declaration of independence.[36] Other groups that followed suit include the Kurds in Iran and Iraq; the Sikhs and Kashmiris in India; the Kachins, Karens, and Arakanese in Myanmar; the Azeris in Iran; the South Tyroleans and Sardinians in Italy; and the Pashtuns in Pakistan. Most of these movements were brutally suppressed by their central governments. Although some resistance leaders pleaded for external support, western governments proved generally unwilling to intervene on their behalf. When the Karen secessionists sought aid from the British, for example, they were advised to "throw [their] lot in with Myanmar." Shortly thereafter, the army arrested the leaders of the uprising, looting and pillaging Karen villages. The Nagas suffered a similar treatment at the hands of the Indian government—approximately 150,000 people died between 1954 and 1964 as a result of the crackdown.[37] Although the United Nations had promised the people of Kashmir and Jammu that they would be able to determine their own fate through a national plebiscite, it did not interfere when India and Pakistan instead divided the region between themselves in 1949. Other would-be separatists took their cue from these developments and moderated their demands in light of the meager support offered by the international community.

In the meantime, communist countries united with newly independent states in a protracted campaign to reinterpret Article 1(2) as a prohibition against colonial rule. After a long period of opposition—during which time colonialism gradually lost legitimacy as a practical and ethical form of government—Western governments finally joined the movement to de-colonize Africa and Asia. To facilitate the process, the UN General

Assembly adopted the Declaration on the Granting of Independence to Colonial Countries and Peoples in 1960. The document asserted that "all peoples" had the right to self-determination and decreed that all "forms and manifestations" of colonialism be brought to an end.[38] Although the resolution was meant to apply to colonized peoples only,[39] it was not long before the success of de-colonization inspired minority organizations in sovereign states to use the principle of self-determination to challenge their national governments.

As the Cold War began to wind down, movements that had mobilized on the basis of class gradually changed their tactics in light of the decline of ideological conflict and the growing salience of self-determination. The Parti Quebecois began as a socialist movement against the economic dominance of the "200 [Anglo-Canadian] families" that supported discrimination against Francophones. By 1980, however, the Parti had become a movement for Quebecois secession.[40] Similarly, the native Hawaiian movement—which had originated as an economic campaign against the destruction of farmland—had by the 1990s "evolved into a larger struggle for native Hawaiian autonomy."[41] The Sri Lankan Tamil movement, too, was initially based on demands for social and economic justice—including the end of racial quotas in civil service employment and university admissions. The campaign escalated to demands for secession in the late 1970s. The Tamil United Liberation Front (TULF) electoral platform of 1977 declared that "The Tamil nation must take the decision to establish its sovereignty in its homeland on the basis of its right to self-determination." It promised that if elected, TULF would gain the independence of Tamil Eelam "by peaceful means or by direct action or struggle."[42] The Kurdistan Workers Party (PKK) in Turkey originally called for overthrowing *both* Turkish and Kurdish capitalists. The PKK Manifesto of 1978 pointed out that "the Kurdish feudal lords welcomed [Turkish exploitation of Kurds], since the limited exploitation offered to them under a feudal system was not sufficient."[43] By 1984, however, the PKK had begun to call for Kurdish sovereignty, accusing Turkey of destroying the Kurdish national identity through state-sponsored assimilation. Other groups that shifted their mobilizational frame from class to nationalism included the Kurds in Iraq, the Moros in the Philippines, the Assamese and Tripuras in India, and the West Papuans and Acehnese in Indonesia.

A behavioral bifurcation again appeared between the strong and the weak minorities. Whereas the leaders of territorially compact groups increasingly used segregationist rights to bargain with their governments, the representatives of territorially dispersed groups began to rally around integrationist rights. During the 1960s, UN principles of nondiscrimination combined with the example of the U.S. civil rights movement to mobilize disadvantaged minorities around the world.[44] The Aboriginals of Australia, for example, organized "freedom rides" into rural areas known for racial prejudice. They also wrote their own version of "We Shall Overcome," which was sung at protest rallies.[45] In Colombia, a political party that represented blacks self-consciously "base[d] its platform on its perception of the North American civil rights movement." A second "model[ed] its actions after the Black Islam and Black Panther movements of North America."[46] Allison Brysk writes:

> An international discourse of racial equality linked to the U.S. civil rights movement was filtering through Latin America; Brazilian Indians were apparently inspired by the North American Indian movement's 1973 protest at Wounded Knee. . . . [Meanwhile,] anthropologists and aid workers radicalized by the 1960's social movements . . . questioned the relationship between their enterprise and imperialism and used their positions to reach out to local populations.[47]

The 1970s witnessed a massive rise in the mobilization of indigenous communities and other marginalized minorities. Examples include indigenous groups in Panama, Colombia, Peru, Paraguay, Chile, Mexico, and Argentina; the Aboriginals in Australia; the Maoris in New Zealand; the Berbers in Algeria; the Assamese and Scheduled Tribes in India; the Biharis and Chittagong Hill Tribes in Bangladesh; and the Indians in Malaysia and Sri Lanka. The growth of minority activism was particularly striking in Central and South America, where indigenous congresses, coalitions, and federations formed at both the national and international levels to pressure their governments for concessions. Rodolfo Stavenhagen writes that "[i]n the 1960s, not more than a smattering of indigenous organizations existed; by the beginning of the 1990s, dozens of such groups have been identified as established and representative associations in every country. Hundreds probably exist continent-wide."[48] International advocacy networks assisted indigenous groups in negotiating with their governments over land, cultural, and linguistic rights as well as labor conditions. Meanwhile, nongovernmental organizations (NGOs) convened high-profile conferences to draw international attention to the plight of indigenous communities, leveraging their power at the substate level.[49] Indigenous leaders responded to these political openings by seeking direct representation in international organizations and by articulating their demands in public fora as a means of attracting additional support for their cause.

The Zapatistas in Mexico have made particularly brilliant use of such tactics.[50] Zapatista Leader Subcommandante Marcos gained notoriety for staging theatrical events for the media as a means of improving the group's bargaining position vis-à-vis the Mexican government. At the end of the UN International Year of the World's Indigenous Peoples in 1993, the Zapatistas launched an uprising to broadcast their plight to the global community.[51] In 2001, Marcos led a March of Indigenous Dignity—modeled after the 1963 March on Washington—through Mexico's southern states and into Mexico City. Mexican President Vicente Fox responded to the outpouring of international sympathy in the wake of these maneuvers by scaling back the government's military presence in Chiapas and by releasing dozens of imprisoned rebels—a key demand of Zapatista leaders for reentering peace talks.[52]

Ethnic Bargaining in the Cyber-Age

The steady increase in minority mobilization around the world appears to have peaked in the early 1990s—mainly as the result of massive upheavals in the former East bloc. The collapse of communism and subsequent breakup of the Soviet Union and Yugoslavia led to dire predictions that nationalism would destabilize the entire Eurasian continent.[53] To prevent internecine warfare on their eastern frontiers, West European governments called for enhanced minority protections within existing state borders. In 1991, the European Community (EC) announced "a common position on the process of recognition" of new states, affirming the principle of self-determination and minority rights so long as they were exercised within "existing frontiers which can only be changed by peaceful means and by common agreement."[54] Not surprisingly, these declarations did little to halt the dissolution of Yugoslavia—Slovenia and Croatia declared independence in 1991 and Bosnia-Herzegovina and Macedonia in 1992.

Patrick Thornberry observes that "[a]s the burgeoning number of entities revealed themselves, international organizations competed to 'do something about' minorities"; the 1992 UN Declaration on Minority Rights, for example, was ratified by the General Assembly in "the blink of an eyelid."[55] West European governments joined in the effort by creating institutions for conflict management and by expanding minority rights to placate restive minorities with irredentist kin states. In 1990, the Conference on Security and Cooperation in Europe (now the Organization for Security and Cooperation in Europe, OSCE) adopted the Copenhagen Document, which committed signatory states to greater minority protections. Two years later, the OSCE established the office of the High Commissioner on National Minorities (HCNM) to detect and resolve nascent ethnic conflicts within OSCE member states. In 1994, the Council of Europe (CoE) adopted the

European Charter for Regional or Minority Languages as well as the Framework Convention for the Protection of National Minorities—the first legally binding instrument for enforcing minority rights on the international level. Under the Framework Convention, signatory states were required to report periodically to the CoE on the status of minorities within their borders.[56]

At the Copenhagen Summit in 1993, the European Council established a set of objective standards that east Central European countries must meet in order to be admitted to the EU. These standards, which came to be known as the "Copenhagen criteria," include democratic stability, the rule of law, respect for human rights, and the guaranteed protection of minorities. The EU's Association Agreements with several prospective member states also required them to recognize their minority nations.[57] Originally aimed at postcommunist Europe, these initiatives appear to have evolved into general instruments for minority protection. The overall effect has been, as Demetres Christopulos put it, to "emancipate minority rights from human rights"[58]—a step toward recognizing groups themselves as subjects in international law.

Segregationist rights, too, have enjoyed a renaissance since the end of the Cold War. Although Western governments have refrained from recognizing minority rights to territorial autonomy, several covenants have moved in that direction. Article 128 of the Maastricht Treaty, for example, proclaimed that "[the European] Community shall contribute to the flowering of the cultures of the member-states, while respecting their national and regional diversity."[59] Now Article 151 under the Amsterdam Treaty, it obliges the EU to support the development of minority regions throughout Europe. The Copenhagen Document, too, states that

> The participating States note the efforts undertaken to protect and create conditions for the promotion of the ethnic, cultural, linguistic and religious identity of certain minorities by establishing, as one of the possible means to achieve these aims, appropriate *local and autonomous administrations* corresponding to the specific historical and territorial circumstances of such minorities.[60]

Even more dramatic is CoE Recommendation 1201, which asserts that—in addition to their own political parties, schools, and the free use of their mother tongue—national minorities also have the right to political autonomy. Article 11 states that "[i]n the regions where they are in a majority the persons belonging to a national minority shall have the right to have at their disposal appropriate local or autonomous authorities or to have a special status, matching the specific historical and territorial situation and in accordance with the domestic legislation of the state."[61]

Minority representatives have responded to their discursive empowerment by invoking segregationist rights as a means of attracting external support and establishing the legitimacy of their cause. In a rare personal interview conducted during the Bosnian War, General Ratko Mladić, commander of the Bosnian Serb Army, asserted that the Serbs had an historic claim to the territory of the Republic of Serb Krajina: "We just want the international community, if the Muslims and Croats are given the right to [create a] federation or confederation, to recognize the same right of the Serb people to be on our own land with our own people. We are not creating our country in Asia or America or Africa; we're just doing so on our ancestors' land."[62]

The Chechen separatists, too, have used the discourse of minority and human rights to gain outside support for their resistance. On April 16, 1996, the *Nezavisimaya Gazeta* published a direct appeal from Chechen President Dzhokhar Dudaev "calling on the peoples of the G7 states, the Vatican, the Islamic world, and all upholders of human rights and freedoms, not to let the G7 summit take place in Moscow in April while there [are] still Russian troops in Chechnya."[63] Chechen leaders have repeatedly requested OSCE mediation and UN intervention to help resolve the conflict and thereby achieve independence for the region. In the mid-1990s, Hungarian minorities in Slovakia, Romania, and Serbia used *both* the CoE Recommendation 1201 and the Framework Convention to justify their demands for local self-government.

Technological advances in the 1990s have also contributed to minority empowerment. The spread of Internet, satellite, and wireless technologies have facilitated the growth of transnational networks used to mobilize logistical and financial support for autonomy struggles in remote locations.[64] According to Jeff Delisio, webmaster for the Free Tibet Home Page, "[t]here is an effort underway now to improve the online services in Dharamsala, the home of the Tibetan Government-in-Exile. This will enable a more direct link between Tibet supporters and the officials and organizations where the bulk of Tibetans reside."[65] Indeed, it is through increased access to the global media that Tenzin Gyatso, the fourteenth Dalai Lama, was able to organize the international Free Tibet movement in the 1990s.

The Native Hawaiian movement, too, gathered momentum via the Internet with numerous websites dedicated to the pursuit of Hawaiian sovereignty. These include weblinks to legal documents, historical accounts of the native people, and contact information for key international organizations and U.S. representatives who may be lobbied for support. The campaign provided impetus for the Apology Bill that was passed by Congress in 1993 to apologize for the illegal U.S. annexation of the Hawaiian kingdom in 1893. For its part, the Hawaiian state government passed legislation in the mid-1990s to promote the development of a "Hawaiian Nation." The U.S. departments of State, Justice, and the Interior also began to negotiate with the Hawaiian government over arrangements for Native Hawaiian autonomy.[66]

Taken together, these developments have helped create what has been called the "Fourth World," a self-conscious community of "[n]ations forcibly incorporated into states which maintain a distinct political culture but are internationally unrecognized."[67] This informal alliance of unrecognized nations has gained momentum in cyberspace, inspiring new independence movements and magnifying the voices of old ones. They sometimes even work in concert. One of the most visible efforts to bargain collectively is the Unrepresented Nations and Peoples Organisation (UNPO), which was established in 1991 as a kind of "shadow United Nations" for aspiring nation-states. Like the UN, the UNPO has a founding covenant, a general assembly, and a secretary general. According to its homepage, the UNPO is

> an international organization created by nations and peoples around the world who are not represented as such in the world's principal international organizations. . . . The UNPO offers an international forum for occupied nations, indigenous peoples, minorities, and even oppressed majorities . . . [empowering] them to represent themselves more effectively.[68]

Its other activities notwithstanding, a central aim of the UNPO has been to obtain statehood for its member nations. Six of its founding members—Armenia, Belarus, Estonia, Georgia, Latvia, and Palau—have since been inducted into the United Nations—a goal to which many UNPO members aspire. In 2005, the UNPO represented over 60 nations and peoples with over 150 million people—ranging from the Cabindans in Angola to the Chins in Myanmar to the Kosovar Albanians in Yugoslavia. The UNPO homepage also contains links to its member websites—each of which displays a self-styled flag and country name, a description of its independence struggle, and relevant UN documents. There are also links to advocacy organizations such as Amnesty International and Human Rights Watch as well as offices of the U.S. Congress, the UN, and the EU.[69]

UNPO lobbying has helped raise the visibility of marginalized groups. Pitching one's cause to powerful states and international organizations has also prepared separatist leaders for international diplomacy in the unlikely event that they *do* obtain sovereignty. This has occurred in a few cases. When NATO countries began to negotiate with the Yugoslav government on behalf of Kosovar Albanians in 1998, the Kosovo Liberation Army (KLA)—

previously blacklisted by the U.S. State Department as a terrorist organization—obtained de facto diplomatic recognition in the West as the legitimate representative of the Kosovar Albanians. The independence leaders of East Timor, a former UNPO member, received unexpected international support when José Ramos Horta—a prominent champion of East Timorese independence—was awarded the Nobel Peace Prize in 1996. Fretilin Leader José António Amorim Dias later recalled: "Before the peace prize, we would visit embassies and they would send out the number two or three. Now [their] doors are open to us."[70] In a letter dated April 20, 2002, East Timor's newly established Ministry of Foreign Affairs invited the UNPO to its independence celebrations. The letter reads in part:

> Dear Friends at UNPO Netherlands,
> It is our greatest pleasure to let you know that East Timor will become an independent nation on 20 May 2002. This day marks the culmination of a courageous and inspiring quest by the people of East Timor, and the birth of a new nation. At the same time, it is an opportunity to acknowledge the remarkable contribution, over many years, of our friends in the NGO and Solidarity Movement around the world and the international community in general to this endeavour, and to recognise their continuing willingness to assist.[71]

Equally important, transnational networks have enabled minority organizations to identify potential allies whose interests intersect—however fleetingly—with their own. Since the 1990s, many secessionist movements have made common cause with Islamic fundamentalist groups, as seen in the involvement of the Afghani mujahideen in the Bosnian Muslim and Kosovar Albanian struggles for independence. In the Philippines, the Abu Sayyaf group was grafted onto the Moros separatist movement by Islamic radicals returning from the Afghan war.[72] In Kashmir, too, the flagging secessionist movement regained momentum with the infiltration of two Islamic fundamentalist groups supported by Pakistan, Pakistani emigrants, and Arab governments and charities in the Gulf. Jason Burke writes of the Kashmiri insurgency,

> When the first demonstrations had started back in 1987, the Kashmiri grievances were largely articulated within a contemporary Western human rights discourse, albeit with a religious and economic undercurrent. The only Islamic activists seriously involved believed in a gradualist political Islam. Seven years later the insurgency had become dominated by the most violent fringe of modern Islamic activism.[73]

Thus, in the same way that they mobilized under the banner of class to gain backing from the U.S. or the USSR during the Cold War, today's secessionist organizations have increasingly adopted the discourse of radical Islam to attract resources from transnational Islamic networks. The growing ease with which loose and/or temporary alliances can now be forged with other nonstate actors represents a novel source of leverage against the state. These actors include diaspora groups, private charities, corporations, advocacy organizations, and secessionist movements in other states—any of which can act as a surrogate kin state to minority organizations seeking to challenge their host government.

Data Analysis: Minority Mobilization in the Postwar Period

A descriptive analysis of the Minorities at Risk (MAR) data set shows a steady rise in minority mobilization since World War II. Figure 1.1 plots the number of *newly* mobilized groups for every five-year period since 1945.[74] A large number of new contenders emerged immediately after World War II, and another large cluster appeared at the close of the Cold War—suggesting that massive political change creates opportunity structures for groups to mobilize collectively for the first time. The largest share of first-time mobilizers in the early postwar years was in sub-Saharan Africa. At the time, European colonial powers were just beginning to retrench from the continent. This fatally weakened their client regimes, paving the way for indigenous groups to challenge their centers over territory or government power. In the

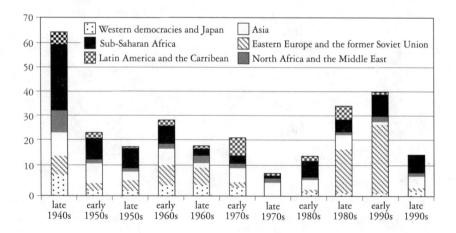

Figure 1.1 Number of newly mobilized groups for each five-year period since 1945

early 1990s, the bulk of newly mobilized groups was concentrated in Eastern Europe, as minority leaders responded to strategic openings created by the collapse of Soviet power to advance claims against their state centers.

Figure 1.2 shows that most of the new mobilizers in the immediate postwar period were powerful groups such as ethnonationalists (large, concentrated groups with a distinctive identity and history of autonomy) and communal contenders (groups competing for control of the central government). In contrast, most new contenders in the 1990s were relatively weak groups, including national minorities (small groups usually well-integrated in the majority society) and ethnoclasses (economically advantaged or disadvantaged ethnic groups).[75] This pattern might be explained by the fact that integrationist minority rights became an influential discursive opportunity structure only after the 1960s, when the U.S. civil rights movement inspired weak groups around the world to mobilize collectively for the first time. Both figures show that the number of new contenders declined sharply at the end of the twentieth century as postcommunist states began to consolidate, thereby narrowing strategic openings at the substate level.

Figures 1.3 and 1.4 depict the *cumulative* number of mobilized minorities for every five-year period since World War II. These figures show a rise in the overall number of mobilized groups since 1945, replicating the findings of Ted Gurr.[76] Although only 67 minorities were politically active in the late 1940s, this number had risen to 230 by the late 1990s. There are two main reasons for this cumulative increase. First, empirical evidence

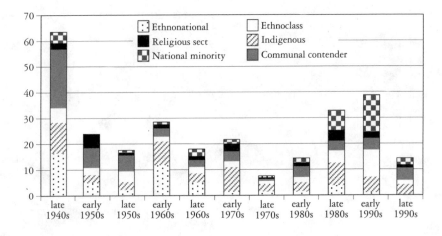

Figure 1.2 Number of newly mobilized groups by type for each five-year period

shows that, once mobilized, groups tend to stay mobilized.[77] The overall number of politically active minorities thus increases over time as new contenders appear on the scene. Second, the growing salience of integrationist rights and the increased activism of international advocacy networks in the 1970s and 1980s mobilized many marginalized groups, including indigenous communities in South America and foreign workers in continental Europe.

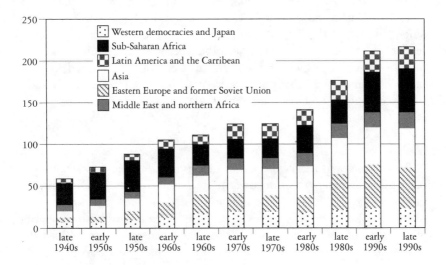

Figure 1.3 Total number of politically active groups by region

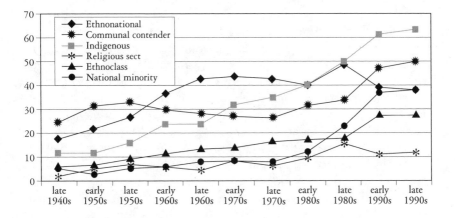

Figure 1.4 Total number of politically active groups by type

Figure 1.4 breaks down the cumulative number of mobilized groups by type. The greatest increases in the total number of mobilized groups can be seen among indigenous groups, national minorities, and ethnoclasses. The number of politically active indigenous groups increased steadily from twelve in the late 1940s to sixty-three in the late 1990s; the number of mobilized national minorities increased from five in the 1940s to thirty-eight in the late 1990s (with the greatest jump in the late 1980s). Finally, the number of politically active ethnoclasses quadrupled from a mere six in the late 1940s to twenty-four in the late 1990s. Such quantum leaps cannot be observed among more powerful groups such as ethnonationalists and communal contenders. This confirms the hypothesis that the steady rise in minority mobilization over the postwar period is driven largely by the increased activism of weaker minorities, which obtained critical leverage from enhancements in the contemporary bargaining framework.

Prior to the twentieth century, the interests of minorities were unambiguously subordinated to those of powerful states and empires. Despite this, the Great Powers established the foundation for integrationist minority rights in a succession of peace treaties used to reconfigure political boundaries in the wake of European wars. The League of Nations regime altered the relationship between states and groups in two important ways. First, the post–World War I European borders were justified on the basis of national self-determination, according to which recognized nations have the right to self-government. This norm gradually evolved into the more controversial strand of segregationist rights, which are used by minority movements today to challenge their host governments. Second, the interwar minorities regime established a mechanism by which group representatives could appeal for legal redress over the heads of their governments. Minority organizations responded to this institutional opportunity structure by flooding the League with petitions for international intervention. They also formed alliances at the substate and transnational levels to leverage their position against their state centers. In these and other ways, minorities used the nascent bargaining framework in the interwar era to launch significant challenges against their governments. Both integrationist and segregationist minority rights fell out of favor in the immediate postwar period due to Nazi Germany's subversive use of collective rights in the 1930s. However, segregationist rights were revived in the 1960s to facilitate the process of de-colonization in sub-Saharan Africa and Southeast Asia. Meanwhile, integrationist rights were given a push in the postwar years by UN working groups, the international human rights campaign, and the U.S. civil rights movement.

The leaders of ethnic groups around the world have responded to these emerging opportunity structures by self-consciously wedding their struggles to the discourse of self-determination and minority rights. The late twentieth century witnessed an unprecedented rise in the number of groups whose representatives were actively bargaining with their host governments over state resources. The post–Cold War alliance of stateless nations known as the UNPO is further indication of this trend as, increasingly, the leaders of smaller and weaker groups advance demands for collective benefits. Minority empowerment has yielded undeniably positive developments, particularly for weak minorities in rich democracies and for indigenous communities whose standards of living have risen as a consequence. However, there has also been a growing trend among the leaders of territorially compact and externally leveraged minorities to escalate their claims against the center—very often leading to ethnic violence and sometimes even reprisals. This is the paradox of minority empowerment. The following chapter describes how the bargaining framework operates on the *micro*-level to produce fluctuations in group claims in individual cases, often in the absence of clear economic or security imperatives.

CHAPTER TWO

The Theory of Ethnic Bargaining

This chapter sets forth the micro-level dynamics of ethnic bargaining. In doing so, it addresses two empirical puzzles in minority politics. First, why do group leaders variously radical-ize and moderate their demands against the state center over time? As noted in the introduction, relatively static features such as historical grievances, cultural differences, and underlying economic disparities cannot account for sudden shifts in the claims put forward by minority representatives. Second, contrary to the expectations of ethnic fears accounts, why do minorities sometimes mobilize when security threats diminish but *fail* to mobilize when they intensify?[1]

The theory of ethnic bargaining seeks to account for both puzzles. I begin with the observation that nationalist conflicts very often take the form of a territorially concentrated minority challenging the state center over collective benefits. Not uncommonly, such disputes also involve one or more external actors that provide aid to the rebelling minority. This strategic configuration bears a first-order resemblance to Rogers Brubaker's model of triadic relations between a national minority, a nationalizing state, and an external national homeland (see fig. 2.1).[2]

According to Brubaker, ethnic conflict occurs as political elites compete for dominance within each of these three "relational fields." The emergence of a radical stance in one field leads to the emergence of a radical stance in the other two fields, and vice versa. Conflict is thus a "contingent" outcome of the "interplay of mutually suspicious, mutually monitoring, mutually misrepresenting political elites," producing a cycle of radicalization that often leads to violence. However ingenious this is as a description of

[38]

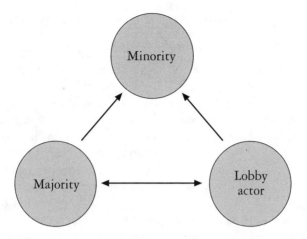

Figure 2.1 The players

ethnic conflict, Brubaker's model is theoretically indeterminate. Because the relational fields are mutually constituted, his theory predicts neither when radicalization is likely to occur nor when a spiral of radicalization is likely to reverse itself. As Brubaker himself acknowledges, "what could not be predicted in these or other cases . . . was just what kind of nationalizing stance, what kind of minority self-understanding, what kind of homeland politics would prevail in the struggles . . . and just how the interplay between the three fields would develop."[3] The ethnic bargaining theory builds on this model by enhancing its predictive capacity.

The Theory of Ethnic Bargaining

The first thing to note is that minority mobilization is a necessary condition for the emergence of ethnic conflict. To see why, imagine what would happen if state authorities target a minority for abuse but the minority does not radicalize. Repression or genocide might result but not sectarian conflict as such. Thus, the extermination of millions of Jews in the Holocaust and the massacre of over one million Armenians by the Ottomans during World War I can be considered genocides but not ethnic conflicts, which imply a two-sided struggle. Now consider a case in which an external actor sends in troops on behalf of a group but, again, the group chooses not to radicalize. Interstate skirmishes or war would be the likely outcome but not minority-majority conflict as such. Minority mobilization is therefore the sine qua non of intergroup conflict and therefore serves as the logical focus of our investigation.

I measure minority radicalization as the extremity of collective demands that minority representatives advance against the center.[4] A group can be said to "make" a particular demand if it is put forward by the party or political leader who enjoys broad support within the minority rank and file. In the context of ethnic bargaining, group claims serve primarily as indicators of state challenge and may be ordered along a continuum of challenge ranging from affirmative action to secession or irredentism. Secession (establishing sovereignty over a portion of state territory) and irredentism (annexation of a portion of state territory by another state) represent the most extreme demands on the continuum; this is because they challenge the integrity of the state itself. Demands for territorial autonomy are less extreme because they call for devolution of state power to minority regions but do not challenge the external borders of the state. Claims of cultural or linguistic autonomy are more moderate still because they call for power-sharing in the spheres of culture and education while leaving unchallenged majority control over the state's politico-territorial institutions. Claims of affirmative action are the least extreme of all because they merely call for greater minority integration into the majority-controlled society (see fig. 2.2).

There is empirical justification for placing group claims on such a continuum. As Donald Horowitz notes, "Groups . . . are not born irredentist or secessionist. They can and do move back and forth from integrated participation in the state of which they are a part to a posture of secession or irredentism."[5] In the course of politicking, minority leaders routinely shift their demands up and down this spectrum to indicate relative radicalization and moderation, respectively. To illustrate, when group representatives abandon calls for territorial autonomy in favor of demands for language

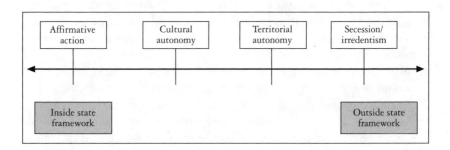

Figure 2.2 Dependent variable: Extremity of minority demands

rights, they signify that the group has de-radicalized its challenge against the state. If, instead, they discard calls for territorial autonomy in favor of secession or irredentism, the group has intensified its challenge. The impetus for these shifts comes mainly from the rank and file, as minority members rally around elites whose claims reflect the perceived power differential between the minority and majority at every point in time.[6]

A number of scholars have already drawn attention the strategic uses of group demands. Donald Rothchild pointed out long ago that minority claims are a part of normal politicking in inter-ethnic societies as groups pursue a more favorable distribution of state resources. In this view, claim-making is not a zero-sum proposition, but rather a routine feature of collective bargaining at the substate level.[7] In his work on post-Soviet Russia, Steven Solnick, too, writes that struggles between the center and periphery constitute an "ongoing bargaining game over the ultimate distribution of powers in the future state."[8] Using a game theoretical model similar to the one set forth below, Rupen Cetinyan concludes that "[s]tronger groups—stronger either because of their independent means or because of those made available through the aid of an outside supporter—should demand, and get, more."[9] All of this suggests that minority demands are less important for what they are than for what they represent from a bargaining perspective.

But why do minorities mobilize around collective demands in the first place? Given that they are usually in a position of weakness vis-à-vis their state governments, mobilization is often a risky proposition. The decision to radicalize must therefore be driven by perceptions of increased power relative to the center. The question then emerges: How do these perceptions come about? On the most basic level, beliefs about minority leverage are a function of structural characteristics, including group size and territorial compactness. These features are both transparent and relatively static and therefore serve as base indicators of group strength.[10] As such, they effectively place limits on the extremity of claims that group leaders may credibly advance against the government. Group traits, however, tell only part of the story. Although size and compactness place limits on a minority's capability—and therefore willingness—to challenge the majority, they cannot predict when (or even if) a minority will radicalize. To explain shifts in demands over time, it is therefore necessary to bracket group traits in order to investigate the influence that nationalist signaling has on minority behavior.

Figure 2.3 illustrates the logic of ethnic bargaining. The minority has the first move for two reasons. First, intergroup conflict is usually initiated when the minority decides to challenge the domestic status quo. Second, due to its strategic vulnerability, the minority is the only player in the game to choose its actions on the basis of the anticipated responses of the other two play-

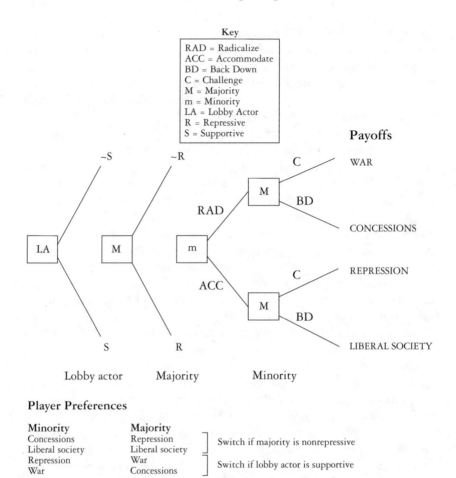

Key

RAD = Radicalize
ACC = Accommodate
BD = Back Down
C = Challenge
M = Majority
m = Minority
LA = Lobby Actor
R = Repressive
S = Supportive

Payoffs

WAR

CONCESSIONS

REPRESSION

LIBERAL SOCIETY

Lobby actor   Majority   Minority

Player Preferences

Minority	Majority	
Concessions	Repression	Switch if majority is nonrepressive
Liberal society	Liberal society	
Repression	War	Switch if lobby actor is supportive
War	Concessions	

Figure 2.3 Decision tree of ethnic bargaining

ers. In contrast, the other actors (usually state governments or organizations) make decisions based on a variety of goals and inputs—which may or may not involve the minority. These include winning the support of their domestic constituents, satisfying powerful interest groups, obtaining trade preferences or international loans, and securing access to scarce resources. Rarely do these powerful players consider the likely minority response to their actions when making their choice.[11] Stephen Saideman provides empirical support for this proposition, showing that Serbia's inconsistent support for the Bosnian Serbs in the 1990s was driven more by domestic political considerations than it was by the needs of its ethnic kin over the border.[12]

Other data analyses indicate that third parties generally do not intervene to "rescue" their co-ethnics, but rather to serve their own geopolitical interests—to gain valuable territory or access to oil or water.[13] Nazi Germany, for example, invaded Bohemia and Moravia not so much to protect its co-ethnics, but rather to expand into central Europe. The host government, too, bases its policies on a wide range of goals. The Slovak government, for example, enacted more liberal minority policies in the late 1990s primarily due to its desire to join the EU.[14]

In light of these empirical regularities, the preferences of both the lobby actor and majority are treated as exogenous to the game. The minority thus begins each round of ethnic bargaining, choosing its action on the basis of the expected responses of the other two players. How does the minority anticipate their reactions? It does so by inferring their preferences from their signals of behavioral intent. On the most basic level, the minority is attempting to determine whether the state majority is repressive (R) or nonrepressive (~R) and whether its lobby actor (assuming one exists) is supportive (S) or nonsupportive (~S).[15]

Figure 2.4 depicts the combinations of these types, yielding four possible states of the world: conflict, opportunity, vulnerability, and peace. The minority's behavior largely depends on which state of the world it believes it is in.[16]

MAJORITY

	Repressive	Nonrepressive
	1	**2**
Supportive	**State of Conflict** The minority radicalizes, risking inter-ethnic conflict	**State of Opportunity** The minority radicalizes, receiving concessions
	3	**4**
Nonsupportive	**State of Vulnerability** The minority accommodates suffering repression	**State of Peace** The minority accommodates, facilitating inter-ethnic cooperation

LOBBY ACTOR (row label spanning left)

Figure 2.4 Minority behavior in four states of the world

1. In the *state of conflict*, the lobby actor has both the incentive and capacity to intervene on behalf of the group; at the same time, the majority favors ethnic discrimination. The minority therefore expects repression if it accommodates the majority. If the group instead radicalizes, it expects its lobby actor to intervene on its side. To avoid confrontation, the majority will then back down and grant the minority concessions. Because the group prefers concessions to repression, it will radicalize to obtain benefits. The danger in this state of the world is that the audience costs to a nationalistic majority of backing down may come to outweigh the benefits of avoiding war, even with the risk of a humiliating defeat. If the minority is unaware of these calculations, it may radicalize to obtain concessions but instead find itself locked into war. Consequently, this combination of types is most likely to lead to intergroup (and even interstate) warfare.

2. In the *state of opportunity*, the minority is in an optimal bargaining position. This is because the majority prefers making concessions to the minority in order to reap the rewards of ethnic harmony. The minority, for its part, enjoys the support of an external lobby actor. The group therefore has a choice between two attractive alternatives. If the group accommodates the majority, the center will refrain from repression, yielding a liberal society. If the minority instead radicalizes, the majority will offer concessions to avoid a confrontation with the group's lobby actor. Because the minority prefers concessions to a liberal society, it will choose to radicalize to obtain rewards.

3. In the *state of vulnerability*, the minority is in the least advantageous bargaining position. Because the majority prefers exploitation to a liberal society, the minority can expect oppression if it accommodates the majority. If it instead radicalizes, the group faces annihilation due to its lack of external patronage. It therefore has a choice between the lesser of two evils. Because it prefers repression to the devastating costs of military defeat, the minority will accommodate the majority and suffer repression. However, the minority is likely to remain mobilized in this state of the world, even if its weakness deters it from overtly challenging the center.

4. In the *state of peace,* there is the greatest potential for inter-ethnic cooperation. This is because the majority prefers a liberal society to minority exploitation. If the minority accommodates the center, it therefore expects ethnic peace. At the same time, the minority has no external leverage with which to extract concessions from the center. Because there are no expected benefits to radicalization, the minority will accommodate the majority, yielding ethnic peace.

Inferring the Likely State of the World

In choosing whether to radicalize, the minority must first ascertain which of the four states of the world prevails. To make things even trickier, the majority and lobby actor preferences toward the minority can change suddenly due to economic shocks, changes in the government, shifts in public opinion, or interest group pressures. In contrast, the preferences of the minority remain relatively stable because it must focus narrowly on ensuring its own survival. The minority is therefore constantly monitoring the other two players for changes in their respective intentions. Because the host state and lobby actor have incentives to misrepresent their preferences, the minority must *infer* these preferences from signals of behavioral intent. Signals are signs—both intentional and unintentional—that communicate a set of preferences.[17] The minority uses these signals to update its beliefs concerning the preferences of the other two players and therefore the prevailing state of the world; the more credible the signal (e.g., the more it commits the majority or lobby actor to a particular set of actions), the more certain the minority is concerning the state of the world. If the minority believes the state of the world has changed, it may alter its behavior accordingly. Because it is continually updating its beliefs concerning the state of the world, the group can be expected to mobilize sporadically so that a society once riven by ethnic violence becomes a model of ethnic cohabitation, and vice versa.

Equilibrium Behavior in an Uncertain World

I use the decision tree in figure 2.3 to show how a minority might act in light of its uncertainty about the state of the world. I do this by comparing the minority's expected utility over two possible actions: radicalization versus accommodation. The expected value of each action is a weighted sum of the values of all the possible outcomes of that action multiplied by their respective probabilities of occurrence. The minority's expected utility of radicalization is thus:

$$EU_m(RAD) = p_2 Con + (1 - p_2)War \qquad (1)$$

In words, the value to the minority of radicalizing is equal to the value of concessions multiplied by the probability that it has a supportive lobby actor plus the value of war weighted by the probability that it has an *un*supportive lobby actor. Similarly, the group's expected utility of accommodation is:

$$EU_m(ACC) = p_1 Rep + (1 - p_1)Lib \qquad (2)$$

This is a weighted sum of the value to the minority of repression multiplied by the probability that the majority is repressive plus the value of a liberal society multiplied by the probability that the majority is nonrepressive. The minority can be expected to radicalize when its expected value of radicalization outweighs its expected value of accommodation:

$$p_2\text{Con} + (1 - p_2)\text{War} > p_1\text{Rep} + (1 - p_1)\text{Lib} \tag{3}$$

Thus, as the likelihood that its lobby actor is supportive (p_2) increases, the probability of obtaining concessions through radicalization also increases. This raises the expected utility of radicalization (the left side of the equation). Meanwhile, as the probability that the majority is repressive (p_1) increases, the likelihood of suffering repression if the group accommodates likewise increases. This lowers the minority's expected utility of accommodation (the right side of the equation).

By assigning concrete values to the preference orderings in figure 2.3 (Concessions = 4; Liberal society = 3; Repression = 2; and War = 1), we can solve for the critical probabilities p_1 and p_2 above which the minority is likely to radicalize regardless of what the majority does. As we see in figure 2.5, as the probability of outside support increases, the likelihood of repression must *decrease* for the group to continue to value accommodation. Strikingly, this diagram also suggests that:

(H$_1$) If the minority is certain that it *lacks* outside support, then it is likely to accommodate the majority, even if it knows that the majority is repressive.

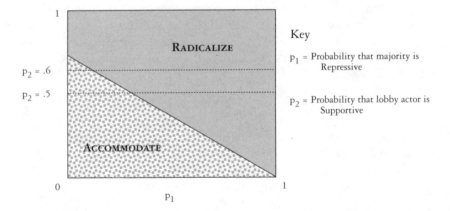

Figure 2.5 Comparative statics of minority behavior

In contrast, if the minority is certain that the majority is *non*repressive, it may still radicalize as long as the estimated probability of outside support is at least two-thirds. This leads to the second hypothesis:

(H₂) If the minority is reasonably confident of outside support, it is likely to radicalize, even if it knows that the majority is nonrepressive.

These hypotheses imply that external actors have a greater impact on minority behavior than host governments. From a policy standpoint, this means that minority protections on the domestic level may be insufficient for resolving an internal conflict if external sources of minority leverage are not first neutralized.

The Spatial Model: Elections and Political Coalitions

I now introduce a spatial model to illustrate the effects that ethnic bargaining has on electoral politics in the host state. Multi-ethnic democracies contain both active and latent political cleavages. Two of the most salient cleavages, class and ethnicity, are represented graphically in figure 2.6. A central assumption in this model is that voters in divided societies have a fixed amount of political capital that they can invest in agents

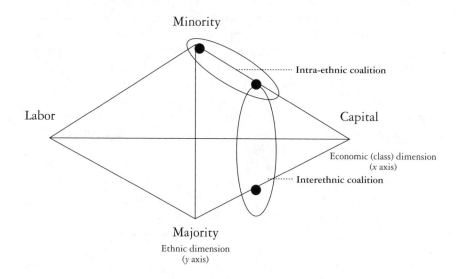

Figure 2.6 Electoral politics in divided societies

who represent their ethnic interests, their economic interests, or some combination thereof. There is thus an implied trade-off between the two issue areas. To win popular support and thereby weaken their competitors, office-seeking minority and majority elites adopt stances that reflect the median preferences of their respective constituencies. These preferences are driven, at least in part, by collective perceptions concerning the prevailing state of the world. In addition to these "opportunistic" elites, there may also be "extremist" elites whose comparative advantage lies almost solely in the dimension of ethnicity or who are personally committed to radical postures—whether or not they resonate with the public. With this in mind, I hypothesize that:

> (H_3) Elites who vary their stances over time in response to changes in ethnic salience are likely to maintain power in divided societies; in contrast, those who retain exclusivist positions despite changes in ethnic salience are likely to fall in and out of political favor.

What determines the level of ethnic salience in divided societies? With respect to ethnic bargaining, the salience of ethnicity can be expected to rise when a minority's host government and/or lobby actor send credible signals of nationalist intent. If, for example, the host government and lobby actor are engaged in a conflict over the minority's status, individuals will be more likely to mobilize on an ethnic basis. Elites respond to the heightened ethnic salience by emphasizing ethnic issues in their political campaigns and public addresses and by forging intra-ethnic alliances. At the same time, inter-ethnic coalitions are likely to fracture as they lose political value. If the host government and lobby actor later drop the minority issue in an effort to normalize diplomatic or trade relations, they have credibly signaled their nonnationalist intent. Politics will then *de*-ethnicize as individuals conclude that their political capital is better invested in other issue areas. Elites respond by forming coalitions across ethnic boundaries to lobby more effectively for these other interests. This yields the following hypothesis for proportional representation (PR) systems of government:

> (H_4) When the minority's host government and/or lobby actor signal nationalist intent, political elites are likely to form intra-ethnic coalitions at the domestic level. If the two major players instead normalize relations, inter-ethnic coalitions are more likely to develop.

This suggests that ethnic cleavages fade rather than disappear as ethnic bargaining de-politicizes and re-politicizes ethnicity over time. Political alignments are thus in constant flux as individuals shift their political capital from one cleavage to the next. It may be, however, that an extended period of non-nationalist signaling will lead an ethnic cleavage to disappear from politics altogether. The evidence in chapter 5 suggests that this may have already happened in the case of the Moravians in former Czechoslovakia.

Research Design

I use the following proxies to test the predictions of ethnic bargaining. I measure minority radicalization as the claims made by political agents who (1) won the plurality of the minority vote in the most recent local or national elections and/or (2) are recognized as the de facto leaders of the group. The claims advanced by these representatives will serve as a moving indicator of the claims supported by the group. Whenever possible, public opinion polls are used to check the validity of this measure. Host government and lobby actor signals are measured as credible signs of policy intent that emanate from the governing officials of these bodies. In order of credibility, these include:

1. *Treaties/pacts.* Binding treaties or pacts are highly credible signals of behavioral intent because they are difficult to reach and costly to violate. By entering into these agreements, the signatories thus credibly commit to adhere to the guidelines set forth in these covenants. The most credible of these include mechanisms for monitoring and enforcement.
2. *Actions/policies.* Although not legally binding, official policies are also a reliable sign of behavioral intent—not only because actions speak louder than words, but also because they are costly signals to send and, once in place, commit a state or organization to a future set of actions. The minority rank and file may infer shifts in host state and lobby actor preferences by observing shifts in their policies.
3. *Public statements.* Public statements are the least credible signs of intent. Because they are cheap to make, they may be little more than empty rhetoric or bluffing devices. Official statements have *some* credibility, however, given that governments or organizations might incur audience costs by reneging on their publicly stated commitments.

Finally, I measure ethnic salience as the extent to which individuals in a society rally around elites—either minority or majority—who assume a hostile position toward the other ethnic group. Domestic coalitions are considered inter-ethnic if mainstream minority and majority representatives engage in political cooperation, particularly if they do so in government. They are considered *intra*-ethnic if there is cooperation within, but not between, minority and majority parties.

At this point, several caveats should be made with regard to the theory of ethnic bargaining. First, I do not argue that individual leaders play *no* significant role in the process of ethnic mobilization. Obviously, it is government leaders who enact repressive policies and the heads of lobby states and organizations who initiate ethnic interventions. Particularly where they can restrict access to independent sources of information, elites can (and often do) succeed in inducing the collective belief that mobilizing along ethnic cleavages will yield the greatest benefits (or the least costs). New democracies are especially vulnerable to nationalist myth-making because opportunistic leaders can exploit their partial monopolies over the media to whip up support for nationalist causes as a means of holding onto power during transition.[18] However, the ability of *minority* elites to play the ethnic card is far more circumscribed due to their limited institutional power as well as the constraints imposed upon them by the group's strategic vulnerability. The argument in this book relates primarily to minority leaders, whose positions are driven primarily from the ground up.

Second, I do not dispute that elites use ethnicity instrumentally to advance their private interests; indeed, I *assume* that political leaders are opportunistic insofar as they seek political power. However, notice that this character flaw—if one can call it that—does not logically predict ethnic extremism; something else must be present in order for ethnic appeals to resonate with the wider population. The ethnic bargaining model addresses this gap by identifying the *conditions* under which radicalism pays political dividends to opportunistic leaders.

Third, it may be objected that host state and lobby actor signals are indeterminate given the contradictory messages and competing voices that emanate from these bodies. However, the minority rank and file generally focus their attention on the recognized *leaders* of these bodies, rather than on peripheral players, for the obvious reason that the intentions of the governing officials are far more likely to be reflected in future policies. This simple rule is used to separate the wheat from the chaff in determining reliable signals of behavioral intent.

Finally, one might question the value of the model for explaining internal conflicts where there are no external lobbyists. In these cases, however, the model simply reduces to a dyadic bargaining game between the minority and majority. In a triadic configuration, minority radicalization is the result of fluctuations in *both* internal and external group leverage. In a dyadic configuration, radicalization is a function of shifts in internal leverage only. Minority size and territorial compactness still serve as preexisting structural determinants of internal leverage, placing limits on the extremity of demands that can be feasibly sought by the group. Fluctuations in mobilization, however, are driven by changes in the *relative power balance* between the group and the center. If the host government is weakened by severe economic recession, civil unrest, or foreign military campaigns, the minority may infer that it is relatively strong vis-à-vis the center and radicalize its demands as a means of obtaining greater concessions.

To conduct this analysis, I divide the seven cases of minority-majority relations into time segments, each of which represents a shift in the demands advanced by minority leaders. I examine these segments in turn to determine whether each shift in claims was preceded by signals from the host government or lobby actor in the direction predicted by ethnic bargaining. If, for example, a bilateral treaty between the minority's host and lobby states is followed closely by a moderation in the minority's demands, this provides support for the bargaining theory. To test the spatial model, I examine periods of inter-ethnic coalitioning to see whether they were preceded by credible signals of non-nationalist intent from both the host government and the lobby actor.

Chapters 4–6 apply joint longitudinal-comparative analysis to paired cases of minority-majority relations to test the explanatory power of ethnic bargaining relative to alternative theories of claim-making; it is also used to test more specific hypotheses concerning the relative influence of the lobby actor and host state on minority radicalization. In doing so, I compare cases that are similar in nearly every relevant respect except the key condition of interest, which is allowed to vary. If this variance is matched by variance in the dependent variable in the manner predicted by ethnic bargaining, this would tend to confirm the theory. I thus combine controlled comparison with longitudinal analysis as a means of addressing the small *N*–many variable problem that plagues qualitative research.[19]

Figure 2.7 shows how longitudinal and comparative analyses are combined to achieve greater control over potentially confounding variables. Thus the vertical axis represents variation in minority behavior over time while the horizontal axis represents variation in minority behavior between the two cases. As shown in the figure, there are four possible patterns of claim-making in the paired studies, each of which indicates a different driver of minority behavior. The first possibility is that the leaders of the two (ethnically

MINORITY CLAIMS
BETWEEN GROUPS

	Same	Different
Same	Static similarities (Cultural traits) 1	Static differences (History of ethnic relations) 2
Different	Synchronized changes (Impact of common lobby actor on host state) 3	Unsynchronized changes (Impact of different lobby actors on host states) 4

MINORITY
CLAIMS
OVER TIME

Figure 2.7 Model of joint comparative-longitudinal analysis

similar) groups make similar demands, despite differing conditions at the substate level. These claims also do not change significantly over time, in spite of changes in the international and domestic environment. Such findings would tend to confirm primordialist arguments that claim-making is driven by relatively static cultural or national traits that the two groups have in common.

The second possibility is that the leaders of the two minorities make different demands that do not change substantially over time. This would lend support to path-dependency arguments that the particular legacy of relations between the minority and majority at the substate level largely determines the goals that minority leaders will seek.

The third possibility is that the leaders of the two groups vary their demands synchronically over time. This would suggest that minority behavior is driven by *dynamic* features that the two groups have in common—their shared lobby actor (if they reside in different states but have the same lobby actor) or their shared host government (if they reside in the same state but have different lobby actors).

The final possibility is that the leaders of the two groups vary their demands *non*synchronically over time. This would indicate that minority claims are driven by dynamic features that the groups do *not* have in common, such as the actions of their different lobby actors (if the groups reside in the same state but have different lobby actors) or the actions of their different host governments (if they reside in different states but have the same lobby actor).

I apply this analytical framework to three paired case studies in postcommunist Europe to isolate the impact of host state and lobby actor behavior on minority mobilization: the Hungarian minorities in Romania and Slovakia (same lobby actor, different host governments), the Vojvodinian Hungarians and Kosovar Albanians in Yugoslavia (same host government, different lobby actors), and the Slovaks and Moravians in Czechoslovakia (same host government, no lobby actors). By analyzing these pairs over time and across space, I test the relative explanatory value of ethnic bargaining against competing accounts of claim-making.

This chapter uses a simple game tree model to illustrate the logic of ethnic bargaining: that minority radicalization is driven by signals of behavioral intent from the host government and/or lobby actor. The minority rank and file use these signals to update their beliefs concerning the other players' intentions toward the minority and thus the prevailing state of the world. Based on these beliefs, they will either radicalize against or accommodate the state center. Because they are continually updating their beliefs concerning the probable state of the world, minorities can be expected to mobilize periodically over time.

This model yields the surprising prediction that, if minority members are reasonably confident of external support, their leaders will radicalize for concessions despite the majority's best attempts to appease them. This stands in contrast to credible commitment expectations that minority radicalization is mainly a function of the center's inability to commit to minority protection. A spatial model is then introduced to illustrate how shifts in ethnic salience affect political coalitioning in multi-ethnic democracies. These micro-level processes are, in turn, embedded in a larger discursive structure that informs the prevailing modes and practices of ethnic bargaining used by minorities to challenge their governments the world over.

CHAPTER THREE

A Full Cycle of Ethnic Bargaining
Sudeten Germans in Interwar Czechoslovakia

The victorious Allied Powers completely reconfigured the map of central Europe after the First World War, establishing boundaries that gave statehood to some groups while denying it to others. The ethnic Germans of Bohemia and Moravia were among those who found themselves on the wrong side of the new national borders. In a few short years, the Sudeten Germans[1] lost their privileged status under the Austro-Hungarian monarchy and became a mere national minority in a binational Czechoslovak state. In the years directly after World War I and before World War II, they supported annexation by Austria and/or Germany. It is easy to infer from this, as many have, that the Sudeten Germans nursed irredentist ambitions throughout the interwar era. However, a careful examination of minority activism over this twenty-year period demonstrates that Sudeten German representatives changed their position considerably over time in reaction to perceived changes in their environment. This chapter shows that the behavior of one of the most notorious fifth-column minorities of the twentieth century is actually consistent with the logic of ethnic bargaining.

I analyze this case longitudinally to determine whether the German minority used signals from the Czechoslovak government and its lobby states (Austria and Germany) to decide whether to radicalize. I first divide the interwar period into six time segments, each representing a shift in minority demands.[2] By examining archival data—including records of debates in the Czechoslovak parliament and the Sudeten German parliamentary club as well as newspaper reports of events on the ground—I assess whether shifts in group demands were preceded by host and/or lobby state signals

Table 3.1. Sudeten German demands in Czechoslovakia, 1918–1938[a]

| Period | Most extreme ↔ Least extreme | | | | | Relative power of lobby state[b] (Germany/Austria) | Perceived Host State Discrimination |
	Irredentism/secession	Territorial autonomy/federalism	Regional autonomy	Cultural Autonomy	Affirmative action		
Late 1918– mid-1919	X					Low/uncertain	High
Late 1919–early 1920		X				Low	High
Mid-1920– mid-1925			X			Low	Med
Late 1925–1929				X	X	Equivalent	Low
1929–1936			X[c]			High	High
1936–1938		X				High	Med
Early 1938	X					High	Low

[a] Low, medium, and high indicate minority perceptions of lobby state support and majority repression. It is difficult to obtain precise measures of these variables because the sources of perceptions differ greatly from one case to the next. The most important thing to note in this respect is the *shifts* in perceived host and lobby state intentions, which should lead to corresponding shifts in minority demands.

[b] As noted in chapter 2, lobby actor support is a joint function of its capacity and willingness to intervene. In this case, the lobby state's willingness to intervene remained more-or-less constant throughout the period of analysis, whereas its capacity to intervene shifted significantly over time. Consequently, shifts in perceived lobby state support of the Sudeten Germans were mostly driven by shifts in relative strength between the lobby state(s) and host state, as indicated here.

[c] Sudeten German claims can only be loosely classified as regional autonomy in this period. Minority leaders kept their demands deliberately vague during this time, making ambiguous calls for "national" autonomy.

in the direction predicted by the model. The six time segments are given in table 3.1.

As shown in the table, Sudeten German demands—measured as the claims of the minority's most popular representatives—shifted dramatically from irredentism after World War I to calls for language rights and affirmative action in the mid-1920s and back to irredentism in the late 1930s. Possible explanations for Sudeten German radicalization include economic deprivation in the 1930s; the ambitions of the Sudeten German Party leader, Konrad Henlein; primordial pan-German revanchism; and German resentment over Czech dominance in the new state. While each of these factors may have played a role, none of them adequately accounts for the peculiar timing of Sudeten German radicalization, nor why interwar Czechoslovakia was mostly marked by peaceful ethnic co-habitation. This analysis demonstrates that Sudeten German radicalization was mainly a function of signals of nationalist intent from the Czechoslovak majority and the minority's lobby states. The remarkable fact that Czech-German relations were largely *harmonious* during this time, despite potentially explosive ethnic tensions, suggests that accommodation is possible even in societies recently torn by war and riven by ethnic hatreds.

Ethnic Bargaining Hypotheses

Minority radicalization is influenced in the first place by internal bargaining leverage, which is largely a function of group size and territorial concentration. For example, if a group fails to meet certain size and compactness requirements for sovereignty, independence would not be feasible. If their position is not seen as credible, minority elites will have trouble mobilizing the external and internal support necessary to extract concessions from the center.

In 1918, the Sudeten Germans numbered over 3 million or 23 percent of the population of Czechoslovakia.[3] In the German-speaking Sudetenland, they made up the overwhelming majority, constituting 90–100 percent of the population in most districts.[4] The group was therefore large and territorially compact. However, it was also territorially noncontiguous, as the Germans resided along the perimeter of the Czech lands. (See map 5.1.) Although their ethnic geography ruled out an independent Sudeten state, annexation by neighboring Austria or Germany *was* feasible. The credibility of these claims translated into greater bargaining power for the Sudeten Germans; their leaders could therefore use irredentism as a credible threat in negotiations with the majority. This does not, however, mean they will necessarily advance such goals. Over the entire interwar period, German leaders only briefly escalated their demands to irredentism.

The bargaining model identifies two important inputs in the minority's decision to radicalize: majority repression and outside support. In the first instance, the minority may mobilize when the government is perceived to be discriminatory, decreasing its utility of accommodation. Signals of repressive intent are more credible when (1) the government has strategic or economic incentives to exploit the minority, (2) the government has a reputation for discriminatory policies, or (3) there has been a power shift from the moderates to the nationalists in government. In other words, when the Czechoslovak majority demonstrates both the capacity and incentive to discriminate, the Germans should be more likely to radicalize. Their ultimate decision, however, rests on their perceived bargaining leverage against the center.

The actions of their lobby actors matter critically in this respect. All things being equal, the extremity of minority demands is likely to (1) increase when the lobby actor is supportive and strong relative to the host state and (2) decrease otherwise. The Sudeten Germans are therefore likely to radicalize when they perceive either Germany or Austria to be supportive and strong relative to Czechoslovakia and accommodate otherwise. Finally, when there is a balance of power between the minority's lobby state and the host state, there is likely to be a political realignment as ethnicity loses political salience. This is because the power of the lobby state serves as a check against majority discrimination while the power of the host state serves as a check against minority radicalization.

I now test these hypotheses using the six time periods outlined in table 3.1.

Sudeten German Claims in the Interwar Period

Late 1918–Mid-1919: The Birth of Czechoslovakia

At the close of World War I, the Sudeten Germans had greater economic incentives to remain in Czechoslovakia than to join either Austria or Germany.[5] Sudeten industrialists, landowners, and the broad middle class were aware that Czechoslovakia had a stronger economy and was more likely to protect private property than either Austria or Germany, both of which were coping with widespread social unrest and were nearing economic collapse. Both states also had strong communist movements, which Sudeten industrialists viewed with distinct unease. Moreover, the Sudetenland produced materials for the Czechoslovak market and was therefore economically dependent on its union with the interior. Finally, if the Sudetenland were annexed by Germany, it would face intense competition from the Reich's more efficient industries, which was sure to damage the region's economy.[6]

This, of course, had to be weighed against the expected costs of discrimination in the new state. The Germans naturally assumed that the Czechs would use their newfound power to redress inequities they had suffered under the previous regime. The Germans had enjoyed extensive economic, cultural, and political privileges under the Austro-Hungarian monarchy, which had ruled the Czech lands from its seat in Vienna. Although the working class was composed of both ethnic groups, the Germans dominated ownership and management positions and held a disproportionate share of the region's wealth.[7] Those without an adequate command of the German language had been excluded from better-paid positions in the civil service and prestigious occupations over which the Germans held a virtual monopoly. The Sudeten Germans had also enjoyed significant electoral advantages in the Bohemian Diet (one of the two local parliaments in the Czech lands) as well as the *Reichsrat* (the imperial parliament in Vienna). Members of parliament were elected through a system of four *curiae* that were weighted according to wealth. In this way, the wealthier Germans were overrepresented in the empire's political bodies, where they used their power to protect their economic position.[8] In exchange for increasing the electoral franchise in 1897 and 1907, the German parties demanded a system of proportional representation that would ensure that the Slavs could not outvote the Germans and Italians in the *Reichsrat*. The Sudeten Germans also secured a veto in the Bohemian Diet by fixing the proportion of representation at fifty-five Germans to seventy-five Czechs, although the Czechs outnumbered the Germans in Bohemia two to one.[9] Thus, Sudeten German privileges in Bohemia and Moravia stemmed from their political dominance in the wider empire.

Toward the end of the war, the Sudeten Germans—anticipating a German victory and the creation of a pan-German state—were by all accounts stunned by the rapid turn of events that reduced them to a national minority in a Slavic state. Their overall reaction was one of horror:

> Suddenly [the Germans] were forced to discover that far from the materializing of Mitteleuropa, the War was lost, and lost to the Slavs. The prospect of being included in an independent Czech State, after all that now lay between Czech and German [*sic*], seemed at first too bad to be true. The War had brought the Sudetendeutschen closer to the Austrian State, and from October 30th, when the Parliament in Vienna claimed to keep their allegiance, they were eagerly Austrian in order not to be Czech. With all their tenets crashing about their ears, the non-Socialist

Germans ... reacted to Wilson and self-determination with almost childish eagerness, though they had long decried the [Czech] "Marxists" for speaking of such things.[10]

On the eve of Czechoslovakia's independence, Sudeten German delegates in the *Reichsrat* called for separate national parliaments for Germans and Czechs in Bohemia. They also announced the formation of local German governments in the border regions as well as a national committee to prepare for the integration of the Sudetenland into Germany. Finally, they appealed to fellow Germans to make every effort to prevent the "forceful incorporation of ethnic Germans into the Czechoslovak state."[11] Czech leaders derided the widening "panic" among Sudeten Germans, claiming that they had more to fear from the "chauvinistic" governments of Austria and Germany than from Czechoslovakia, which would be a liberal, multi-ethnic state.[12]

Nevertheless, plans went ahead with the new German National Assembly, which elected a committee on October 21 to preside over the "German territories" prior to annexation by Austro-Germany. These actions were undertaken with the tacit approval of the nationalist governments of Vienna and Berlin. Shortly after the establishment of Czechoslovakia in October 1918, Austria's Provisional Parliament voted to declare German-Austria a constituent part of Germany as the first step toward creating a pan-German state. Chancellor Karl Renner declared that "in this hour our German people in every district shall know that we are one race and share one destiny," at which point the parliament erupted in wild cheers.[13]

With the encouragement of Austria and Germany, provisional governments were established in the Sudetenland—in Reichenberg, Drumau, Troppau, and Znaim. These were to be transitional arrangements prior to the *Anschluss* between Austria and Germany, at which point the Sudetenland would be incorporated into a greater German nation-state.[14] It became increasingly evident, however, that neither Austria nor Germany could provide the support the minority would need to defy the Czechoslovak government. Both states urged the Germans to resist the Czechoslovak authorities in the face of poor military odds and a harsh winter. However, neither Berlin nor Vienna could offer direct assistance, particularly given their own problems with food shortages and social unrest—not to mention Allied opposition to such plans.

Lacking external aid and facing a severe food shortage in the border regions, the Sudeten governments attempted to negotiate assistance from the Czechoslovak officials who had been authorized by the Allies to distribute food relief throughout the country. In early November, a Sudeten delegation led by Joseph Seliger traveled to Prague to apply for food assistance and to "establish peace and order between the two nations."[15] After making their request, the delegates proposed an arrangement whereby the Czechs and Germans could govern "their own areas" until the boundaries between Germany, Austria, and Czechoslovakia could be redrawn to reflect the ethnic realities. The Czechs retorted that they would dispense food aid to the region on condition that the Germans recognize the Czech National Committee as the legal government of all Bohemia, Moravia, and Silesia. The meeting soon reached an impasse, with the Czech official, Alois Rašín, blurting, "We don't negotiate with rebels!"[16]

Dire food shortages and growing unrest in the borderlands finally forced the Sudeten leaders to petition for outside assistance—first from Germany (which refused their request) and then from Czechoslovakia. The Czechoslovak military responded by occupying the towns in the Sudetenland, quelling the uprisings and quietly dissolving the territorial governments.[17] Over the coming months, the central government gradually asserted military control over the renegade provinces in the face of vociferous protests from Vienna. Austria had hoped to annex portions of south Bohemia and Moravia, which were among the wealthiest, most industrialized areas of central Europe. However, the much-weakened Austrian state was helpless to do anything but watch as the Czechoslovak authorities—with Allied backing—consolidated control over the Sudetenland.

The Sudeten Germans ultimately failed to confront the occupying forces. Although more radical leaders called for armed resistance, the rank and file correctly perceived that their political fate now rested in the hands of the Conference Powers. Austria and Germany had demonstrated that they could not support a resistance against the Czechoslovak state; when Sudeten leaders applied for military assistance in 1919, the war-weary Reich told them "the Sudetendeutschen must satisfy themselves with autonomy."[18] With little hope of external support, the Sudeten Germans inferred that resistance against the Czechoslovak *legionnaires* would be futile at best and catastrophic at worst. Nonetheless, there was still hope for indirect support. Both Austria and Germany promised to apply to the Conference Powers for territorial adjustments on the grounds of mismatched ethnic and political boundaries.[19]

In the meantime, the Czechs had begun to signal nationalist intent. Soon after the establishment of the Czechoslovak state, government officials proclaimed the need to "convince" the Sudeten Germans of the "justice of Czechoslovakia's actions," asserting that the government itself was the best guarantee of the political, economic, and national well-being of the country's inhabitants.[20] President Tomáš Masaryk openly praised the "bravery of our Czech and Slovak *legionnaires*," who had fought on the side of the Allies during the war. He called on them to assist in implementing the conditions of the Paris Peace Conference to "secure the position of the Czechoslovak nation."[21] In these and other ways, the Sudeten Germans were depicted as outsiders and enemies of the new state, which belonged explicitly to the Czechs and the Slovaks. Perhaps the starkest illustration of this was Masaryk's Christmas address in 1918 in which he asserted that "our Germans" must "work with us" in building the new state, adding that "[Czechs and Slovaks] have created the state and this determines the constitutional position of our Germans who originally entered the country as immigrants and colonists."[22]

To the Germans, the president's speech signified that the Czechs intended to even the score with their German compatriots. Radical minority leaders began to quote Masaryk's address—along with Rašín's earlier outburst—as proof of deep-seated Czech animosity toward the German minority. Their claims resonated strongly with the public in light of memories of Czech grievances in the prewar era and the attendant suspicion that the Czechs were planning to retaliate against their former overlords. In view of this, the government's promises to protect the economic, cultural, and political rights of the minority were not credible in the eyes of the Sudeten Germans—the majority of whom, "regardless of their politics and class background, wanted to remain part of Austria."[23]

The Germans rallied around irredentist demands in spite of strong economic disincentives to secede. As noted earlier, German industrialists were particularly dependent on their ties to the Czechoslovak interior, as both the primary market for their goods and the main source of their supplies. Moreover, annexation threatened to cripple Sudeten businesses by forcing them to compete with the more efficient industries of the Reich.[24] Despite this, Sudeten German industrialists were among the most enthusiastic irredentists, gathering in the north Bohemian town of Reichenberg (Liberec) on October 24 to sign a resolution calling for the political union of Deutschböhmen ("German Bohemia," or the Sudetenland) with Austria or, barring that, with the German Reich. Given their poor economic prospects in the Reich, the German capitalists could only have favored this outcome because the costs of Czech discrimination were expected to be extremely high.[25] Believing that the Czech majority was repressive, the Germans thus mobilized along ethnic rather than economic cleavages.

The high point in ethnic tensions came in March 1919, when the new Austrian Republic held its first parliamentary elections. The Czechoslovak authorities prevented Sudeten delegates from traveling to Vienna to participate, and hundreds of Germans from the border regions descended on Prague to demonstrate against the government. On the first day, the rallies dispersed peacefully, but the following day nervous Czech soldiers fired on German protesters in various towns, killing fifty-four people.[26] Despite their bitterness over these incidents, the Germans did not retaliate with violence. Indeed, the momentum toward cooperation with the Czechs seemed barely disrupted by these events.[27] This suggests that repression alone will not incite groups to radicalize if they are bargaining from a position of weakness.

The minority's growing willingness to negotiate with the Czechs was actually driven by events outside the country. In 1919, the Allies were finalizing the political borders of central Europe. Germany had all along refused to abet the Sudeten irredentists, partly to curry favor with the Allied Powers and thereby obtain a more favorable postwar settlement. The Austrian government, however, had strong economic interests in securing the territories of lower Bohemia and Moravia—indeed, it had sought to unite with Germany in part to achieve this aim. From late 1918 to early 1919, Renner repeatedly appealed to the Conference Powers for the unification of Austria, Germany, and the Sudetenland. As the odds of this outcome became increasingly remote, Austria scaled back its claims on Czechoslovakia from "continuous areas of [German] settlement" to border areas with overwhelming German majorities.[28] By spring 1919, however, the Allies had decisively closed the book on a pan-German state.[29]

With the hoped-for *Anschluss* ruled out, Sudeten leaders began to moderate their demands. Despite this, much of the population still favored irredentism. The German parties participated in Czechoslovakia's local elections in June in order to retain their positions in city and district governments in the Sudetenland. The German Social Democrats (DSAP) won 50 percent of the minority vote, followed by a coalition of German nationalist parties with nearly 20 percent.[30] The nationalist parties campaigned foremost on national self-determination, but qualified this by saying that if they "[had] to remain within the state," they would demand territorial autonomy for areas with large German majorities.[31] Although the German Social Democrats were more moderate with respect to cooperating with the Czechs, they too called for union with Austro-Germany. In fact, minority leaders continued to call for irredentism until the end of the Peace Conference—with territorial autonomy as their fallback position.

Although Germany signed its peace treaty in summer 1919, Renner continued to press for a border adjustment between Austria and Czechoslovakia, calling for a national plebiscite in districts with German majorities.[32] Observing this, the Germans in South Bohemia and Moravia held out for an exit option; Austrian and Sudeten German delegations jointly submitted petitions to the Conference Powers on behalf of German communities near the Austrian border. With their appeals falling on deaf ears, Rudolf Lodgman, a popular minority representative, thundered that "if Austria doesn't succeed [in this venture] then Sudeten Germans will join with other 'nations' in Czechoslovakia in a war against the state," emphasizing that this would be very destabilizing for Europe.[33]

At the end of the war, the Sudeten Germans believed that the Czechoslovak government was nationalistic and that their lobby states, Austria and Germany, were supportive. They were somewhat less convinced that their lobby states were strong, although they held out hope that their bargaining leverage would be bolstered by Allied support for national self-determination at the Paris Peace Conference. The minority therefore inferred that the state of the world was one of conflict (fig. 3.1, box 1). Given these beliefs, minority representatives should radicalize their claims to obtain significant concessions. Consistent with this prediction, mainstream German leaders Seliger and Lodgman put forward demands for irredentism in 1918 and 1919.[34] This increased the potential for sectarian conflict, as Czech authorities forcibly occupied the Sudetenland and later prevented Sudeten German delegates from voting in Austria's elections—leading to violent clashes between German protesters and Czech officials.

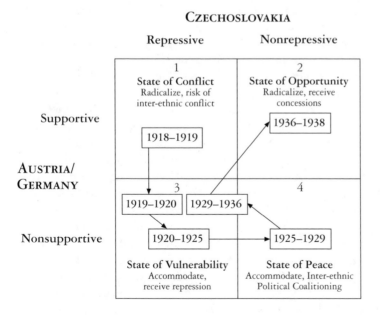

Figure 3.1 Sudeten German claims in interwar Czechoslovakia

Late 1919–Early 1920: Consolidating a Slavic National State

By September 1919, both Germany and Austria had renounced their territorial claims on Czechoslovakia. At this point, Sudeten irredentism lost all credibility as it became clear that the minority's exit option had disappeared. The Sudeten Germans would have to accept their status as a national minority in the new Slavic state. Minority parties responded by scaling back their demands from irredentism to territorial autonomy. The Sudeten German newspaper *Morgenzeitung* wrote that the Germans must fight to the last moment against incorporation into the Czechoslovak state but that, if the Peace Conference decided against them, they would have to fight for autonomy within existing state borders.[35] Minority elites echoed this sentiment, asserting that "nothing now remained for Germans but to work for autonomy and civic freedom [within Czechoslovakia]."[36] Even Rudolf Lodgman, the former proponent of Deutschböhmen, conceded that territorial autonomy was now the only viable option for the minority.

With the exception of a few renegade bases on the border, by 1920 most ethnic Germans had resigned themselves to their future in the Czechoslovak state.[37] Meanwhile, the Czech majority continued to send nationalist signals. In accordance with the wishes of the Allied Powers, the government had enacted a Minority Treaty in September 1919 guaranteeing minorities the right to be educated and conduct official business in their native tongue.[38] However, the treaty was not a credible guarantee of protection. Not only did the Czechs have an incentive to remove the privileges the Germans had enjoyed under the former regime, but they signaled their intention to do so in a thousand different ways. The new banknotes, for example, placed German third on a list of the Republic's four languages—after Ruthenian, a language spoken by about 100,000 people. German street signs were torn down in Prague and other towns across the country.[39] The Czechs appeared determined to exact revenge on those who had once regarded them as social inferiors.

During this period, Sudeten leaders began to realize that their negativist stance[40] toward the government in 1918–1919 had proven extremely costly. Minority elites had refused to participate in the provisional Constituent Assembly in protest of anti-German statements made by Czech leaders and because they were intent on negotiating a position outside the Czechoslovak state. By refusing to cooperate with the Czechs, they had excluded themselves from negotiations over key political and economic legislation. As a consequence, the assembly (a transitional parliament made up entirely of Czechs and Slovaks) passed the Minority Treaty; the state constitution; and important laws on land reform, war debts, capital levies, and education—all without input from the German minority.

Unsurprisingly, the new legislation had an overall negative impact on Germans. One law stipulated that minorities could have their own school only if they could put at least forty pupils in a classroom. Because many Germans lived in predominantly Czech areas, this led to the closure of a number of German schools. Although the government correctly pointed out that the Germans still had more teachers per pupil than Czechs in the Sudetenland, the Germans saw this defense as further evidence of Czech chauvinism. The Land Control Act of 1919 stipulated that no individual could hold more arable land than 150 hectares, or 371 acres.[41] The state confiscated any land in excess of this amount and redistributed it to landless peasants.[42] Although the law affected only a few large landholders, they were almost all German, whereas the beneficiaries were primarily Czech and Slovak. One German tract later claimed that, according to 1938 census statistics, ethnic Germans (who made up 22 percent of the population) had received only 6 percent of the redistributed land. In contrast, 31 percent of German land had been "seized by means of land reform."[43] Many Germans viewed this reform as an ill-disguised ruse to rob Germans of their property.

What troubled Sudeten Germans the most was the 1920 language law that made Czechoslovak the official language.[44] Under the new law, all government correspondence was to be conducted in Czechoslovak and all citizens had to use the language when conducting official business, with the exception of districts where a minority made up at least 20 percent of the population.[45] This reform had a particularly negative impact on ethnic Germans. Whereas most Czechs spoke German, very few Germans had a good command of Czech, which had been seen as a "servant language" not worth the trouble to learn. German civil servants were now commanded to learn Czech within two years or face losing their jobs.[46] These decrees led to public demonstrations across the Sudetenland—to Germans, the language law was an unmistakable sign of discriminatory intent. Although the constitution proclaimed equal rights for members of racial and linguistic minorities, the designation of Czechoslovak as the sole official language belied the constitution's guarantees of equality.[47] Minority leaders also objected to the fact that the constitution treated the sizable German minority as just one of several national minorities, the interests of which were subordinated to those of the Czechs and Slovaks in what increasingly appeared to be a national Slavic state.

We now turn to the question of external support. By now Austria and Germany had completely withdrawn from Sudeten German affairs. They were both economically and strategically weak relative to Czechoslovakia and therefore unwilling to provoke a confrontation with the new state. As noted earlier, Germany had steadfastly rejected pleas for paramilitary support prior to and during the occupation of the Sudetenland in 1918.

Germany quite simply could not afford to send nationalist signals when it needed a favorable settlement from the Allies to rebuild its shattered economy and put down widespread social unrest. The minority's odds of gaining external assistance became even more remote after Berlin committed itself to a position of nonintervention under the Treaty of Versailles, the abrogation of which entailed serious consequences.

Austria—considered less threatening than Germany and with a justifiable claim on lower Bohemia and Moravia—continued to press for border revisions right up until it signed its peace treaty in 1919. Almost immediately thereafter, Prague and Vienna negotiated several important agreements. The first was a military alliance against Hungary, which was threatening to attack both Czechoslovakia and Austria. More importantly, Renner promised to discontinue all support for Sudeten irredentism in return for much-needed food and coal supplies. In defending the deal, he proclaimed that Austria remained interested in the "liberation of Deutschböhmen *within Czechoslovakia.*"[48] These were highly credible signals that neither Austria nor Germany was willing to intervene on behalf of the minority. Meanwhile, the Czechoslovak government continued to signal nationalist intent toward its ethnic Germans.

Sudeten leaders responded to these changes by moderating their claims. As noted earlier, the German Social Democratic Party (DSAP) enjoyed the greatest support among the Sudeten Germans during this time, having captured one-half of the minority vote in Bohemia in the 1919 local elections.[49] I therefore use the goals advanced by the DSAP as a loose proxy for the position of the Sudeten Germans as a whole. At its first party congress in 1919, the DSAP leadership voiced support for the Czechoslovak state but demanded territorial autonomy for national minorities. Josef Seliger, the DSAP party chairman,[50] advocated the creation of a "corporate body through which each nationality would govern itself by means of a national council and a government." These "governments" would be responsible for the "legal regulation of the nationalities, administration of the educational system, [and] maintenance of ethnic culture."[51] The popular resonance of this position is evidenced by the fact that practically all German parties had adopted this position by late 1919.

In 1919, the minority's lobby states committed themselves to a position of nonintervention; at the same time, Czechoslovakia passed a number of laws that harmed ethnic Germans disproportionately. The minority therefore inferred that the state of the world had become one of vulnerability (fig. 3.1, box 3), leading minority elites to moderate their demands while remaining mobilized along ethnic lines due to the continued salience of ethnicity. This was in fact what occurred. The DSAP, the most popular Sudeten German party, shifted its demands from irredentism in the first several months of Czechoslovakia's existence to the pursuit of broad territorial autonomy by late 1919. Despite their moderated stance, the Sudeten Germans still voted their ethnic interests first and foremost. Minority representatives now entered parliament with the aim of shaping legislation in their favor.[52]

Mid-1920–Mid-1925: Sudeten German Integration

The German parties participated in the first national elections in April 1920, winning 72 seats in the 300-member Chamber of Deputies and 37 seats in the 150-member Senate.[53] Despite their substantial presence in parliament, the Germans were not given a place in the government. In fact, the country was actually run by five Czechoslovak parties (known as *Pětka,* "The Five"): the left-wing Social Democrats, the right-wing National Democrats, the National Socialists, the Agrarians, and the Populists (Catholics). Each Czechoslovak party had a minority German counterpart and each had its roots in the former Habsburg regime.[54] The *Pětka* had even managed the country during the transition—initially under the extremist National Democrats and later under the more moderate Social Democrats.[55]

The Czechoslovak and German Social Democrats won the pluralities of their ethnic constituencies, with 26 and 11 percent of the vote, respectively.[56] As head of the largest party, Vlastimil Tusar was invited to form the government. He first tried to establish a coalition with the German Social Democrats. However, the Germans demanded a guarantee of territorial autonomy in return for their participation.[57] Tusar could not agree to this condition—first, because of the practical problem of how to demarcate Czech territories from German territories and, second, because he faced considerable opposition from the more extremist Czechoslovak National Socialists and National Democrats who protested the government's "special treatment" of an already privileged minority. For his part, Seliger, the DSAP leader, risked losing the support of his constituents were he to ally with the Czechs before first obtaining broad concessions from the center.

The platforms of the German parties in 1920 reflected the salience of ethnicity: every German party in parliament had based its campaign on gaining "national autonomy."[58] Although the German leaders now grudgingly accepted the necessity of working within existing borders, they still opposed the existence of Czechoslovakia. Rudolf Lodgman addressed the newly elected assembly on behalf the German parliamentary club as follows: "Germans in Bohemia, Moravia and Silesia did not willingly join the

Czechoslovak Republic. . . . Deutschböhmen was incorporated forcibly by the Czechs, violating the Germans' rights to national self-determination."[59] Lodgman, who led the negativist parliamentary bloc (to which the majority of German parties belonged), demonstrated the resonance of his position when he called on all "immigrants and colonists" to leave the chamber when President Masaryk appeared to give his parliamentary address. All German deputies except the German Social Democrats got up and left the room.[60]

Having failed to form a coalition with his German counterparts, Tusar was compelled to establish a government with Czechoslovak parties across the political spectrum. Before long, the unwieldy alliance began to break down. Divisions appeared among the Social Democrats over whether they should cooperate with the right-wing parties; several leftist Social Democrats renounced "any kind of participation in a coalition government which also includes bourgeois [i.e., Agrarian] parties."[61] To complicate matters further, the spring and summer of 1920 brought significant social unrest as workers went on strike for higher wages and food relief. The government also faced strong criticism from both the right and the left over its position of neutrality during the 1920 Soviet-Polish war. From the perspective of the left, Prague was not sufficiently supportive of the Soviets. The government's controversial foreign policy together with "unacceptable" concessions to right-wing parties ultimately convinced the leftist Social Democrats that they could not simultaneously support Bolshevism and remain in the Tusar government.[62] The resultant split in the Social Democratic Party coupled with external opposition to scuttle the improbable coalition in September 1920.[63] The president then appointed a caretaker government of technocrats, which held power until September 1921.

In the meantime, chronic food shortages and labor strikes had begun to radicalize the general public. In the midst of this social unrest, Czech-German tensions periodically erupted into overt conflict. On the second anniversary of Czechoslovakia's independence, German demonstrations led to armed clashes between the Germans and the Czech *legionnaires* in the border regions. This was followed by German riots in the Sudeten towns of Reichenberg and Teplice. In Prague, street violence led to the ransacking of Jewish and German stores and monuments. On December 10, leftist leaders mobilized trade unions across the country to march on the capitol, successfully shutting down utilities and public transportation in several cities.[64] The government responded to the growing rebellion by issuing emergency decrees and passing a law against terrorism. It put down the strikes, quelled unrest in the border areas, and strictly curtailed the activities of the leftists, who were now out of government. The new legislation was used to prosecute and harass those who spoke out against the government—namely, the

Sudeten Germans and the Marxists.[65] Their shared plight helped bring the two groups together, and the left-wing Czechoslovak and German Social Democrats united in 1921 to become the first Czech-German political alliance of the interwar period.

At this point, the parliament was effectively gridlocked because Sudeten German and other opposition parties had blocked government legislation through most of 1921. Despite the government's inefficacy, new elections were considered unwise in a climate of ethnic divisiveness and social upheaval. Moreover, since the split of the Social Democratic Party, no single party was strong enough to form a new government. After several months of negotiations among the five leading Czechoslovak parties, a provisional arrangement was reached whereby Edvard Beneš, leader of the National Socialists and sitting foreign minister, became the prime minister of a new all-national government in September 1921.[66] Beneš was given this position largely to pacify the Sudeten Germans as a means of consolidating the still-fragile multi-ethnic state. Right away, Beneš initiated negotiations with Sudeten leaders over state compensation for Austrian war bonds (held mostly by ethnic Germans) and confiscated Sudeten German property. He also held discussions over appointing Germans to the territorial administrative committee of Czechoslovakia. These meetings were roundly condemned by Czech nationalists, who declared that Beneš and Masaryk were "more interested in pleasing the Germans than their own people."[67]

Masaryk now began to speak out in favor of inter-ethnic cooperation. While denouncing German demands for territorial autonomy, Masaryk asserted in his 1922 New Year's address that Czech-German discord was the final major challenge facing the state. He advocated greater German participation in government and public life as a means of forging a genuine multi-ethnic society.[68] Masaryk's repeated entreaties for closer Czech-German relations, together with Beneš's attempts to address minority concerns, suggested that the Czechs were beginning to moderate their position toward the minority. This led to a rift among Sudeten Germans over the desirability of cooperating with the Czechs.[69] Czech and German deputies began to collaborate in parliament along economic lines. Immediately after Masaryk's address, the National Assembly for the first time passed legislation that had been initiated by a German deputy.[70] The split between German activists and negativists came to a head in November 1922, when Lodgman announced at a meeting of the German parliamentary club that it was the duty of every German deputy to be disloyal to the Czechoslovak state. When the German Agrarians protested this statement, Lodgman walked out of the meeting, and the club was formally split between those who favored cooperating with the Czechs and those who did not.[71]

At this point, most Czechoslovak parties were still unwilling to form alliances with their German counterparts, even if this meant forgoing opportunities to be in power. This was largely due to the Czechs' reluctance to trust a minority that only a few years previously had threatened armed resistance against the state. Perhaps more significantly, Czechoslovak parties and their constituents were committed to creating a *Czechoslovak* state— a project in which minorities could play no role. Ensuring the national character of the state involved three major reforms: land redistribution, language regulations, and the transfer of civil service posts from Germans to Czechs and Slovaks.[72] These tasks were not completed until 1926, at which point the German parties finally entered government.[73]

Nationalizing legislation in the early 1920s reinforced German perceptions that the Czechoslovak government was discriminatory. Meanwhile, Austria and Germany convincingly signaled their unwillingness to support the minority. The Sudeten Germans therefore inferred that the state of the world was still one of vulnerability, leading them to continue to moderate their demands while remaining mobilized due to the high salience of ethnicity. However, emerging signs of Czech conciliation also led to perceptions that the state of the world might be shifting toward one of ethnic peace (fig. 3.1, box 4). As a result, a split appeared in the German parliamentary club between those who retained a separatist stance and a larger group that now advocated cooperating with the Czechs. That a greater number of Germans were beginning to favor collaborating with Czechoslovak parties is demonstrated by the results of the 1924 communal elections in which activist parties registered gains, whereas negativist parties suffered losses.[74] This signifies an overall trend toward minority accommodation, consistent with the predictions of the bargaining model.

Late 1925–1929: The Locarno Treaty and German-Czech Détente

In 1925, an economically resurgent Germany concluded a treaty with France (Czechoslovakia's ostensible patron) and Great Britain. In it, Germany guaranteed its western borders in return for Allied demilitarization of the Rhineland. The treaty also included a timetable for Germany's entry into the League of Nations. Although Berlin promised to conclude similar treaties with its neighbors to the east, the Locarno Accords did not guarantee Germany's eastern borders. This was an important diplomatic coup for Germany and a serious blow to Poland and Czechoslovakia. At the same time, Beneš had been promoting the Geneva Protocol, a collective security arrangement whereby signatory states pledged to come to one another's aid in the event of invasion by an aggressor country.[75] The protocol ultimately foundered on Britain's unwillingness to guarantee the security of Poland and Czechoslovakia, which were seen as remote and strategically vulnerable. The British were far more concerned with securing Germany's western frontiers, which they regarded as vital to their national interests. Under the provisions of Locarno, France was no longer compelled to come to the aid of Czechoslovakia or Poland in the event of a German attack; indeed, it could not intervene at all until after the League of Nations had failed to resolve the conflict. Britain and France had thus sacrificed Poland and Czechoslovakia to ensure the peace of Western Europe—more than a decade before the Munich Agreement!

These agreements were said to have created a "Locarno spirit" of cooperation and mutual understanding between the Czechs and Germans in Czechoslovakia.[76] This characterization is somewhat misleading. Prior to 1925, Germany was diplomatically isolated, with France guaranteeing Czechoslovakia against a German attack. Under this arrangement, the Czechs had no need to appease—or even protect—the Sudeten German minority. After Locarno, however, the German minority could be certain of Czech conciliation. This is because the withdrawal of the French guarantee rendered Czechoslovakia vulnerable to German revanchism. Prague was therefore dependent on Berlin's goodwill for its security, which meant that discrimination against the German minority was now out of the question. At the same time, the Sudeten Germans could infer with reasonable certainty that Germany was nonsupportive. Because its immediate interests lay in demilitarizing the Rhineland and easing its reparations payments, Germany could ill afford to antagonize the West by interfering in Czechoslovakia's domestic affairs.[77] Berlin therefore reassured the Czechs that it had renounced all territorial claims on the Sudetenland and encouraged the German minority to cooperate with the Czechoslovak government.[78]

Locarno thus created powerful security incentives for Prague to appease its German minority; meanwhile, the minority's lack of external support effectively ruled out ethnic rebellion. This mutual check on extremism undermined the credibility of nationalist rhetoric on both sides. The results of the 1925 elections—held three weeks after the signing of the treaty—provide confirmation for this hypothesis. The most activist (pro-government) minority party, the German Agrarians, obtained the plurality of the German vote, whereas support for the negativist bloc remained low and stagnant. Rudolf Lodgman, the "father of Sudeten German nationalism," even lost his own seat in the Chamber of Deputies to a vocal proponent of German activism![79]

With a mutual security guarantee at the international level, power-sharing at the substate level was now a real possibility. The all-national Czechoslovak government dissolved in 1926 as the salience of ethnicity decreased relative to that of economic interests. In October, the Czechoslovak Agrarians and the Czechoslovak Christian Socialists formed a right-wing coalition with their German counterparts; the leaders of the two German parties (Franz Spina and Robert Mayr-Harting) were even given cabinet positions.[80] In this so-called Gentlemen's Coalition, the Christian Socialists agreed to vote for higher agricultural tariffs in return for Agrarian support for increased funding of the clergy—their complementary economic interests thus held the alliance together.[81] The German members of government adopted a resolution in September 1926 pledging to cooperate with the government so that "the German people in Czechoslovakia can acquire their rightful share of power and full equality in national, cultural, and economic affairs."[82] While in government, the German parties sought broadly integrationist goals, including linguistic rights and cultural autonomy for the German minority. At a German Christian Socialist party congress in Liberec, Mayr-Harting stated categorically that the pursuit of irredentism "is just as dangerous as declaring a revolution."[83] Meanwhile, Spina, the German Agrarian leader, dedicated himself to advancing the educational rights of Germans, designing proposals for educational autonomy in preparation for negotiations over school reform.[84] The German leaders thus followed a strategy of ethnic accommodation—making concrete demands that could be easily satisfied within the existing state framework. In this way, they avoided antagonizing their Czech allies while securing tangible benefits for their constituents.

The late 1920s was marked by a profound degree of Czech-German cooperation as parties reached across the ethnic divide to achieve common economic goals. German deputies eschewed more extreme demands for autonomy and sided with the Czechs against Berlin's accusations that the government was not adequately protecting minority rights.[85] Strikingly, the German parties in government even supported the administrative reforms of 1927 that abolished the commune system in favor of four large provinces— Bohemia, Moravia-Silesia, Slovakia, and Ruthenia. These reforms helped meet *Slovak* demands for autonomy, but they represented a major step backward for Sudeten German autonomy. This is because ethnic Germans were a minority in each of the four new provinces, whereas they had dominated several of the smaller communes. The German deputies had backed the legislation out of narrow party interests—the reforms gave the central government the authority to appoint fully one-third of the delegates to the provincial diets, ensuring a strong position for both the German Agrarians and the German Christian Socialists at the local level.[86] This calculation demonstrates how normalized politics had become in a society recently riven by ethnic conflict.

The German parties in government were continually attacked by German nationalists for selling out the interests of ordinary Germans to remain in power. By the late 1920s, however, economic issues were so much more salient than ethnicity that negativism completely lost its resonance with the Sudeten German rank and file. Even the Sudeten German Nazi Party proclaimed its willingness to collaborate with the Czechs "given the right conditions."[87] At a regional party congress in April 1927, Spina spoke out in favor of inter-ethnic harmony: "The rule of the majority means a system of cooperation between nations, a system that should be lasting. In such a system, a policy of conservatism and stability is essential for economic reasons."[88] The leaders of the most popular German parties (the Agrarians and Social Democrats) made a number of similar pronouncements, touting the virtues of inter-ethnic partnership and citing harmonious relations between the Czechs and Germans dating back to the fourteenth-century reign of Charles IV. In 1928 and 1929, the German Social Democrats joined forces with the Czechoslovak Social Democrats, the Communists, and the National Socialists in opposing the Czech-German bourgeois government.[89] This constituted a complete realignment of political coalitions in Czechoslovakia from the ethnic to the economic axis (see fig. 3.2).

The Locarno Accords created a détente between Prague and Berlin, diminishing the salience of ethnicity and paving the way for inter-ethnic coalitioning at the substate level. Because Germany was no longer constrained from attacking its eastern neighbor, the Czech majority could no longer afford to

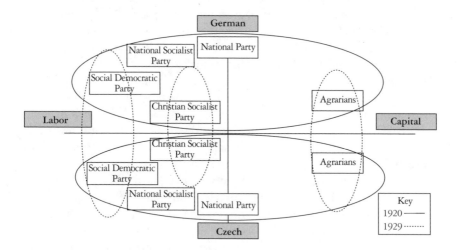

Figure 3.2 Political coalitions in Czechoslovakia

antagonize Germany by discriminating against its co-ethnics. Meanwhile, Germany was intent on reducing its war reparations and demilitarizing the Rhineland and therefore could not afford to attack the Czechs without provocation. Observing this, the Sudeten Germans could be reasonably certain that their lobby state was nonsupportive and that the Czech majority was nonrepressive, leading them to infer that the state of the world was one of ethnic peace (fig. 3.1, box 4). The ethnic bargaining model therefore predicts further minority moderation and the emergence of inter-ethnic alliances. The results and aftermath of the 1925 elections provide support for this hypothesis. Negativist German parties continued to lose ground to activist parties that favored cooperating with the Czechs; the leading German nationalist, Rudolf Lodgman, even lost his parliamentary seat to a vocal proponent of German activism. Right-wing Czech and German parties formed a coalition government based on compatible economic interests, whereupon left-wing Germans joined forces with left-wing Czechs to oppose the ruling coalition. Throughout this period, the German parties in government advanced moderate demands that could be easily accommodated within the existing state framework.

1929–Early 1936: Re-radicalization of the Sudeten Germans

The 1929 elections represent a high-water mark in Czech-German cooperation. Following the electoral victories of the Czechoslovak and German Social Democrats, the DSAP (having regained its status as the most popular German party) was invited to join a Red-Green Socialist-Agrarian coalition; Ludwig Czech, the DSAP leader, was given the Social Welfare Portfolio. The Czechoslovak Social Democrats had lobbied hard to get their German counterparts into the coalition. For their part, DSAP leaders offered to join the government unconditionally. This stands in marked contrast to negotiations between the two parties in the early 1920s, when the DSAP had demanded guarantees of territorial autonomy in exchange for its participation in government—leading to an impasse.

This situation had reversed itself by the mid-1930s. In just a few short years, the majority of Sudeten Germans switched their allegiances from the activist parties in government to the negativist Sudeten German Party (SdP). In 1929, the activist parties had won over 80 percent of the ethnic German vote, giving them fifty-four electoral mandates; the negativists had won only eight mandates.[90] In 1935, in contrast, the activist parties won only twenty-two mandates against the SdP's forty-four mandates. This meant that over 60 percent of ethnic Germans now *opposed* cooperating with the Czechs.[91] This dramatic shift cannot be explained as a reaction to unpopular government policies because no such shift could be seen among the Czechs, whose voting behavior remained much the same between 1929 and 1935.

The conventional wisdom concerning Sudeten German radicalization is that the 1933 Nazi *Putsch* in Germany led to a parallel rise in support for the Sudeten Nazi party. In this view, Hitler and his henchmen used the latently irredentist Sudeten Germans to organize a fifth column of subversives in preparation for Hitler's takeover of Bohemia and Moravia.[92] This account implies that the Germans were at heart disloyal citizens of Czechoslovakia and that the rise of Nazi Germany finally enabled them to pursue their secret irredentist longings. This is not only an oversimplification of events, but also dangerous, as it was used to justify the expulsion of as many as 3 million Germans from Czechoslovakia in 1945.

Sudeten German radicalization was actually rooted in a domestic crisis that predated the Nazi takeover. Relations between the Czechs and Germans had been remarkably stable until the effects of the global depression caught up with Czechoslovakia.[93] The dramatic slump in world grain prices in the early 1930s placed a great strain on the agricultural economies of Eastern Europe, forcing them to reduce their industrial imports from Czechoslovakia.[94] The Sudeten economy suffered tremendously as a result, because the most export-intensive industries in the country (glass and textiles) were concentrated in the region. Even more damagingly, Germany (Czechoslovakia's most important trading partner) reduced imports from its eastern neighbor by 75 percent between 1929 and 1930.[95] Czechoslovakia's drop in exports led to a significant trade deficit in 1932. Without hard currency to purchase raw materials from abroad, the country's industrial sector—concentrated in the Sudetenland—faced imminent collapse.[96]

Germany's financial crisis had a particularly bad effect on the Sudetenland. Many Sudeten businesses were financed by German banks. When these banks became insolvent, Sudeten German capitalists were compelled to seek assistance from Czech banks, which became increasingly reluctant to assume the credit risk. Their plight was exacerbated by the historically competitive relations between the Czech and German business communities.[97] Meanwhile, official unemployment increased from 42,000 in 1929 to nearly 1 million in 1933, at which point roughly one-quarter of the Czechoslovak labor force was out of work. Due to the severely depressed Sudeten economy, ethnic Germans were overrepresented in the unemployment statistics; although Sudeten Germans made up a little over 20 percent of the state population, more than 50 percent of the unemployed were ethnically German.[98]

In the midst of economic hardship, it was tempting for the Sudeten Germans to believe that their suffering was due to Czech neglect of the conditions in their community or, worse, a conspiracy on the part of the Czech government to force the long-reviled minority to take the brunt of the economic downturn.[99] Stories about ethnic discrimination began to circulate, despite the fact that the minister of Social Welfare—himself an ethnic German—had implemented a welfare program specifically designed to help people in the depressed Sudeten regions.[100] The growing resentment among the minority rank and file was not lost on their nationalist leaders, whose charges of Czech discrimination enjoyed particular resonance in the worst-hit areas of the Sudetenland. Premier Milan Hodža observed,

> [N]ationalistic German radicals made the disastrous economic plight the basis of a political claim against the Czecho-Slovak Republic. . . . They succeeded in catching the ear of the unemployed, who listened avidly in spite of the fair 'dole' which the Czecho-Slovak Government shouldered to the utmost limit.[101]

The Sudeten German National Socialist (Nazi) Party, in particular, attracted significant support by pledging to fight "national oppression." In spite of repeated attempts by the government to address their complaints, ordinary Germans were drawn to the Nazi Party, particularly in areas of severe economic downturn; the party's membership doubled between 1930 and 1932.[102]

As the Nazis and German Nationalists gained popularity, they became increasingly strident in their condemnation of the Czechoslovak state. Government authorities responded by taking legal action against them, finally disbanding the parties in 1933. At the same time, Konrad Henlein, an obscure gymnastics instructor from the town of Asch, established a cultural organization known as the *Sudetendeutsche Heimatfront* (Sudeten German Home Front), which received generous backing from Sudeten industrialists and German organizations.[103] The *Heimatfront* absorbed much of the rank and file of the recently defunct Nazi Party. With his wooden speeches and monotonic delivery, Henlein had none of the notorious charisma of Adolf Hitler. To the Sudeten German people, however, he seemed simple and sincere and came to symbolize the German everyman to his adherents, who placed their trust in his professed dedication to the German *Volk*. At this point, the negativists enjoyed far greater support than those who counseled patience and cooperation with the Czechs in a shared economic crisis. Richard Freund illustrates the bind facing German activists with the following anecdote:

> I have seen a German Deputy, who had staked his career on appealing for loyal co-operation with the Czechs, in tears while he told a Czech

Minister . . . "You ask us to trust you," he said, "and we accept your assurance that our unemployed men shall not fare worse than yours. What would those 40 or 50 jobs have mattered to you? To my town they would have been a symbol of hope. How can I now go before my constituents and ask them to be patient and loyal? They will shout me down and join the Henlein Party."[104]

While activist leaders appealed for calm, Henlein set out to establish a movement that would encompass all German parties, organizations, and unions—declaring that the Sudeten Germans "must unite to protect our people, our homeland and our jobs and to rise again: as 'one.' "[105] Henlein mobilized support by appealing to the frustrations of the unemployed. In a public address in Schluckenau on July 22, 1934, he proclaimed:

I feel deeply connected to [the common worker]; at the same time, there must not be anyone among us who is not ready to demonstrate his commitment to social justice by making the ultimate sacrifice. In this respect, I refer above all to the many tens of thousands of healthy men who are willing to work but have no jobs, to every young man who sees no future in front of him. . . . To secure the right to employment for all men who are willing and able to work is the most urgent task of any truly popular movement. . . . They can ban us, they can repress us, but no one can prevent workers from joining our ranks in ever increasing numbers, because our movement will ensure the [German] worker a better future than class-warfare and class-hatred.[106]

It was not difficult to persuade ordinary Germans that disparities between the Czechs and Germans were due to Czech discrimination and that their only alternative was to join the Henlein movement. Their plight appeared even grimmer when contrasted with the brighter prospects of their compatriots just over the border, lending further credibility to Henlein's claims of discrimination. As the effects of the depression wore on, it became increasingly difficult for activist leaders to defend their collaboration with a government seen as culpable for German suffering. Henlein thus gradually siphoned off activist support by persuading ordinary Germans that the German parties in government were too engrossed in internecine warfare (*Brüderkrieg*) to defend the Germans against discrimination. Henlein was well aware that the depression was working in his favor and later boasted that he and his henchmen had deliberately aggravated the economic crisis in order to incite animosity against the Czechs.[107]

When speaking of the German radicals, it is important to make a distinction between the Sudeten Nazi Party and the *Heimatfront*. One might easily assume that the Sudeten Nazis had simply reestablished themselves as the *Heimatfront* after they were disbanded in the 1930s.[108] If the *Heimatfront* were merely a smokescreen for the Sudeten Nazi party, it would be easier to conclude that Henlein had colluded with the Nazis in Germany from the beginning to subvert the Czechoslovak state.[109] An examination of the sequence of events, however, reveals that Sudeten German irredentism was instead a contingent outcome of incremental shifts in the bargaining leverage of the Sudeten German minority against the Czech majority.

Henlein's movement was actually divided between traditionalists and radicals. The *Heimatfront's* original base of support had centered on the apolitical *Turnvereine* ("gymnastics societies"); its traditionalist leadership had come out of the *Kameradschaftsbund* (KB, "cultural union"), an elite prewar organization based on the mystical ideals of Othmar Spann, who believed that the Germans were destined to rule central Europe. Far from seeking union with Germany, the traditionalists advocated political autonomy for ethnic Germans *within* Czechoslovakia.[110] In contrast, the radicals (mostly former Sudeten Nazis) favored irredentism. Although the German government made financial contributions to the *Heimatfront* (even underwriting Henlein's 1935 election campaign), these monies came from a variety of agencies with different agendas vis-à-vis the Sudetenland. In fact, both the radicals and the traditionalists had allies in the German government with whom they collaborated in a fight for dominance in both states.[111] This internecine warfare was exacerbated by Hitler's Social Darwinist approach to policy making. Rather than establishing a clear directive at the outset, Hitler would often give his backing to the winners of internal power struggles, reasoning that the most effective approach would ultimately prevail. This method also ensured that no single individual or agency could gain control over the country's foreign affairs.[112]

The Reich still had no wish to antagonize the Great Powers by encouraging irredentism in Czechoslovakia. The Sudeten Nazis' frequent and open contacts with the German government had, however, begun to raise suspicions concerning Hitler's intentions toward Germany's eastern neighbor. The Reich therefore set up a traditionalist-oriented *Volksdeutscher Rat* (VR) to assist the *Verein für Deutschtum im Ausland* (VDA) in supervising the affairs of Germans abroad. It was thought that their relative autonomy and nonpolitical orientation would prevent irredentist elements from infiltrating these bodies and radicalizing Germany's foreign policy.[113] Hitler also instructed the Nazi party and state agencies to refrain from unauthorized interference in Sudeten affairs and to reject all requests from Sudeten leaders for political or military assistance. Although he publicly expressed concern for the rights of Germans in Czechoslovakia, Hitler privately informed Hans Knirsch, the Sudeten Nazi leader, that they would have to solve their problems on their own because it would be a long time before the Reich could provide any assistance.[114] Indeed, far from working hand-in-hand with Hitler, Henlein could barely get an audience with him, let alone assurances that he could depend on the Führer's support in the event of a government crackdown or internal party coup.

Henlein gave an indication of the party's aims in another address in Schluckenau in 1934:

> A true democracy entails the free development of personality, including the personality of a group. Because we do not live in a nation-state, but rather in a nationalities-state, democracy necessitates that not only the individual, but also every ethnic group, has the right to freely develop. A true democracy entails decentralization, which means [national] self-administration. We will not stand behind bad democracies; rather, we will fight for a true democracy.[115]

The demand for autonomy was central to the SdP's 1935 election campaign.[116] On the strength this platform, the SdP garnered more support than any other German party, with 60 percent of the minority vote.[117] That Henlein still favored working with the Czechs is evidenced by the fact that he attempted to form a governing coalition with the Czech Agrarians and Hlinka's Peoples Party in Slovakia. In return for joining the alliance, Henlein demanded guarantees of Sudeten German national autonomy and self-administration, while disavowing any interest in irredentism or frontier revision.[118] What exactly did national autonomy entail? Although Henlein was somewhat vague on this point, he asserted that autonomy meant self-administration in German affairs, including educational and local self-government. He qualified this by noting that the preservation of the state "[ruled out] the establishment of a Sudeten German parliament or anything of that sort."[119] Henlein's position reflected the prevailing sentiments of the Sudeten Germans at large, who preferred territorial autonomy to irredentism.[120] Johann Wolfgang Brügel himself concedes that the victory of the SdP in 1935 did not mean that the Sudeten Germans desired territorial annexation, which in any case had been ruled out by the Reich. Rather, the German minority had rejected the activist parties in government, which they believed had failed to protect them from economic discrimination. As late as 1935, therefore, the majority of Germans supported demands as moderate as regional autonomy within Czechoslovakia.[121]

In the early 1930's, disproportionate economic suffering in the Sudetenland led to minority perceptions that the Czechoslovak government was discriminatory. Although Hitler's intentions were somewhat unclear, the Reich appeared unlikely to intervene on behalf of the German minority. Taken together, these perceptions induced the belief that the state of the world had moved from one of ethnic peace to one of vulnerability (fig. 3.1, box 3), in which case the rank and file should still support relatively moderate demands while mobilizing along ethnic lines to protect against discrimination. This is in fact what happened. Although the majority of Germans had voted for activist parties in 1929, in 1935 they threw their support behind Henlein's negativist party, representing a shift toward remobilization. Meanwhile, demands for national autonomy gained greater support than demands for linguistic or cultural autonomy, which had been popular in the late 1920s. Significantly, however, the Germans still favored accommodating the Czech majority, given their perceptions of low bargaining leverage. Finally, the spatial model predicts that the increased salience of ethnicity would hamper the construction of inter-ethnic coalitions. Consistent with this prediction, the SdP ultimately broke off negotiations with Czech and German parties over forming a government. Henlein recognized that maintaining the support of his constituents required remaining outside government, which had become highly unpopular with ordinary Germans.

Mid-1936–1938: The Path to Irredentism

In March 1936, Hitler sent his forces into the Rhineland, in direct violation of Germany's treaty promises. Apart from verbal protests, Britain and France did nothing to sanction the Reich. A few months later, Hitler intervened in the Spanish Civil War and concluded a treaty with Austria committing it to follow the lead of German foreign policy. These events indicated that Germany was beginning to pose a threat to its neighbors. The Allies' tepid response to these actions signaled to central European countries that they could no longer rely on the Great Powers to defend them against a German invasion. Czechoslovakia now faced Germany from a position of weakness.

The Reich's newly aggressive foreign policy had direct consequences for the internal feud between the moderates and radicals in the SdP. Up until this point, most of the party rank and file had supported the moderates. However, as Germany gradually flexed its muscles beyond its borders, the SdP radicals not only gained greater support from the German government, but also greater credibility in the eyes of the Sudeten Germans. This is because their irredentist agenda appeared increasingly compatible with

Germany's evolving international stance. To combat the growing power of the radicals, the moderates attempted to win British and French support for resolving the "Sudeten German problem." In 1936, Henlein and other moderate leaders (including Walter Brand and Heinrich Rutha) traveled to London to lobby the British government to pressure Czechoslovakia to grant broad concessions to the Germans. They saw this as the best means of bolstering popular support for the Sudeten moderates while undermining the radicals' claim that the Czechs were repressive. Henlein and his deputies made numerous trips to England, testifying before politicians and journalists that the Sudeten minority wanted nothing more than reconciliation with the Czechs and that neither the SdP leadership nor the Sudeten German population had any interest in irredentism.[122] British dignitaries and journalists were encouraged to visit Czechoslovakia, where they were given tours of the depressed areas of the Sudetenland. This generated significant international sympathy for the "Sudeten German plight," and Britain began to urge a three-way German-Czechoslovak-SdP resolution of the "Sudeten problem." At the same time, the SdP moderates joined the moderates in the Reich to lobby for a nonaggression treaty mandating that the minority's problems be solved within the Czechoslovak state.[123]

Despite their best efforts, the popularity of the radicals continued to rise. Rudolf Sandner, an SdP deputy, noted that the public outcry for the dismissal of Rutha, Brand, Karl Hermann Frank, and other SdP moderates indicated that "the groundwork for a rebellion is being systematically created."[124] German cultural organizations also underwent radicalization; notably, the leader of the *Hochschülerschaft*, a prominent student group in Prague, favored the Nazification of German youth. The radicals were becoming increasingly disloyal to Henlein's moderate line and increasingly successful in mobilizing support for their position.

To stymie the growing rebellion in their ranks, the SdP leaders announced the expulsion of several prominent radicals, including Anton Kreissl, who had been working as an agent for Hans Krebs, the former head of the National Socialists now based in Germany. Divisions in the party were becoming a concern for the German government as well, as it increasingly viewed a united Sudeten front as vital to the success of German maneuvers abroad. Just as the party was about to split, the Reich brokered a pact between the two camps whereby two expelled SdP radicals were reinstated and sent to Berlin while Brand, an SdP moderate and close ally of Henlein, was sent to England. However, this did little to quell the growing unrest on the ground: the radicals had taken over the local party organizations and were using the widespread economic discontent to turn ordinary Germans against both the Czechs and the SdP moderates.[125]

In Berlin, meanwhile, the moderates were losing the battle over German foreign policy. In 1935, the *Büro Kursell* was created to serve as a liaison between the formerly autonomous VDA (the organization supervising Sudeten German affairs) and Joachim von Ribbentrop, Rudolf Hess's plenipotentiary in foreign affairs. This allowed the radicals to infiltrate the VDA as they had other government agencies.[126] When Henlein went in search of patrons in the Reich, he now found that the most powerful officials were invariably radical. In October 1937, Henlein's most important moderate ally in the Reich was dismissed as head of the VDA and replaced with *Schutzstaffel* (SS) sympathizers, signaling that the moderates had finally been defeated.

To make matters worse, Henlein's closest advisor and fellow moderate, Heinz Rutha, was arrested by Czech authorities on charges of homosexuality; he later committed suicide in his jail cell. With Brand in England and Rutha dead, Henlein had his back against the wall. A skirmish between radical SdP deputies and Czech police at Teplitz-Schönau finally pushed him into the radical camp. On October 17, 1937, an SdP deputy exiting a political meeting was assaulted by a Czech police officer, who hit him with a truncheon. Enraged, the deputy grabbed a truncheon from another officer and retaliated, after which he and his colleagues were carried off to jail. The minority press interpreted this event as proof that the government was anti-German.[127] With still no word of personal support from Hitler, Henlein was forced to respond to the ensuing public outcry or face political death. He therefore wrote an open letter to Beneš in which he condemned the officers' role in the incident, denounced the government, and demanded that Sudeten German autonomy be established immediately.[128] Henlein recognized that moderation was no longer a viable position in Sudeten politics and followed the lead of the Reich's emerging foreign policy by formally requesting German annexation of the Sudetenland.[129] He thus joined the ascendant radical faction in the SdP and thereafter worked closely with irredentists on both sides of the border. This analysis demonstrates that elite radicalization was largely a response to resurgent anti-Czech agitation at the grassroots level. Radicalism among the rank and file was in turn driven by Germany's renewed activism in foreign affairs.

Seeing this, Czechoslovak leaders accelerated their efforts to reach out to the Sudeten Germans. Formal negotiations between minority and government representatives were initiated in 1936, just as Germany began to flex its muscles on the international stage. Beneš, now president, proclaimed his willingness to listen to German demands and traveled across the Sudetenland to better acquaint himself with minority grievances. At the same time, Prime Minister Hodža (himself an ethnic Slovak) attempted to implement a system of extensive national autonomy.[130] In these and other ways, government leaders proved amenable to compromise in the wake of the 1936 crisis.

The remilitarization of the Rhineland in 1936 not only gave credence to the irredentist position within the German government—helping the SS gain control of foreign policy—but also signaled to the Sudeten Germans that their lobby state was strong and supportive. This, together with growing perceptions that the Czech majority was conciliatory, should induce the belief that the state of the world was one of opportunity (fig. 3.1, box 2), leading Sudeten elites to up the ante against the Czechs. There is substantial support for this prediction. Positioned to extract ever-increasing concessions from their government, the German leadership had little incentive to negotiate a compromise. Having made a number of offers with little success, Hodža finally requested that the German parties in government produce a concrete list of demands. They responded in January 1937 with a memorandum of Sudeten German grievances. Among other things, they called for major investment in the Sudetenland, greater representation in civil service, and self-administration of the German regions.[131] Following month-long talks between Czech and German ministers, the government issued the *Memorandum of 18 February,* which promised to meet these demands. However, the settlement was dead on arrival: the SdP refused to accept the memorandum and staged demonstrations in protest, claiming that the document was mere government propaganda.[132]

Hodža realized that any viable deal necessitated the support of the SdP. He therefore invited Henlein to lay out the party's demands so they could hammer out an agreement. Again, the government came away frustrated. Hodža later observed that "the new German radical opposition did not seem able to lay down a strict political programme," adding tartly that although "criticism may be the salt of opposition, salt is far from being a meal."[133] Unable to nail down Henlein's position, the government attempted to address the source of minority discontent as a means of undermining Sudeten radicalism. However, this was seen as too little too late. As Freund pointed out, "If the genuine German grievances had been tackled years ago, Henlein and his friends might not have found the Sudeten electorate receptive to desperate counsels. But taking things as they are, any constructive collaboration between the authorities and the Henlein Party presents almost insuperable difficulties."[134]

With growing indications of lobby state support, the Sudeten Germans were unmoved by government promises of welfare relief and civil service employment. Given their present bargaining power vis-à-vis the Czech majority, there was conceivably no limit to the concessions they could now extract from the government.

The 1938 Anschluss—Closing the German Ranks

The union of Germany and Austria in 1938 rendered a pan-German state geographically feasible, bolstering the credibility of Sudeten irredentism. Although the *Anschluss* was actually the outcome of a number of contingent events, the Sudeten Germans saw it as an unmistakable sign that Germany intended to expand into Czechoslovakia. Rumors flew across the Sudetenland that annexation was imminent and could occur as early as April in commemoration of the Führer's birthday.[135] Henlein responded by publicly ratcheting up his demands. In April 1938, he gave a public address in Karlsbad in which he repeated his party's rejection of the Minorities Statute, the government's most recent proposal for addressing German grievances. (He had dismissed the proposal before even learning of the substance of the offer!)[136] While insisting that his demands consisted of nothing more than territorial autonomy, Henlein now proclaimed that all ethnic Germans had the right to pursue "German *Volkstum* and the German *Weltanschauung*"—references to Hitler's rationale for German expansion. These comments were interpreted as a thinly veiled call for irredentism.[137]

Observing these events, the government intensified its efforts to appease the Germans in hopes of heading off a looming crisis. Although the state had made significant progress in addressing the grievances laid out in the 1937 memorandum, Sudeten leaders remained unimpressed. The government even offered to implement broad territorial autonomy in a desperate attempt to meet SdP demands or at least diminish Henlein's appeal in the eyes of his supporters. In June 1938, the government presented Sudeten leaders with a plan for de facto federalization along ethnic lines. One proposal consisted of reviving the old administrative system of *župas* (self-governing counties):

> Each župa would . . . [include] within its boundaries people of one race only. A kind of administrative and legislative headquarters would be provided with power to unite all those župas with common interests into a larger body for dealing with the administration and legislation concerning the aforesaid common interests. . . . In practice, a number of župas including adequate German majorities would be able to unite into a German minority self-government for dealing with all those matters which were not necessarily reserved for . . . the State.[138]

In making this unprecedented offer, Hodža reasoned that "in the critical year of 1938 a compromise between Centralism and Decentralism was to be preferred . . . [so that] the union [could be] preserved."[139] Every concession from the government, however, was met with a more extreme demand.[140]

In this way, the SdP avoided ethnic compromise as a means of retaining the support of its constituents, who continued to radicalize in response to increasingly bellicose signals from Germany. The dynamics of ethnic bargaining ultimately delivered SdP leaders into the hands of the Reich to be used as instruments of German expansion.[141]

It should be noted that not all Sudeten Germans supported irredentism; many stood to lose, economically or otherwise, by refusing to cooperate with the Czechs. The SdP leaders were well aware of the variation in the preferences of ordinary Germans. They also knew that they needed the support of *all* ethnic Germans to bargain effectively in this high-stakes game. The Henleinists therefore attempted to alter the preferences of would-be traitors to achieve consensus and thereby prevent defection. One technique they used was to offer financial incentives to adhere to the party line. Because the SdP exercised de facto control over local governments across the Sudetenland, allegiance to Henlein translated into much-needed jobs and business contracts. The SdP also employed scare tactics to frighten dissenters into towing the party line. The infamous whisper campaign of 1938 (most likely organized by Reich agents and Henlein party functionaries) spread rumors throughout the Sudetenland of Hitler's imminent invasion.[142] This led many moderate Germans to throw their support behind Henlein in anticipation of a Nazi takeover. Still other methods included boycotting the businesses of "national traitors," disrupting activist party events, and indoctrinating pupils with Henleinist principles.[143] Many employers threatened to fire workers who opposed the SdP. The commercial boycotts were especially effective. The following leaflet was distributed in a suburb of Karlsbad in 1938:

GERMANS, TAKE NOTICE!

The Baumgartl dairy, opposite the Brown House, is a disguised Jewish-Communist centre. Baumgartl uses Czech milk which is delivered to him by the Red Defence leader Josef Grüner. Baumgartl himself is a Communist, but pretends to credulous people to be a supporter of the Henlein party. Germans! Buy only German milk from German shops! Boycott Baumgartl and his associates![144]

The target of this attack was a German activist who refused to join the SdP even after repeated threats and boycotts resulted in significant losses to his business. Henlein supporters often stood in front of dissenters' shops in order to enforce these boycotts. Anti-Henleinists were threatened with the loss of their jobs, apartments, and services that were under SdP control.

In addition to direct threats, numerous posters, leaflets, and newspaper articles announced that German moderates were being watched and would suffer the consequences of "betraying" the German nation. The following message was posted all over the town of Ingelsberg in June 1938, warning Germans of the consequences of sending their children to Czech schools:

> Should this warning not receive attention by various German parents, then we shall take good note of those scoundrels, and shall persecute them as traitors to their own nation, and they will not be accepted any more into our determined, iron German ranks. The gallows are already waiting for the traitors and ruffians Schmidt and Vogel. . . . We greet our Führer, beloved everywhere with the oath of fidelity: "Down with the traitors of the Nation! Long live our Führer! Sieg Heil![145]

These and other threats were made in German-speaking areas throughout the state. Efforts to achieve ethnic solidarity intensified in the months following the *Anschluss*. By 1938, the German moderates had either joined the ranks of the SdP or left the Sudetenland. The pressure to support the SdP became so great that the activist parties themselves left the coalition government and joined the Henlein movement![146] This about-face on the part of German moderates—who until 1938 had vehemently opposed Hitler and the fascist movement—demonstrates how rapidly the activist position lost currency among ordinary Germans in the wake of the *Anschluss*. Sudeten German activism had become not only politically infeasible in light of Germany's growing bellicosity but also dangerous given the persecution of German moderates.[147]

This apparently unified support for the SdP lent credibility to Henlein's claims that the Sudeten Germans desired national liberation. It also bolstered Hitler's arguments at Munich that the minority had the right to join its national homeland. At this point, Sudeten German activism was nothing short of heroic—German antifascists who clashed with Henlein's storm troopers in the weeks preceding the Munich Agreement were either wounded or killed. As Bauer observes,

> It was not easy for German anti-Fascists to side with the Czechs in those days of national fanaticism, Fascist terror, and mass hysteria. Political activity meant constantly 'swimming against the current.' Standing for the defence of the Republic meant being branded as an 'agent of Czech imperialism,' as a 'national traitor.' [148]

In truth, ethnic Germans were far from united in their support of either Henlein or annexation by Nazi Germany.[149] However, fears of Nazi persecution and the SdP's proven capacity for monitoring and punishing dissent rendered opposition nearly impossible in the months leading up to the Nazi invasion.

The Sudeten Germans interpreted Berlin's foreign policies from 1936 to 1938 as credible signals of interventionist intent. These events included: (1) the Reich's remilitarization of the Rhineland, (2) Hitler's public speeches condemning the oppression of the Sudeten minority, and (3) the 1938 *Anschluss*. Following each event, there was a visible shift toward radicalization as measured by the claims advanced by SdP leaders against the Czechoslovak government. Given calculations that their lobby state was both strong and supportive and that the Czech majority was conciliatory, ethnic Germans had good reason to believe that the state of the world had become one of opportunity (fig. 3.1, box 2). To retain the support of his constituents, Henlein continued to escalate his demands against the government. In doing so, Henlein and his allies presented the international community with the image of an oppressed minority, which Hitler ultimately exploited to advance his war aims.

This chapter examines Sudeten German claims in interwar Czechoslovakia to test the bargaining hypotheses developed in chapter 2. This analysis demonstrates the added value of ethnic bargaining as a theory of minority mobilization, particularly relative to theories that focus on ethnic entrepreneurship, economic incentives, or cultural differences. Empirically, it casts doubt on the popular fifth column theory that the 1938 Sudeten crisis was the result of a premeditated Hitler-Henlein plot to overthrow the Czechoslovak state.

Instrumentalist theories often mistake elite maneuvering as the *cause* of ethnic mobilization rather than the *by-product* of more fundamental forces that drive both elite and grassroots behavior. By examining shifts in Sudeten German claims over time, I show that mobilization is largely driven by the dynamics of minority-majority bargaining. For example, Rudolf Lodgman, the radical father of Sudeten separatism, moderated his demands from irredentism to territorial autonomy once Germany and Austria had renounced their claims on the Sudetenland in 1919. After the 1925 Locarno Treaty established a détente between Czechoslovakia and Germany, the value of cooperating with the Czech majority began to outweigh the value of remaining mobilized along ethnic lines. Seeing this, Lodgman scaled back his claims further to cultural and linguistic autonomy and entered the Czechoslovak parliament as a minority representative.

Czech-German relations in the 1930s provide further evidence for the grassroots origins of ethnic mobilization. In 1929, when ethnic salience was at an all-time low, negativist German parties garnered only a small fraction of the ethnic vote. In 1935, however, in the wake of disproportionate German suffering that lent credibility to accusations of Czech discrimination, the negativist SdP attracted over 60 percent of the German vote. The sudden reemergence of Sudeten German nationalism cannot be attributed to elite manipulation for personal gain—negativist political agents had been active *throughout* the interwar period, but enjoyed popularity only periodically. Neither their rhetoric nor their mobilizing tactics altered substantially in the intervening years. Nor does personal charisma explain their surge in support—by all accounts, Henlein was a stiff and uninspiring politician, notwithstanding his tremendous popularity.

This analysis also shows that the 1938 takeover did not begin as a premeditated plot on both sides of the border. Henlein was not by nature a rabid nationalist and had originally sought inter-ethnic compromise with the Czechs. The rising popularity and organizational power of the SdP radicals (bolstered by increasingly nationalistic signals from Germany as well as the growing influence of the radicals in the Reich government) gradually pushed Henlein into a position of intransigence vis-à-vis the Czechoslovak state as he strove to maintain the support of his constituents while fending off radical challengers. The defeat of Henlein's moderate allies in the Reich finally ruled out activism as a viable position in Sudeten politics. It was not until 1938, however, that Hitler decided to use the radicalized Sudeten minority as a justification for expanding into Czechoslovakia; minority mobilization thus preceded Hitler's scheme for expansion. Because the Sudeten German case is widely seen as an exemplar of elite-manufactured conflict, these findings stand as significant counterevidence to instrumentalist theories of mobilization.

Purely economic explanations also fail to account for the specifics of this case. Economic opportunism predicts that the Sudeten Germans would support those positions expected to advance their economic interests. German industrialists stood to lose from irredentism in 1918 due to their dependence on access to Czech markets as well as their fear of competition from the more efficient Reich industries. Despite this, they became leading advocates of annexation. Many Sudeten Germans had economic disincentives to support irredentism in the late 1930s as well—due to their dependence on the Czech economy or because they benefited from a liberal, pro-market government. Nevertheless, there was little internal opposition to Henlein's movement.

What is missing in these accounts is the crucial dimension of power, which is central to the ethnic bargaining theory. The German industrialists

Table 3.2. Summary of competing theories, Sudeten Germans in Czechoslovakia

Theory	Prediction
Primordialism (cultural/linguistic differences; preexisting "national" identity; ethnic hatreds)	**Correctly predicts** the lines of conflict in interwar Czechoslovakia, the ethnic ties between Sudeten Germans and Austria and Germany, and the grievances upon which the minority would ultimately mobilize; **Cannot account for** dramatic shifts in Sudeten German demands, nor for shifts in interethnic cooperation over this period
Economic Theories	**Incorrectly predicts** that Sudeten Germans would refrain from irredentism after World War I due to their much better economic prospects in Czechoslovakia; **Incorrectly predicts** that many Sudeten Germans would oppose German revanchism in the late 1930s due to their economic dependence on the Czechoslovak interior
Ethnic Entrepreneurship Theories	**Incorrectly predicts** that Sudeten Germans would remain radicalized in the early 1920s due to the manipulation of opportunistic, charismatic leaders (Lodgman); **Does not explain** why Lodgman himself soon discarded this posture to enter the Czechoslovak parliament; **Does not explain** why Henlein moved from relatively moderate calls for minority autonomy in the mid 1930s to irredentism by the late 1930s
Security Dilemma/Ethnic Fears	**Correctly predicts** that Sudeten Germans would radicalize after the establishment of Czechoslovakia to avoid reprisals by the Czechs; **Does not explain** why the minority rapidly demobilized after 1919 despite the lack of change in majority threat; **Correctly predicts** that Sudeten Germans would re-radicalize in the early 1930s in response to growing fears of economic discrimination; **Does not explain** why the minority continued to radicalize even after Czechoslovak leaders credibly signaled their intent to accommodate the minority
Ethnic Bargaining	**Correctly predicts** that Sudeten Germans would moderate their demands when Austria and Germany ruled out border claims on the Sudetenland, signaling a drop in the minority's bargaining leverage; **Correctly predicts** further moderation in minority demands after a détente was reached between their host and lobby states in 1925; **Correctly predicts** that Sudeten Germans would radicalize their demands against the Czechoslovak center in the 1930s in tandem with signals of growing support from their lobby state, Germany

in 1918 and many ordinary Germans in 1938 supported irredentism against their economic interests due to their fear of reprisals. Minority elites by themselves, however, are rarely able to enforce such solidarity. What generated near ethnic unity in 1938 was the popular perception that the once-marginalized radical leaders now enjoyed the backing of a strong nationalist lobby state—Germany. Because of this, moderate Germans feared that opposition to Henlein would ultimately be punished by the Nazi government after the German takeover. They responded en masse to elite pressures only *after* Germany overtly signaled its support for the Sudeten radicals.

Ethnic fears theories broadly predict that the Sudeten Germans would radicalize when the Czechs failed to credibly commit to protect their rights and accommodate when they succeeded in doing so. However, minority leaders deescalated their demands from irredentism to territorial autonomy in 1919 not because the government had committed to minority protection but, rather, because their lobby states had failed to provide them with external leverage. Although it is true that the Germans remobilized in the early 1930s in response to perceptions of economic discrimination, they did not become truly radicalized until after Nazi Germany had begun to signal its support for the minority. With Berlin at their back, Sudeten German representatives continued to escalate their claims in spite of the government's repeated efforts to broker an ethnic compromise—leading ultimately to the 1938 crisis.

CHAPTER FOUR

Triadic Ethnic Bargaining

Hungarian Minorities in Postcommunist Slovakia and Romania

After the Treaty of Trianon stripped Hungary of two-thirds of its land and population in 1920, a national mythology developed around the nearly 2.5 million Hungarians now residing in contemporary Serbia, Slovakia, and Romania—the primary beneficiaries of the postwar border adjustments. Hungarian revanchism led Budapest to join the Axis Powers in World War II, allowing it to regain some of its lost territories before losing them again at the end of the war. Although Hungary's involvement with its diaspora was limited during the Cold War, the fall of communism in 1989 led politicians and opinion leaders to revisit Trianon in domestic debates over the country's identity.[1] Public ruminations over possible revisions to the widely reviled treaty generated anxieties on the part of Hungary's neighbors while raising the ambitions of Hungarians abroad.

Although few have called for outright border adjustments, the Hungarian minorities in postcommunist Romania and Slovakia have mobilized around claims for language rights and even territorial autonomy. Why are these claims being made now? Some scholars argue that the immutable desire to exist as a separate group leads to demands for autonomy.[2] Others have pointed out that minorities have economic incentives to obtain education and language rights.[3] Although both propositions have some basis in fact, they do not explain why the claims of Hungarian leaders have *varied* from calls for police protection to language rights to territorial autonomy, and back. This chapter shows that the main drivers of Hungarian radicalization are minority perceptions of relative power vis-à-vis the state majority. These perceptions are driven in turn by the expected behavior of the minority groups' lobby actor, Hungary, and their respective host governments, Romania and Slovakia. To complicate matters,

Table 4.1. Hungarian demands in (Czecho)Slovakia, 1989–2003[a]

	Most extreme	↔			Least extreme	
Period	Irredentism/ secession	Regional/ territorial autonomy	Cultural autonomy	Affirmative action	Support from lobby actor (Hungary)	Host state repression (Slovakia)
1989–mid-1992			X		Low	Low
Late 1992–1993		X			High	High
1994		X			High	Low
1995–Early 1998				X	Low	High
Mid-1998–2003			X		Low/ uncertain[b]	Low

[a] Low, medium, and high indicate minority perceptions of lobby state support and majority repression. It is difficult to obtain precise measures of these variables because the sources of perceptions differ greatly from case to case. The most important thing to note is the *shifts* in perceived host and lobby state intentions, which should lead to corresponding shifts in minority demands.

[b] Uncertainty over lobby state support is the result of mixed signals from the 1998–2002 Fidesz government, which sought to extend benefits to Hungarians abroad while maintaining good relations with the Slovak and Romanian governments.

intergovernmental organizations (such as NATO, the OSCE, the CoE, and the EU) have used carrots and sticks to influence the policies of these governments toward their minorities. This dynamic may be depicted as a series of concentric waves rippling inward from the suprastate to the interstate to the substate level.

To test these hypotheses, I break the two cases of minority behavior into a series of time segments, each representing a temporal shift in the demands made by the most popular minority leaders. I then use media reports, elite interviews, campaign platforms, and survey data to assess whether each observed shift in minority radicalization was preceded by a shift in perceived host and lobby state intentions with respect to the group. In the course of this analysis, I pay close attention to the influence of supranational players—primarily NATO and the EU, but also the OSCE and the CoE—in altering the dynamics of ethnic bargaining at the substate level. As tables 4.1 and 4.2 indicate, minority claims in Romania and Slovakia fluctuated considerably from the time of transition in 1989 until Slovakia and Hungary were admitted to the EU in 2004. These shifts cannot be explained by minority grievances or fears of repression alone. They were instead driven by host and lobby state signals, which informed minority perceptions of the

Table 4.2. Hungarian demands in Romania, 1989–2003[a]

Period	Most extreme				Least extreme	
	Irredentism/ secession	Regional/ territorial autonomy	Cultural autonomy	Affirmative action	Support from lobby actor (Hungary)	Host state repression (Romania)
1989–early 1990			X		Low	Low
Mid-1990–early 1992				X	Low	High
Mid-1992–1995		X			High	High
1996–2003			X		Low/ Uncertain[b]	Low

[a] Low, medium, and high indicate minority perceptions of lobby state support and majority repression. It is difficult to obtain precise measures of these variables because the sources of perceptions differ greatly from case to case. The most important thing to note in this respect is the shifts in perceived host and lobby state intentions, which should lead to corresponding shifts in minority demands.

[b] Uncertainty over lobby state support is the result of mixed signals from the 1998–2002 Fidesz government, which sought to extend benefits to Hungarians abroad while maintaining good relations with the Slovak and Romanian governments.

prevailing state of the world and therefore whether to radicalize against or accommodate the majority.

Slovakia and Romania as Ideal Comparative Cases

Postcommunist Slovakia and Romania offer a useful comparison for both methodological and substantive reasons:

- Both countries had many domestic features in common, including a similar level of economic development, a legacy of communist rule, and the experience of rapid political and economic reform.
- The populations of both countries supported membership in Western organizations, generating electoral incentives for their leaders to meet NATO and EU accession criteria.
- Both countries had at least some experience of Hungarian suzerainty under the prewar Habsburg regime as well as Hungarian irredentism in the twentieth century.
- Both countries engaged in ethnic assimilation during the Cold War and both became nationalizing states in the postcommunist period.

There were also important similarities between the groups themselves. In both countries, they constituted the largest national minority. They also made up the largest Hungarian settlements outside Hungary and enjoyed close ties with their co-ethnics over the border.[4] Hence, the two minority groups were similarly situated with respect to their host governments as well as their shared kin state. Therefore, *differences* in the behavior of the two groups are likely to be related to factors at the substate level, whereas *similarities* are likely to be the result of the common impact of their lobby state. Furthermore, their shared culture, language, and national identity can be ruled out as possible explanations for variation in minority claims both over time and between the two cases (see figure 2.7).

This investigation is also useful for substantive reasons; this is because these are textbook cases of intractable language conflicts. Such disputes pose an interesting empirical puzzle due to the seemingly trivial issues over which they are waged. At various times, minority Hungarians have staked all their political capital on bilingual place-names or report cards for their children. The behavior of the Romanian and Slovak governments is more puzzling still, because they attracted international opprobrium and risked delaying their admission to the EU and NATO in return for the questionable benefits of restrictive language policies. I will show that these conflicts had less to do with the use of language than they did with minority-majority bargaining over the distribution of institutional power in the new states.

Ethnic Bargaining Hypotheses

The limits on the demands a group may credibly advance are largely determined by internal sources of power, including group size and territorial concentration. For example, if a minority does not meet certain size and compactness requirements for independence, its demands for statehood are unlikely to be seen as realistic, undermining their usefulness as tools for extracting concessions from the center.

According to the 1991 census, ethnic Hungarians in Romania numbered about 1.7 million, or 7 percent of the population. The minority was concentrated in the northwest region of Transylvania but dominated only two of the state's forty-one counties—Covasna and Harghita. The Hungarian community in Slovakia numbered about 570,000 people, or 11 percent of the population, and was concentrated along the Hungarian border from Bratislava to Ukraine. Although almost all ethnic Hungarians lived within this so-called Hungarian Belt, they made up only one-third of the region's population.[5] The Hungarian groups in both states were therefore too small and geographically dispersed to achieve statehood. However, since there were Hungarian majority districts clustered along both borders, they *could* advance credible claims for border adjustments. Moreover, because they were concentrated in particular regions (see map 4.1), territorial autonomy was also a feasible aim for both groups.

This does not mean, however, that they would necessarily advance such claims; tables 4.1 and 4.2 show that the leaders of both minorities have varied their demands considerably since 1989 as a joint function of host and lobby state signals of behavioral intent. A group may mobilize in the first place when it perceives the government or majority to be repressive. The ultimate decision to radicalize, however, rests with the minority's perceived bargaining leverage vis-à-vis the center. This, in turn, is largely driven by signals of support from external lobby actors.

Hungary was the primary lobby actor for the Hungarian minorities in postcommunist Slovakia and Romania. Hungary's current borders were established by the 1920 Treaty of Trianon. As punishment for allying with the Central Powers during World War I, the treaty drew over 3 million Hungarians outside a truncated Hungary, where they became citizens of Romania, Czechoslovakia, Yugoslavia, Italy, Austria, and Ukraine. During the interwar period, "Trianon and its children" served as a potent symbol in shaping Hungary's national identity. Trianon was later used to justify Hungary's alliance with Nazi Germany as well as its revisionist incursions into Yugoslavia and territorial acquisitions in Slovakia and Romania. Forced to return the territories after the war, Hungary maintained cordial relations with its neighbors until the 1980s, when Romania's assimilationist policies toward ethnic Hungarians in Transylvania galvanized demonstrations in Hungary.[6]

By 1990, Hungary had reestablished itself as the national homeland and champion of Magyars everywhere; as a result, the Hungarian diaspora began to look to Budapest for patronage and protection as early as the late 1980s. In contrast to the Sudeten German case (chap. 3), the balance of power between the minority groups' host and lobby states did not change appreciably in the decade or so following 1989. Fluctuations in minority claims are therefore more likely to be a function of changing host and lobby state *intentions* toward the minority than of changes in their relative capabilities. All other things being equal, minority leaders in Slovakia and Romania should radicalize their demands when Budapest sends credible signals of support and moderate their demands when it indicates a lack of support. If both Hungary and the host government signal non-nationalist intent, Hungarian minority leaders should moderate their demands. The associated decline in

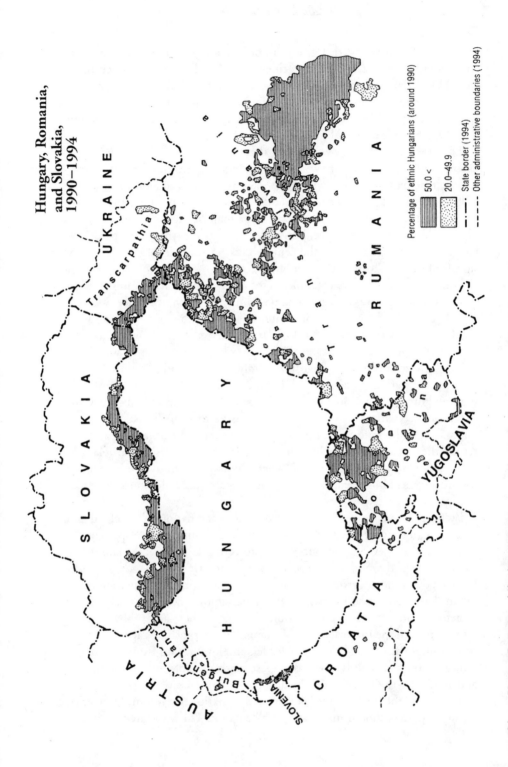

Hungary, Romania,
and Slovakia,
1990–1994

UKRAINE

Transcarpathia

SLOVAKIA

AUSTRIA

Burgenland

SLOVENIA

H U N G A R Y

CROATIA

T r a n s y l v a n i a

R U M A N I A

V o j v o d i n a

YUGOSLAVIA

Percentage of ethnic Hungarians (around 1990)

50.0 <

20.0–49.9

State border (1994)

Other administrative boundaries (1994)

Map 11. Hungarians, Romania, and Slovakia, 1990–1994

ethnic salience should also induce political coalitions to form across ethnic lines.

What about other external actors? As noted in chapter 2, the minority's lobby actor need not be a kin state. It may be any powerful state, organization, interest group, or military alliance that intervenes or threatens to intervene on behalf of the minority against its host government. In contemporary Europe, potential lobbyists include the EU, NATO, the CoE, the OSCE, and various NGOs. Significantly, however, these bodies did not act, nor did they claim to act, on behalf of the Hungarian minorities. Although they certainly influenced minority behavior in these cases, they did so *indirectly* by altering the preferences of the groups' host and lobby states—the main principals of ethnic bargaining.[7] I therefore focus on the actions of Hungary, Slovakia, and Romania, although I pay close attention to the ways in which external actors such as NATO and the EU influenced their preferences through incentives and constraints. We can now test these hypotheses using the cases of Hungarian minorities in postcommunist Romania and Slovakia.

The Hungarians in Postcommunist Slovakia

1989–Mid-1992: The Velvet Revolution and the Czechoslovak Split

In November 1989, popular demonstrations swept the dissident playwright Václav Havel and his opposition movement, the Civic Forum (CF), into power in what became known as the Velvet Revolution. In the final weeks of the dying regime, the Czech Civic Forum and the Slovak Public Against Violence (PAV) joined forces against the communist leadership. The revolution itself took place in an atmosphere of profound interethnic cooperation that extended across the country. An ethnic Hungarian deputy recalled a poignant example involving Hungarian minority activists who had just returned to Bratislava from the scene of the revolution in Prague. When they stood up to address a pro-democracy rally and no interpreters could be found, Slovak demonstrators shouted out, "Don't translate, we understand you!"[8] Over the coming months, a number of rallies were held to promote inter-ethnic cooperation, and Havel famously spoke out against xenophobia and racial intolerance.[9] Minorities were permitted to establish their own parties and encouraged to run on the broad-based CF and PAV candidate lists in the 1990 elections. Although Slovak nationalism had already emerged as a political force by mid-1990, the Slovak leadership remained quite liberal. The government did pass a language law in late 1990 placing restrictions on the use of Hungarian in public administration.

However, the law was widely seen as a compromise between Slovak nation-alists and ethnic Hungarians.[10] The law was also consistent with prevailing European norms concerning the use of minority languages.[11] Throughout the first electoral cycle, Slovak representatives focused primarily on revising the federal constitution, property restitution, market reform, and privatiza-tion.[12]

In Hungary, meanwhile, the communist system formally ended in 1989 following a series of roundtable talks between communist party leaders and opposition groups. The "October Constitution," published in the party's official gazette in October 1989, declared an end to state socialism and single-party rule. By the end of the year, there were over sixty new par-ties, with the Hungarian Democratic Forum (MDF) leading the move-ment for reform. During its first six months in office, the caretaker govern-ment pushed through economic and political legislation to consolidate the still-tenuous transition. The government also negotiated the withdrawal of Soviet troops from Hungarian territory and began to make diplomatic overtures to the West. Unsurprisingly, given the nature of these reforms, the most salient political cleavage in the 1990 elections was ideological:

> In one of the January editions of his regular radio commentary spot, István Csurka (MDF) warned about "the New Lenin Boys who revile Lenin," whilst on the eve of the elections Gáspár Miklós Tamás (Free Democrat) . . . admonished voters that if the Free Democrats did not win then the country would not see a change of régime or democratic government but at best changes in leadership: Backwater and fear—or Free Democratic majority. There is no third way," he wrote.[13]

Ideological debates such as these dominated the political discourse in the immediate postcommunist period while the issue of Hungarians abroad re-ceded into the background.

With both Budapest and Prague preoccupied with regime change, the Hungarians in Slovakia should infer that the state of the world was one of ethnic peace (fig. 4.1, box 4), leading them to support moderate aims in co-operation with the Slovaks. Consistent with this expectation, minority leaders maintained an integrationist stance in the first years of transition. Indeed, the Slovaks and Hungarians formed an inter-ethnic caretaker government shortly after the revolution.[14] The first Hungarian party, the Independent Hungarian Initiative (IHI), "defined itself as liberal, placing . . . the greatest emphasis on upholding individual rights."[15] The second Hungarian party, the Forum of Hungarians in Czechoslovakia, actually *joined* the PAV. Both parties ran on the PAV candidate list in the 1990 elections. Zsuzsa Csergő observes that from

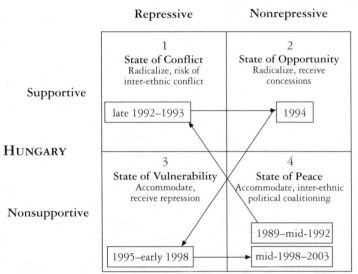

Figure 4.1 Hungarian minority behavior in Slovakia

the 1989 revolution to the June elections, "there was no evidence of an emerging ethnic division in the political arena between Slovaks and Hungarians."[16] Despite a smattering of anti-Hungarian rallies in early 1990, relations between the two groups remained remarkably calm with regular collaboration between Hungarian and Slovak politicians in parliament.[17] After the first elections, the Slovak leadership even invited the IHI to join the ruling coalition. This alliance remained in power until the 1992 elections, with a Hungarian vice chairman of parliament and a Hungarian deputy prime minister.[18]

Minority demands, too, remained quite moderate during this period. In the first electoral cycle, Hungarian leaders sought the restoration of minority schools, expansion of the minority press, and reestablishment of faculties of Hungarian history and culture.[19] They pursued these goals quietly, however, mainly through backdoor negotiations with government leaders. Minority representatives thus restricted their demands to cultural and linguistic autonomy in the early days of regime change. Meanwhile, political coalitions formed across ethnic lines, confirming the model's predictions.

Late 1992–1993: Constructing a National Slovak State

Vladimír Mečiar's Movement for a Democratic Slovakia (MDS) claimed victory in the 1992 elections and formed a ruling coalition with the ultra-nationalist Slovak National Party (SNP) in preparation for the 1993 Czechoslovak split. Ethnic Hungarians had bitterly opposed the breakup of Czechoslovakia because they regarded the federal government in Prague as a vital guarantor of their rights.[20] The wording of the new Slovak constitution only seemed to confirm their fears. Edwin Bakker notes, "Following the first phrase— 'We the Slovak People'—at every turn, the Slovak nation is given a preeminent position. . . . [T]he term 'nation' does not refer to all the people living within the territory of the Slovak Republic. Rather, it refers to the Slovak nation, as opposed to those members of minorities and ethnic groups living in Slovakia."[21] Although the constitution contained provisions for minority protection, the government seemed to be doing everything in its power to intimidate the ethnic Hungarians. For example, Slovak Transportation Minister Roman Hofbauer ordered the removal of Hungarian street signs ostensibly because they violated traffic and other safety regulations. The government also seemed bent on assimilating its Hungarian minority. A year into the new administration, the Cultural Association of Hungarian Workers of Czechoslovakia (CSEMADOK; the peak Hungarian cultural association in Slovakia) observed that Mečiar's government displayed "an obvious intention to damage the Hungarian-language school system."[22] Stefan Wolff writes:

> Since the inception of the new Slovak state in 1993, a growing lack of funding for Hungarian cultural organisations and activities has been claimed by minority representatives to cause gradual erosion of Hungarian culture in Slovakia. The simultaneous stepping-up of efforts to increase the prominence of Slovak culture, especially in mixed Hungarian and Slovak areas, is seen as an attempt of gradual assimilation.[23]

With the government promoting Slovak culture and restricting support for Hungarian educational and cultural development, the Hungarians had reason to believe that the Slovak leadership intended to repress the minority.

In Hungary, meanwhile, the Democratic Forum (MDF) had won the first multiparty elections with 43 percent of the vote, making MDF Leader József Antall the new prime minister. Robert J. Patkai notes that Antall "pursued a policy that was virtually the polar opposite of that of the communists. The Antall government put the fate of the ethnic Hungarians first in its foreign policy aims, causing some degree of alarm in the host-states."[24] Antall listed the government's priorities as forging ties with the West, increasing regional cooperation, and protecting Hungarian minorities in neighboring countries. He also emphasized that protecting co-ethnics abroad would not be subordinated to other foreign policy goals. As if to underscore this point, Antall declared himself "the prime minister of 15 million Hungarians," including about 5 million outside Hungary's borders. Although he later qualified this by saying that he saw himself only as the "spiritual" leader of 15 million Hungarians, the damage had already been done: "[Antall's] words were taken as a clear sign of a rebirth of Hungarian irredentism by the governments and majority populations in the neighboring countries. Antall's statements were problematic—not so much because they were proof of his irredentist intentions, but because they encouraged those who harbored such ideas and stirred up fear."[25]

In 1992, Hungary began to lobby aggressively on behalf of Hungarians outside its borders. In February, Defense Minister Lajos Für proclaimed that the preservation of the Hungarian "linguistic nation," was an "essential element" of Hungary's national security.[26] Although most Hungarian citizens wanted to join the EU as soon as possible—which required good relations between Hungary and its neighbors—there was a rising level of nationalism within Hungary toward the Hungarian diaspora.[27] Antall responded to these competing electoral pressures by forswearing irredentism while calling for increased autonomy for Hungarians abroad.[28] The government also maintained regular contact with ethnic Hungarian parties in Slovakia and Romania.[29] Slovakia's Coexistence Party enjoyed particularly close ties with the Antall government.[30] Government-sponsored foundations and agencies began to fund Hungarian associations in neighboring countries; the Office for Hungarian Minorities Abroad was set up to coordinate these activities.[31]

In mid-1992, Bratislava and Budapest began bilateral talks in anticipation of Slovak independence; the status of Hungarians in Slovakia loomed large in these negotiations. Returning from one such meeting in September, Mečiar defiantly declared that minority issues were Slovakia's internal affair and that ethnic Hungarians had no need for cross-border contacts with Hungary. Hungary countered by inviting a delegation of minority parties to Budapest for high-level talks with the government. On the eve of the Czechoslovak split, Budapest proclaimed that local self-government was the best means of guaranteeing the rights of ethnic Hungarians and, by extension, preventing secession.[32] Hungary also used its leverage in international organizations to lobby for Hungarian minorities. Already a member of the Council of Europe (CoE), Hungary threatened to veto Slovakia's admission to the CoE if it did not enact minority legislation immediately.[33] The standoff between the two governments lasted through the end of the year.[34]

Given strong signals of support from Hungary and indications of repressive intent from Slovakia, the minority should believe the state of the world to be one of conflict (fig. 4.1, box 1), leading Hungarian elites to radicalize their demands against the center. At the same time, increased ethnic salience on the ground should cause inter-ethnic alliances to fracture. In line with these predictions, minority representatives accelerated their demands considerably during this period. In summer 1992, Miklós Duray, the Coexistence Party leader, called for "political autonomy" for Hungarians in the event of Slovak independence. When Hungary threatened to veto Slovakia's admission to the CoE, the Hungarian minority parties drafted a memorandum to the CoE demanding that Slovakia be denied membership on the grounds of failing to protect minority rights.[35] They maintained this position right up until the CoE brokered a compromise between the two states in 1993. In response to government efforts to remove bilingual street signs and redistrict Hungarian regions, thousands of ethnic Hungarians gathered in the border town of Komárno in early 1994 in their first-ever popular protest. Minority representatives also issued a memorandum calling for the establishment of a Hungarian province with "an independent self-government and public administration."[36] These demands were enshrined in the campaign platform of the coalition of Hungarian parties going into the 1994 elections.[37]

These elections represent a high-water mark in minority radicalization. By now, most minority leaders had joined Duray in calling for territorial autonomy. The moderate Hungarian Christian Democrats (HDCM) began to assume a more extreme stance as well, asserting that "regions with 300,000—500,000 inhabitants . . . can be an ideal model for self-governing societies independent from the [Slovak] state."[38] Even the liberal IHI (now the Hungarian Civic Party) abandoned its pro-government position, having failed to reestablish its alliance with the Slovak PAV in 1992. Every major Hungarian party thus ran on a platform of regional or territorial autonomy in the 1994 elections.[39] We may therefore conclude that the minority leaders had radicalized their position against the Slovak government.

1994: The Liberal Interregnum

In the context of a growing economic crisis and increasing international isolation, the Slovak opposition finally gathered enough votes to oust Mečiar from power in March 1994, installing a liberal government with the backing of the Hungarian parties. This time, the government's promises of minority protection were credible because it depended on the minority's support in parliament for its survival. Almost immediately, Hungary restarted treaty talks with the new Slovak government headed by Josef Moravčík. In April, Moravčík announced that Hungary and Slovakia must resolve their disputes over minority rights in order to gain entrance to the EU, adding that Slovakia would apply for EU membership later that year.[40] True to its word, the government pushed through two new laws favored by Hungarians—one permitting name registration in one's mother tongue and the second allowing bilingual place names for towns and villages. The Slovak leadership had initiated the legislation to comply with CoE and EU recommendations and maintain the support of its Hungarian allies in parliament.[41] During a two-day visit to Slovakia in late 1994, CoE Representative Tarja Halonen stated that the administration had "fulfilled and *in some ways exceeded*" its promises of minority protection, among other things.[42] One observer noted: "There were no radical changes in Moravčík's government. The main thing was a change in the atmosphere. There was a lowered level of suspicions, a lack of ethnic provocations by officials and members of the Slovak government. It was possible to [engage in] constructive ethnic dialogue."[43]

Despite Slovakia's emerging conciliatory stance, Budapest continued to triangulate, reiterating the government's intention to consult with the Hungarian minority parties before submitting *any* bilateral treaty to parliament.[44] With a new pro-minority Slovak leadership and Hungary indicating its continued support for the minority, the Hungarians should believe that the state of the world had become one of opportunity (fig 4.1, box 2), leading them to mobilize around more radical demands. They are also more likely to obtain concessions in this state of the world, given the presence of a non-repressive majority.

Consistent with this expectation, Hungarian representatives escalated their demands to territorial autonomy. When the Slovak leadership offered to include Hungarian parties in the coalition government, Pál Csáky, the head of the Hungarian coalition, demanded guarantees of territorial self-administration in return for their participation. Specifically, he called for the creation of three autonomous territorial units in which Hungarians would be in the majority.[45] One minority representative despaired of his leader's extremist stance: "The problem with Duray, and also Csáky, is that they don't believe in real cooperation with the Slovaks. This is why I'm nervous. Because if you don't believe that real cooperation is possible, then your position is [always] the same. If your vision is that you will always be an isolated minority fighting for your rights, then that is a gloomy perspective."[46]

Nevertheless, Csáky's demands resonated strongly with the Hungarian rank and file. Surveys taken in the summer of 1994 indicated that 58 percent of ethnic Hungarians now supported territorial autonomy for Hungarian regions.[47] The Slovaks were aware that their Hungarian compatriots had radicalized—54 percent of Slovaks in the north and 56 percent of Slovaks in the south agreed with the statement, "Hungarians keep reinforcing their demands."[48] If minority behavior were a straightforward function of grievances or fears, then the Hungarians should have *moderated* their claims during this time. Instead, they radicalized against a relatively liberal government in response to perceptions of sustained external support. The Moravčík government, meanwhile, attempted to meet the minority's demands as far as it was able.[49]

1995–Early 1998: Slovakia's Janus-Faced Strategy

The MDS rode to victory in the fall 1994 elections, and Mečiar reassumed the premiership with the nationalist SNP as his junior partner. To international audiences, Mečiar proclaimed his support for minority rights, but for domestic consumption, he embarked on a series of policies targeting the Hungarian community. In 1995, the Education Ministry announced plans for an alternative education program under which all schools, including those in exclusively Hungarian regions, would be obliged to teach certain mandatory subjects in Slovak. Later that year, the government introduced a new language proposal that would require the use of Slovak in almost every area of public life.

Over the following two years, the Mečiar government introduced a number of additional initiatives that were seen as damaging to the Hungarian community. The Ministry of Culture issued a memo instructing museums to replace Hungarian signs with signs in English. The licenses of two Hungarian-language theaters in south Slovakia were revoked, and state funding for Hungarian cultural associations was radically reduced. More significantly, the parliament passed a law that redrew Slovakia's electoral districts, making Hungarians a numerical minority in every district.[50] Apart from the law's electoral implications, this also meant that ethnic Hungarians had fewer rights to use their native language in public life.[51] Mečiar further exacerbated tensions at a party rally in September 1997 when he suggested that Slovakia's minority issues could be resolved by expatriating Hungarians to Hungary.[52] The minority took these actions as clear signs of repressive intent; the overwhelming majority of Hungarians felt their situation had worsened significantly since the 1994 elections.[53]

As Slovak leaders turned up the heat, Hungary began to *withdraw* its support from the Hungarian minorities in neighboring states. This shift occurred under the new socialist-liberal government, which had come to power in 1994. On assuming premiership, Gyula Horn proclaimed that the government would no longer put the issue of Hungarian minorities above finalizing state treaties with Romania and Slovakia.[54] Horn "signaled his government's [conciliatory] intentions by visiting Bratislava just weeks after taking office in August 1994."[55] To expedite matters, Budapest ruled out the possibility of border adjustments and dropped its insistence that Slovakia grant territorial autonomy to its ethnic Hungarians as a condition of normalized relations. According to Miroslav Kusý, "[b]oth governments needed the bilateral treaty in this period, and it was necessary to give some sign of goodwill to the EU—this was why the treaty was signed so hurriedly. It was hurriedly prepared, and signed in Paris with great [fanfare]."[56] By decoupling Hungary's foreign policy from its diaspora issues, Horn was able to conclude a bilateral treaty with Slovakia in a matter of months.

With Hungary backing away from its co-ethnics and Slovakia resuming its policies of minority intimidation, ethnic Hungarians had strong reason to believe that the state of the world had become one of vulnerability (fig. 4.1, box 3), leading them to support more moderate demands in response to their diminished bargaining leverage. Consistent with this expectation, minority leaders soon abandoned calls for Hungarian self-administration and focused instead on combating specific policies of discrimination. Hungarian teachers and parents gathered in towns across southern Slovakia to protest the government's new education law.[57] A second Komárno meeting was held in 1995 to rally against the alternative education plan. They petitioned the CoE and the EU to intervene on their behalf and drafted counterproposals to each government initiative. The Hungarians thus followed a largely defensive strategy during this period.[58] Kálmán Petőcz justified their moderated position as follows: "You simply have to be very patient with the Slovaks—they have lived fifty years as an isolated nation—since 1938 under Hitler's rule, then 45 years under communism. Absolutely isolated . . . at this point, Hungarians are treated as second-class citizens in their own state . . . "[59]

The new Hungarian Coalition (Strana Mad'arskej Koalície, SMK) adopted a program going into the 1998 elections that reflected this moderation.[60] Instead of making overtly separatist demands, the SMK advocated a plan that would give the minority a degree of autonomy by way of *general decentralization and democratization of the state*.[61] Edit Bauer, a Coexistence Party representative, observed that "[o]ur manifesto does not place a major emphasis on minority issues, but rather on the issue of renewing democracy and the rule of law. If these goals are met, then the problems of minorities will be solved as well."[62] On the strength of this moderate agenda, the SMK gained almost the entire Hungarian vote, with only a tiny percentage going to other parties.[63] We may therefore infer that the Hungarians had de-escalated their claims in spite of heightened government discrimination—in confirmation of the model's predictions.

Mid-1998–2003: Slovak Liberalization

The 1998 elections were held in the midst of mounting public anxiety over Slovakia's growing diplomatic isolation, government corruption, and consequent demotion from the first-wave EU-accession countries. Although Mečiar's party had won a plurality of the vote, parties across the political spectrum formed a government under Mikuláš Dzurinda's Slovak Democratic Coalition (SDK) in a bid to oust Mečiar from power. The SMK was invited into the governing coalition, even though Dzurinda already had a parliamentary majority without it.[64] The Hungarians received three ministerial positions in Dzurinda's twenty-member cabinet. The Human Rights and Minorities portfolio went to Pál Csáky, a man who had once demanded a separate political status for Hungarian regions. The SMK also received the deputy speakership of parliament, the chairmanship of the parliamentary committee for human and minority rights, and four departmental secretaryships. These gestures were taken as credible signs that the new leadership favored building a liberal society.

In the meantime, Hungary appeared to be moving in the opposite direction. The nationalist Fidesz (Fiatal Demokraták Szövetsége, Alliance of Young Democrats) party won the 1998 elections, and Viktor Orbán became the new prime minister. As the self-described inheritor of Antall's earlier nationalist government, Orbán had campaigned on the promise to reach out to Magyars abroad. Orbán eventually made good on his pledge by initiating the so-called status law.[65] This law, passed by the Hungarian parliament in 2001, extended numerous benefits to Hungarians in Slovakia, Romania, Ukraine, Yugoslavia, Croatia, and Slovenia. In its original form, the law included the right to work in Hungary for three months each year. It also made scholarships, travel subsidies, medical and pension benefits, and financial aid available to individuals and organizations in the diaspora.[66]

Although Romania and Slovakia reacted very negatively to these developments, Hungary managed to maintain a working relationship with its neighbors both before and after the law was passed.[67] Moreover, Orbán affirmed that it was in Hungary's interests to see its neighbors admitted to the EU as soon as possible.[68] In contrast to the previous nationalist government, which had attempted to block Slovakia's admission to the CoE, the Fidesz government actually *supported* Slovakia's application to the EU and NATO, even holding discussions with the Czechs about how to get Slovakia re-inducted into the first-wave accession countries.[69]

To understand Orbán's mixed signals during this time, it is important to bear in mind that the status law had been primarily intended for a domestic audience. As the 2002 elections approached, Orbán attempted to reconnect with his supporters by honoring his promise to push through a status law on behalf of minorities in neighboring countries. However, the government began to distance itself from the law once it became clear that it might inhibit the government's ability to achieve its other goals—namely, EU integration. When formal negotiations over EU accession began in 1998, Hungarian legislation received a thorough going-over to see whether it complied with EU standards. From the very start, the status law attracted significant criticism from international bodies. Before it was even passed, the CoE pointed out that the law did not conform to European principles of nondiscrimination because it extended benefits on an ethnic basis to citizens of Austria—then an EU member. The parliament obligingly rewrote the proposal to exclude Austria from the scope of the law. After it was passed, the CoE asserted that the law *still* did not meet European standards, so the government promised to amend it. Hungary also pledged to negotiate with Romania and Slovakia over implementing the law in a way that would not discriminate against non-Hungarians. Hungarian Foreign Ministry Spokesman Tamás Tóth affirmed Hungary's conciliatory intentions toward its neighbors: "[The status law] would be an internal affair of Hungary [if it did not have] external implications. So that's the core of the problem. That's why it's difficult, because this is a Hungarian law, but we want to make it in a way that it would be acceptable for the neighbors . . . [so that the benefits] will not be limited to ethnic Hungarians but also [extended] to Slovaks."[70]

Despite their strong condemnation of the law, Slovak leaders maintained an ongoing dialogue with Hungary throughout the crisis. Slovak leaders stated that, although they regretted Budapest's decision to act unilaterally with respect to its diaspora, they would not retaliate. Deputy Foreign Minister Jaroslav Chebo offered, "I think nobody here has got in mind . . . any countermeasures to be introduced to somehow oppose the intention of the Hungarian legislators. But anyway, we have to find out a way in which the support—the cooperation between Hungary and the ethnic Hungarians living in Slovakia—can be conducted in a way that is compatible with Europeanism as such."[71] In the end, the government effectively gutted the law in response to sustained international criticism.[72] The amended law was shorn of most of its original benefits, including the right to work permits and access to health care and pensions in Hungary. Diaspora Hungarians could still obtain identity certificates, but these would not be official identity cards.[73] The status law had thus been reduced to little more than a symbol, mainly as a result of EU conditionality.

The predictions of ethnic bargaining would seem to be indeterminate in light of Hungary's mixed signals. However, I argue that the status law was *not* a credible sign of interventionist intent for two reasons. First, Hungary maintained cordial bilateral ties with Slovakia throughout this period, in contrast to the previous Antall administration, which had refused to declare its borders inviolable and declined to normalize relations with Slovakia over minority issues. Second, the status law would have dispensed benefits within Hungary proper and therefore had no direct bearing on the minority's relations with its host government. Finally, by removing the most objectionable portions of the law, Hungary had shown that it was willing to renege on its promises to ethnic Hungarians abroad in order to meet the conditions of EU accession.

With a noninterventionist lobby state and conciliatory host government, the Hungarian minority had reason to believe that the state of the world was one of peace (fig. 4.1, box 4), leading minority representatives to advance integrationist demands in cooperation with the Slovak majority. Consistent with this prediction, Hungarian leaders pursued a modest agenda of cultural autonomy. They formulated their demands in the framework of actual legislation such as a language law that would expand the minority's right to use its mother tongue in official business; they also sought the establishment of Hungarian educational facilities in south Slovakia.[74] A new language law was passed in summer 1999 with the support of their Slovak allies in government. Although the SMK was not entirely satisfied with the law, and had yet to obtain Hungarian faculties, its leaders refrained from radicalizing. Instead, they joined Slovak parties in pushing through a raft of reforms that had no direct bearing on minority issues. Despite accusations by Hungarian nationalists that the party had "sold out Hungarian interests in the name of Slovak democracy," the SMK gained a valuable reputation as a dependable junior partner. In 1999, Dzurinda praised the SMK as "the most stable part of the government."[75]

In the 2002 elections, the SMK received an overwhelming popular mandate from its constituents with over 11 percent of the vote. It was consequently invited into the second Dzurinda government, and Pál Csáky was appointed deputy prime minister, indicating a level of ethnic accommodation not seen since the early days of the revolution.[76] In this position, Csáky defended Slovakia's minority policies and argued for the country's swift accession to the EU. Strikingly, Csáky himself favored amending Hungary's status law to comply with European standards, stating that the dispute could be resolved "within 48 hours" if both Hungary and Slovakia demonstrated the "political will to do so."[77] He even acted as a mediator in bilateral negotiations over the law in 2002.[78] From these events, we may infer that Hungarian minority leaders retained their moderate stance while using their leverage in government to obtain concessions in the areas of language and education. Moreover, they did so in cooperation with the Slovak leadership, in line with the predictions of ethnic bargaining.

The Hungarians in Postcommunist Romania

1989—Early 1990: The Revolution and Its Aftermath

In December 1989, opponents of Ceauşescu's regime—both Romanians and ethnic Hungarians—rallied in support of László Tőkés in the Romanian border town of Timişoara. Tőkés, the dissident pastor of the Hungarian Calvinist Church, had preached against totalitarianism as well as xenophobia; mixed marriages between Hungarians and Romanians were commonplace in his congregation. When Romanian authorities, fearful of his growing popularity, attempted to remove Tőkés, a crowd of about 5,000 Hungarians and Romanians gathered around the pastor's house in defiance of the regime. Thus began a four-day standoff between Tőkés's unarmed supporters, on one side, and the Securitate (the Romanian secret service), the militia, and the army, on the other. Several hundred citizens of both ethnicities died in this and subsequent battles.[79] By December 20, the army had gone over to the side of the revolutionaries, and the next day about 10,000 Hungarian and Romanian civilians and soldiers gathered in the town's main square chanting, "We are ready to die!"[80] The revolution quickly spread to Bucharest and other cities across the country.

In a little over a week, Nicolae Ceauşescu was overthrown, and the Romanian authorities established the National Salvation Front (NSF) to oversee the transition. The NSF set up a caretaker government, which made overtures to the Hungarian minority.[81] Ion Iliescu, NSF leader and head of the interim government, sought ethnic Hungarian support by promising to implement minority protections. On January 5, the NSF "solemnly declared that it would guarantee individual and collective rights and freedom for ethnic minorities," pledging to establish a ministry for minorities.[82] Interethnic cooperation was evident at the grass roots level as well; shortly after the revolution, Romanians assisted the Hungarians in reopening a Hungarian radio station that had been closed since 1985.

The Hungarian government, too, assumed a non-nationalist posture during this time, extending diplomatic and material support to *all* citizens of Romania regardless of ethnicity. In response to the revolutionary crisis, Hungary sent humanitarian aid over the border, including much-needed food and medical supplies.[83] Romanians initially greeted Budapest's overtures with mistrust; however, a spirit of ethnic harmony arose as it became clear that Hungary was offering unconditional assistance to all. Army and border guards became friendly and courteous to visitors from Hungary "almost overnight."[84] At the same time, the NSF government established relations with the Hungarian government, and Budapest and Bucharest entered an unprecedented period of cooperation. A *New York Times* reporter wrote exuberantly of these events:

> During the fighting in Romania, Hungarians wept for those killed by Ceauşescu's forces and were anguished when the revolution seemed to falter. They shared joyfully the final success of those they were thinking of as brothers. There is now the chance that out of fearful bloodshed two adjacent countries, with intermingled, once quarrelling populations, can make their land fit for heroes to live in with reciprocal amity.[85]

With Hungary providing support to/backing the NSF and the NSF pledging to protect minority rights, ethnic Hungarians should believe that the state of the world was one of ethnic peace (fig. 4.2, box 4), leading Hungarian representatives to pursue moderate aims in cooperation with the government. Indeed, the Democratic Alliance of Hungarians in Romania (DAHR)—the only major Hungarian political organization in the

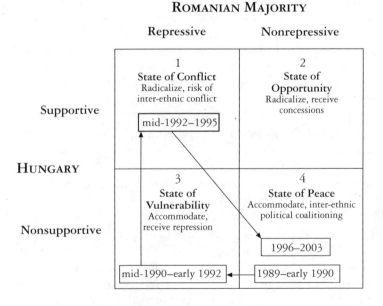

Figure 4.2 Hungarian minority claim-making in Romania

postcommunist period—strongly supported Iliescu and the NSF in the months following the revolution. The DAHR was founded in December 1989 as a broad-based coalition of political platforms, cultural and youth organizations, and educational institutes. It had a well-established political hierarchy, and its leaders were directly elected from the bottom up—its program thus serves as a reasonable proxy for the preferences of Hungarians as a whole.[86]

The DAHR assumed a strongly conciliatory posture toward the new Romanian government. It recognized the NSF as the sole legal authority of Romania and proclaimed that it was every citizen's duty to support the achievements of the December revolution regardless of national origin.[87] In the beginning, prominent Hungarian leaders, including Tőkés and Géza Domokos, were themselves members of the NSF. Ethnic Hungarians were given places in the caretaker government, and it was even rumored that Tőkés would become the first Romanian minister of minorities. In return for their support, the DAHR leaders called for expanded minority education, the reestablishment of a Hungarian university in Cluj, and the right to use Hungarian in official business in Transylvania.[88] Despite their outspoken demands, they promised to pursue these goals in cooperation with the government.

Mid-1990–Early 1992: Constructing a National Romanian State

Romania's inter-ethnic tranquility was disrupted in early 1990 when clashes broke out in the Transylvanian town of Târqu-Mureş. On March 19, supporters of the nationalist *Vatra Românească* (Romanian Cradle) attacked representatives of the Hungarian community with axes and clubs. On the second day of the violence, the Hungarians began to retaliate. The army finally intervened on March 21 to end the crisis, but not before eight people had been killed and more than three hundred injured—mostly Hungarians.[89] Iliescu downplayed the seriousness of the attacks, calling them "regrettable events," and delayed an official inquiry into the conflict. By siding with the *Vatra Românească* and other right-wing elements that enjoyed strong support in Transylvania, Iliescu hoped to boost the government's flagging popularity in the region. The *Vatra Românească* was also given considerable column space in pro-government newspapers, where it openly disseminated its anti-Hungarian views. Partly because of this, its opinions came to be associated with the NSF itself.[90]

The NSF emerged victorious in the May 1990 elections and aligned itself with the nationalist parties, including the National Unity Party of Romanians (PUNR), the political wing of the *Vatra Românească*. Soon after the elections, NSF leaders began to renege on their promises to the Hungarian minority. In 1990, the parliament approved a law that further restricted minority education.[91] The government also removed DAHR representatives from the Mures County Council and the Târqu-Mureş City Council and replaced them with *Vatra Românească* members.[92] The two main nationalist parties, the PUNR and the Greater Romania Party (GRP), repeatedly introduced legislation to disband the DAHR, branding the Hungarian deputies as national traitors and stooges for the Hungarian government. Prime Minister Petre Roman even assisted the GRP in launching *România Mare,* a xenophobic weekly publication that enjoyed a wide readership.[93]

In late 1991, the parliament passed a constitution that pronounced Romania a "sovereign and independent, unitary and indivisible Romanian national state" [Article 1(1)], founded on "the unity of the Romanian people" [Article 1(4)]. It also ruled out autonomy for Hungarian regions.[94] The NSF continued to cooperate with the nationalist parties throughout the first electoral cycle, effectively abandoning the DAHR in favor of the Romanian ultra-nationalists.

Hungary maintained a remarkably noninterventionist stance during this period, all things considered. Budapest condemned the "explicitly anti-Hungarian atrocities" in Târqu-Mureş and accused the Romanian government of sanctioning national chauvinism. However, it refrained from direct confrontation and instead appealed to international bodies to sanction Bucharest. The government wrote a letter to the UN secretary general, stating, "The Hungarian side does not wish to interfere in the internal affairs of Romania, nevertheless, we cannot remain silent about the severe violations of minority rights embodied in several international instruments. . . . the international community should render assistance to curb the Romanian nationalist actions violating the provisions of the UN Charter."[95]

Despite his manifest displeasure with the Romanian government, Antall affirmed his wish to negotiate a bilateral treaty with Bucharest.[96] To expedite matters, the government attempted to contain cross-border tensions with Romania. When the World Federation of Transylvania organized a protest march in Timişoara on the sixtieth anniversary of Trianon, Antall warned that the demonstrations could harm the status of Hungarians in Romania.[97] With almost 80 percent of the Hungarian public favoring accession to NATO, the CoE, and the EC, the government endeavored to resolve disputes over minority issues through bilateral diplomacy rather than direct intervention.[98]

Given Hungary's noninterventionist signals and Romania's increasingly nationalist orientation, the Hungarians should perceive the state of the world to be one of vulnerability (fig. 4.2, box 3), leading them to accommodate the majority while remaining mobilized along ethnic lines. As predicted, the minority largely refrained from radicalization. An ethnic fears approach might expect the Hungarians to pursue some degree of separatism in the wake of Târqu-Mureş as a means of guarding against future aggression. Instead, DAHR representatives tried to negotiate better police protections and expanded minority education; DAHR leaders joined moderate Romanians in calling for guarantees of minority rights in accordance with the Helsinki Final Act. At the first DAHR congress in April 1990, Acting President Domokos declared that it had not been a mistake to support the NSF government and called for continued cooperation with liberal Romanian parties. The DAHR went into the 1990 elections on a platform of ethnic accommodation.[99]

Hungarian representatives maintained their conciliatory posture through 1991. When restrictions were placed on the minority press in February, the Hungarian deputies reacted mildly, proclaiming their solidarity with Romanian moderates. Right-wing elements in the NSF and the *Vatra Românească* also launched a campaign to ban the DAHR, accusing it of fomenting irredentism. In response, the DAHR Congress issued an "Appeal to the Entire Romanian Society" pleading for inter-ethnic calm and voicing concerns that in the "atmosphere of suspicion that has been created . . . anti-Hungarian feelings may be ignited at any time through false accusations or misrepresentation of minority demands."[100] At the second DAHR congress in May 1991, Tőkés (now honorary chairman of the DAHR) declared that Hungarians "do not want to be the minority facing the majority nation, we want to become the equal partners of Romanians in [a] common homeland."[101] The organization made a point of eschewing calls for territorial autonomy, noting that such an arrangement would leave many Hungarians outside autonomous minority regions.[102] In the absence of external backing, the Hungarian leadership thus maintained a position of accommodation even in the face of majority threat.

Mid-1992–1995: Bilateral Treaty Talks

Iliescu's new Party of Social Democracy in Romania (PDSR) prevailed in the 1992 elections but failed to gain an absolute majority in parliament. Iliescu therefore established a minority government with the support of the two nationalist parties. Meanwhile, Gheorghe Funar, the PUNR leader, was elected mayor of the Transylvanian capital of Cluj, where he began to change the names of Hungarian streets and monuments, ban Hungarian street signs, and generally restrict DAHR activities in town.[103] Despite domestic and international condemnation of these activities, Iliescu declined to sanction Funar for his behavior, even though the PUNR was a close government ally—election results and opinion polls at the time indicated considerable popular support for ethnic extremism.[104]

Around this time, Hungary began to intervene more aggressively on behalf of its co-ethnics in the context of bilateral treaty talks with Romania. Budapest's increasingly confrontational posture was evidenced by Defense Minister Lajos Für's announcement that Hungary "should do everything in [its] power, using all legal and diplomatic means, to end the threat to the minorities and guarantee their survival."[105] Already a member of the CoE, Hungary threatened to block Romania's admission to the body if it failed to improve its treatment of ethnic Hungarians. It also refused to sign a treaty with Romania without a side agreement on minority protection. Romania responded by complaining of Hungarian meddling in its domestic affairs, accusing Budapest of conspiring to annex Transylvanian territory.[106] The talks soon reached an impasse.

The two governments resumed their negotiations in March 1993, but not before a DAHR delegation was invited to Budapest, where minority representatives were assured of Hungary's support for the minority's "legitimate aspirations," including "*internal self-rule* in accordance with Romanian and international law."[107] Budapest and Bucharest reached another stalemate over minority issues, with each side accusing the other of intransigence. The Socialists came to power in Hungary in mid-1994 with the two sides still trying to hammer out a compromise. Just as negotiations began to look promising, the nationalist elements in Romania turned up the heat. The parliament passed a controversial education law that would force Hungarians in Romania to learn at least some Romanian, and in July the mayor of Cluj approved a request for an archeological excavation under Hungarian national monuments. DAHR leaders again traveled to Budapest to appeal for support and were promised that (1) Hungary would consult with minority leaders before it signed a bilateral treaty and (2) any acceptable treaty *must* include protections for ethnic Hungarians. The government continued to meet with minority representatives throughout 1995, repeatedly assuring them that Budapest supported autonomy for Hungarian regions in Romania.[108]

With Hungary assuming a more interventionist posture and Romania signaling a strongly nationalist orientation, the Hungarian minority should perceive a state of the world of conflict (fig. 4.2, box 1), leading DAHR representatives to radicalize in response to perceptions of heightened leverage. In line with this prediction, the Hungarians lost little time in accelerating their demands. Shortly after the 1992 elections, DAHR leaders issued the Cluj Declaration, in which they called for self-determination and communal autonomy for Hungarian regions.[109] The declaration represents the most radical minority demand to date and attracted criticism not only from Romanian nationalists but also from their moderate Romanian allies in the Democratic Convention (DC).[110] Meanwhile, pressure mounted on the ground for assuming a more confrontational stance to the government. When Funar ordered the removal of Hungarian place names in Cluj, 5,000 people marched through the city in protest.[111] This was the first time in more than fifty years that Hungarians in Transylvania had demonstrated over minority issues.

DAHR leaders stopped short of demanding territorial autonomy at their 1993 party congress, limiting their demands to *communal* autonomy.[112] Territorial autonomy did not enjoy the backing of the Hungarian government at the time; Romanian moderates, too, considered claims for territorial autonomy too incendiary. Such calculations were also apparent in the choice of the new DAHR leadership. At the DAHR convention, party representatives elected Béla Markó as president—someone who, as *Expres* put it, "is more radical than [current president] Domokos and more moderate than László Tőkés."[113] The Hungarian rank and file thus selected a more radical leader to press their radicalized agenda, but were careful not to overplay their hand.[114]

As treaty talks threatened to stall once again over minority issues, Béla Markó took advantage of the minority's heightened leverage by escalating his demands to territorial autonomy where "compact Hungarian populations live." Markó called on Hungary to insist that provisions for such arrangements be included in its basic treaty with Romania.[115] In January 1995, the DAHR further upped the ante by creating a council to coordinate local governments for Hungarians under one autonomous zone. When bilateral talks restarted in fall 1995, Markó sought and received assurances from the Hungarian prime minister that Budapest would continue to support autonomy for ethnic Hungarians in Romania. Bishop Tőkés went even further, proposing that Romania devolve power to Hungarian regions along the lines of South Tyrol.[116] Hungarian minority leaders thus radicalized their position in reaction to the increased leverage they enjoyed in the context of eleventh-hour treaty negotiations between Hungary and Romania.

Ethnic tensions in Romania ran high during this period. Perceptions of minority extremism led to fissures in the fragile coalition between the DAHR and Romanian moderates in the DC. One DC representative proposed that the Hungarians be ejected from the convention if they failed to recant their calls for territorial autonomy.[117] This led to a formal split between the DAHR and the DC, demonstrating that inter-ethnic coalitions are difficult (if not impossible) to sustain in a climate of high ethnic salience.

1996–2003: Liberalization and Uneasy Coexistence

Treaty talks between Hungary and Romania dragged into 1996. The main sticking point was Romania's refusal to sign the CoE Recommendation on Minority Protection; it was feared that the provision for minority self-government would provide a legal basis for Hungarian separatism.[118] In 1995, the United States, EU, and CoE began to insist that the two governments settle their differences as a prerequisite for full membership in NATO and other European bodies.[119] In 1995, NATO issued a document that read in part: "States which have ethnic disputes or external territorial disputes, including irredentist claims . . . must settle those disputes by peaceful means in accordance with OSCE principles. Resolution of such disputes would be a factor in determining whether to invite a state to join the Alliance."[120] The United States urged Bucharest in particular to make concessions to its Hungarian minority, noting that its failure to do so had hindered the country's accession to NATO.[121] In March 1996, the U.S. secretary of state announced that NATO was now ready to expand eastward provided that these countries resolved their disputes with their neighbors, among other things.[122] Debates in the Hungarian parliament now raged over whether the government should simply sign a treaty with Romania and be done with it. The Hungarian government had become increasingly willing to compromise on diaspora issues to conclude a basic treaty with its neighbor.[123]

The Romanians were even more eager to join the EU and NATO. Opinion polls conducted in 1996 showed that 95 percent of the population favored NATO membership and 97 percent EU membership.[124] With NATO indicating its willingness to consider Romania's application that year and fall elections fast approaching, Iliescu launched a desperate bid to start Romania down the path toward accession, even if this meant granting concessions to the ethnic Hungarians. In August, the two governments reached a compromise: "Mr. Iliescu, eyeing Romania's November 3 presidential elections and in need of a foreign-policy victory, proposed that an annex be added to the treaty, clearly stating it did not allow for collective rights. Hungary, over the protests of many Hungarians in Romania—and aware that preliminary NATO talks begin this winter—agreed to the annex."[125]

Hungary had thus effectively reneged on its promises to the Hungarian minority, sending a strong signal of noninterventionist intent. Romania, too, began to change its orientation toward the minority. Despite Iliescu's efforts to recapture popular support by moving to the center, the moderate DC emerged victorious in the 1996 elections. To shore up their base of support and establish their liberal credentials, DC leaders invited the DAHR into the governing coalition even though they had a bare parliamentary majority without it.

With relations between Budapest and Bucharest normalized and the moderates in control of the Romanian government, the Hungarian minority should infer that the state of the world had become one of ethnic peace (fig. 4.2, box 4), leading minority representatives to moderate their demands. At the same time, political alliances should form across ethnic lines. True to this expectation, DAHR leaders abandoned their demands for territorial autonomy in exchange for concrete amendments to Romania's education and language laws. The DAHR worked closely with its Romanian allies to achieve these goals and obtained positions in the government.[126] Meanwhile, the party began to diversify its platform. Whereas previously it had focused almost exclusively on matters of interest to the minority, the DAHR now adopted policies on a range of issues, including budgetary reform, privatization, taxation, monetary and fiscal policy, and EU and NATO integration.[127] Tibor Szatmári, public relations head of the DAHR office in Bucharest, said of this time:

> [A]fter being in government, we realized there are different ways of securing the rights of Hungarians and avoiding discrimination. In the past, autonomy was the solution to discrimination against Hungarians and lack of investment in these regions. Now, Hungarians have a *Hungarian* minister of territorial development—*he* is the guarantee that there will be no more discrimination against Hungarians.[128]

The new government succeeded in meeting most of the DAHR's language and cultural demands over the next two years, sometimes against considerable opposition. When they failed to obtain the necessary votes to pass the controversial amendments, the government issued emergency decrees.[129] The Romanian leadership also fulfilled its campaign promise to reopen the Hungarian consulate in Cluj, which had been closed since 1988.[130] The DAHR and its Romanian partners even tentatively agreed that a Hungarian university would be established in Târqu-Mureş. Mainstream minority leaders had thus moderated their demands from territorial autonomy to cultural and linguistic rights. Moreover, they were working with the Romanian leadership to achieve their goals.

Impact of the Hungarian Status Law in Romania

As noted above, the 1998 elections in Hungary brought the nationalist Fidesz party to power with Orbán as the new prime minister. Both during and after the elections, Orbán and other Hungarian politicians asserted that Budapest "represented Hungarians both at home and abroad" and that Hungary had a moral obligation to lobby for the rights of beleaguered Hun-

garians in neighboring countries. After years of debate, the Orbán government finally introduced the proposed status law in the run-up to the 2002
elections. With broad popular support, the proposal was passed in 2001
with the backing of all major parties in parliament.

In assessing the impact of these events on ethnic relations over the border, it is important to remember that Orbán's nationalism differed fundamentally from that of the previous Antall government, which had refused
to normalize relations with Romania over its treatment of ethnic Hungarians
and had attempted to block the country's admission to the CoE. In contrast, Orbán maintained an open dialogue with Romania throughout his
term of office, supporting the country's accession to European bodies and negotiating with Bucharest over how best to implement the status law.[131] In
response to complaints that the status law violated Romanian sovereignty,
Orbán assured his Romanian counterpart that their differences could be
resolved through negotiations.[132] Indeed, just months after the status law
was enacted, Hungary and Romania signed a Memorandum of Understanding making *all* Romanians (not just ethnic Hungarians) eligible for
three-month work permits in Hungary.[133] The government finally excised
the controversial portions of the law in 2002.

In Romania, interethnic cooperation continued to grow. The DAHR
obtained a number of new positions in government, including the portfolios of Health and the Protection of National Minorities. In 1999, the
parliament finally approved long-sought amendments to the education
and local administration laws, institutionalizing the emergency decrees
of 1997.[134] When Iliescu regained power in 2000, many feared a return
to his nationalist policies of the early 1990s. However, Iliescu recognized
which way the wind was blowing and exchanged his xenophobic nationalism for a tamer brand of European socialism. His new Social Democratic
Party (PSD) aligned itself *not* with the GRP, its earlier ally and second
most powerful party in parliament, but with the DAHR. The government
signed a Political Protocol with DAHR leaders promising them more than
they had enjoyed under the previous regime in return for their support in
parliament. The protocol was reaffirmed in 2002.[135] During his first two
years in office, Iliescu made good on several of his pledges to the Hungarians—pushing through key legislation on property restitution and local
administration.

With Hungary signaling its lack of support (having placed EU accession
over the interests of its diaspora) and Romanian leaders working closely
with DAHR representatives in parliament, the bargaining model predicts
that minority leaders would continue to seek moderate goals in cooperation with the Romanian government. Although most of this period

was indeed marked by inter-ethnic cooperation, Orbán's early nationalist signals *did* appear to have influenced minority behavior in Romania. Indeed, an open split emerged in the DAHR as the radicals attempted to use their ties with nationalist elements in Hungary to undermine the mainstream Markó leadership. These tensions surfaced at a DAHR party congress in June 1998, immediately after Fidesz had swept to power. One observer noted that Orbán's nationalist campaign in Hungary appeared to have increased popular support for the radicals.[136] Before the assembled delegates, the radicals proclaimed—to audible sounds of assent—that the moderates had sold out the interests of ordinary Hungarians to secure a place in government. They then revived an old demand for a Hungarian university in Cluj as well as territorial autonomy for Hungarian regions.[137] The growing mutiny within the rank and file led mainstream DAHR leaders to escalate their demands against the Romanian government in order to maintain the support of their constituents in the context of a leadership challenge.

For the most part, however, the DAHR moderates stayed the course in government—working with their Romanian partners to hammer out concrete legislation related to Hungarian interests. In doing so, they retained the support of the minority rank and file; according to a 2000 opinion poll, 85 percent of DAHR supporters favored the leadership's decision to stay in government.[138] Like its counterpart in Slovakia, the DAHR even acted as a mediator in the dispute between Hungary and Romania over minority issues. As tensions arose over how to implement the status law in Romania, Markó adopted a neutral position, stating only, "[w]e would favor a very simple, clear, and objective preparation procedure on Romania's territory."[139] When in late 2003, the Fidesz party (now out of government) expressed its support for the radicals' demand of territorial autonomy, Markó denounced Fidesz interference in Romanian affairs as "an unwise move" that would harm the interests of the Hungarian minority.[140] One member of the Romanian government offered this evaluation: "DAHR is not an extremist party, although there are certain extremists included. Generally, I perceive them as a moderate party with European values. . . . [the] DAHR is a pragmatic party, and they have programs the goals of which are not only ethnically oriented, but European."[141] The gradual normalization of the DAHR is well documented as its leaders focused increasingly on issues that concerned the entire citizenry.

From this discussion, we may conclude that the deepening rapprochement between Romania and Hungary in the context of EU and NATO conditionality led the minority leadership to seek moderate goals in cooperation with the Romanian majority. This is consistent with the expectations of ethnic bargaining given minority perceptions that the state of the world was one of ethnic peace.

Comparing the Hungarian Movements

I now provide a comparative analysis of the two Hungarian minority movements to evaluate the competing theories of minority claim-making. Primordialist theories would expect both groups to pursue a degree of separatism in the postcommunist period due to their cohesive national identities as well as their linguistic, regional, religious, and cultural distinctiveness. Thus, the minority groups should seek a separate status once they have the opportunity to do so. Although these theories correctly anticipate the lines of conflict as well as the basis upon which people mobilized, they explain neither why both groups failed to pursue autonomy before 1992 nor why they abandoned autonomy demands in the late 1990s to gain more moderate benefits such as property restitution and Hungarian faculties.

Economic opportunism also fails to account for Hungarian claim-making in these cases. Both minority groups were concentrated in agricultural areas, which were less developed than the state as a whole. Regional economic data show that the agricultural regions of south Slovakia had a relatively high rate of unemployment in the 1990s, ranging from 18 to 21 percent (Slovakia's overall unemployment rate was 13–15 percent).[142] Economic factors alone predict that Hungarians in Slovakia would not seek territorial autonomy because the regions stood to lose from severing their ties with the comparatively rich Slovak center. In Romania, the Hungarian regions had unemployment rates ranging from 4.3 percent in Covasna to 8 and 8.2 percent in Harghita and Mureş counties, respectively (Romania's overall unemployment rate was 6.6 percent).[143] Although these differences are relatively slight, the Hungarian regions in Romania were somewhat worse off than the country as a whole and therefore would be ill-advised to seek fiscal autonomy from the center. Finally, the material benefits to minority members of expanded Hungarian language education and the right to use their language in official business may explain why these demands were made in the first place. However, they do not explain why they were periodically exchanged for autonomous demands or abandoned altogether.

Elite arguments generally hold that charismatic leaders manipulate ethnic divisions in society to gain or maintain power or wealth. An analysis of elite behavior in these two cases is illuminating in this respect. Both groups had charismatic leaders who called for noncooperation with their governments. Slovakia's minority extremists included Miklós Duray and, to a lesser extent,

Pál Csáky; Romania had Bishop Tőkés. Interestingly, all three men changed their political positions markedly over the period of observation. In the early to mid-1990s, Csáky and Duray called for noncooperation with the Slovaks and a separate political status for Hungarian regions. Both later abandoned these positions in favor of more moderate demands and even joined successive post-1998 Slovak governments (Csáky serving as deputy prime minister of Slovakia). In Romania, Bishop Tőkés originally advocated ethnic tolerance and integration, but later championed territorial autonomy and federal status for Hungarian counties. He was sidelined by the late 1990s once Hungary and Romania normalized bilateral relations, paving the way for inter-ethnic cooperation in Romania. These patterns suggest that minority elites must adapt their position to the prevailing bargaining dynamic between the minority and the center or succumb to marginalization or political irrelevance.

According to ethnic fears explanations, minorities pursue separatist agendas as a means of protecting themselves against assimilation, discrimination, or annihilation. These accounts, however, do not tell the whole story. The Hungarians in Slovakia, for example, faced their greatest threat during the 1995–1998 Mečiar period, when the government undertook a campaign of linguistic and cultural assimilation, treating the Hungarians like a fifth-column minority. Minority leaders responded by petitioning international bodies and organizing protests; however, they failed to radicalize their claims against the center. In Romania, the minority faced its greatest danger after the 1990 Târqu-Mureş clashes when the government aligned itself with Romanian ultra-nationalists. Rather than launching a separatist bid, however, Hungarian representatives sought promises of police protection and a full investigation into the conflict in cooperation with Romanian moderates. These cases show that minorities often *accommodate* threatening governments, contrary to the expectations of ethnic fears theories.

Ethnic bargaining provides the most satisfactory account of minority claim-making in the two cases. In Slovakia, the Hungarians began to radicalize in 1992 as Hungary initiated treaty negotiations with the new Slovak state. Budapest called on Bratislava to sign the CoE recommendation allowing for minority self-government and threatened to block Slovakia's admission to the CoE if it failed to do so. Hungarian representatives responded to their heightened leverage by pushing for territorial autonomy; they maintained this position even after a pro-minority government had come to power in 1994. Minority leaders muted their demands once Hungary and Slovakia had concluded a treaty, indicating that the minority no longer enjoyed external leverage. Consistent with the predictions of the spatial model, periods of non-nationalist signaling (the immediate post-

Table 4.3. Summary of competing theories, Hungarians in Slovakia and Romania

Theory	Hungarians in Slovakia	Hungarians in Romania
Primodialist theories (cultural/linguistic differences; pre-existing "national" identity; ethnic hatreds)	**Incorrectly predicts** that ethnic differences between Hungarians and Slovaks would lead to *constant* claims for autonomy since 1989	**Incorrectly predicts** that ethnic differences between Hungarians and Romanians would lead to *constant* demands for autonomy since 1989
Economic arguments	**Correctly predicts** that Hungarians would not seek secession due to their relative economic backwardness **Does not explain** why they would favor *territorial autonomy*, nor why they would do so *only* in the mid-1990s	**Correctly predicts** that relatively poor Hungarians would not seek secession **Does not explain** why they would favor *territorial autonomy*, nor why they would do so *only* in the mid-1990s
Ethnic entrepreneurship theories	**Incorrectly predicts** that Hungarians would continue to radicalize in response to extremist elites (Csáky and Duray); **Does not explain** why these elites moderated their demands after 1998, cooperating with successive Slovak governments	**Incorrectly predicts** that Hungarians would continue to radicalize in response to extremist elites (Tőkés) **Does not explain** why Tőkés began to lose popular support in the late 1990s
Security dilemma/ ethnic fears	**Incorrectly predicts** that Hungarians would advance most radical claims when the Slovak government was most threatening (the 1995–1998 Mečiar period); the minority actually moderated its demands during this time	**Incorrectly predicts** that Hungarians would advance most radical claims when the Romanian government was most repressive (the 1990–1996 period); the Hungarian minority radicalized only *after* 1992 in response to signs of support from Hungary
Ethnic bargaining	**Correctly predicts** that Hungarians would radicalize claims when Hungary lobbied on their behalf in the context of 1992–1994 treaty talks with Slovakia **Correctly predicts** that Hungarians would moderate their demands during the periods of lobby state non-intervention (1989–1992; 1995–2003)	**Correctly predicts** that Hungarians would radicalize claims when Hungary lobbied on their behalf during 1992–1996 treaty talks with Romania **Correctly predicts** that Hungarians would moderate their demands during periods of lobby state non-intervention (1990–1992; 1996–2003)

communist period and the post-1998 period) coincided with political co-alitioning between the minority and majority elites on a nonethnic basis.

Ethnic bargaining provides a fuller account of minority behavior in Romania as well. Before Budapest began to lobby for its co-ethnics in 1992, Hungarian leaders had advanced very moderate demands, even in the face of ethnic intimidation and violence. Hungary began to intervene on behalf of the minority in 1992 in the context of treaty talks with Romania. The DAHR responded to its increased leverage by calling for communal and then territorial autonomy. Once Hungary and Romania had signed a bilateral treaty, however, the DAHR exchanged these autonomy demands for a place in government. In line with the predictions of the spatial model, periods of normalized relations between Hungary and Romania coincided with periods of inter-ethnic coalitioning at the substate level (the immediate postrevolutionary period and the post-1996 period). Table 4.3 summarizes this comparative evaluation.

A comparative analysis of minority claims in Romania and Slovakia demonstrates the explanatory power of ethnic bargaining. Periods of minority radicalization coincided with periods of international tension between the minority groups' host and lobby states. In the context of bilateral treaty talks, Hungary lobbied for collective rights on behalf of its co-ethnics, negotiated joint positions with diaspora leaders, and threatened to block their host states' admission to the CoE if they failed to grant concessions to their minorities. With Hungary at their back, the leaders of both minority groups escalated their demands to internal self-determination. When they did not enjoy the support of Hungary, however, Hungarian representatives assumed a position of accommodation even in the face of ethnic intimidation or assimilation. This complicates standard ethnic fears accounts of minority mobilization. It also provides support for the hypothesis that external lobbyists tend to have a greater impact on minority mobilization than do host governments, consistent with the predictions of the bargaining model.

Finally, this chapter demonstrates the key role played by international organizations in promoting liberal regimes in contemporary east central Europe and thus the conditions for inter-ethnic peace. The carrots of EU and NATO accession were vital for inducing compromises between Hungary and its neighbors over their Hungarian minorities. When NATO increased its pressure on the candidate countries in the mid-1990s, moderate non-nationalist forces were catapulted into positions of power in both Slovakia and Romania.[144] Strikingly, it was the xenophobic Mečiar who finally concluded a bilateral agreement with Hungary in 1995 and the antiminority Iliescu who signed the controversial CoE Recommendation on Minority Rights in 1996. When Iliescu regained office in 2000, he formed an alliance not with the resurgent nationalist parties but with the DAHR—a coalition that would have been unthinkable in the early 1990s. External organizations also convinced Hungary to alter its incendiary status law on ethnic Hungarians in neighboring countries in the early 2000s. These events demonstrate that NATO and EU conditionality was consequential in altering the preferences of the Hungarian, Romanian, and Slovak governments toward the Hungarian minorities. The resurgence of nationalism in Hungary and Romania in the late 1990s might have led to civil or even international conflict had not the EU, NATO, CoE, and OSCE continued to pressure these governments to negotiate compromises with one another. The policy lesson is that external actors aiming to protect the rights of minorities would do well to focus on altering the preferences of the powerful players engaged in ethnic bargaining rather than intervening directly on behalf of beleaguered minorities. To do otherwise is to risk encouraging minority rebellion while raising the salience of ethnic divisions in already divided societies.

CHAPTER FIVE

Dyadic Ethnic Bargaining

Slovak versus Moravian Nationalism in Postcommunist Czechoslovakia

The 1989 Velvet Revolution gave rise to not one but two regional movements in Czechoslovakia: one in Slovakia and the other in Moravia (see map 5.1).[1] Although their beginnings were similar in many ways, the two movements yielded remarkably different outcomes. Slovak nationalism continued to grow in strength and culminated in the dissolution of Czechoslovakia, whereas the Moravian regional movement quickly lost momentum and ultimately disappeared from the political map. A number of scholars have investigated the causes of the Slovak secession. Explanations for the 1993 Czech-Slovak split range from latent Slovak nationalism[2] to economic incentives[3] to elite opportunism[4] to institutions that deepened the ethnic divide.[5] Strikingly, however, there has been almost no scholarly investigation into the simultaneous surge of Moravian nationalism. Although largely stillborn, this movement serves as a useful contrast to the much-studied Slovak movement; because they began in the same period under similar circumstances yet yielded very different outcomes, the two cases may be fruitfully compared to test the propositions of ethnic bargaining. As in previous chapters, I have broken each case into a series of time segments, each of which represents a shift in the most salient demands sought by minority representatives (see tables 5.1 and 5.2). I then analyze each period in turn to determine whether the model can account not only for the differences between Slovak and Moravian claims but also for the fluctuations within each movement over time.

The two cases provide an excellent controlled comparison due to their many similarities. The groups shared a legacy of subordination under the Austro-Hungarian Monarchy, twenty years of coexistence in the First

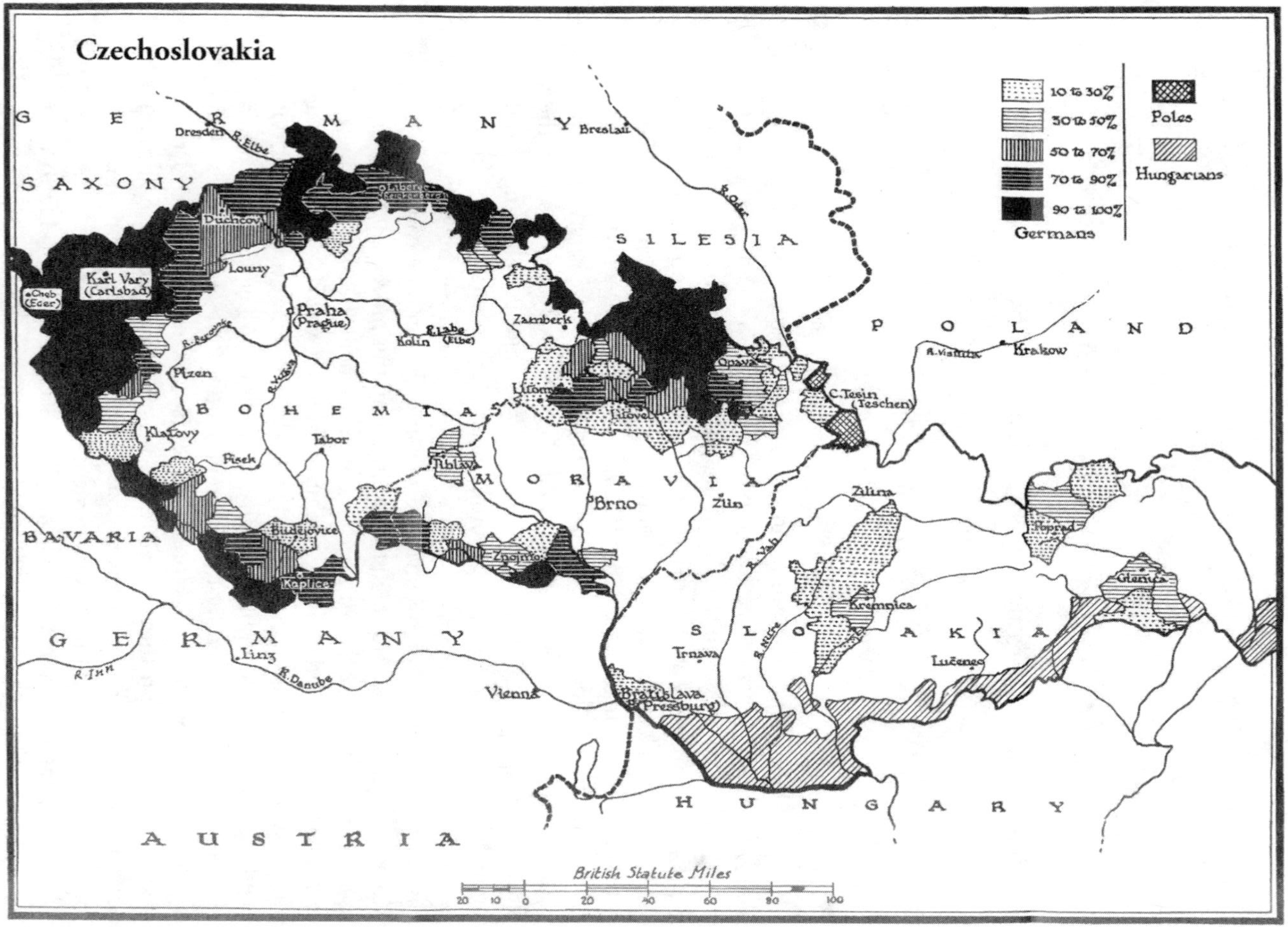

Map 5.1 Czechoslovakia

Table 5.1. Slovak demands in Czechoslovakia, 1989–1992[a]

Period	Most extreme		↔		Least extreme		
	Separate state	Confederal state	Authentic federalism[b]	No claims	Internal leverage	Perceptions of Czech discrimination
Late 1989				X	Uncertain	Low
Mid-1990– late 1990			X		High	Low
Early 1991– mid-1992		X			High	High

[a] Low, medium, and high indicate minority perceptions of internal leverage and majority discrimination. It is difficult to obtain precise measures of these variables because the sources of perceptions differ greatly from case to case. The most important thing to note is the shifts in these variables, which should lead to corresponding shifts in minority demands.
[b] Refers to a federal state in which the republics have an equal share in state power.

Table 5.2. Moravian demands in Czechoslovakia, 1989–1992a

Period	Most extreme		↔		Least extreme		
	Federal republic	Territorial autonomy	Cultural autonomy	No claims	Internal leverage	Perceptions of Czech discrimination
Late 1989			X		Low	Low
Early 1990– early 1991	X	X			Medium	Uncertain/ Medium
Mid-1991– late 1992				X	Low	Low

[a] Low, medium, and high indicate minority perceptions of internal leverage and majority discrimination. It is difficult to obtain precise measures of these variables because the sources of perceptions differ greatly from case to case. The most important thing to note is the shifts in these variables, which should lead to corresponding shifts in minority demands.

Czechoslovak Republic, and forty years of communist government. They also had the common experience of Prague-centrism and rapid market and democratic reform. Finally, there were charismatic, ethnic entrepreneurs who agitated for autonomy in both regions. A key difference between the two groups was that the Slovaks enjoyed institutional power as a constituent republic in the socialist federation, whereas the Moravians did not. Although this status was, for all practical purposes, moot under single-party rule, it gave the Slovaks considerable leverage in the context of democratic transition.

In the following sections, I explore the impact that differential Slovak and Moravian institutional power had on the claims their representatives advanced against the Czech majority in the context of constitutional nego- tiations.[6] In doing so, I demonstrate the predictive power of the ethnic bar- gaining model in a case of *dyadic* bargaining—where there are no external lobbyists. As I show, it is the group's internal bargaining leverage against the center, filtered through the opportunity structure[7] of constitutional talks, that best accounts for the different trajectories of the Slovak and Moravian movements as well as the variation within each movement over time. This case comparison illustrates the vital role played by national institutions in empowering the Slovaks to bargain for advantages, whereas the Moravians (who had no such institutions) could not. In the context of transition, in- stitutional empowerment accounts for both the robustness of the Slovak movement as well as the failure of the short-lived Moravian movement.

Ethnic Bargaining Hypotheses

In the Moravian and Slovak cases, ethnic bargaining reduces to a dyadic game between the minority and majority. The upper limits on the claims minority representatives may credibly seek are, as before, determined by the group's structural features, including its size and territorial compactness as well as its institutional status in the state. *Shifts* in claims, meanwhile, are driven by changes in the perceived balance of power between the minority and majority at the substate level as well as perceptions of majority inten- tions. Using the principles of ethnic bargaining, we can make general pre- dictions concerning the trajectories and relative strength of the two move- ments in postcommunist Czechoslovakia.

The Slovaks

The creation of Czechoslovakia in 1918 was a realpolitik project of epic proportions. At the close of World War I, a group of Czech and Slovak émigrés persuaded the victorious Allied Powers to establish a bina- tional Czech-Slovak state from the ruins of the Habsburg Empire based on historic ties between the two Slavic peoples. Slovak elites calculated that the union would afford them military protection against Hungary, whose leaders militated against the loss of territory under the Treaty of Trianon.[8] The federation also promised to augment the numerical supe- riority (and thus electoral advantage) of the Czechs and Slovaks over the Germans and Hungarians minorities, which were virulently opposed to

Slavic suzerainty. For these reasons, the federation has often been called a marriage of convenience.[9]

The union was troubled from the start. Having endured centuries of Hungarian domination, the Slovaks now found themselves subordinated to Prague under a unitary Czechoslovak state; this remained a source of discontent throughout the interwar period. There were economic concerns as well. The Czechs had developed a competitive economy under the Austrian half of the Habsburg regime with three-fifths of the empire's industrial facilities and two-thirds of its industrial workers. The Czech lands also boasted a thriving commercial sector, a prominent intellectual elite, and sizable middle class.[10] Slovakia, by contrast, had remained relatively underdeveloped under Hungarian rule; its economy consisted mainly of subsistence farming and a small industrial sector.[11] After 1918, Slovakia lost its economically protected status and was forced to compete with the more productive industries of the Czech lands. This led to further de-industrialization, fueling accusations of Czech exploitation.[12] The lack of well-trained public officials in the region also led to an influx of Czech professionals, which only added to Slovak resentment.[13] Perceptions of Czech chauvinism were reinforced by the state's constitutional design. Despite Czech promises to create a federation of coequal partners, the 1920 constitution was highly centralized and contained no provisions for Slovak autonomy. Moreover, the federal government itself was based in Prague and dominated by Czechs.[14]

During World War II, Slovakia declared its independence and became a Nazi satellite state under Josef Tiso's fascist regime. After Tiso was overthrown, Slovakia was reincorporated into the Czechoslovak state with the promise of Slovak autonomy. This promise, however, remained largely unfulfilled until the normalization period of the 1970s.

Opportunities for renegotiating the constitution emerged in the 1960s as the economy began to falter and the regime grew increasingly fragile. In 1968, the Slovaks began to call openly for a symmetrical federation. Following the Soviet-led crackdown, a federal framework was finally agreed on that would give the region a considerable degree of autonomy. In 1969, Czechoslovakia was declared a federal socialist state with the Czech and Slovak republics as equal partners.[15] The constitution also gave the Slovaks veto power over federal legislation, although single-party rule rendered this meaningless in practice.[16]

By the time of transition, the Slovaks enjoyed considerable internal leverage as a large, compact group of 5 million people (one-third of the state population). Almost all Slovaks resided in the Republic of Slovakia, which was nearly 90 percent ethnically Slovak. The group was therefore sufficiently large and compact to make credible demands for secession. A second source of leverage was, as Valerie Bunce put it, the Slovaks' "long history of contestation over the boundaries of the state and over the definition and the rights of nations and national minorities" in Czechoslovakia.[17] From Slovak agitation in the First Republic to their brief independence in World War II to the conflict over Slovakia's status in 1968–69, the Slovaks had built up a reservoir of national consciousness and mobilizational resources with which to bargain with the Czechs during the next political opening.[18]

The third source of internal leverage was Slovakia's institutional status—specifically, its effective veto over federal legislation. The federal government consisted of the House of People, which was divided proportionately between the Czechs and Slovaks (two Czechs to every Slovak), and the House of Nations (hereafter, the Czech and Slovak National Councils), which was divided equally (one Czech to every Slovak). Article 42 of the federal constitution explicitly prohibited outvoting of one republic by the other on issues "pertaining to national interest." On such matters, the Czech and Slovak deputies were to vote separately in the House of Nations. The legislation could be adopted only if a majority of deputies in *both* houses approved it.[19] Under this system of dual vetoes, a minority of deputies in either house could block any proposed amendment to the constitution. Thus, not only were the Slovaks sufficiently large and compact to credibly pursue secession, but they also had a strong mobilizational legacy as well as the institutional power to obstruct federal legislation. They were therefore well positioned to use extreme demands to extract major concessions from the center.

The Moravians

One of the three historic Czech lands, Moravia makes up the eastern half of present-day Czech Republic with roughly 40 percent of its territory. Although more significant at the turn of the twentieth century, the Moravian identity was still salient at the time of the 1989 revolution, with almost half of the region's inhabitants declaring themselves Moravian as a write-in choice in the 1991 census. Unlike the Slovaks, Moravia had lost its political institutions long ago, although there was a collective memory of historical autonomy under Habsburg rule. Indeed, it could be argued that the Moravian nation is actually much older than the Czech nation (which encompasses modern-day Moravia and Bohemia). The Great Moravian Empire of the tenth and eleventh centuries covered the entire Moravian region as well as large swaths of Bohemia and Slovakia. With its own literary culture, church, political capitol, and folk heroes, the empire boasted one of the oldest civilizations of east central Europe.[20] Czechs, Moravians, and Slovaks all trace their national heritage to the Great Moravian Empire.[21]

During the Middle Ages, Bohemia and Moravia coexisted peacefully under a succession of Bohemian kings. In the late fifteenth century, Moravia and Silesia were given to the Kingdom of Hungary, although they were later returned to Bohemia. For centuries, Moravia remained culturally and politically separated from Bohemia. The Moravians were relatively untouched by the Hussite movement that ushered in the Age of Reformation in Bohemia. The National Revival of the eighteenth and nineteenth centuries was also far more pronounced in Bohemia than in Moravia, while the pressures of Germanization were more strongly felt in Moravia than in Bohemia. This all contributed to a higher religiosity among the inhabitants of Moravia. Moreover, industrialization and urbanization began in Bohemia before it did in Moravia, leading to a divergence in the regions' economies.[22] After the 1848 revolutions, Moravia became a separate crown land under the Austrian Empire where it enjoyed an extensive degree of self-government with its own regional diet; Bohemia and Moravia were even allocated their own seats in the imperial *Reichsrat*.[23] With the codification of the Slovak language in the early 1800s, Moravian nationalists began to demand linguistic separation from—or at least a presence in—the Czech language. Their efforts were vehemently opposed by Czech intellectuals, who had no desire to see their centuries-old *bibličtina* (the high Czech language) contaminated by "common" elements.[24]

After World War I, Moravia, Bohemia, Silesia, Slovakia, and Ruthenia were cobbled together to create Czechoslovakia. Although Moravia was made an administrative land in the interwar republic, the Moravian identity was not very salient during this time. This was because the Czechs and Moravians had to cooperate to deal with the restive German minority in their border regions. The Moravian identity might have reentered politics after World War II, but by then the Communist Party had begun to consolidate control over the state. Because the Moravians had been known for supporting noncommunist parties, the communist leadership decided to squelch the Moravian problem once and for all by abolishing the lands system in 1949 and dividing the country into smaller districts that would be directly subordinated to the central government.[25]

By the time of the 1989 revolution, Moravia had no institutional status whatsoever. Moreover, because the region was sandwiched between Bohemia and Slovakia, territorial separation was not a credible posture for Moravian leaders (unless the Slovaks were to secede first). Hence, although large and territorially compact, the Moravians were unlikely to call for anything more than republican status within the federation.

The Slovak Movement in Postcommunist Czechoslovakia

Late 1989: The Velvet Revolution

The 1989 revolution took place in an atmosphere of remarkable ethnic harmony. Following a series of demonstrations in November 1989, the Czech Civic Forum (CF) and the Slovak Public Against Violence (PAV) forced the demoralized communist leadership to resign.[26] The Communist Party pulled its deputies out of the Federal Assembly, and a binational transitional government was established under President-elect Václav Havel (a Czech) and Federal Assembly Chairman Alexander Dubček (a Slovak).[27] The Czech and Slovak leaders of the transitional government announced that they intended to cooperate closely to achieve regime change. Indeed, the two movements would have merged were it not for Czech concerns that the CF would be perceived as dominating the reform process in Slovakia.[28]

Unlike other titular nations in postcommunist Europe, the Czechs did not assert a dominant position in the new state, despite the fact that they outnumbered the Slovaks two to one and wielded effective control over civil institutions and the military. The Czech leadership instead recognized the Slovaks as co-equals in a binational state. The draft constitution of February 1990 (and every draft thereafter) even included the right of the republics to secede from the union, entitling the Slovaks to opt out at any time. International lawyers had advised against such a provision, warning presciently that it would lead to "ethnic and factional struggle" and "reduce the prospects of compromise and deliberation in government."[29] One advisor recalled, "The reaction to our arguments [against establishing a constitutional right to secede] on the Slovak side was one of surprise: to them this was a non-issue, a closed matter beyond debate. The Czech members responded with an air of resignation: that course was the only way—'a cavalry,' 'a route through Balkanization'—toward a new and one would hope, lasting relationship."[30] The Czechs thus signaled their conciliatory intent both during and after the 1989 revolution.

Slovak leverage was still not an issue at this point. After a few failed attempts to draft a new constitution in the pre-election period, negotiations over the federation were postponed until after the June elections, effectively neutralizing the Slovak veto for the time being.

Given Czech signals of nonrepressive intent and delayed negotiations over the federal constitution, Slovak leaders should infer that the state of the world was one of ethnic peace (fig. 5.1, box 4), leading them to advance relatively moderate demands in cooperation with the Czechs. And this is borne out. At the time, the PAV was by far the largest political formation in Slovakia, representing groups ranging from environmentalists to Catholic dissidents to reformed communists. It featured every major Slovak politician, including Alexander Dubček, Fedor Gál, Ján Čarnogurský, and Vladimír Mečiar. Soon after the revolution, the PAV issued an official proclamation entitled "A Chance for Slovakia" that called for political reform, press freedoms, and other civil liberties. On November 26, the PAV put forward a twelve-point declaration of the movement's goals; only two of these related to the Slovak nation as such. The other ten points called for civic freedoms, the removal of communist propaganda from schools and other public institutions, the restoration of private property, and so on.[31] Moreover, the PAV affirmed its commitment to working alongside the Czechs in achieving these aims.[32]

In the first half of 1990, PAV and CF elites cooperated in pushing through a raft of political reforms including term limits, rules for political parties, and a new electoral system.[33] For the most part, conflict between the Czechs and Slovaks took a backseat to economic and political concerns.[34] Surveys conducted at the time indicate that the PAV's nonethnic stance resonated strongly with ordinary Slovaks. In an opinion poll conducted in early 1990, 40 percent of the respondents felt that the most important task facing the country was economic reform, 29 percent felt it was improving the environ-

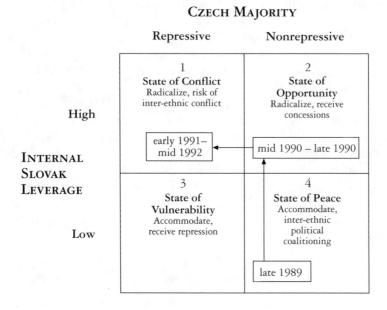

Figure 5.1 Slovak claims in postcommunist Czechoslovakia

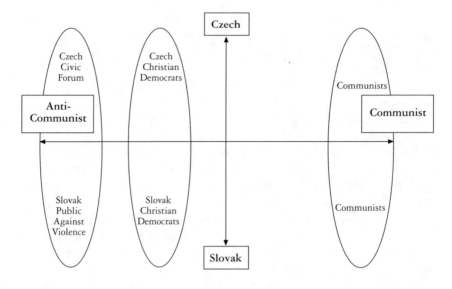

Figure 5.2 Political coalitions in Czechoslovakia after the 1990 elections

ment, and 16 percent believed it to be democratic and civic reform.[35] Thus, in the months following the revolution, the Slovaks favored pursuing a non-ethnic agenda in cooperation with the Czechs.

Given a state of the world of ethnic peace, we should also see political alliances forming across ethnic lines. Consistent with this prediction, the pro-federal CF and PAV emerged victorious in the June elections, together winning 170 of the 300 seats in the Federal Assembly. They were followed by the Communist Party with 47 seats. Figure 5.2 shows that nationalism was not yet a salient divide. The winners of the 1990 elections—the CF-PAV, Communists, and Christian Democrats—were either federal or pro-federal parties with nonethnic programs. There were signs that ethnicity was gaining political salience, however. Slovak voters surprised pundits and politicians alike by awarding the secessionist Slovak National Party (SNP) with nearly 14 percent of the popular vote, making it the fourth most powerful party in Slovakia.[36]

Mid-1990–Late 1990: Czech-Slovak Negotiations—The Opening Rounds

The first sign of the coming ethnic conflict was the so-called hyphen war in April 1990. In a seemingly innocuous vote to remove the word Socialist from Czechoslovak Socialist Republic, several Slovak deputies proposed that the state be renamed Czech-Slovak Federal Republic, triggering a parliamentary mud fight. In the midst of the conflict, Havel wrote an open letter to the Federal Assembly calling for reconciliation. In it, he advocated the recognition of Slovak identity: "All of us know that this 'hyphen,' which seems ridiculous, superfluous and ugly to all Czechs, is more than just a hyphen. It in fact symbolizes decades, perhaps even centuries of Slovak history."[37] Some time later, Havel organized a goodwill trip to Slovakia, with CF and PAV deputies in tow, in a bid to improve national relations and persuade the Slovaks of the importance of economic and political reform.[38] The Czech premier, Petr Pithart, too, announced his willingness to compromise with his Slovak counterparts in reconfiguring the state.[39] To this end, the newly elected federal government pledged to loosen the centrist state framework to promote the autonomy of the republics.[40] By now, Slovak institutional leverage had kicked in with the start of the constitutional negotiations. These talks served as a kind of political opportunity structure whereby the Slovaks could flex their newfound institutional power to extract concessions from the center.

With their powerful legislative veto and a conciliatory Czech leadership, the Slovaks had reason to believe that the state of the world was becoming one of opportunity (fig. 5.1, box 2), leading them to escalate their demands for concessions. Consistent with this expectation, Slovak representatives did radicalize—first during the "hyphen war" and again at the first round of constitutional negotiations in Trenčianské Teplice.[41] In the case of the name dispute, Slovak deputies hardened their stance only after the debate had become public, with Czech and Slovak intellectuals exchanging insults in the major newspapers. In the midst of this controversy, thousands of people demonstrated in Bratislava for Slovak sovereignty. Protesters rallied before the Slovak National Council, where a petition was read aloud accusing the Czechs of denying the existence of the Slovak nation. The Slovak premier, Rudolf Schuster, responded to the public outcry by promising the assembled crowd that the Slovak deputies would "heed their demands."[42] Schuster was not the only Slovak leader to change his political tune in reaction to events on the ground. In a stunning departure from his earlier pro-federal stance, Christian Democratic Leader Ján Čarnogurský advocated the eventual dissolution of the federation so that the Czech and Slovak Republics could enter the European Community as "two little stars" in the EC constellation.[43] Meanwhile, PAV leaders, anxious to shore up support for their pro-federal line, organized counter-demonstrations in favor of the federation and wrote editorials warning of the risks of extremism.[44] The dispute ended when the two sides agreed on a new name: the Czech and Slovak Federal Republic.

The constitutional talks in Trenčianské Teplice provided the next political opening for the Slovaks. There, representatives of the two National Councils and the Federal Assembly met in the first of a series of meetings that would stretch over two years. At issue was the division of powers between the republic and the federal governments. Although the negotiators met behind closed doors, Slovak Premier Vladimír Mečiar was said to have played a masterful hand. He unexpectedly presented a full constitutional draft to the Czechs in a dramatic take-it-or-leave-it offer, giving the Czechs little choice but to reject it out of hand.[45] The proposal called for an "authentic" federation of sovereign republics that delegated certain powers to the federal government. At the same time, however, Mečiar was careful to disavow secessionist demands, declaring, "A split in the country must not occur, [as] we see how nationalism develops in the USSR or Yugoslavia."[46] Mečiar thus cleverly staked out a middle ground between a strong federation (advocated by mainstream PAV leaders) and full Slovak independence (favored by the SNP). Not coincidentally, his position exactly mirrored median Slovak preferences at the time—in late 1990, more than 50 percent of Slovaks supported an "authentic" federation with strong republics. Čarnogurský later recalled that "Mečiar was always an opportunist in politics, and since the idea of an independent Slovakia was not acceptable to [most] people in 1990, he stood up against it."[47]

A power-sharing agreement that reflected Slovak demands was hammered out at a subsequent meeting between the heads of the three governments in Prague. As the federal assembly debated whether to approve the document, Mečiar threatened that if the Czechs did not pass the proposal "as is," the Slovak National Council would immediately declare sovereignty. That this was a bluff is evidenced by the fact that Mečiar later *denied* having made such threats, claiming that "however the situation might develop, Slovakia has always confirmed its interest in a common state."[48] The resulting treaty represented a major concession to the Slovaks because it devolved considerable power to the republics. The federal government was left with only a few competencies—including foreign affairs, defense, banking, and taxation. The Czech premier justified these concessions as the only way the federation could be saved, warning that national conflict could "end with the disintegration of the state."[49] These events show that the Slovaks had effectively utilized their institutional leverage to extract concessions from the Czech center.

Early 1991–Mid-1992: National Polarization and the Czech-Slovak Split

By the end of 1990, factional divisions had begun to emerge in the Czech CF. The largest of these was the Interparliamentary Club of the Demo-

cratic Right—a group committed to liberal market reform and privatiza-
tion. The club soon achieved dominance within the CF and engineered the
election of Václav Klaus as the new CF leader. Klaus declared his intention
to transform the CF into a center-right party—leftist groups and individuals were accordingly sidelined or removed from positions of power. Klaus
defended his actions by claiming that his position "corresponded with the
wishes of the vast majority of the movement's supporters." In early 1991,
the faction formally split off from the CF to become the Civic Democratic
Party (CDP), which called for rapid economic reform with an eye toward
joining the EC. According to Klaus, his party "would not be led by dream-
ers but would be characterized by realism and pragmatism."[50] Although the
government was still in the hands of pro-federalists, it was becoming clear
that their days were numbered.

In January, the government kicked off its program of market reform by
removing price controls on most goods. The Slovaks feared that they would
bear the brunt of these reforms because their economy consisted mainly of
state-subsidized heavy industry. Indeed, there were already signs of the divergent impact that liberalization would have on the two republics. By April, the
rate of unemployment in the Slovak Republic was double that of the Czech
Republic.[51] Although this was still only 3.8 percent, the perception of Czech
discrimination had begun to take hold in the Slovak imagination—a view
actively cultivated by the local media.[52]

Not surprisingly, the Slovaks became increasingly skeptical of government-led reform. Whereas 51 percent of Slovaks had favored rapid market
reform in 1990, only 23 percent approved of such reforms in early 1992;
the corresponding figures for the Czechs were 60 percent in 1990 and 50
percent in early 1992. A growing percentage of Slovaks also preferred slowed
privatization and increased state intervention.[53] Significantly, a survey in
late 1990 indicated that fully 60 percent of Slovaks (but only 41 percent of
Czechs) were willing to go on strike if reforms led to major price hikes.[54] As
if to make good on this threat, hundreds of workers gathered in Bratislava in
January to protest rising unemployment and the increased cost of living.[55]
More ominously, the Slovaks also began to take a dimmer view of national
relations. In October 1990, only 32 percent of Slovaks had agreed with the
statement "Czechs and Slovaks will never trust one another"; by May 1991,
this had increased to 52 percent![56]

Despite their growing sense of victimization, the Slovaks wielded substantial leverage against the Czechs in the context of continuing constitutional
talks. This leverage combined with perceptions of Czech discrimination to
convince Slovak leaders that the state of the world was becoming one of
conflict (fig. 5.1, box 1). Given these beliefs, they should continue to radical-

ize their demands for concessions. With a less conciliatory Czech leadership, however, such actions are less likely to yield concessions and more likely to lead to conflict.

As expected, Slovak representatives drove up their demands against an increasingly hostile Czech center. The two sides met again in early 1991 to decide whether the federation would be formulated from the top down or the bottom up. Unexpectedly, Čarnogurský broke with other Slovak representatives by insisting that the republics establish their own constitutions *first* and then delegate powers to the federal government.[57] This amounted to a call for confederation—a clear upping of the ante. He also proposed replacing the government's program with an "alternative economic program," capitalizing on popular opposition to market reform.[58] Public support for the Christian Democrats swelled in the wake of these maneuvers. Ultra-nationalist groups issued an open memorandum to the Slovak National Council calling for a unilateral declaration of sovereignty, and several thousand people demonstrated in Bratislava in favor of independence. Surveys conducted from October 1990 to May 1991 showed a seven-point decrease in support for a federal model and a corresponding rise in support for either confederation or independence.[59]

Prime Minister Mečiar responded to this challenge by urging the PAV to radicalize its own stance. A series of scandals then led to Mečiar's expulsion from government. On the day he was ousted, several members of the government resigned and approximately 50,000 people rallied on his behalf. Opinion polls at the time revealed that 81 percent of the Slovak public trusted Mečiar more than any other politician.[60] Now out of government, Mečiar and his supporters established a new party, the Movement for a Democratic Slovakia (MDS), which called for advancing Slovak interests and slowed economic reform. In an effort to outbid the outbidder, Čarnogurský (the new Slovak premier) responded by adopting exactly the same program as the MDS.[61]

The Slovak leadership appeared to be radicalizing with each new round of constitutional talks. In the wake of another round of negotiations in September, Mečiar made the following statement: "Considering . . . the efforts of many nations of central and Eastern Europe to emancipate themselves, the time has come for the Slovak Republic to demand its right to *self-determination* and achieve *sovereignty.* Postponing this matter is a grave political [mistake] that will leave Slovakia outside an integrated Europe."[62] Mečiar then demanded the resignation of the head of the Slovak government for continuing to negotiate with the "oppressor nation." Given the positive public reaction to these remarks, the deputy chair of parliament announced that the government might adopt a constitution before the talks were concluded—this would amount to a declaration of independence. These demands resonated strongly with the Slovak rank and file. According to one survey, public support for a functioning federation had decreased dramatically over the course of the year—the percentage of Slovaks who preferred a federal model had dropped from 40 percent in January 1991 to 26 percent in November. At this point, more Slovaks favored a confederation over any other state form.[63] The results of these polls were published widely, reinforcing elite perceptions that the Slovak public had radicalized. Given the lack of popular support for full independence, however, the leadership was careful not to overplay its hand. Despite the National Council's repeated calls for sovereignty, motions to declare independence were defeated by narrow margins in 1991 and 1992. It is possible that Slovak leaders engineered these votes to increase the credibility of their secessionist threats.

In the meantime, the Czech leadership was becoming increasingly hostile to Slovak demands. Deputy Prime Minister Jan Kalvoda threatened that if an agreement over the division of powers was not reached soon, the Czech National Council would dissolve the state. He estimated that there was now only a 50 percent chance of saving the federation.[64] Years later, Kalvoda offered insight into the Czech perspective: "Relations between the Czechs and Slovaks gradually changed for the worse. On the Czech side, the feeling gradually emerged: if they want to go, let them go. On the Slovak side, people said, we must be free at any cost, we must get out of bondage."[65]

By the end of 1991, negotiations had reached an impasse, largely because the Czechs had become far less willing to accommodate the Slovaks.[66] Recognizing the mounting potential for stalemate, Havel invited a delegation of Czech and Slovak deputies to his summer cottage in Hrádeček to hammer out a solution. The talks lasted for several days, but produced little more than a tepid agreement that the federation should be saved. It became clear that the Czechs had hardened their position. Allison Stanger notes that:

> [i]t was representatives *from the Czech delegation* rather than the Slovaks—especially deputy chair of the Czech National Council, Jan Kalvoda—who served as the principal obstacle to consensus in November 1991. While [an earlier meeting] had produced mutual understanding that a [state treaty] was necessary, the ensuing discussion of the Havel plan foundered on the question of the [treaty's] legal significance, or put another way, *what both parties had earlier actually agreed upon.*[67]

That the Czechs were no longer willing to honor the concessions they had already agreed to shows that their bargaining range had narrowed and that the odds of reaching a settlement had correspondingly diminished.

In early 1992, a joint commission from the Czech and Slovak National Councils proposed a compromise arrangement that would recognize the sovereignty of *both* republic and federal governments. This time, however, the Slovak representatives opposed the plan—Mečiar called it a "betrayal of the contemporary national movement."[68] Slovak deputies then blocked the passage of the first three chapters of the proposed constitution, and further negotiations were suspended until after the June 1992 elections. Stanger points out that "[the Slovaks'] voting behavior can . . . be explained by simple self-interest: Why should a minority with extraordinary power voluntarily vote it away, particularly when that power might be used as a bargaining chip in unrelated negotiations?"[69]

After the elections in June, talks over the federation passed to the new heads of the Czech and Slovak governments—Klaus and Mečiar. Compromise was highly unlikely at this point because the two leaders had staked out incompatible policy positions to appeal to their respective constituencies.[70] According to an opinion poll released in January, 55 percent of the Slovak electorate now supported explicitly nationalist parties.[71] Meanwhile, Klaus's pro-reform party, the CDP, enjoyed *twice* as much support in the Czech Republic as the next most popular party.[72] Revealingly, the pro-federal PAV and CF had virtually vanished from the political scene.[73]

With Klaus and Mečiar elected on irreconcilable platforms, the end of the federation appeared to be a real possibility. Despite this, Mečiar continued his attempts to bargain with the Czech leadership as he had a strong popular mandate to extract concessions from the center. He confessed, "[I]f we talk about independence it is not because we want it, but because we must."[74] Consequently, in a meeting with Klaus in June,

> Mečiar made a series of demands in the name of Slovak nationalism that came very close [to]—but stopped short of—a call for political independence. Klaus responded that these demands were incompatible with either a viable single state or economic reform. Therefore, Slovakia should go its way and free the Czech lands to pursue reform unburdened. Mečiar was clearly stunned; he had intended to use the threat of separation to extract concessions. Instead he was being given a divorce. But Slovakia is entirely unprepared for independence, and Mečiar knows it.[75]

The Slovak leader had probably failed to realize that, at this point, Klaus could make this unpopular move without political fallout by blaming it on Slovak intransigence. Seeing this, the Slovaks desperately tried to backpedal. In August, the Slovak deputies drafted yet another constitutional proposal to save the federation. However, by then it was too late—the Czechs had already opted out.

Institutional leverage had thus interacted with the opportunity structure of constitutional talks to induce Slovak elites to escalate their demands in hopes of gaining major concessions. Challenging the center, however, became a much riskier proposition with the emergence of Czech leaders who were much less willing to accommodate the Slovaks to save the federation. This dynamic contributed significantly to the Czech-Slovak split—an outcome that few had foreseen in the early days of the revolution and that the majority of Czechs and Slovaks opposed—even at the time of the split.

Consistent with the predictions of the spatial model in a state of the world of conflict, political agents now eschewed inter-ethnic alliances in favor of national blocs. By 1992, the communist-anticommunist divide had completely lost resonance with the disappearance of the old regime. Political elites now confronted new choices, including the pace of economic reform and the future of the federation—issues on which Czechs and Slovaks as a whole had somewhat divergent preferences. With the newly salient Czech-Slovak divide and a republic-level electoral system, Czech and Slovak parties assumed the positions of their median ethnic voters and dug in. To give ground in the interest of preserving the union would have been political suicide in a climate of national conflict. Thus, political formations crystallized along ethnic lines (see fig. 5.3).

The Moravian Movement in Postcommunist Czechoslovakia

Late 1989: The Velvet Revolution in Moravia

The postcommunist movement for Moravian autonomy had an earlier incarnation in the constitutional negotiations of 1968–1969. Dr. Boleslav Bárta, a psychologist known to his followers as the "father of Moravian nationalism," played a leading role in both campaigns.[76] Both the Prague Spring and the Velvet Revolution had created political openings for the Moravians to renegotiate their status in the federation. Unlike the Slovaks, however, the Moravians had no institutional power with which to bargain during these openings—their leverage derived almost solely from the support of the Czechs and the Slovaks—the two principals of the talks. In 1968, Moravian leaders put forward the Moravian Declaration calling for a tripartite federation of equal republics—Bohemia, Slovakia, and Moravia-Silesia. Although this proposal was met with some sympathy, it was ultimately rejected on the grounds that Moravians were "ethnically Czech" and therefore not in need of a separate status. The truth of the matter was that neither the Czechs nor the Slovaks favored a tripartite state—the Slovaks because they feared being outvoted by two republics whose interests were

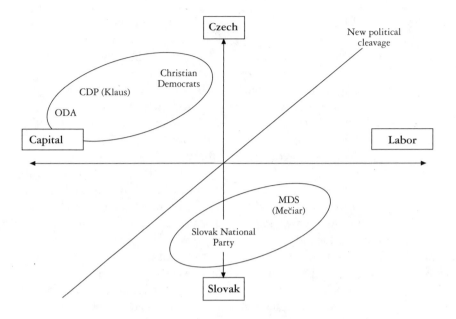

Figure 5.3 Political coalitions in Czechoslovakia after the 1992 federal elections

usually aligned and the Czechs because they opposed further devolution of state power. Therefore, the 1969 constitution established no autonomy for Moravia, which meant that the Moravians had no institutional power with which to bargain at the time of the transition.[77] As a consequence, Moravian leverage with respect to the Czechs was highly contingent in the early postcommunist period.

The transitional authorities sought to cooperate with the Moravians. Both before and after November 1989, the Czech CF reached out to its Moravian counterparts. CF leaders in Prague worked closely with their affiliates in Moravia and Silesia to coordinate demonstrations and strikes against the dying regime. In predominantly Catholic Moravia, a vibrant movement for religious freedom had grown up in the 1980s, feeding grass-roots opposition to the regime. This translated into high rates of participation in the local CFs.[78] The CF in Prague lent support to smaller CFs throughout the country, generating a high degree of trust between the Czech and Moravian dissidents.

With their still uncertain bargaining position and close ties to the new Czech leadership, Moravian elites had reason to believe that the state of the world was one of ethnic peace (fig. 5.4, box 4), leading them to pursue moderate goals in cooperation with the Czech majority. Consistent with

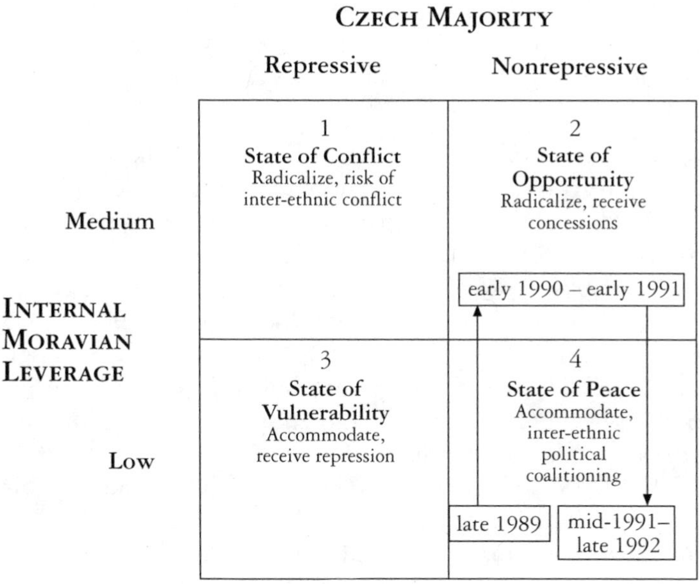

CZECH MAJORITY

Repressive   Nonrepressive

	Repressive	Nonrepressive
Medium	**1** State of Conflict Radicalize, risk of inter-ethnic conflict	**2** State of Opportunity Radicalize, receive concessions
Low	**3** State of Vulnerability Accommodate, receive repression	**4** State of Peace Accommodate, inter-ethnic political coalitioning

INTERNAL
MORAVIAN
LEVERAGE

early 1990 – early 1991

late 1989 | mid-1991–
late 1992

Figure 5.4 Moravian claims in postcommunist Czechoslovakia

this expectation, Moravian elites generally limited their demands to civic reform and the recognition of Moravian identity in the early days of the transition. Shortly after the November revolution, a lawyer by the name of Dr. Miroslav Richter formed the Moravian Civic Movement (MOH) to promote the region's interests. In the beginning, the MOH focused on regime change at the local level. As the Central Committee's hold on power began to weaken, Richter and his supporters took over the regional communist headquarters in Brno, throwing party functionaries out of their offices. The MOH then proceeded to set up its own headquarters in the building under the banner of "rehabilitating the Moravian nation."[79] On November 20, the organization put forth its manifesto, which began:

[W]e have decided to establish the Moravian Citizens Movement (MOH) as a free and independent association of citizens living in Moravia. The MOH aspires to be a democratic association of thinking citizens who want to actively participate in the healing of . . . deformities and injuries resulting from forty years of inadequate government and Marxist ideology. . . . We proclaim solidarity with all people . . . who want to work together in these days to promote justice, freedom, equality [and] harmony . . . in the interest of tolerance and love, and achieving a genuine society of people.[80]

Offering membership to "every citizen of Czechoslovakia," the MOH proclaimed that its primary goal was to facilitate democratic transition. In January 1990, MOH leaders organized a party congress at a hockey stadium in Brno, and around 6,000 people gathered to hear them speak.[81] Richter addressed the assembled crowd: "We want nothing more, nor less, than rehabilitation of our nation, which is directly descended from the Great Moravian Empire. We have the right to lead our lives as Moravians, a right that is held by Slovaks, Czechs and all other ethnic groups."[82] Meanwhile, the SMS set up its own headquarters in Brno; in spring 1990, the SMS was registered as a party called the Movement for Self-Government of Moravia and Silesia (HSD-SMS) with Bárta as its leader. The party announced its intention to run in the June elections.

It was generally expected that Bárta and Richter would join forces to represent Moravian interests in the federal and Czech governments. However, it soon became clear that the two men had different constituencies, strategies, and visions for the movement. Richter's group consisted mainly of young people, many of whom had participated in the mystical student movement in the 1980s that promoted and celebrated Moravian identity. Bárta's party, on the other hand, was largely made up of people who had worked under the former regime.[83] They therefore ran on separate candidate lists.

Despite their differences, both men came out strongly in favor of democratic and civic reform—advocating close cooperation with the CF in Prague to realize the aims of the revolution. The MOH even sent a delegation to the CF Assembly in Olomouc to discuss the possibility of joining the CF candidate list in the upcoming elections.[84] These actions are consistent with the model's prediction of inter-ethnic cooperation in a state of the world of ethnic peace.

Early 1990—Early 1991: The Moravian Surprise

The Moravian movement gained momentum as talks over the federation got underway. Bernard Wheaton and Zdeněk Kavan observed that "[r]egional 'nationalism' in Moravia and Silesia was . . . partly sparked off by the confrontation of the Czechs and Slovaks [during the "hyphen war"] on the question of autonomy."[85] Inspired by the flare-up of Slovak nationalism over Slovakia's status in the federation, demonstrations were organized in Brno and other Moravian towns to lobby for Moravian autonomy. These activities were decried in the Czech press as part of an insidious effort to destroy the state during a time of economic and social crisis.[86]

Whereas the mainstream media either mocked or condemned the growth of Moravian nationalism, Czech leaders (most notably Czech Premier Petr Pithart and President Václav Havel) indicated that they would be willing to work with Moravian representatives to satisfy their national aspirations. There seemed to be an implicit consensus, at least among political elites, that the Moravians had at least some claim to autonomy. An editorial in *Lidové noviny* pointed out that the territorially concentrated Moravians and Silesians (like the Czechs and Slovaks) were generally perceived to be state-bearing nations, in contrast to other smaller minorities (such as the Hungarians and the Roma), which had no such claim to a separate status.[87] Zdeněk Jičinský, the Federal Assembly chairman, conceded that Moravian nationalism was understandable given the harsh centralism of the former regime, adding that the "Moravian-Silesian question" was a classic example of the reemergence of regional interests after a period of harsh totalitarian rule. He concluded that it would now be possible to recognize Moravia and Silesia under a "functioning federation."[88] In this and other ways, the Czechs signaled their willingness to accommodate Moravian demands.[89]

The initiation of constitutional talks, together with signs of support from the Czech leadership, led Moravian elites to believe that the state of the world was becoming one of opportunity (fig. 5.4, box 2). They should therefore radicalize their demands to obtain concessions from the center. Consistent with this prediction, MOH leaders began to call for territorial autonomy in spring 1990. They also announced that they had decided not to run on the CF candidate list in the June elections. They made the latter decision for two reasons. First, the CF had rejected the MOH's condition for cooperation: a promise to devolve power to local governments.[90] Second, Moravian elites could see that they were profiting from their anti-Prague rhetoric. They could ill afford to undermine this position by going on the same list as the Prague-based CF. Despite their earlier identification with the CF, the new clarion call of Moravian leaders was that the CF had little to do with the lives of ordinary Moravians. A local scholar of the movement described the Moravian mindset as follows:

> [When] the revolution began with the Civic Forum, the dissidents, those people who were active against the regime—to the Moravian mind this was something strange. [W]hen Klaus came with his movement, the people here said: "That's all in Prague, we are Moravians, we want our own community . . . we want our own economy because we have our fields

and factories in Brno. Now all this will go to Prague. Businessmen in
Prague will get rich with our money."[91]

The sentiment seemed to be that the CF was for Czechs whereas Moravian
parties were for Moravians. Moravian elites also promulgated the view
that the region was subsidizing the rest of the country.[92] In light of these
beliefs, it is unsurprising that calls for a separate status resonated strongly
with the Moravian public. A survey conducted in early 1990 showed that
fully 60 percent of Moravians supported some form of territorial autonomy for Moravia within the Czech Republic, 27 percent favored full republican status for Moravia, and only 10 percent was satisfied with the status quo.[93] To compete for the median Moravian voter, the MOH and the
HSD-SMS ran on almost identical platforms in the 1990 elections: broad
territorial autonomy with a Moravian-Silesian parliament, local governing
structures, and autonomous financial institutions.[94]

In the end, the Moravian vote went to the HSD-SMS—the most successful party in the region after the CF. With 10 percent of the overall vote in the
Czech Republic, the party obtained representation in the Federal Assembly
and twenty-two seats in the Czech National Council. This made it the third
most powerful party in the Czech Republic. The HSD-SMS was therefore
invited to join the Czech government and given a position in the cabinet.[95]
Moravian leaders believed that the Czech leadership needed Moravian support in their negotiations with the Slovaks, and that they enjoyed the support
of influential Czech politicians. President Havel had met with HSD-SMS
deputies shortly after the elections to discuss Moravian autonomy and the
role that the party might play in Czech politics. Havel repeatedly avowed
his support for the restoration of the "historical lands," suggesting that
Moravia might be granted territorial autonomy within the Czech Republic.
Given these signals, HSD-SMS representatives judged him sympathetic to
the Moravian cause. Moreover, in the run-up to the elections almost every
Czech party had proclaimed support for devolving power to the regions.[96]
Bárta now declared his intention to hold the Czechs publicly accountable
for the promises they had made during their campaigns.[97]

He soon made good on his word. At one of the first meetings of the new
Federal Assembly, Bárta proposed a constitutional amendment to allow for
territorial autonomy within the Czech Republic. His proposal was met with
little enthusiasm—excluding Havel, few Czech leaders favored institutionalizing Moravian autonomy in the constitution.[98] In August, HSD-SMS deputies introduced legislation in the Czech National Council that would give
territorial autonomy to Moravia-Silesia, Bohemia, and the greater Prague
area within the Czech lands.[99] Although the prime minister was willing to

consider the proposal, the majority of CF deputies rejected it outright. This led to considerable bitterness on the side of the Moravians, who believed they had been promised autonomy in exchange for their support for the CF government. In response to unrelenting pressure from HSD-SMS deputies, the Czech government finally established a commission in early September to examine the various proposals for administrative reform—these ranged from tripartite federation to territorial autonomy to the current unitary state. It was clear, however, that devolving power to the regions went against Czech interests insofar as doing so undermined federal control of the state. The government therefore postponed a vote on the matter until January, at which point it was put off until February. By continuing to defer a decision on Moravian autonomy, the Czech leadership managed to retain HSD-SMS support in parliament without actually granting them concessions.

Meanwhile, fissures began to emerge within the Moravian movement over its desired strategies and goals. The biggest conflict was between Bárta's HSD-SMS, which favored territorial autonomy within the Czech Republic, and Jiří Bílý and others in the Moravian National Party (MNS; formerly the MOH),[100] who advocated a tripartite Czech-Moravian-Slovak federation.[101] What this came down to was a dispute over whether the Moravians could best extract concessions at the republic or at the federal level. Bílý later speculated that Bárta's campaign for autonomy within the Czech Republic had cost them the support of the Slovaks because it signaled that the Moravians would be likely to ally with the Czechs in a tripartite federation.[102]

The federal government announced its 1991 budget in January, which included austerity measures and projected sharp rises in prices and unemployment. The reforms threatened to harm the steel manufacturing and coal mining areas of northern Moravia and Silesia in particular. Moravian leaders saw this as an opportunity to leverage their position in government. On January 26, the HSD-SMS organized protests in Moravian towns and cities calling for "an immediate change in the 1991 budget, [regional autonomy for] Moravia and Silesia by March 31, 1991, and a new federal arrangement of Czechoslovakia by the end of 1992."[103] Meanwhile, Václav Tomis, a Moravian deputy, accused the government of discriminating against Moravia by allocating 3.2 billion crowns to Bohemia that should have gone to Moravia and Silesia.[104]

The views of ordinary Moravians appear to have radicalized as a result of these developments. Surveys conducted in early 1991 showed increased popular support for a more extensive form of Moravian autonomy. The Institute for Public Opinion Research in Prague reported that the percentage of respondents in the Czech Republic preferring a tripartite federation had doubled in the first few months of 1991 to 50 percent; in Moravia and

Silesia, the figure is likely to have reached 64 percent.[105] If these estimates are correct, the proportion of Moravians now favoring a tripartite state had doubled from the previous year.

The Moravian elites viewed the apparent radicalization of their constituents as a source of bargaining leverage. In the midst of particularly tense negotiations between the Czechs and the Slovaks, Moravian deputies escalated their claims from territorial autonomy to republican status. A few Czech leaders attempted to respond to their demands—Pithart and Havel began to speak openly in favor of a tripartite arrangement.[106] In an effort to address their economic grievances, the government reallocated a portion of state funds from the richest districts in the Czech Republic to some of the poorest; districts in Moravia-Silesia were the recipients of two-thirds of these funds. The government also promised a grant to the city of Brno to build a hospital.[107]

Nevertheless, these gestures were seen as tepid at best, and the HSD-SMS deputies judged that remaining in the Czech government was no longer likely to pay political dividends. They therefore left the coalition, claiming that they had "assessed all aspects" of the situation and concluded that "the coalition [had] been . . . weakened by the [now Klaus-dominated] Civic Forum."[108] When the government announced an indefinite suspension of talks on Moravian autonomy, the HSD-SMS countered that it would boycott all future government sessions. Bárta then took his anti-Czech message to the street, and approximately 60,000 people gathered in the towns of Brno, Ostrava, and Olomouc to rally for autonomy and protest budgetary discrimination. This was a shrewd gamble on Bárta's part to force the government's hand by demonstrating broad constituent support for his position.[109] His tactic appeared to have paid off—the government pledged that the issue of Moravian autonomy would be taken up in the coming weeks. The Moravian deputies reciprocated by returning to parliament.

In May, the Czech National Council held the promised debates on Moravian autonomy. Four different proposals were considered, but the council ultimately postponed a vote on the matter, arguing that the region must first develop a degree of self-government.[110] With this circular logic, the Czechs again sidestepped the issue of autonomy without making concrete concessions to the Moravians.

Mid-1991–Late 1992: Decline of the Moravian Movement

Shut out by the Klaus-led government, the Moravian leaders now attempted to leverage their position at the federal level. Both the Czechs and the Slovaks had tossed about the idea of a tripartite state—the Slovak Christian Democrats had even offered guarded support for a trifederation, as long as it consisted of a state treaty among Bohemia, Moravia-Silesia, and Slovakia. However, as the deadline for the new constitution approached, Moravian leaders were increasingly sidelined by both the Czechs and the Slovaks, who were more concerned with securing a favorable position for their own republics in the future federation. In summer 1991, Moravian representatives began to complain that they were being excluded from the power-sharing talks.[111] What was worse, Bárta died unexpectedly during key negotiations in Budmerice, leaving the party rudderless at a crucial moment in the talks.[112]

They were also losing hope of gaining Slovak support. In late 1991, HSD-SMS leaders traveled to Bratislava, where they met with Čarnogurský and Mečiar, both of whom confirmed that the tripartite model was no longer on the table.[113] It became clear that what little leverage they had enjoyed from their position in government during the talks had yielded little in the way of concessions and was about to disappear. Moreover, claims of economic discrimination were losing resonance among ordinary Moravians—market reforms had failed to produce a clear economic divide between Bohemia and Moravia as they had between the Czech and Slovak economies.[114]

Given perceptions of low leverage and absent credible signs of Czech discrimination, Moravian deputies had strong reason to believe that the state of the world had become one of ethnic peace (fig. 5.3, box 4), in which case they should moderate their demands. Political alliances should also form between Czech and Moravian parties as the regional cleavage loses its political salience. This prediction is borne out by subsequent events. By mid-1991, public demonstrations for Moravian autonomy had all but disappeared. Lacking obvious signs of popular support in the run-up to the June 1992 elections, the new HSD-SMS leader, Jan Kryčer, scaled back his demands to administrative reforms that would strengthen local governments in Moravia. Kryčer indicated his willingness to work in the margins to obtain modest benefits for the region. He acknowledged that the movement had lost much of its base of support and that the "[1992] elections [was] the last opportunity to achieve autonomy for Moravia and Silesia . . ."[115] Moravian leaders were thus well aware that once the negotiations over the federation ended, so too would any possibility for extracting meaningful concessions from the Czech center.

In the run-up to the 1992 elections, HSD-SMS representatives made a last-ditch overture to the Slovaks by announcing that their party would support Alexander Dubček for the federal presidency because Havel had betrayed the Moravian cause. The party also continued to submit proposals for regional and cultural autonomy to the Czech National Council and even appealed to the UN to support Moravian autonomy based on their right to self-determination.[116] However, the Klaus government ignored all of these proposals and shut HSD-SMS leaders out of negotiations over the new Czech constitution, which did not even allow for the possibility of regional autonomy. As the deadline for the federal constitution approached, Moravian representatives lost what little support they had on both sides.[117]

Given the apparent disappearance of the Czech-Moravian cleavage, Kryčer attempted to broaden the electoral appeal of his party by allying with *non*ethnic parties—consistent with the predictions of the spatial model.[118] The HSD-SMS formed a coalition with the MNS and the Democratic Workers Party to run in the 1992 elections—the coalition was a flop; it won just 5 percent in the Czech Republic and failed to meet the threshold for entering the Federal Assembly.[119] The absence of Czech discrimination combined with the closure of the political opportunity structure to undermine support for the movement. Ordinary Moravians appear to have calculated that their political capital would be better spent on republic-wide parties than on regional parties, which at this point had little hope of returning benefits to their constituents.

In the June 1992 elections, the Moravians voted in much greater numbers for nonethnic parties (including the Communists, the Democratic Left, and the Czechoslovak People's Party) than they had in 1990.[120] Moravian leaders responded to the apparent shift in voter preferences by assuming positions on other issue dimensions. Between 1993 and 1997, Moravian parties multiplied, split, and formed electoral coalitions with a variety of nonethnic parties. They incorporated a mix of ethnic, social, and economic planks into their platforms as a means of regaining the support of their constituents. Despite their best efforts, the popularity of the regional parties continued to decline. In the 1994 local elections, electoral support for the party (now renamed the Czech-Moravian Party of the Center) plummeted to 1 percent.[121] In 1996, they finally failed to meet the 5 percent threshold for entering the Czech parliament and slid into political obscurity.

There are various explanations for the failure of the Moravian movement. One possibility is that it lacked a strong leadership and clear policy agenda. Years later, Dřímal and Bílý speculated that, had Bárta not been rocked by charges of StB collaboration or had they pressed for a tripartite state rather than territorial autonomy (which they believed had cost them Slovak support), the movement would have grown in strength. Dřímal claimed that the Czech leadership, too, was responsible for undermining the movement. He pointed out that Pithart, who had promised to help the Moravians achieve their goals if the HSD-SMS supported the government, repeatedly let them down by siding with right-wing CF deputies against successive proposals for Moravian autonomy.[122] Czech stonewalling thus prevented the Moravian elites from fulfilling their electoral promises.[123] According to Bílý, internal divisions as well as the party's failure to return benefits to its constituents led ordinary Moravians to lose faith in the movement.[124]

Although certainly plausible, these accounts are not satisfactory. Leadership problems and internal disputes are endemic to *all* national movements. They do not, however, necessarily diminish the popularity of separatism, as seen in the cases of elite struggles in Kosovo, Palestine, and Eritrea. Moreover, Moravian leaders were mired in scandals and internal conflicts even as their star was continuing to rise. The present analysis shows that Moravian demands were largely driven by perceptions of internal leverage. HSD-SMS leaders called for territorial autonomy in 1990 when polls showed that a majority of Moravians supported a separate status within the Czech Republic. They ratcheted up their demands to republican status in the wake of demonstrations that swept across Moravia and as Czech and Slovak leaders signaled that they might consider a separate status for Moravia in the federation. They later moderated their demands as the Czechs and Slovaks withdrew their support for a trifederation and as constitutional talks drew to a close. Following the negotiated split of 1992, they scaled back their demands to state subsidies for Moravian cultural institutions and monuments. In 1998, long after the movement had disappeared, Moravian leaders made a rather pathetic request for a seat on the Czech Council for National Minorities—a request that was duly denied.[125]

Comparing the Slovak and Moravian Movements

I now return to the question posed at the beginning of the chapter: Why did the Moravian movement—which began at the same time and under similar circumstances as the Slovak movement—disappear in less than three years, whereas Slovak nationalism continued to grow in strength, culminating in the 1993 Czechoslovak split? The two movements had several features in common that justify comparison:

- They began at the same time, in the same state, under the same central government.
- Both regions had been subordinated to Prague-centric rule (with the important difference that Slovakia had gained institutional status in the federation in 1969).

- Both Slovakia and Moravia could claim a national past—with a national literature, folk heroes and mythology as well as a history of political autonomy. There was a tradition of nationalist uprisings in both regions dating back to the early 1800s (with Slovak campaigns being more pronounced).
- Both regions' economies were based on agriculture and state-subsidized heavy industry, making them vulnerable to market reform.
- Both movements had charismatic leaders willing to exploit anti-Prague sentiments to gain and maintain political power.

Given their many similarities, it might be reasonably asked why these movements yielded such different outcomes.

Essentialist accounts hold that the Czechoslovak split was the outgrowth of latent Slovak nationalism that found expression after the collapse of the communist regime. In this view, the Slovak movement grew in strength because the Slovaks had a strong national tradition as well as a history of grievances against the Czechs.[126] In contrast, the Moravian movement was unlikely to gain momentum because it was based on a *regional* rather than a national identity; Moravianness was thus an "artificial" nationalism fabricated by elites to serve their narrow interests.

It is important to note in this respect that the Moravians had many of the same claims to antiquity (and thus national past) as the Slovaks. They had a legacy of autonomy movements in the nineteenth century, national myths and symbols, a regional capitol, universities, and a history of self-government. Like the Slovaks, the Moravians saw themselves as distinct from the Czechs. Public opinion polls showed that a large proportion of people living in the region "felt" more Moravian than Czech, with nearly half of the region's inhabitants declaring themselves Moravian as a write-in choice in the 1991 census.[127] The region was also largely rural and Roman Catholic—in contrast to the relatively secular Bohemia. In this and other respects, the Moravians were actually more similar to the Slovaks than they were to the Czechs.

However, the greater strength of the Slovak national identity at the time of transition undoubtedly accounts for much of the difference between the two movements. While having the requisite raw material on which to base a nationalist movement, the Moravian identity had not been nurtured in the same way as the Slovak identity under the former regime. With the national consciousness and mobilizational momentum gained from periodic struggles against the Czechs, the Slovak movement was easily set into motion in 1990. Still, this difference does not explain the *timing* of the Slovak movement, nor does it explain the peculiar fluctuations in Slovak and Moravian mobilization over this short period of time.

Do economic factors account for the differential success of the two movements? The most applicable economic explanation, relative deprivation theory, holds that disadvantaged groups mobilize around collective grievances in order to redress economic disparities and prevent further exploitation.[128] In this view, the Slovaks, bearing the brunt of market reform, mobilized around secessionist demands as a means of escaping depredation by the more advanced Czech center.[129] The Moravians, by contrast, failed to politicize their identity due to the absence of significant inequalities between Bohemia and Moravia.

This may appear to fit the facts of the case; however, economic hardship alone cannot account for the differences between the two movements. Although market reforms were indeed hurting the Slovaks disproportionately, the difference between Czech and Slovak suffering was, as yet, relatively insignificant. Slovak unemployment was only a few percentage points higher than Czech unemployment by the time of the split, and average food prices in Slovakia were only 4 percent higher than in the Czech Republic in 1991.[130] Hence, there was little actual deprivation on which to mobilize.

Slovakia's real economic problems lay, for example, in converting its many armament factories to civilian uses, which required significant capital. Seceding from the wealthier Czech lands could only hinder the Slovaks in achieving this goal, particularly as the Czechs effectively subsidized the Slovak economy. Prague had long provided Bratislava with technical support and transfer payments—assistance that continued even after the revolution. Indeed, the federal government had worked for decades to close the economic gap between the two regions, with the result that, by the 1980s, these disparities had narrowed considerably.[131] Statistics show that as late as 1989 nearly one-tenth of Slovakia's per capita income was made up of net transfer payments from the Czech lands.[132] In her analysis of Slovak secessionism, Milica Bookman concludes, "in Slovakia, [the] level of income is relatively low, the dependency on the nation state is high, the net outflows seem to be negative, and the degree of decentralisation very low. *It seems therefore that the secessionary aspirations in Slovakia are not based on economic factors,* but that the importance of the nationalistic and political elements is overriding in the demands for increased autonomy."[133] In other words, the Slovaks had strong economic incentives to remain in the union. In contrast, the Moravians were probably net contributors to the federation. Despite this, Slovak autonomy became increasingly popular after 1990, whereas Moravian autonomy gradually lost popular support. From a strictly economic perspective, we should have seen the opposite.

In a certain sense, market reforms *did* influence group mobilization in that they signaled the policy intentions of the Czech center toward the respective regions. Thus, the reforms were important not so much because of their direct material impact—which was still relatively slight—but, rather, because of what they signified in terms of future government policies.

Instrumentalism or elite opportunism is often cited as a central factor in the Czechoslovak split. A key piece of supporting evidence is that majorities of *both* Czechs and Slovaks opposed the split from the beginning of the talks until the time it was negotiated. If they had acted according to the wishes of their constituents, the split should not have occurred! Mečiar contributed to the split by adopting increasingly intransigent positions vis-à-vis the Czechs in response to Slovak nationalism.[134] As Abby Innes and Ellen Comisso rightly point out, Klaus, too, played an influential role, as he made the final decision to partition the state, having tired of the obstructionist Slovaks.[135] Czech and Slovak leaders thus engaged in a strategic game fueled by political ambition and mutual distrust, ultimately leading to the state's breakup.[136]

In a similar vein, Shari Cohen posits that in postcommunist Slovakia, as elsewhere in postcommunist Europe, the collective amnesia created by the previous regime produced an ideological vacuum in which only those elites who could adapt to a fluid political environment could survive. These mass-elites (opportunists willing to use nationalism instrumentally) therefore triumphed over ideological elites (leaders who championed an ideology regardless of its popularity). Mečiar was a mass-elite, exploiting Slovak nationalism as it gained traction in Slovak public opinion.[137]

Elite behavior was undoubtedly a factor in the Czechoslovak split, particularly once federal negotiations passed to the heads of the Czech and Slovak governments after the 1992 elections. But to say that the breakup was the result of a high stakes game between self-interested elites merely begs the question as to why they expected to profit from *this* game and not another. Elite opportunism implies that individual leaders take on popular agendas for instrumental reasons. However, it says nothing about what those agendas are likely to be. The Moravian-Slovak comparison illustrates the hole in these arguments. Opportunistic politicians dominated both Slovak and Moravian political landscapes at the time of transition: Bárta and Dřímal bore a striking resemblance to Mečiar in the sense that they were clever, charismatic, had populist appeal, and adopted a range of positions in response to subtle shifts in public opinion. However, nationalist leaders gradually *lost* popular support in Moravia while they gained support in Slovakia. Without understanding *why* a radical position resonates with the public at some times but not others, it is impossible to explain, let alone predict, the success of a nationalist project.

Institutions explain much of the divergence between the two movements. As previously noted, the Slovaks were given autonomy in 1969 in return for their support for the reconstructed regime. This promoted Slovak nationalism in several ways. First, the divided political elite and separate republican institutions led the Slovaks and Czechs to experience the transition differently. According to Bunce, "It was not just that more Czechs than Slovaks took to the streets; it was also that their publics and the leaders of their Communist parties and their opposition movements had quite different perspectives on what the future should entail."[138] This provided impetus to the Slovak autonomy movement in the context of negotiations over the state. Second, the republic-level electoral system created incentives for Slovak politicians to appeal exclusively to Slovak voters in freely contested elections. The Moravian parties, in contrast, were forced to compete with Czech parties in a pooled electorate; they therefore had disincentives to base their platforms on a narrow regional identity. Third, national institutions served as a mobilizational focal point around which a Slovak autonomy movement could coalesce and gain momentum; the Moravian leaders had no such devices with which to coordinate their movement.

Finally, as Stanger, Sharon Wolchik, and Leff point out, the Slovak veto and regional parliament drove up the minority's reservation value of accommodation, increasing the likelihood of state breakup.[139] With no institutional status in the federation, the Moravians, by contrast, were not a veto player. This limited the extent to which they could exploit the opportunity structure of constitutional reform to extract concessions, effectively undermining the salience of Moravian identity and the force of Moravian nationalism.[140]

Thus, the differential success of the Slovak and Moravian autonomy movements is mainly a function of their differential institutional endowment, national identity and mobilizational resources. However, the timing of these movements is explained by the *interaction* between this internal leverage and the external leverage represented by the political opportunity structure of constitutional reform. It is the position of each group within these negotiations, together with shifting perceptions of Czech intentions, that largely accounts for the fluctuation in these movements over time. The Slovaks perceived government-led market reform in early 1991 as a sign of Czech discrimination against the Slovak economy. This, combined with perceptions that they enjoyed considerable leverage against the center in the context of negotiations over the federation, led Slovaks to believe that the state of the world was becoming one of conflict. They responded by hardening their stance against the Czechs, propelling the two sides toward constitutional impasse.

The Moravians perceived an increase in leverage when they entered the Czech government in 1990 as federal talks were getting underway. This, along with signs that the Czech leadership was willing to accommodate Moravian demands in return for their political support, led HSD-SMS leaders to believe that the state of the world was becoming one of opportunity, inducing them to accelerate their demands to territorial autonomy. By 1992, the political opportunity structure had all but disappeared along with credible signs of Czech discrimination. Believing the state of the world to be one of ethnic peace, Moravian elites responded by de-escalating their demands to state subsidies for Moravian cultural associations and monuments. Table 5.3 summarizes this comparative evaluation.

This chapter shows that elite incentives, economic variables, and cultural differences cannot adequately explain why the Moravian movement for autonomy—so promising in early 1990—quickly faded away, whereas its sister movement in Slovakia led to the Czechoslovak split. Both regions contained opportunistic elites willing to adopt whatever agendas would bring them to power. However, national agendas continued to gain popularity in Slovakia, whereas they completely fell out of favor in Moravia. Economic theories also do not account for the trajectories of the two movements because Slovakia was a net beneficiary of state subsidies, whereas Moravia was most likely a net contributor. The Moravians, therefore, had stronger economic incentives to pursue autonomy than the Slovaks, predicting the reverse of what actually occurred. Finally, cultural differences between the Czechs and Slovaks do not adequately explain the greater force of the Slovak movement because the Moravians, too, were culturally distinct from the Czechs (although to a lesser extent). In some ways, the Moravians had closer affinities to the Slovaks because both regions were strongly Roman Catholic, with large rural populations and a strong aversion to Prague-centrism. Although the Moravian identity was not nearly as strong as the Slovak identity at the time of transition, the Moravians had ample raw material on which to mobilize a national movement, including a Moravian history and folklore, a legacy of autonomy movements, a memory of self-government, and even a myth of national origin. Despite this, support for the movement dwindled in the early 1990s, whereas Slovak nationalism continued to grow in strength.

The different trajectories of the two movements are best explained through the prism of ethnic bargaining, which holds that minority radicalization is driven by perceptions of minority leverage and majority intent. Although external actors certainly influence minority perceptions of power, this chapter demonstrates the applicability of the bargaining model to cases in which there are no outside lobbyists. Besides a less robust national identity and history of national struggle, the Moravians were less empowered than the Slovaks because they had no institutional status in the federation. They were therefore forced to rely on the two principals of the talks (the Czechs and Slovaks) to leverage their bargaining position within them. Shut out of federal negotiations by early 1992, Moravian deputies responded to their diminished power by ratcheting down their demands to government support for Moravian cultural institutions within the Czech Republic. The

Table 5.3. Summary of competing theories, Moravians and Slovaks in Czechoslovakia

Theory	Prediction
Primordialism (cultural/linguistic differences; preexisting national identity; ethnic hatreds)	**Correctly predicts** a stronger national movement in Slovakia than in Moravia due to the Slovaks' stronger national consciousness **Does not explain** shifts in either movement over time
Economic theories	**Incorrectly predicts** that the Moravians would be more likely to support separatism than the Slovaks, as the Moravians were probably net contributors to the federal budget, whereas the Slovaks were net beneficiaries
Ethnic entrepreneurship theories	**Incorrectly predicts** successful autonomy movements in both Slovakia and Moravia, as there were nationalist, opportunistic, charismatic leaders in both regions
National Institutions	**Correctly predicts** that Slovak nationalism would be stronger than Moravian nationalism **Does not explain** shifts in either movement over time
Ethnic bargaining	**Correctly predicts** that Slovak nationalism would be relatively stronger than Moravian nationalism as the Slovaks had institutional leverage, whereas the Moravians did not **Correctly predicts** fluctuations in claim-making as a function of changes in the opportunity structure of constitutional talks

Slovaks, however, moved in the opposite direction. Although Czech and Slovak leaders had worked together to dismantle the communist regime, negotiations over the federal constitution created an opportunity structure in which the Slovaks had incentives to bargain hard for maximal side payments for remaining in the federation.[141] Even when they perceived that the Czechs were becoming less conciliatory, their leverage induced them to continue radicalizing for concessions despite the growing likelihood of deadlock. This dynamic ultimately led to the dissolution of the state, an outcome undesirable to all.

CHAPTER SIX

Ethnic Bargaining in the Balkans

Secessionist Kosovo versus Integrationist Vojvodina

This chapter serves as an initial test of the applicability of the ethnic bargaining model outside central Europe. Yugoslavia provides a useful laboratory for this plausibility probe because it differs in important ways from its northern neighbors while having many other characteristics in common. Yugoslavia, like Czechoslovakia, Romania, and Hungary, experienced forty years of communist rule that denied all unofficially sanctioned forms of national expression. Unlike these other countries, however, Yugoslavia has a recent history of internecine warfare—with violent rather than peaceful secessionist conflicts. Hence, this probe into the Balkans holds many regional factors more or less constant while allowing the degree of ethnic violence to vary. I can therefore determine whether the model retains its explanatory leverage where minority-majority relations have been negotiated largely outside of civic channels.

Within Yugoslavia, I provide a comparative analysis of the Albanians in Kosovo and the Hungarians in Vojvodina (see map 6.1) from the beginning of the Balkan conflicts in 1988–89 to the democratic transition in 2000. In comparing the Kosovar Albanians and Vojvodinian Hungarians, I effectively control for many factors that have been used to account for minority radicalization. The two groups had the same history of authoritarian rule, the same host government, similar Balkan identities, similar institutions of regional autonomy, external national homelands, and opportunistic minority elites.[1] Notwithstanding their many commonalities, the two minorities sought qualitatively different demands from one another and from themselves over time, as shown in tables 6.1 and 6.2. I can therefore bracket these

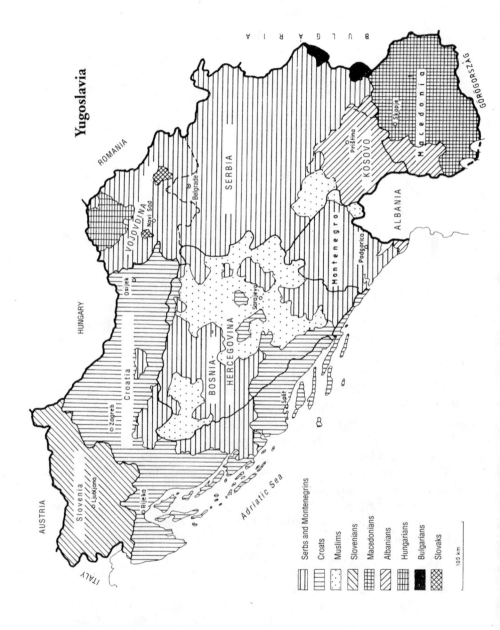

Yugoslavia

Serbs and Montenegrins
Croats
Muslims
Slovenians
Macedonians
Albanians
Hungarians
Bulgarians
Slovaks

100 km

AUSTRIA
ITALY
Slovenia
Ljubljana
Rijeka
Croatia
Zagreb
Osijek
HUNGARY
VOJVODINA
Novi Sad
ROMANIA
Belgrade
SERBIA
BOSNIA-HERCEGOVINA
Sarajevo
Split
Adriatic Sea
Montenegro
Podgorica
KOSOVO
Priština
ALBANIA
Skopje
Macedonia
BULGARIA
GÖRÖGORSZÁG

Table 6.1. Hungarian demands in Vojvodina, 1989–2002[a]

	Most extreme		↔	Least extreme		
Period	Irredentism/ secession	Regional/ territorial autonomy	Cultural autonomy	No claims	Support from lobby actor (Hungary)	Host state repression (FRY/Serbia)
1989–1992		X			Medium	Medium
1993–1999				X	Low	High
2000–2002			X		Low	Low

[a] Low, medium, and high indicate minority perceptions of lobby state support and majority repression. It is difficult to obtain precise measures of these variables because the sources of perceptions differ greatly from case to case. The most important thing to note is the shifts in perceived host and lobby state intentions, which should lead to corresponding shifts in minority demands.

Table 6.2. Albanian claims in Kosovo, 1988–2002[a]

	Most extreme		↔	Least extreme		
Period	Irredentism/ secession	Federal state	Regional/ territorial autonomy	No claims	Support from lobby actor (Albania/ NATO)	Host state repression (FRY/Serbia)
1988–1992	X				High	High
1993–1997		X			Low	High
1998–1999	X				High	High
2000–2002	X				High	Low

[a] Low, medium, and high indicate minority perceptions of lobby state support and majority repression. It is difficult to obtain precise measures of these variables because the sources of perceptions differ greatly from case to case. The most important thing to note is the shifts in perceived host and lobby state intentions, which should lead to corresponding shifts in minority demands.

variables to better isolate the causes of fluctuations in group claim-making both over time and across cases.

This chapter addresses the following question: Why, given their many similarities, did one minority mobilize periodically for secession in the 1990s, whereas the other did not? This analysis reveals that variation in group demands over time and across space may be largely attributed to the different levels of support offered by the minorities' respective lobby actors: Hungary in the case of Hungarians in Vojvodina, and Western governments and NATO in the case of the Albanians in Kosovo. Before testing the predictions of ethnic bargaining in each of the two cases, I first determine the internal bargaining leverage of each minority against the Serbian majority.

Ethnic Bargaining Hypotheses

Hungarians in Vojvodina

The largest ethnic minority in the region, Hungarians in Vojvodina are descended from the Magyar tribes that invaded the Danube Basin and Pannonian plain between the seventh and ninth centuries. Vojvodina had been part of the Hungarian Kingdom for many centuries when the Turks conquered it in the 1500s. Gaining control over much of the territory in the early eighteenth century, the Habsburgs began to resettle the region with non-Hungarians in a bid to change its ethnic balance.[2] This, together with the in-migration of Slavs following the collapse of Turkish rule, gradually turned the Hungarian majority into an ethnic minority in the region. The nineteenth century saw considerable tensions between the Hungarians and other groups, culminating in the armed uprisings of national minorities during the 1848 revolutions. After the *Ausgleich* in 1867, Hungary imposed assimilationist policies on minorities throughout the kingdom, giving rise to the myth of the "millennial Magyar crime of national repression."[3] At the close of World War I, Vojvodina was detached from Hungary and most of it was given to the multinational Kingdom of Serbs, Croats, and Slovenes—later renamed Yugoslavia. Belgrade exercised direct rule over the region between the two world wars, during which time Kosovo and Vojvodina enjoyed no autonomy whatsoever. When Germany invaded Yugoslavia in 1941, the country was dismembered, and Hungary occupied much of the territory of Vojvodina—an outcome welcomed by the ethnic Hungarians of the region.[4]

Once the Axis Powers were defeated in World War II, Vojvodina was returned to Yugoslavia. The postwar government adopted a Soviet-style multinational constitution with six republics under a strong federal government: Serbia, Slovenia, Croatia, Bosnia, Montenegro, and Macedonia. The Autonomous Province of Vojvodina and the Autonomous Region of Kosovo-Metohija were established within the Serbian Republic. Although Vojvodina and Kosovo were given the powers to enact provincial laws, set social policies, elect judges, and pass legislation in their respective regions, they were effectively ruled from Belgrade.[5] The situation began to change in the mid-1960s, when a series of constitutional amendments upgraded Kosovo and Vojvodina to the status of quasi-republics. The 1974 Constitution gave them the same rights, privileges, and responsibilities as the republics themselves. Relations between the Hungarians and the Serbs in Vojvodina remained more or less harmonious under Josip Broz Tito's policies of ethnic appeasement. Following his death in 1980, however, the Serbian leadership began to assert greater dominance over both the federal government and the provinces, particularly once Slobodan Milošević assumed control of the Serbian Communist Party in 1986.

By the late 1980s, roughly 95 percent of Yugoslavia's ethnic Hungarians resided in Vojvodina.[6] Because they made up only 17–20 percent of the region's population, their leaders are unlikely to have pressed for Vojvodinian statehood, which would have made the Hungarians a minority in a Serb-dominated state.[7] Indeed, the Hungarians had no legitimate claim to Vojvodina in the first place, due to their minority status in the province. However, given the fact that the Hungarians dominated many districts on or near the border with Hungary, they could have feasibly pursued irredentism by calling for a slight border adjustment between Hungary and Yugoslavia. They could also have advanced credible claims for territorial autonomy for Hungarian-majority localities.

Albanians in Kosovo

The region of Kosovo was originally settled by Illyrians, who are believed to be the forebears of the modern-day Albanians. In the second century BCE, the Romans conquered the region and incorporated it into their empire. When the Roman Empire fell, it became part of the Byzantine Empire. The Slavs arrived on the scene in the seventh century CE. When Serbian rulers expanded their domain in the thirteenth century, they added the region to their empire. In the fourteenth century, the Ottomans began to drive the Slavs northward, consolidating control over the southern Balkans. Over the next four hundred years, Kosovar Albanians (most of whom had converted to Islam) enjoyed limited autonomy under the Ottoman Empire. Although they had an uneasy relationship with their Turkish overlords—against whom they periodically revolted—they began to view their status in the empire as protection against the rising powers of Serbia, Macedonia, and Greece, all of which had claims on Kosovo.[8]

During the Balkan Wars of 1912–1913 and World War I, Serbia and Montenegro defeated the Ottoman army and incorporated Kosovo into the new Yugoslav state. The government attempted to alter Kosovo's ethnic balance in the interwar period, settling some 70,000 Serbs in the region.[9] In 1941, Kosovo was transferred to Italian-occupied Albania but was returned to Yugoslavia after the war. Under the postwar constitution, the region was granted provincial autonomy, although on paper only. In a series of reforms in the 1960s and under the 1974 Constitution, Kosovo acquired de facto republican status with its own government, judiciary, police force, constitution, schools, and economic institutions.[10] The Albanians also obtained education and language rights. It is important to note that interstate relations between Albania and Yugoslavia were practically nonexistent during the Cold War. Albania's Stalinist leader, Enver Hoxha, had sealed the borders in 1948 and maintained a generally hands-off policy toward the Albanian diaspora in Kosovo.[11]

By the late 1980s, the Albanians in Kosovo numbered 1.8 million people; the province itself was 90 percent ethnically Albanian. The minority was therefore sufficiently large and territorially concentrated to form a viable state. Because the region was overwhelmingly Albanian and had autonomous institutions, the minority also had a legitimate claim to self-government. Concentrated along the border with their kin state, the Kosovar Albanians could advance credible demands for irredentism as well. This range of possibilities suggests that their internal leverage against the center was considerable.

Hungarians in Vojvodina

1989–1992: The Window of Opportunity

In October 1988, Milošević dissolved Vojvodina's provincial assembly. The heads of schools, cultural organizations, courts, and law enforcement agencies in Hungarian-majority districts were replaced with ethnic Serbs or Hungarians loyalists. Vojvodina's autonomy was effectively revoked under the 1990 Serbian constitution and most executive, judicial, and administrative competencies were transferred to the Serbian government.[12] The authorities also closed many Hungarian schools and classes and clamped down on minority newspapers and radio and television stations. The local media, now under Belgrade's control, aired inflammatory reports that the Hungarians were plotting to secede from Yugoslavia, intensifying anti-Hungarian sentiment on the ground.[13]

At the same time, Hungary began to sound a nationalist chord vis-à-vis its co-ethnics in neighboring countries. Prime Minister József Antall announced in 1990 that he was "in spirit" the prime minister of Hungarians throughout the world, including the 5 million living outside Hungary. As Yugoslavia teetered on the brink of collapse in 1991, Antall asserted that Hungary's southern borders applied to Yugoslavia *but not to Serbia,* implying that Hungary might make territorial claims on the region if Yugoslavia disintegrated.[14] When accused of fomenting irredentism, the government denied having territorial aspirations toward Vojvodina. Nevertheless, it claimed that it had a duty to "protect the rights" of Hungarians outside its borders, stating, "[w]e never said that the minority question was the *only* factor in interstate relations, but we find it impossible to have good relations with a country that mistreats its Hungarian minority."[15] It also came to light that Hungary had been covertly aiding the secessionist movements in Yugoslavia; Budapest had been sending arms to the Croats and Muslims while helping to train anti-Serb guerilla fighters.[16] With signs of increased Serbian repression and increased interventionism on the part of their kin state, ethnic Hungarians should believe that the state of the world was becoming one of conflict (fig. 6.1, box 1), leading them to radicalize their demands against the Serbian center.

Consistent with this prediction, the new Democratic Community of Vojvodina Hungarians (DCVH), headed by the ambitious and charismatic András Ágoston, radicalized its demands from cultural autonomy to territorial autonomy in the space of two years. Formed in 1990, the DCVH quickly became the dominant Hungarian party in Vojvodina. At its first party congress in August 1990, the delegates adopted a program of cultural autonomy, defined as "the guaranteed collective rights of the Hungarian

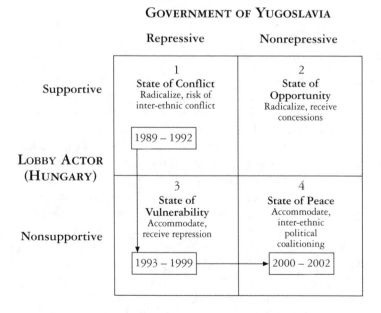

Figure 6.1 Hungarian claims in postcommunist Vojvodina

minority through the equal use of language and freedom of the press."[17] The DCVH ran on this moderate platform in the December 1990 elections, winning an estimated 80 percent of the Hungarian vote.[18] Given its broad popular support, the DCVH position thus serves as a reasonable proxy for Hungarian claims in the early 1990s.

The Hungarian government became increasingly vocal in lobbying for its co-ethnics as the Yugoslav wars got underway. In response, Ágoston ratcheted up his demands, issuing a formal memorandum in April 1992 that called for "tri-partite autonomy" for Hungarians in Serbia. The plan envisioned the creation of a Hungarian Autonomous District, which would preside over 56 percent of Vojvodina's ethnic Hungarians. Its capitol in Novi Sad would administer public education, local budgetary affairs, the judiciary, law enforcement, and other economic and social matters. The proposed district had its own coat of arms and flag—with the red, white, and green colors of Hungary's national flag.[19] Ágoston called for the same level of autonomy for Hungarians in Serbia that the Serbs in Croatia and Bosnia-Herzegovina stood to gain under Lord Peter Carrington's proposed peace plan.[20] Campaigning on this platform, Ágoston won an overwhelming victory in the 1992 elections, receiving eighteen out of sixty seats in Vojvodina's parliament with more than 90 percent of the Hungarian vote.[21] In light of this victory, we may infer that Ágoston's position largely reflected the preferences of ordinary Hungarians, indicating that they had indeed radicalized in confirmation of the model's prediction.

1993–1999: *Ethnic Intimidation and War*

In the early 1990s, Belgrade began resettling Serbian refugees from the Yugoslav wars in Vojvodina and Kosovo. During the Bosnian war, an estimated 200,000 Serbs were resettled in Vojvodina, particularly in areas with high concentrations of ethnic Hungarians.[22] To make matters worse, the ultranationalist Serbian Radicals had gained control of Novi Sad's municipal government, adding to the minority's sense of insecurity. The Hungarians endured systematic intimidation throughout the war, including bombings, beatings, death threats, and threats of rape. In some cases, people were forcibly evicted from their homes or coerced into house-swapping agreements with Serbian refugees from Croatia and Bosnia.[23] Ethnic Hungarians were also disproportionately drafted to fight in Yugoslavia's wars where they were often sent to the front. Due to these and other policies, some 35,000 Hungarians fled the region during this time. Because those who left were mostly men, tens of thousands of families were separated as a consequence.

In the meantime, Hungary had begun to moderate its stance toward the Hungarians in Vojvodina. As attacks against the minority escalated, the new

Socialist government in Budapest made it clear that it would not intervene on the minority's behalf. Asked what Hungary would do if Vojvodinian Hungarians became the victims of ethnic cleansing, Foreign Minister Géza Jeszenszky stated, "I can say only that Hungary is not in a position to be seen as a threat by any of our neighbors. . . . At most, we are capable of deterring a possible aggressor for a few hours or days . . . until the United Nations or some other international help comes."[24] The new leadership thus signaled a major shift in the country's policies toward Hungarians abroad. In his election campaign, Prime Minister Gyula Horn had pointedly asserted that he aspired to be the prime minister of only *10.5* million Hungarians (i.e., those within the country's borders) while having a "deep feeling of responsibility for the fate of Hungarians living abroad."[25] This statement was made in deliberate contrast to Antall's proclamation in 1990. At the same time, Hungarian Foreign Minister László Kovács indicated that Hungary was eager to normalize relations with its neighbors, asserting that this was Hungary's most urgent foreign policy goal.[26] The protection of the Hungarian diaspora was now only *one* of Hungary's foreign policy objectives rather than its overriding aim.[27] Budapest thus distanced itself from Ágoston and disentangled its foreign policy from minority issues in Vojvodina.

In light of growing Serbian repression and Hungary's new passivity, the Hungarians in Vojvodina should believe that the state of the world was becoming one of vulnerability (fig. 6.1, box 3), leading them to moderate their stance against the center. Consistent with this expectation, the DCVH—still advocating territorial autonomy—began to fragment after its disappointing run in the 1993 republican elections. Now seen as too radical, Ágoston rapidly lost the support of his constituents. Following two splits in the DCVH, he was removed from his leadership position. A second party, the Alliance of Hungarians, now became the mainstream voice of the Hungarian minority, with József Kasza (the affable mayor of Subotica) as its self-described moderate leader.[28] Oriented toward accommodation, he promised to negotiate directly with the Serbian authorities over the minority's status.[29] In a statement capturing the position of the Hungarians during this time, Kasza said, "We look for the little openings. . . . We work in the background, and through our personal contacts in the ministries in Belgrade."[30]

In 1999, NATO bombs rained down on Yugoslavia in a three-month air war to force Milošević to withdraw from Kosovo. Vojvodina, too, was targeted in these attacks as bombs hit factories, power stations, television and radio stations, government buildings, bridges, and trains—terrorizing the population and crippling the local economy.[31] Novi Sad sustained much of the damage in these raids, which destroyed its bridges, electricity, water supply and infrastructure over a period of weeks. One board member of the Novi Sad City Council observed that many of the targets of the attacks "had no military uses," pointing out that the first two bridges that were ruined were walking bridges, one of which "was barely strong enough to support buses."[32] To make matters worse, the Hungarian minority once again found itself scapegoated by the Serbian ultra-nationalists, who viewed the conflict as a battle for survival against a fifth-column minority. Belgrade, meanwhile, signaled its tacit approval of these activities.

During this time, Budapest refused even to meet with Hungarian representatives to discuss the minority's plight. Instead, Hungary gave its full support to the NATO campaign, despite the fact that its co-ethnics suffered as a direct result.[33] Facing a repressive majority and lacking external support, the minority had reason to believe that the state of the world was still one of vulnerability, in which case it should refrain from radicalizing even in the face of significant threat. Consistent with this prediction, Kasza (still the most popular minority representative) spoke out against NATO strikes but *not* against Serbian intimidation. He stated publicly that Orbán's support of NATO air strikes was "irresponsible and incomprehensible," adding that "Hungary should fulfill its NATO obligations . . . without sacrificing the Vojvodina Hungarians."[34] He thus staked out a position *against* his national homeland and *in favor* of the Yugoslav government. With no leverage against the center, the minority had little choice but to support its host government. This is consistent with the model's prediction that a weak minority is likely to lay low rather than radicalize in response to ethnic persecution.[35]

2000–2002: Inter-ethnic Coalitioning in Vojvodina

After Milošević' was expelled from office in 2000, the new Yugoslav president, Vojislav Koštunica, staked out a comparatively pro-minority stance. In late February, the head of Vojvodina's provincial parliament, Nenad Čanak, announced that he was preparing to enter talks with Serbian parties over restoring autonomy to Vojvodina.[36] Kasza's Democratic Alliance was invited into the ruling coalition, and Kasza was made deputy prime minister of Serbia with the portfolio of minority affairs and local government. Meanwhile, Hungary maintained its noninterventionist stance vis-à-vis the minority, focusing instead on fostering ties with the new government in Belgrade.

Given Serbian signals of nonrepressive intent and Hungary's continued hands-off policy toward the minority, ethnic Hungarians should believe with greater probability that the state of the world was one of peace (fig. 6.1, box 4), inducing parties to form coalitions across ethnic lines. In line with this expectation, Kasza's party joined non-Hungarian parties at the local level to call for Vojvodinian autonomy on a *nonethnic basis*. Tamás Korhecz, a Hungarian leader in the province of Vojvodina, observed that regime change in

Belgrade had laid the foundation for a historic reconciliation between the two groups. They now worked together to achieve greater autonomy for the region—a project that linked the interests of the Hungarians with those of the Serbs in Vojvodina. With the salience of ethnicity declining relative to economic interests, the Hungarian rank and file threw their support behind leaders who favored coalitioning across ethnic lines to lobby more effectively for the economic interests of *all* Vojvodinian residents. Indeed, the party's proposal for restoring autonomy to the region aimed at improving the status of people belonging to all ethnic groups. Partly because of its inclusive scope, such legislation actually became easier to get through the Serbian parliament. In February 2002, provisions for cultural autonomy were granted to ethnic Hungarians and some two hundred competencies were restored to Vojvodina under the Omnibus Act of 2001.[37] Consistent with the model's predictions, political coalitions thus formed across ethnic lines as Hungarians allied with Serbs and other groups to secure benefits for all inhabitants of the region.

Albanians in Kosovo

1988–1992: The Window of Opportunity

Kosovo emerged as a touchstone issue in Serbian politics in the 1980s as the economy weakened and the federation grew increasingly fragile. The once-marginal view that other ethnic groups had benefited at the expense of Serbs had gradually become a mainstream perception. This view was articulated in the infamous draft memorandum of the Serbian Academy of Sciences and Arts, which was leaked to the press in 1986. The memorandum asserted that "[t]he physical, legal, and cultural genocide of the Serbian population of Kosovo and Metohija is a worse historical defeat than any experienced in the liberation wars waged by Serbia from the First Serbian Uprising in 1804 to the uprising of 1941."[38] Slobodan Milošević (by now the head of the Serbian Communist Party) played on this hot-button issue to increase his popularity with the Serbian rank and file. In Priština, he proclaimed that the Kosovar Serbs were "oppressed by injustice and humiliation" and that Yugoslavia and Serbia would never surrender Kosovo.[39] To make good on this pledge, the government pushed through a raft of laws in 1989–1990 that restricted the sale of property to ethnic Albanians, created incentives for Serbs and Montenegrins to settle in Kosovo, and encouraged family planning and out-migration for Kosovar Albanians. In 1990, Belgrade revoked Kosovo's provincial autonomy, dissolved its assembly, shut down Albanian newspapers and radio and television stations, changed the street names from Albanian to Serbian, and introduced a new Serbian curriculum for schools and universities in Kosovo. The Serbian government thus signaled a strongly repressive intent toward the Albanian minority. At the same time, no state or organization intervened overtly on behalf of the Kosovar Albanians.

With the government indicating discriminatory intent and the minority group lacking external patronage, the Albanians should perceive a state of the world of vulnerability, leading them to accommodate the majority. Contrary to this expectation, the Albanians actually *radicalized* their demands to full republican status (fig. 6.2, box 1). After first knuckling under to Serbian pressure to pass antiminority laws, in July 1990 114 members of the now defunct Kosovar Assembly declared republic status for Kosovo within the Yugoslav federation.[40] Hundreds of thousands of Albanians participated in strikes and protests in support of the declaration and against Belgrade. The demonstrations gathered momentum over the following months as Albanians engaged in sporadic clashes with local authorities. In a bold act of defiance, the shadow Kosovar Assembly organized a referendum on Kosovo independence in September 1991, obtaining near-unanimous approval.

It may appear that these actions were *not* predicted by the bargaining model because there were no outside actors overtly lobbying for Kosovar

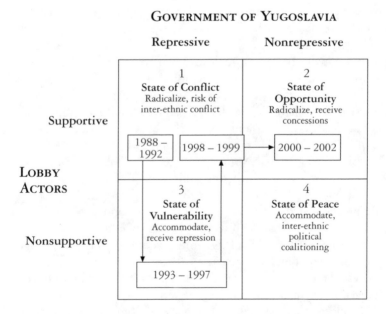

Figure 6.2 Minority behavior in Kosovo

independence during this time. However, there is evidence to suggest that the organizers of the miners' strikes in Trepča and other demonstrations against the regime *did* enjoy external backing.[41] Moreover, while denying aspirations for a Greater Albania, the Albanian premier, Ramiz Alia, strongly protested Serbian policies toward Kosovo, which he denounced as blatant discrimination against the Albanian minority.[42] Slovenian President Milan Kučan, too, publicly supported the minority, declaring that the miners in Trepča were "defending" a multinational Yugoslavia with their actions. He thus aligned Slovenia's struggle with that of the Kosovars.[43]

On the heels of the Slovenian and Croatian declarations of independence in 1991, Albanian minority leaders declared independence for Kosovo and established a shadow government, which set up parallel Albanian clinics, schools, and a local administration. The government collected a 3 percent levy on the income of more than 600,000 Albanian exiles in Europe and about 300,000 in North America.[44] Albania recognized Kosovo's independence immediately, and Sali Berisha—then a presidential candidate—made the status of Kosovar Albanians a central theme in his election campaign, promising that once in power he would "bring down the Balkan wall" and work to unify Kosovo and Albania.[45] After winning office, Berisha invited the provisional head of the shadow government to Tirana and proclaimed that Kosovo had the right to self-determination.[46] Meanwhile, Western diplomats Lord David Owen and Cyrus Vance initiated bilateral negotiations with the leader of the Democratic Alliance of Kosovo (DSK) and acting head of state, Ibrahim Rugova.

Serbian repression may appear to account for the radicalization of Kosovar Albanians during this time. However, the precise timing of their independence claims indicates that minority radicalism occurred in anticipation of (1) intervention by external actors who had begun to speak out on behalf of the Albanian minority and (2) the imminent collapse of the Yugoslav federation—both of which led Kosovar Albanians to believe that they enjoyed significant leverage against the center.[47]

1993–1997: Ethnic Intimidation and War

Discrimination against the Kosovar Albanians continued apace in the mid-1990s. Serbian irregulars escalated their persecution of Albanians in what came to be known as a program of "quiet ethnic cleansing."[48] In 1993, Commission on Security and Cooperation in Europe (CSCE) human rights monitors were forced to leave the province, and the local government imposed a Serbian curriculum on schools throughout Kosovo—teachers who started Albanian schools were beaten or arrested.[49] Belgrade continued the process of Serbianization by dismissing ethnic Albanians from positions in hospitals, state-run enterprises, the judiciary, the police force, media outlets, and schools; tens of thousands of Albanians were thrown out of work as a consequence. Restrictions were also placed on the minority with respect to private property and the freedom of movement. As a result of these measures, some 300,000–400,000 Albanians fled the province between 1990 and 1995, and the ethnic balance in Kosovo began to shift in favor of Serbs.[50] Throughout, Albanians were routinely brutalized, harassed, and imprisoned on trumped-up charges—there were even reports of torture and summary executions.

In the meantime, the Kosovar Albanians had begun to lose their already meager external patronage. As the conflict in Bosnia heated up, Kosovo effectively dropped off the international radar. Western governments—eager to avoid further entanglements in the Balkans—pressured Albania to recognize Yugoslavia's southern border and make nice with Belgrade. Fearful of losing Western aid, Berisha withdrew his support for Kosovar self-determination and called on minority leaders to reach an accommodation with Belgrade.[51] By the mid-1990s, Western attention was riveted on the evolving Bosnian war. The message to ethnic Albanians was clear: solve your problems with the Serbs diplomatically; we do not need another headache in the Balkans. Tim Judah characterizes Kosovo politics between 1992 and 1997 as "both dull and bizarre." Police repression never let up, but Serbian authorities allowed Rugova to "govern" the region unmolested; he conducted his affairs as though he were a "real president."[52]

With Serbia sending strong signals of nationalist intent and western governments urging a compromise with Belgrade, the model predicts that Kosovar leaders would perceive the state of the world to be one of vulnerability (fig. 6.2, box 3) and respond by moderating their demands to avoid confrontation with a much more powerful actor. In line with this expectation, the Kosovar Albanians gave almost unanimous backing to the pacifist Rugova and his policy of negotiating a status for Kosovo *within* the federation. Rugova justified his more moderate position as follows: "We would have no chance of successfully resisting the army. In fact, the Serbs only wait for a pretext to attack the Albanian population and wipe it out. *We believe it is better to do nothing and stay alive than to be massacred.*"[53] While the Kosovo Liberation Army (KLA) was mobilizing militants abroad, Rugova retained almost full support of the populace at home.

Within the province itself, there was an emerging consensus—even among relative extremists—that the Albanian minority should moderate its position vis-à-vis the government in light of recent events. Kosovar leaders gave their backing to the "Three Republic Solution" in 1996. The plan was publicly endorsed not only by Rugova but also by the hero of violent resistance Adem Demaçi, who had just been released from twenty-eight years of Serbian imprisonment. Under the proposal, Kosovo would be a constituent member of a tripartite federation consisting of Serbia, Montenegro, and Kosovo; Demaçi's name for the proposed federation was Balkania. He even attempted to form an alliance with the Serbian opposition leader, Vuk Drašković, to broaden support for the plan—reaching across ethnic lines in the belief that moderation would yield dividends.[54] The Kosovar Albanians thus ratcheted down their demands from independent statehood to a republic status within Yugoslavia, consistent with the predictions of ethnic bargaining.

1998–1999: The Violent Resistance

In 1997, Albania descended into chaos with the collapse of massive pyramid schemes in which hundreds of thousands of people had invested their life savings. People took to the streets in anger, and the opposition Socialists took advantage of the situation by mobilizing criminal networks, secret police, and former army officers to seize areas in the south of the country. The government soon lost control of the situation, and ammunition depots were thrown open to the public. Before long, the country was awash with nearly a million *kalashnikovs*. These events had a significant impact on the political climate in Kosovo. One writer notes:

> What finally transformed the KLA from a wannabe IRA into the fighting force that it became was *the disintegration of Albania.* . . . The KLA absorbed thousands of weapons from the looted armoires of the Albanian military and police. . . . The convulsive dissolution of Albania led to changes in high places. Sali Berisha was deposed and replaced by Rexhep Mejdani, who had an even more sympathetic ear to separatist demands. Berisha himself later allowed the KLA to use his property, around Tropoja, as staging grounds and supported the cause . . . unequivocally.[55]

Even before he was ousted, Berisha had resumed his nationalist posturing in an effort to shore up support for his crumbling regime. In Albania's daily satellite broadcast to Kosovo, Berisha attacked Rugova's passivity toward the Yugoslav government.[56] Now out of office, Berisha returned to his home in northern Albania, where he began an outspoken campaign against the Socialist government for its lack of "nationalist credentials and legitimacy."[57] With the aid of local authorities, he allowed the KLA to set up training camps in the Albanian border areas of Tropoja and Bajram Curri, where

KLA fighters were permitted to move about openly. Many KLA recruits wore Swiss military fatigues, having flown directly from Switzerland to the Tirana airport to train near the Albanian border.[58] The KLA even paid Albanian army officers to help organize the resistance against Yugoslavia.[59] These fighters—financed with proceeds from drug and arms trafficking as well as the Homeland Calling Fund based in Switzerland and Germany— set up checkpoints near the border where they actively recruited Kosovar refugees, many of whom later returned to Kosovo as trained fighters. The KLA also enjoyed the support of Albanian locals, who furnished them with safe houses and hid them from the Serbs. The new Albanian prime minister, Fatos Nano, was initially conciliatory toward the Yugoslav government. Later, however, he too began to refer to the KLA not as terrorists but, rather, as "people of Kosovo taking up arms in order to defend their lives and property," adding that "their organisational structure is a reality that should not be ignored."[60]

The situation in Kosovo remained in an uncomfortable stasis in the late 1990s, with the government assuming a largely reactive, rather than offensive, response to KLA attacks. Despite this, Serbian authorities and irregular troops continued to harass ethnic Albanians, signaling that the Serbs still harbored repressive intent toward the minority.

With a nationalizing Serb center and increased external backing, the Kosovar Albanians should believe that the state of the world was becoming one of conflict (fig. 6.2, box 1), leading them to radicalize against the Yugoslav government for a reward. Consistent with this prediction, the minority rank and file began to transfer their loyalties from the relatively moderate Rugova to the KLA militants. Even before KLA leaders came out into the open, people on the ground had begun to mobilize around more extreme demands. In 1997, just months after the collapse of the pyramid schemes in Albania, students from the Priština University initiated some of the first public protests against Yugoslav authorities since the early 1990s. The demonstrations quickly swelled to 20,000 students and culminated in violent clashes with the police. The students operated independently of Rugova's shadow government and refused to discontinue their activities despite the president's best efforts to quell them.[61] The organizers defended their actions by claiming that there had been no improvement in the status of Albanians since 1992, blaming the "passivity" of Kosovar elites.[62] At the funeral of the first KLA fighter to die in uniform in late 1997, KLA men took off their masks in public for the first time and called for Kosovo liberation; the assembled crowd of 20,000 mourners answered with shouts of "KLA, KLA, KLA!"[63] The militia had thus entered the Kosovar political arena, and its message of resistance was beginning to resonate with ordinary Albanians. When Serbian forces attacked members of a clan believed to be associated with the insurgency, killing about 100 people, the Kosovar Albanian rank and file spontaneously joined the rebellion. The KLA had not anticipated the uprising, but reacted quickly by distributing arms and organizing militias.[64] KLA men in northern Albania also began to send volunteers, uniforms, and arms over the border. At this point, village elders announced that the Albanians were now at war with the Serbs and began to organize, proclaiming "we are all KLA now," whether or not they were actually affiliated with the militia.[65]

Rugova responded to the grassroots mobilization by radicalizing his own position. Having repeatedly postponed presidential and parliamentary elections in Kosovo for fear of provoking the Serbs, Rugova now arranged for the elections, scoring an overwhelming victory on a platform of Kosovar independence.[66] He also hardened his stance against the Yugoslav authorities. When Milošević offered to negotiate directly with the shadow government over the region's status, Rugova refused—he could not be seen to negotiate for autonomy when he had just been elected on the promise of achieving Kosovar statehood.[67] Over the coming year, NATO, the United States, and other Western leaders stepped up their support for the Albanian minority as more and more Serbian atrocities came to light. In 1998, U.S. special envoy to the region, Robert Gelbard, and his assistant, Richard Holbrooke, began direct talks with Hashim Thaçi, the KLA leader, to coordinate a war strategy against Yugoslav forces.[68]

The KLA militants responded to NATO backing by escalating their attacks against Yugoslav irregulars. At the same time, thousands of ordinary Kosovar Albanians joined in the armed resistance:

> In effect, western leaders, convinced that sooner or later the Serbs and Albanians would be compelled to back down from all-out war and would be forced to compromise, were marching their troops to the top of the proverbial hill. When by March 1999, and many more threats later, there was still no compromise, there was also no way back—and, short of a humiliating climbdown, force had to be used. In the meantime, *more and more Kosovars were becoming ever more convinced that, like the Fifth Cavalry, NATO would soon be appearing on the horizon ready to rescue them.*[69]

By rallying around the extremist KLA militants, the minority rank and file effectively radicalized their stance in response to perceptions of western support. Although it would have been sensible for the Serbian leaders to back down at this point given repeated NATO warnings, Milošević could not be seen to go back on the public commitment he had made to the Serbian population to stand up to bullying foreign powers. KLA radicalization therefore met with Serbian intransigence, ultimately leading to the Kosovo war. This is consistent with expectations of the ethnic bargaining model in a state of the world of conflict.

2000–2002: Moving toward Kosovo Statehood

After Milošević was ousted in 2000, the new Serbian president, Vojislav Koštunica, came to power on a relatively pro-minority platform with the promise of negotiating with Albanian leaders over Kosovo's status. In December 2000, Koštunica announced that he would renew diplomatic relations with Washington under the new Bush administration, pledging to negotiate directly with U.S. officials "immediately after the new year" to resolve clashes in the buffer zone between Serbia and Kosovo.[70] In January, Yugoslav authorities announced that they had agreed to reduce the number of forces in the buffer zone, signaling Belgrade's willingness to cede control of the region to international bodies.[71]

In the meantime, NATO continued to back KLA militants even after the war had ended. Although the peace settlement mandated that the militia be disarmed, the United States and its allies gave the KLA effective control over the protectorate in the guise of the new Kosovo Protection Corps (KPC)—a security force that consisted mostly of former KLA fighters.[72] When NATO assumed command of the five occupation zones in postwar Kosovo, the KPC was allowed to take over police stations, border patrols, and other strategic locations.[73] The organization eventually gained control of twenty-three of the protectorate's thirty municipalities under the UN interim administration (United Nations Mission in Kosovo, UNMIK).[74] Not surprisingly, as many as three-quarters of the Serbs who had lived in Kosovo before March 1998 fled the region in fear of reprisals.[75]

Given Serbia's newly liberal stance and NATO's sustained backing of the Albanian militants, the Kosovar Albanians should perceive the state of the world to be one of opportunity (fig. 6.2, box 2) and continue to radicalize to obtain rewards. This is in fact what occurred. Although Rugova's pacifist Democratic League of Kosovo obtained more than 60 percent of the vote in the 2000 elections, the Albanians no longer envisioned Kosovo as part of Yugoslavia. There was a rising level of popular support for radicalism, as Albanians in the border regions (together with former KLA fighters) mobilized for a Greater Albanian state. Events in the Preševo Valley just outside of Kosovo bear this out—the months-long insurgency in the region suddenly mushroomed to 2,000 fighters in February 2001. At the same time, a newly formed National Liberation Army engaged in clashes with authorities in northern Macedonia, particularly in Tetevo, where Thaçi had a large residence. Six groups of armed Kosovar Albanians numbering about 1,000 crossed the border into Macedonia with the aim of ethnically cleansing the region and attaching it to Kosovo, south Serbia, and Montenegro to create a "greater Kosovo."[76] It is clear that perceptions of sustained external backing, rather than government repression, drove Albanian radicalization during this period.

Comparing the Vojvodina and Kosovo Movements

I now conduct a comparative analysis of the two cases to assess the relative explanatory power of the competing theories of minority radicalization. First, cultural differences cannot account for the different behavior of the two groups because there were significant linguistic, cultural, and religious differences between the minority and majority in both provinces. Ethnic distinctiveness does not explain why the Kosovar Albanians periodically supported secessionism, whereas the Vojvodinian Hungarians maintained an overall integrationist stance. Both minorities also had strong national identities and affinities with their co-ethnics over the border. However, only the Kosovar Albanians seriously entertained notions of uniting with their homeland state in the post–Cold War period.

It may be objected that the Hungarians could not have realistically pursued secession because they made up only 17 percent of the population of Vojvodina and therefore had no legitimate claim to the region. Nevertheless, although small, the minority was also territorially concentrated, with seven Hungarian-majority districts on or near the border with Hungary (see map 6.1). Hence, the minority could have feasibly sought a border adjustment on the grounds of mismatched ethnic and political boundaries. Hungary even had an historical claim to Vojvodina because the Habsburg military frontier had separated the region from the rest of Serbia. Despite this, the Hungarians carefully avoided all calls for territorial separation.

Albanian radicalism also cannot be attributed to ancient hatreds because the Hungarians, too, harbored grievances against the Serbs (although to a much less extent). For centuries a part of the Hungarian Kingdom, Vojvodina had been detached from Hungary under the 1920 Treaty of Trianon—an act still widely regarded as a political crime by Hungarians both inside and outside of Hungary. During World War II, as many as 40,000 Hungarian civilians were tortured and summarily executed when Serb partisans recaptured Vojvodina from the occupying Hungarian Army.[77] Moreover, like the Albanians, the Hungarians had been the victims of Serbian assimilation and resettlement policies through most of the twentieth century. In sum, although the Kosovar Albanians had greater grievances and a more robust legacy of national struggle than the Vojvodinian Hungarians, there were sufficient historical grievances on which to mobilize a Hungarian secessionist movement—an event that did not occur.

Geographical theories of secessionism hold that ethnic islands surrounded by enemy territory are vulnerable to majority attack, creating incentives for their national homelands to rescue them in the context of political instability.[78] Such theories were used to explain Serbian irredentism in Bosnia and Croatia—Serb forces punched through walls of enemy groups in order to rescue marooned Serbian communities in the new states. According to this logic, Hungary should also have intervened to rescue Hungarians in Vojvodina because Hungarian-majority districts were surrounded on all sides by Serbs.[79] Ethnic geography in Vojvodina therefore predicts irredentist mobilization, particularly as Serbian extremists began to systematically harass the Hungarian minority—resettling Serbian refugees in Hungarian areas and provoking tens of thousands of Hungarians to flee during the Bosnian and Croatian wars. This, however, did not occur.

In Kosovo, there were no such vulnerable pockets of ethnic Albanians. To the contrary, the Kosovar Albanians were territorially concentrated near the Albanian border, making them "easy to rescue" by their homeland state. According to Posen's theory, this very ease of rescue should have deterred Serbian aggression, ensuring ethnic peace.[80] However, not only did this ethnic geography fail to deter Serbian attacks, but Albania failed to rescue its beleaguered kin from these attacks. Despite the fact that Yugoslavia had no nuclear deterrent, Albania maintained a hands-off policy toward its co-ethnics in Kosovo—even during Serbia's ethnic cleansing campaign in 1999.

Economic theories predict the exact reverse of what happened in the two cases. With small reserves of oil, fertile land, and a well-developed economy, Vojvodina was one of the richest regions in Yugoslavia. If we accept that Slovenia and Croatia pursued secession to improve their economic position, the same should hold for Vojvodina. Purely economic considerations predict that the Hungarians would seek significant autonomy (if not secession) from Serbia to avoid subsidizing a relatively backward center. Instead, mainstream Vojvodinian leaders steadfastly rejected secessionist and irredentist claims throughout the 1990s, even in the face of crippling economic sanctions. In contrast, Kosovo—the most backward region in Yugoslavia—periodically pursued secession throughout the same period, despite the fact that the region was woefully unprepared for independence. In sum, economic theories predict that the Vojvodinian Hungarians would be separatist and the Kosovar Albanians integrationist—the exact opposite of what actually occurred.

According to ethnic entrepreneurship theories, ethnic groups mobilize with the emergence of nationalist, charismatic leaders who are willing to play the ethnic card for private gain. The Hungarians had such a person in András Ágoston; the Albanians in Hashim Thaçi. By all accounts, Ágoston was exactly the kind of leader who could successfully rally the minority rank and file around the myth of an external threat to gain and maintain political power. Charismatic and popular, Ágoston was regarded as a natural leader in the early 1990s, when he and his party garnered 80–90 percent of the Hungarian vote. However, with growing signs of Serbian repression and diminished patronage from Hungary, both Ágoston and his ethnic agenda rapidly lost popular support. In the new climate of ethnic insecurity, Jószef Kasza, a moderate who advocated cooperation with Belgrade, assumed the mantle of leadership, having won a plurality of the ethnic vote in the 1996 elections. In Kosovo, meanwhile, Rugova and other ethnic Albanian leaders moderated their positions as external support for the minority dried up in the mid-1990s. When NATO and cross-border assistance began to emerge in 1998, however, Rugova ratcheted up his demands to full independence, refusing to negotiate with the Serbian government over autonomy. Although elites undoubtedly played an important role in the two cases, their agendas were largely a function of bargaining considerations.

Constructivist or institutional theories also cannot account for why the Albanians in Kosovo were more radical than their Hungarian counterparts in Vojvodina. The regions had enjoyed the same level of autonomy under the Yugoslav federation, with their own courts, police forces, constitutions, and local assemblies. Despite these similarities, the Vojvodinian Hungarians refrained from secessionist demands, whereas the Kosovar Albanians periodically embraced them.

Ethnic fears or credible commitment theories correctly predict minority radicalization in both regions in the late 1980s, in response to Belgrade's campaign of Serbianization. However, they cannot explain why the minorities later moderated their stance in the mid-1990s, when majority repression had, if anything, actually increased. Indeed, ethnic fears theories incorrectly predict Hungarian radicalism *throughout the 1990s* as Serbian nationalists and paramilitaries harassed and intimidated the minority—forcing many of them to hand over their homes to Serbian refugees. Tens of thousands of Hungarians fled the country as a result of these policies. Ethnic fears theories predict that the Hungarians would radicalize in reaction to this climate of ethnic insecurity. Instead, minority representatives maintained their loyalty to Belgrade throughout the Croatian, Bosnian, and Kosovar wars.

Ethnic bargaining largely accounts for the variation in minority claims both between the two cases and within each case over time. The Hungarians eschewed separatist demands in the post–Cold War period in view of their limited external patronage and because their kin state, Hungary, hewed to a pro-Belgrade line through most of the 1990s. Although the minority did mobilize in 1988 when the government revoked Vojvodina's autonomy, these demands were *not* made on an ethnic basis until the Antall government began to argue in favor of Hungarian autonomy. When Budapest moderated its position in 1993, the minority understood that it would now have to negotiate directly with the Serbian government. Minority representatives responded by ratcheting down their demands, even as the authorities stepped up their campaign of repression. When Koštunica came to power in 2000, the salience of ethnic cleavages diminished markedly, increasing the value of inter-ethnic coalitions. The ethnic bargaining model predicts that political alliances would form across ethnic lines, which occurred in Vojvodina in 2001.

In Kosovo, minority leaders escalated their demands in the late 1980s in anticipation of support from Slovenia, Albania, and possibly even Western governments against the Yugoslav center. Having lost its allies in the mid-1990s and facing a repressive center, Rugova moderated his stance while seeking an accommodation with Serbian leaders. When the KLA obtained external backing in 1997–1998, the minority rank and file switched their allegiances to militant elites who pursued secessionism through violence. The Kosovar Albanians continued to press these demands even after a relatively pro-minority government had come to power in 2000. This is because sustained international support lent the Albanians considerable bargaining leverage against Belgrade. Table 6.3 summarizes this comparative evaluation.

This chapter shows that the bargaining model retains its explanatory leverage in a case of ethnic violence, suggesting that the drivers of peaceful intergroup conflict and violent ethnic warfare may be very similar. Minority radicalization in both cases was largely driven by perceptions of bargaining leverage, which is a function of internal leverage (group size, territorial compactness and autonomous institutions) and external leverage (assistance from exile organizations, military alliances, and/or kin states). Because Hungarians made up a minority of the population of Vojvodina and because Hungary did not actively call for a border revision, neither secession nor irredentism was a credible posture for the group. Minority leaders therefore limited their claims to territorial autonomy. In contrast, ethnic Albanians made up the vast majority of Kosovo's inhabitants; secession was therefore a feasible political program for Kosovar Albanians.

Table 6.3. Summary evaluation of competing theories, Hungarians and Albanians in Yugoslavia

Theory	Vojvodina Hungarians	Kosovar Albanians
Primordialism (cultural differences; national identity; ethnic hatreds; group traits)	**Incorrectly predicts** that cultural differences between Hungarians and Serbs would lead to separatist claims in the 1990s; Hungarians in Vojvodina actually rejected separatism altogether, hewing to moderate demands throughout the 1990s. The group's minority status in Vojvodina **correctly predicts** that the Hungarians would be unlikely to sue for independent statehood. **Does not explain** fluctuations in the demands that they did advance.	**Correctly predicts** that cultural differences between Albanians and Serbs would lead to separatist demands in the 1990s, but does not explain why these demands shifted over time. The group's majority status in Kosovo and its territorial compactness **correctly predict** that the Albanians would be able to sue for statehood. **Does not explain** fluctuations or timing of independence claims
Ethnic geography	Presence of ethnic "pockets" of Hungarians in Vojvodina **incorrectly predicts** that Hungary would intervene to rescue its co-ethnics in order to preempt Serbian victimization in the context of political instability.	High concentration of Albanians near the border with Albania **correctly predicts** that Tirana would not directly intervene to rescue its co-ethnics due to the minority's "ease of rescue," but not why Albania declined to intervene when this geography failed to deter Serbian aggression against the minority
Economic theories	**Incorrectly predicts** that Hungarians would seek a separate status during the 1990s to preserve their economic advantages from depredations by the center	**Incorrectly predicts** that Albanians would *not* seek autonomy or secession during the 1990s due to Kosovo's economic backwardness
Ethnic entrepreneurship theories	**Incorrectly predicts** that Hungarians would support secession or territorial autonomy in the 1990s in response to the charismatic nationalist leadership of Ágoston, who agitated for Hungarian separatism	**Correctly predicts** that Albanians would support secession in the late 1990s due to the efforts of their charismatic nationalist leader, Thaçi **Does not explain** why Albanians favored the *noncharismatic, pacifist* Rugova through most of the 1990s
Ethnic fears/Credible commitment	**Incorrectly predicts** that Hungarians would radicalize most when the majority posed the greatest threat to the minority (during the Bosnian and Kosovar wars)	**Correctly predicts** that Albanians would radicalize for independence in response to increased repression in 1990 and during the Kosovo war **Does not explain** why Albanians failed to react to earlier Serbian repression, particularly during the Bosnian war

Table 6.3—continued

Theory	Vojvodina Hungarians	Kosovar Albanians
Constructivism (institutionalization of national identity)	**Correctly predicts** that Vojvodinian Hungarians would seek some degree of political autonomy due to their possession of national institutions. **Does not explain** why they quickly suppressed these demands in the 1990s.	**Correctly predicts** that Kosovar Albanians would seek some degree of political autonomy due to the possession of national institutions **Does not explain** fluctuations in these demands, nor why their demands were more extreme than those of the Hungarians, who had the same institutional status
Ethnic bargaining	**Correctly predicts** that Hungarians would not radicalize for more than territorial autonomy in the 1990s due to their limited internal leverage and because no external actor (including their kin state) overtly lobbied on their behalf	**Correctly predicts** that Albanians would radicalize for secession when they received external support for such goals (from co-ethnics in Albania, exile groups abroad, and NATO) **Correctly predicts** that they would *not* radicalize without such support, even in the face of significant majority threat

Because the two minorities had the same central government but different lobby actors, this comparison also helps to isolate the relative impact that outside actors have on minority claims (see fig. 2.7). In the case of Vojvodina, Hungary (an applicant to both NATO and the EU) assumed a generally hands-off policy toward its co-ethnics. As a consequence, mainstream minority leaders moderated their demands and ultimately even backed the Belgrade regime during the NATO war. In the case of Kosovo, Albania was counseled restraint by Western governments in the 1990s and duly refrained from intervening on behalf of its co-ethnics. The international community also began to turn away from the Albanian minority, inducing Kosovar leaders to moderate their demands. In the late 1990s, however, NATO aligned itself with the KLA, leading the minority rank and file to rally around Albanian militants as Kosovar leaders radicalized their demands to secession.

The explanation as to why the Albanians pursued their demands through violence, whereas the Hungarians did not, may be as simple as the groups' relative access to arms. The disintegration of the Albanian state in 1997 led to the distribution of 1 million small arms, many of which were smuggled over the border into Kosovo. Moreover, the region's mountainous terrain and the existence of KLA training bases in Albania offered a ready means for the minority to pursue its agenda through violence. Most importantly, the intervention of NATO and mercenary soldiers financed through the Homeland Calling Fund leveraged the minority against the center, providing it with a means of defense against a repressive government. The Hungarians in Vojvodina, however, had no such access to armaments—which also helps explain why Hungarian demands remained relatively moderate. As noted in the introduction of this book, minorities are far less likely to advance secessionist demands if they cannot back them up through force. Indeed, separatist claims and the use of violence are strongly correlated.

Viewing minority radicalization as a function of bargaining leverage can assist policy makers in identifying both the sources and the timing of group mobilization. This, in turn, is essential for interrupting the spiral of ethnic conflict. By (1) counseling external patrons or national homelands to watch what they signal to minorities in the course of domestic politicking (as Hungary did vis-à-vis its co-ethnics in Vojvodina and as NATO might have done vis-à-vis the Kosovar Albanians), (2) challenging the norms that support kin state involvement in minority-majority relations, and (3) making aid or membership in international organizations conditional on sustained inter-ethnic cooperation at both the domestic and regional levels, we may come closer to constructing lasting solutions to minority conflicts in today's world.

CHAPTER SEVEN

Conclusion and Policy Implications

W hat are the lessons of this book for resolving ethnic conflict? This question is of paramount importance in a world where sectarian divides do not observe political boundaries. Many of the most intractable conflicts in the postwar period have been fought over group claims for greater political autonomy or independent statehood, including the decades-long conflicts in Palestine, Sri Lanka, Northern Ireland, Kashmir, Sudan, Turkey, and Myanmar, to name but a few. Nearly always waged in the name of national emancipation or historical injustice, it is tempting to view these wars as somehow predetermined or fated to happen. We might, then, conduct an autopsy on the state itself to identify the mortal flaw in the country's history of ethnic relations or in its economic or political institutions. This book demonstrates, however, that such preexisting structural factors are neither sufficient nor are they perhaps necessary for minority mobilization.[1] The critical mechanism of conflict is instead the group's perceived bargaining leverage against the state center at any given time, suggesting a strongly contingent—rather than predestined—quality to minority claim-making. Moreover, insofar as groups are leveraged from the outside, the impetus of such campaigns is very often external to the state itself.

Despite its strongly theoretical bent, this work is also intended for a policy audience. The present chapter therefore draws implications from the ethnic bargaining model for managing internal conflicts in today's world. I begin by noting that a sound understanding of the mechanisms underlying separatist conflict is necessary for arriving at effective remedies; indeed, the different theories of conflict point toward very different prescriptive solutions.

Primordialist or essentialist theories generally hold that claims of self-determination should be taken at face value. In this view, demands for autonomy are a natural, and somewhat inevitable, by-product of nationalism. Once a group has developed a certain degree of national consciousness—often due to domination by another group—the minority is bound to pursue self-determination until it achieves nation-state status. Because of the strength of its identity, and sometimes the depth of its grievances, the seceding minority is unlikely to abandon its struggle until it is granted some degree of self-government. From this, we might conclude that autonomous institutions are the only answer to separatist violence—serving as a compromise solution between no independence (which the group would not accept) and full statehood (which the central government would not accept). These remedies have been applied to war-torn regions such as Kosovo, Palestine, East Timor, West Sahara, Bosnia, Chechnya, and are currently being considered in other places as well.[2]

The inevitability thesis of nationalist conflict must, however, be questioned in light of the fact that most contemporary campaigns for independence emerged only after minority rights and national self-determination had begun to gain normative traction in the global political discourse. Demands for sovereignty mushroomed in the wake of the de-colonization movements of the 1960s and 1970s, suggesting that such movements are more a function of discursive minority empowerment than they are of indigenous desires for self-government. Moreover, the fact that group representatives pursue secessionism at some times but not others is further proof that claim-making is more strategic than primordial in nature. If it is true that claims for self-determination are *not* a reflection of deeply rooted preferences, then there may be less-destabilizing solutions to territorial conflicts short of providing halfway houses to statehood.[3]

Economic theories hold that groups mobilize in reaction to real or perceived disparities in wealth or income. The theory of relative deprivation predicts that when one group enjoys a disproportionate share of the country's wealth, and particularly when such disparities appear to widen, subordinate groups may rally around demands for collective compensation once they have the opportunity to do so. The Tamil uprising, for example, began in the 1980s partly due to resentments over racial quotas implemented by the Sri Lankan government. Economic grievances or disparities in wealth and income have also been cited as major factors in the radicalization of the Palestinians, the Kurds in Iraq and Turkey, the native Hawaiians in the United States, the Southerners in Sudan, the Moros in the Philippines, the Catholics in Northern Ireland, the minorities in Myanmar, the Assamese in India, the Chechens in Russia, and the Kosovar Albanians in the former Yugoslavia.

Such theories suggest the need for policies that reduce economic dispari-ties in order to encourage disaffected groups to reintegrate into society.[4] Sri Lanka attempted to do exactly that when it eliminated quotas that discrimi-nated against Tamils in university admissions and civil service employment. However, these gestures were seen as too little too late and ultimately failed to stem the tide of Tamil radicalism. In the 1990s, the Tamil Tigers morphed from a ragtag insurgency into a formidable fighting force, taking over large stretches of territory in the northern and eastern regions of Sri Lanka. Simi-larly, Canada's linguistic concessions to the Francophone minority failed to prevent the growth of separatism in the province of Quebec. The Sudeten German and Slovak cases examined in this book also demonstrate that ef-forts to address inequalities often do not succeed in demobilizing groups. I do not mean to argue here that movements based on collective grievances are somehow suspect or that there is no need for governments to implement minority rights or redress material inequities. To the contrary, minority pro-tections are critical to the stability of divided societies and, when imple-mented early, may even prevent an ethnic divide from becoming politically salient. My point is rather that, logically speaking, grievances over the eco-nomic status quo are unlikely to generate sectarian conflict on their own. One need only consider the impoverished, but politically inactive, Roma minorities across Europe to see the truth in this statement.[5] Conversely, there are many examples of minorities that mobilized in the *absence* of such disadvantages—including the Serbs and Croats in postcommunist Bosnia, the Slavs in Moldova, and the South Ossetians and Abkhazis in Georgia. Therefore, it should not come as a surprise that efforts to combat economic grievances by themselves often fail to produce the desired results.

Entrepreneurship theories yield rather indeterminate policy prescrip-tions. If we believe that elites themselves are the problem—the "bad apple" theory of ethnic violence—then military tribunals[6] or outright military in-tervention[7] might be necessary to remove these individuals from power and thereby resolve the conflict. However, most entrepreneurship arguments ac-knowledge that the political environment plays at least a permissive role in encouraging nationalizing behavior or allowing ideologues to assume power. If this is true, elite behavior might be altered simply by changing the elites' incentive structure. Indeed, Stuart Kaufman proposes that third parties "aim at finding a way to restrain the belligerent elites, most likely through some combination of inducement and deterrence."[8] V. P. Gagnon, Jr., too, recommends that conflicts be addressed at their root by altering the domes-tic political arena in which elites operate.[9] Both Gagnon and Kaufman thus acknowledge that elites and their agendas derive largely from their political environment—a position that is actually consistent with theories of conflict that *de-emphasize* the role of particular leaders.

Much of the conflict resolution literature is based on ethnic fears theories of ethnic war. According to security dilemma logic, sectarian conflict emerges at the substate level when groups are unable to determine whether the other side is defensively or offensively oriented. This uncertainty leads to spirals of conflict as each side operates on worst-case assumptions concerning the other's motives.[10] Neither side will disarm until the costs of victimization are radically reduced, most likely through external security guarantees.[11] Such guarantees can take many forms, of which territorial partition and population transfers represent a kind of last resort. As its most well-known advocate, Chaim Kaufmann argues that severe ethnic conflicts create security dilemmas so intense that they cannot be resolved without separating the warring groups into "defensible enclaves."[12] Critics counter that ethnic partition entails unacceptable costs—population transfers invariably lead to significant loss of life, and territorial partition risks transforming internal conflicts into even deadlier inter-state wars. Territorial partition may also encourage secessionism elsewhere, while creating authoritarian statelets whose leaders are not accountable to the people they claim to represent.[13] Moreover, it is not even clear that ethnic partition can resolve the problem for which it was designed. In his analysis of 125 civil wars, Nicholas Sambanis concludes that wars terminated by partition were no less likely to recur than wars ended through other means.[14]

A second variant of the ethnic fears approach predicts that a minority may try to secede during political transition if the state majority cannot credibly commit to follow through on its promises to the minority under the new regime.[15] The majority is unable to make its promises credible because there is nothing to prevent it from reneging on these pledges once the minority has disarmed and (re)entered the state. The minority therefore has a strong *dis*incentive to submit to majority control so long as it anticipates greater rewards from exiting the state through secession. Pieter van Houten posits that the presence of an active kin state may help solve the majority's commitment problem because the majority is unlikely to violate a minority that enjoys the backing of a strong homeland state.[16] UN peacekeeping troops or other occupation forces might also assist in resolving the commitment problem by compelling the government to follow through on its pledges to the minority under the new regime.[17]

Others suggest the use of *internal* security guarantees such as power-sharing arrangements. Arendt Lijphart posits that a minority veto and other consociational structures might serve as a credible protection against discrimination, making minorities less apprehensive about their future in a majority-dominated state.[18] However, while sometimes the only viable means of post-conflict reconstruction, divided decision-making tends to undermine democratic stability by promoting legislative deadlock, increasing bureaucratic inefficiency, and reducing the ability of government to adapt to changing social and economic conditions.[19] Marie-Joëlle Zahar offers support for this contention in the case of Lebanon, demonstrating that power-sharing arrangements did little to secure peace in that state and may have actually *increased* sectarianism in the context of successive foreign interventions.[20] Public education, civic institutions, and confidence-building measures have also been suggested as methods of managing ethnic fears at the substate level.[21]

If these remedies sometimes fail in achieving their desired aims, it may be because insecurity or group fears do not tell the whole story of internal conflict. Opportunism must also be taken into account as an important driver of minority mobilization. In contrast to security dilemma expectations that guarantees of protection promote moderation, the ethnic bargaining model predicts that a minority may still radicalize if it believes it enjoys significant external backing. The logical corollary to this is that a minority with very *low* bargaining leverage (due to territorial dispersion or lack of outside support) is unlikely to mobilize against the center—even in the face of significant threats. This is because the minority prefers low-level discrimination to the dire consequences of challenging the center from a position of weakness.

Solving the Paradox of Minority Empowerment

This, then, is the paradox of minority empowerment. Partisan intervention on behalf of beleaguered groups may perversely encourage minority rebellion, culminating in minority reprisals that leave the group worse off than it was before.[22] It is crucial to note in this respect that third-party intervention into domestic conflicts is hardly a rare occurrence. According to one recent study, one-fifth of the 165 internal wars waged from 1946 to 2004 involved troops from an outside state. An additional 80 conflicts involved external assistance short of troops (including military funding, logistical assistance, and the provision of arms and training bases to insurgent groups).[23] This means that fully *70 percent* of the civil conflicts since World War II have featured external aid to one or both parties. The authors also note that "a vast majority (21) of external interventions were carried out by neighboring states. This type of intervention dominated through the whole 1946–2004 period." Indeed, from 1989 to 1998, the only external actors involved in such conflicts were neighboring countries.[24] This demonstrates the importance of third parties—and particularly neighboring states—in prosecuting and possibly prolonging domestic armed conflict.

Does this mean that outside actors should stand aside as venal governments repress their minorities? Not if they can muster a nonpartisan intervention. In this view, the identity of the intervener may be more important than the method of intervention in determining the final outcome. I expect that mediators are more likely to succeed when they do not have a dog in the fight. The intervener should not, for example, have salient ethnic affinities to either side of the dispute because such ties are likely to be regarded with suspicion by the other side while sending the wrong message to its presumed protégés.[25] For example, when the nationalist Antall government attempted to block Slovakia's admission to the CoE in the early 1990s over its treatment of ethnic Hungarians, minority leaders responded by escalating their demands to territorial autonomy and ethnic relations in Slovakia hit a low point. Hungary also refused to normalize relations with its neighbors until they agreed to sign CoE Recommendation 1201 giving national minorities the right to political autonomy. Minority elites reacted by calling for a separate political status for Hungarian-majority districts. This served as grist for the nationalist mill on both sides of the border. The xenophobic Greater Romania Party in Romania and the Slovak Nationalist Party in Slovakia gained popularity and political influence in the wake of these events, helping to push through legislation that further restricted minority education and language rights.

Military patronage is particularly dangerous because the group is likely to view this as a rare window of opportunity through which it can gain an important strategic advantage. If the group confronts the center in expectation of external support that never materializes, retribution can be devastating. For example, the 1991 Shi'ite and Kurdish uprisings in Iraq were triggered by veiled promises of U.S. assistance in the wake of the First Gulf War. When the U.S. failed to come to their aid, Saddam Hussein brutally suppressed the rebellions and retaliated against both groups. Even if the anticipated assistance *does* appear, this may still wreak havoc by providing cover for the government to carry out programs of ethnic cleansing. When NATO intervened on behalf of the Kosovar Albanians in 1999, for example, Serbian forces conducted a massive sweep of the province. As soon as the OSCE monitors were evacuated (just days before the strikes), hundreds of thousands of Kosovar Albanians fled to Albania and Macedonia ahead of ground attacks. The U.S. State Department documented the fallout from this campaign, noting that ethnic cleansing in the region "dramatically accelerated in mid-March 1999" [ten days before the bombing] and that more than 300 villages were burned and about 500 residential areas partially burned during the campaign. The report continues: "Serbian forces have made Pristina, the capital of Kosovo, a ghost town [after the start of the war]."[26] All of this suggests that military interventions generally do more harm than good and should be avoided where possible.

Finally, third-party mediation is more likely to succeed if it is carried out by a major rather than a minor power. In the same way that the intervention of a parent carries more weight in a sibling dispute than the intervention of a third sibling, a great power is likely to be taken more seriously by the warring parties than a medium or smaller power. This is because powerful states have potent tools at their disposal—big carrots as well as sticks—to push *both* sides to the bargaining table. By making aid packages, government contracts, or trade preferences conditional on sustained ethnic peace, great powers can create strong incentives for both sides to work together to resolve their differences. At the same time, they can severely punish one or both sides for refusing to cooperate. The greater influence of major powers in mediating conflict was particularly evident in the Kosovo case. The OSCE, the High Commissioner on National Minorities (HCNM), and the Council of Europe had pushed for negotiations between the Albanians and the Milošević government for nearly a decade. It was only with the intercession of the United States and its NATO allies that the two sides finally came together for talks in Rambouillet in 1999. Finally, when great powers intervene, the world is literally watching. To gain sympathetic coverage in the international media and to win over global public opinion, both parties must make a show of conciliation. However calculated these gestures may be, they can actually help in getting the two sides to the bargaining table.

To summarize these policy recommendations:

- Third-party mediators of ethnic conflicts should not have ties to either party of the dispute. Interventions by partisan actors may encourage their protégés to overreach, creating the conditions for military reprisals.
- Forceful interventions should only be carried out by major powers (with the consent of the international community). Major powers are likely to be more successful than other mediators due to the potent inducements and threats they have at their disposal.

As a general rule, military intervention on behalf of beleaguered minorities is likely to be counterproductive. Where interventions are deemed necessary (to prevent genocide, for example), they are best accomplished by disinterested major powers, which have the wherewithal to threaten and cajole both sides to enter into negotiations. Kin state interventions, on the other hand, are unlikely to help resolve ethnic disputes and may even *exacerbate* the sectarian divide.

The Spatial Model of Ethnic Coalitioning

The spatial model introduced in chapter 2 suggests various strategies for consolidating ethnic peace in divided democracies. The model predicts that when the minority's external lobbyist signals its intent to intervene, ethnic salience is likely to increase at the domestic level, leading mainstream political elites to ally with ethnic extremists to shore up their nationalist credentials and thereby maintain constituent support. If these signals later disappear, ethnic salience is likely to decrease, leading politicians to form coalitions *across* ethnic lines as economic or ideological cleavages become relatively more salient.

The Sudeten German case serves as an apt illustration of this dynamic. At the close of World War I, Austria and Germany sent signals of irredentist intent to their co-ethnics in Czechoslovakia while the government in Prague labored to consolidate a Slavic state. In this climate of heightened ethnic salience, Czech-German political coalitions became virtually impossible— neither the Czechoslovak Social Democrats nor the Czech bourgeois parties were able to form alliances with their German counterparts. The mainstream Czechoslovak parties therefore formed an ungainly all-national coalition—a lame duck government doomed to legislative paralysis.

After Germany and France had normalized relations under the Locarno Treaty in 1925, however, Czechoslovakia could no longer afford to antagonize Germany. At the same time, the Reich government was in no position to provoke the West by intervening in Czechoslovakia's internal affairs. Both Prague and Berlin therefore had powerful incentives to reach détente. The Sudeten German issue was consequently dropped, diminishing the salience of the Czech-German cleavage in domestic politics. Almost immediately, minority-majority coalitions began to form across ethnic lines. In 1926, the Czechoslovak Agrarians and Christian Socials joined their respective German counterparts to form the first Czech-German government in the interwar period. In the mid-1930s, as Germany again began to signal interventionist intent, the minority rank and file gradually abandoned the moderate minority parties in government and threw their support behind Henlein's Sudeten German Party, which refused to cooperate with the Czechs. By the time of the 1938 *Anschluss*, inter-ethnic coalitions in Czechoslovakia had become all but impossible—even the moderate German parties had left the government to join the Henlein movement.

The spatial model has predictive power in postcommunist Czechoslovakia as well. After the 1989 revolution, the transition government in Prague focused on dismantling the power structure of the former regime and enacting democratic reforms. Consequently, the most salient cleavage was ideological—in the 1990 elections, the main Czech and Slovak political organizations joined together in an anticommunist coalition against the binational Communist Party. Inter-ethnic cooperation gradually broke down over the following year as continuing talks over the federal constitution grew increasingly contentious. Czech efforts to reform the unwieldy system of dual vetoes in parliament signaled to the Slovaks that the Czechs intended to create a unitary Prague-centered state; meanwhile, the Czechs viewed Slovak intransigence in the reform process as naked opportunism. The results of the 1992 elections reflected the heightened salience of the Czech-Slovak cleavage relative to the communist-reformist divide—support for pro-federal parties dropped into the single digits, whereas parties emphasizing national issues won the plurality of votes in their respective republics. Weeks later, perfunctory talks over the federation between Czech and Slovak leaders resulted in stalemate, precipitating the split.

It seems clear from these and other examples that divided democracies are most stable when nonethnic issues dominate the political arena. If this is true, what (if anything) can third parties do to heighten the salience of nonethnic cleavages? The cases examined in this book suggest a few possibilities: organizations such as NATO and the EU could make membership, subsidies, trade preferences, and other developmental assistance contingent on guarantees of minority protection or ethnic power-sharing.[27] This method is likely to be most effective when the requirements are clearly specified, and when the rewards are credible, substantial and communicated directly to the people, so that the citizens of divided democracies understand the consequences of supporting nationalist elites.[28] This strategy has already enjoyed some success. In 1998, Slovak opposition parties united across the political spectrum to oust Vladimír Mečiar, a man who had been repeatedly reelected on a platform of Slovak nationalism. This outcome can be attributed, at least in part, to warnings by the EU Commissioner for Enlargement Gunther Verheugen that Slovakia would be excluded from the first wave of EU accession unless its leaders demonstrated a commitment to economic reform and minority rights.[29]

The case of Romania provides an even clearer example of the effectiveness of third-party conditionality. In the early 1990s, Romania was ruled by the nationalist authoritarian leader, Ion Iliescu, while the democratic opposition remained relatively weak. However, once Western leaders began to send credible signals to the Romanian public in 1995 that NATO (and eventually EU) membership would be forthcoming if its government improved (among other things) its protection of minorities, the voters rejected Iliescu in the 1996 elections in favor of the liberal reformer, Emil Constantinescu. In a watershed moment, the Hungarian party was then invited into the ruling coalition, despite the fact that the government already had a parliamentary majority without it.

A second remedy involves institutional change. Rather than deepening the ethnic divide through consociational arrangements such as minority vetoes and ethnically-based cantons, electoral rules could be altered to make minority support a requirement of majority rule. To accomplish this, outside parties might make foreign aid or other benefits to a country dependent on election reform. Ethnic power-sharing might also be engineered through a system of cross-voting so that no party could govern without gaining a certain percentage of the minority vote.[30] Alternatively, a "power-dividing" strategy might be followed by creating multiple cross-cutting jurisdictions in different policy areas to diffuse majority power while implementing strict checks on the limits of majority rule.[31] Whatever the chosen remedy, the population should be informed of the benefits it stands to gain by supporting such changes—in this way, a grassroots movement could be mobilized to push the necessary reforms through parliament.

Caveats and Further Avenues of Research

Several qualifications should be made at this point. First, I have tested the bargaining model using a relatively small number of cases from central and Eastern Europe. This raises the question as to whether the principles of ethnic bargaining can be generalized to cases beyond Europe. The obvious next step would be to apply the model to cases in other regions around the world in order to determine the extent to which ethnic bargaining retains its explanatory value with respect to conflicts that emerged under different historical, political, social, and economic circumstances.

Second, the proposition that ethnic entrepreneurs are largely epiphenomenal to ethnic mobilization requires qualification. An important assumption I have made is that the polity in question is minimally democratic and that the people have access to independent sources of information. Elite discretion is significantly circumscribed under these conditions for two reasons. First, in functioning democracies, political leaders can be held accountable to their constituents through free and fair elections; they are therefore necessarily responsive to shifts in public opinion. Second, without control of the popular media, politicians are usually less able to manipulate public opinion. This is because the rank and file are able to use alternative sources of information to verify their leaders' assertions concerning the intentions of the government and outside parties. Where these conditions hold, the ability of elites to manipulate public opinion is significantly constrained. Public opinion is instead driven by many inputs, meaning that popularly elected elites must adapt their positions to constituent preferences in order to stay in power. In contrast, politicians in *non*democracies tend to exercise far more control over public opinion due to their ability to restrict public access to alternative sources of information. Elites in nondemocracies can therefore be expected to play a far more consequential role in the process of ethnic mobilization. If true, this hypothesis has important policy ramifications and suggests a promising line of research into the ways in which ethnic bargaining plays out in nondemocracies.

Elites also play an indispensable role in the construction of identities that serve as the basis for mass mobilization. Intellectuals and politicians help shape and strengthen national identities through public education campaigns and through speeches and writings that are disseminated on the ground. They may also influence the choice of strategies for collective action. In the postcommunist period, Roma intellectuals attempted to establish a pan-European Roma identity to unite the Roma populations throughout east central Europe. Through seminars sponsored by the EU and the CoE, Roma activists trained community leaders to petition international, state, and local bodies for legal redress; organize public protests; and attract media attention to their cause. Individuals have played a far less central role in mobilizing the Hungarian minorities, the Kosovar Albanians, and the Slovaks in the contemporary era. This is because these groups already had well-developed national identities, active kin states, cultural associations, and sometimes even political parties or autonomous institutions by the time of transition.

Finally, it appears that different *sources* of minority leverage have a qualitatively different impact on minority behavior. If a group derives its strength from uncertain or mercurial external patrons—such as Hungary in the case of Hungarian minorities—mainstream leaders are more likely to advance vague demands such as political autonomy, which can be adapted to a range of bargaining positions and a variety of different audiences. The use of ambiguous claims also allows minority leaders to avoid entrapment at a time when their leverage is in flux or otherwise uncertain. When their source of power is *internal*, however, such as when the government depends on minority support for its survival (e.g., the 1994 Slovak government and the 1996–2000 Romanian government), minority elites are more likely to advance specific demands that are amenable to negotiation. This is because their position in power holds them at least partly accountable for the government's policies, particularly in the area of minority rights. They therefore have an incentive to deliver concrete goods to their constituents, requiring them to establish and work for a realizable set of goals. These include (among other things) university instruction in the minority language, bilingual curricula, minority teacher training, and subsidies for cultural associations. By identifying the conditions under which minority leaders have incentives to broker compromises with their governments rather than merely posture, external mediators can determine well ahead of time whether the parties to a conflict are in a position to negotiate in good faith.

This book develops and tests a theory of minority claim-making that challenges predominant ethnic fears, grievances, and instrumentalist understandings of ethnic mobilization. According to the theory of ethnic bargaining, group claims serve primarily as a means by which minority representatives challenge their state governments over the distribution of resources—the extremity of demands thus fluctuates in tandem with minority beliefs concerning the group's prevailing bargaining power against the center. Two important predictions emerge from this theory. First, if a minority believes its leverage against the majority to be sufficiently high (such as when a powerful external patron sends credible signals of interventionist intent), minority elites are likely to radicalize against the majority even in the face of credible promises of protection. This goes against the expectations of ethnic fears theories that minorities mobilize mainly in reaction to signs of repression or majority threat. It also accounts for the puzzling cases of Sudeten German irredentism in the late 1930s and Slovak separatism in the early 1990s. Both groups mobilized around extremist demands in response to perceptions of heightened leverage, despite credible guarantees of protection from the majority as well as economic disincentives to secede.

Second, groups that do *not* enjoy at least a minimum degree of power vis-à-vis the majority are likely to remain quiescent even in the face of significant repression. This provides insights into the puzzling behavior of the Vojvodinian Hungarians, who supported the Belgrade regime throughout the 1990s despite considerable ethnic intimidation. It also sheds light on the motives behind Kosovar Albanian attempts in the mid-1990s to reach a compromise with the Yugoslav government in the midst of systematic attacks on the ethnic Albanian population.

The analysis in this book yields clear policy lessons as well. It suggests that separatist minorities are unlikely to negotiate a settlement with the center so long as they enjoy significant external backing or cross-border support. Although we might expect that an interventionist kin state or other lobby actor would help the center in solving its commitment problem toward a secessionist minority, the model indicates instead that the presence of an interventionist lobby actor is more likely to exacerbate, rather than ameliorate, ethnic tensions. This is because signals of external support are likely to increase the minority's perceived bargaining leverage against its host government, creating incentives for the group to ratchet up its demands for ever-increasing concessions from the center. This dynamic can be seen most clearly in the case of the Sudeten Germans, whose leaders accelerated their demands to irredentism against a conciliatory Czech government in the late 1930s. Indeed, most of the intractable civil conflicts around the world have been embedded in larger *regional* conflicts. A short list of examples include Turkey and Greece with respect to Cyprus, India and Pakistan with respect to Kashmir, Israel and its Arab neighbors with respect to the Palestinians, England and Ireland with respect to Northern Ireland, Russia and Georgia with respect to Abkhazia, and Azerbaijan and Armenia with respect to Nagorno-Karabakh. Rather than focusing primarily on internal ethnic relations, mediators would therefore do well to take an *outside-in* approach to resolving ethnic disputes—choking off external sources of support and neutralizing regional disputes before inducing minority guarantees at the substate level. In the course of any mediation, third parties should avoid sending signals of partisan support to either side of the conflict.

This book also challenges widely held assumptions concerning the role of elites in ethnic conflict. The Slovak premier, Vladimír Mečiar, radicalized from a pro-federalist stance in 1990 to a separatist stance in 1992. In contrast, the Sudeten German leader Rudolf Lodgman moderated his demands from irredentism in 1918 to regional autonomy in 1921. Both cases indicate that office-seeking leaders are likely to adopt those positions that best resonate with their constituents *at every point in time*. Extremist demands are therefore less a function of internal dispositions of the leaders themselves than they are of conditions on the ground that create incentives for radicalization. In light of this, third parties might focus more on altering the environmental factors that generate grassroots extremism than on removing ill-behaved elites from power.

The spatial model, too, offers policy recommendations for divided democracies. On the most general level, it supports the carrot (as opposed to the stick) approach to conflict resolution. If inter-ethnic cooperation is inversely correlated with ethnic salience, then mediators should attempt to increase the salience of other cleavages over that of ethnicity. Threatening a government with sanctions if it fails to improve its treatment of minorities (the stick approach) may perversely *increase* the salience of ethnicity by lending credence to accusations that the minority is colluding with hostile outside powers. By contrast, offering rewards for ethnic peace that can be enjoyed by the entire population is likely to *de*-politicize ethnic divisions by creating incentives for all citizens to support inter-ethnic alliances.

On the systemic level, the discourse of ethnic bargaining must be re-framed before the level of sectarian violence can be permanently reduced. The empirical record shows that the majority of serious internal conflicts have been waged over territorial claims—demands based on segregationist rights, which were revived in the second half of the twentieth century to facilitate de-colonization. The increased legitimacy of separatism since the 1970s has greatly assisted nonstate actors in mobilizing both internal and external support for independence movements—contributing to the problem of failed states, the spread of refugees and disease, and the strengthening of global terrorist networks. The consequences of lending further legitimacy to separatism will be grim. It is widely acknowledged that it is not possible for every nation to achieve self-determination through statehood (or even autonomy) because nations themselves are forever multiplying, giving rise to new competing claims over territory. Major powers, international organizations, and NGOs should therefore work to de-emphasize segregationist rights in favor of integrationism. Over the longer term, the promotion of multistate citizenship—undergirded by an enhanced and enforced system of universal human rights—would go a considerable distance toward negating, or at least complicating, our identification with pieces of territory. Governments, meanwhile, should be pressured to decouple membership in an ethnic community from citizenship in the state. Such measures might gradually undermine the legitimacy of national self-determination, over which many of the bloodiest conflicts of the twentieth century have been waged.

Notes

Introduction

1. Peter Wallensteen and Margareta Sollenberg counted 110 armed conflicts worldwide from 1989 to 1999. According to their statistics, 54 of these conflicts were fought along explicitly ethnic lines. See Peter Wallensteen and Margareta Sollenberg, "Armed Conflict, 1989–99," *Journal of Peace Research* 37 (2000): 635–49.

2. A *minority* is defined here as a group that is numerically inferior to the politically dominant group in the state. *Minority demands* refer to calls by legitimate representatives of the minority against the state or local government for goods that may be collectively enjoyed by the minority rank and file. Such claims vary in intensity from affirmative action to cultural autonomy to regional autonomy to secessionism or irredentism.

3. This book follows Donald Horowitz's definition of ethnicity as an identity "based on a myth of collective ancestry, which usually carries with it traits believed to be innate" (Donald Horowitz, *Ethnic Groups in Conflict* [Berkeley: University of California Press, 1985], 41). Such traits may be linguistic, regional, religious, racial, cultural, or any other characteristic upon which a communal bond can be formed. An ethnic group can now be defined as a community whose membership is based on the possession of a trait that is taken to be ascriptive and thus largely inherited.

4. It should be noted that this theory is intended only to explain the mobilization of minorities that are geographically concentrated and therefore likely to use territorial demands in bargaining with the center. In contrast, geographically dispersed groups (such as the Tutsis and Hutus in Burundi and Rwanda, the Mainland Chinese in Taiwan, and the Shi'is and Sunnis in Lebanon) are likely to employ a different set of demands because they cannot lay claim to a particular territory. Given the different bargaining dynamic at play, conflicts that involve non-territorially concentrated minorities fall outside the scope of the theory.

5. This model builds on Rogers Brubaker's triadic nexus of national minority, nationalizing state and national homeland. Rogers Brubaker, *Nationalism Reframed: Nationhood*

and the national question in the New Europe (Cambridge, U.K.: Cambridge University Press, 1996).

6. Foundational studies in this field include Alexis Heraclides, *The Self-Determination of Minorities in International Politics* (London: Frank Cass, 1991); Donald Horowitz, *Ethnic Groups in Conflict;* Joseph Rothschild, *Ethnopolitics: A Conceptual Framework* (New York: Columbia University Press, 1981); Donald Rothchild and Victor A. Olorunsola, eds., *State Versus Ethnic Claims: African Policy Dilemmas* (Boulder: Westview, 1983); Hurst Hannum, *Autonomy, Sovereignty, and Self-Determination: The Accommodation of Conflicting Rights* (Philadelphia: University of Pennsylvania Press, 1990).

7. For examples of such arguments, see Edward Shils, "The Integrative Revolution: Primordial, Personal, and Sacred Ties," *British Journal of Sociology* 8 (1957): 130–45; Clifford Geertz, "The Integrative Revolution: Primordial Sentiments and Civil Politics in the New States," in *Old Societies and New States,* ed. Clifford Geertz (New York: Free Press, 1963), 105–57.

8. Although most of these theories address the specific phenomenon of intercommunal violence, the causal mechanisms they identify should apply to ethnic mobilization of any kind.

9. A classic formulation is given by Walker Connor, *Ethnonationalism: The Quest for Understanding* (Princeton: Princeton University Press, 1994).

10. Roger D. Petersen, *Understanding Ethnic Violence: Fear, Hatred, and Resentment in Twentieth-Century Eastern Europe* (Cambridge, U.K.: Cambridge University Press, 2002), 1.

11. Stuart J. Kaufman, *Modern Hatreds: The Symbolic Politics of Ethnic War* (Ithaca: Cornell University Press, 2001), 30.

12. Ibid. Donald Horowitz advances a similar social psychological explanation for ethnic riots, arguing that while "ancient hatreds" do not themselves determine ethnic violence, these riots could not occur in the absence of fear, anxiety, intergroup hostility, an event that provokes a group to rage, and justification for violence. Donald L. Horowitz, *The Deadly Ethnic Riot* (Berkeley: University of California Press, 2001).

13. Stephen Van Evera, "Hypotheses on Nationalism and War," *International Security* 18 (1994): 40–41. Barry Posen makes a similar argument concerning the link between locally intermingled ethnic populations and secessionism; see Barry R. Posen, "The Security Dilemma and Ethnic Conflict," in *Ethnic Conflict and International Security,* ed. Michael Brown (Princeton: Princeton University Press, 1993), 108–9.

14. Toft tests this hypothesis using a series of case studies as well as a data analysis that shows a positive and robust correlation between group rebellion and territorial concentration. Monica Duffy Toft, *Geography of Ethnic Violence: Identity, Interests, and the Indivisibility of Territory* (Princeton: Princeton University Press, 2003).

15. For theories of advanced-region secessionism, see Daniel S. Treisman, "Russia's 'Ethnic Revival': The Separatist Activism of Regional Leaders in a Postcommunist Order," *World Politics* 49 (1997): 212–49; Peter Alexis Gourevitch, "The Reemergence of 'Peripheral Nationalisms': Some Comparative Speculations on the Spatial Distribution of Political Leadership and Economic Growth," *Comparative Studies in Society and History* (1979): 303–23. On backward-region secessionism, see Michael Hechter, *Internal Colonialism: The Celtic Fringe in British National Development, 1536–1966* (London: Routledge, 1975); Ernest Gellner, *Nations and Nationalism* (Ithaca: Cornell University Press, 1983), chaps. 6–7. Donald Horowitz synthesizes the two approaches, claiming that under certain

conditions *both* relatively rich and relatively poor minorities can be expected to mobilize for independence (*Ethnic Groups in Conflict,* chap. 6).

16. See Ted Robert Gurr, *Minorities at Risk: A Global View of Ethnopolitical Conflicts* (Washington, D.C.: United States Institute of Peace Press, 1993), 123–24; Ted Robert Gurr, *Why Men Rebel* (Princeton: Princeton University Press, 1971); Ted Robert Gurr and Will H. Moore, "Ethnopolitical Rebellion: A Cross-Sectional Analysis of the 1980s with Risk Assessments for the 1990s," *American Journal of Political Science* 41 (1997): 1079–103; Will H. Moore and Keith Jaggers, "Deprivation, Mobilization, and the State: A Synthetic Model of Rebellion," *Journal of Developing Societies* 6 (1990): 17–36.

17. Yoshiko M. Herrera, *Imagined Economies: The Sources of Russian Regionalism* (Cambridge, U.K.: Cambridge University Press, 2005), chap. 1. Using large-N logit analysis, James Fearon and David Laitin find that income inequalities between groups have no significant impact on the likelihood of internal conflict. James D. Fearon and David D. Laitin, "Ethnicity, Insurgency, and Civil War," *American Political Science Review* 97 (2004): 85.

18. Paul Collier and Anke Hoeffler, "Greed and Grievance in Civil War," *Oxford Economic Papers* 56 (2004): 563–95; Fearon and Laitin, "Ethnicity, Insurgency, and Civil War," 86–88.

19. For institutionalist accounts of secessionism, see Henry E. Hale, "The Parade of Sovereignties: Testing Theories of Secession in the Soviet Setting," *British Journal of Political Science* 30 (2000): 31–56; Svante E. Cornell, "Autonomy as a Source of Conflict: Caucasian Conflicts in Theoretical Perspective," *World Politics* 54 (2002): 245–76; Ronald Grigor Suny, *The Revenge of the Past* (Stanford: Stanford University Press, 1993); Yuri Slezkine, "The USSR as a Communal Apartment, or How a Socialist State Promoted Ethnic Particularism," *Slavic Review* 53 (1994): 414–53. See also Philip G. Roeder, "Soviet Federalism and Ethnic Mobilization," *World Politics* 43(1991): 196–232; Valerie Bunce, *Subversive Institutions: The Design and the Destruction of Socialism and the State* (Cambridge, U.K.: Cambridge University Press, 1999); and Gurr, *Minorities at Risk,* 76–82.

20. Suny, *Revenge of the Past,* 126.

21. Dmitry P. Gorenburg, *Minority Ethnic Mobilization in the Russian Federation* (Cambridge, U.K.: Cambridge University Press, 2003), 258.

22. Roeder, "Soviet Federalism and Ethnic Mobilization."

23. Philip G. Roeder, *Where Nation-States Come From: Institutional Change in the Age of Nationalism* (Princeton: Princeton University Press, 2007).

24. Bunce, *Subversive Institutions,* 32.

25. Susan Woodward's analysis of the breakup of Yugoslavia is a notable exception in that she traces the impact of IMF and World Bank interventions on nationalist movements in 1980s Yugoslavia. See Susan L. Woodward, *Balkan Tragedy: Chaos and Dissolution after the Cold War* (Washington, D.C.: Brookings Institution Press, 1995), 47–81.

26. In some cases (e.g., the South Tyroleans in Italy, the Basters in Namibia, the Azeris in Iran, and the Sikhs in India), demands for statehood were abandoned quickly because they lacked the credible threat of force and therefore were not taken seriously by their host governments. In other cases (e.g., minorities in Bosnia and Myanmar, the Uzbeks in Kyrgyzstan, the Jurassians in Switzerland, and the Moros in the Philippines), secessionist threats *were* taken seriously, and the groups were ultimately bought off, co-opted, or both. In still other cases (e.g., the Ibos in Nigeria and the Basques in Spain), secessionism was dealt with through brutal suppression. Governments can be seen to change their strategy from suppression to concessions

and back, in response to shifts in the perceived balance of power between the minority and the center.

27. For examples of these arguments, see Paul Brass, *Ethnicity and Nationalism: Theory and Comparison* (New Delhi: Sage, 1991); Valery Tishkov, *Ethnicity, Nationalism, and Conflict in and after the Soviet Union: The Mind Aflame* (London: Sage, 1996). The theory of ethnic outbidding was most famously articulated by Kenneth Shepsle and Alvin Rabushka, *Politics in Plural Societies: A Theory of Democratic Instability* (Columbus: Charles Merrill, 1972).

28. V. P. Gagnon, Jr., "Ethnic Nationalism and International Conflict: The Case of Serbia," *International Security* 19 (1994/95), 134. In a more recent formulation, Gagnon argues that Yugoslav elites who were threatened by calls for political pluralism and other reforms in the early 1990s used violence strategically as a means of reconceptualizing the political space around ethnic issues and thereby *demobilizing* popular movements for reform. See V. P. Gagnon, Jr., *The Myth of Ethnic War: Serbia and Croatia in the 1990s* (Ithaca: Cornell University Press, 2004).

29. Valery Tishkov, *Ethnicity, Nationalism, and Conflict in and after the Soviet Union, The Mind Aflame* (London: Sage, 1997), 210.

30. For example, societies recently traumatized by war or impoverishment are more likely to respond to the divisive politics of authoritarian leaders or firebrands who play on latent societal divisions to further the interests of a narrow constituency. Besides Weimar Germany, salient examples include postcommunist Romania, Slovakia, Croatia, and Serbia.

31. Posen, "The Security Dilemma and Ethnic Conflict."

32. Ibid., 118–19.

33. See James D. Fearon, "Commitment Problems and the Spread of Ethnic Conflict," in *The International Spread of Ethnic Conflict: Fear, Diffusion, and Escalation,* ed. David A. Lake and Donald Rothchild (Princeton: Princeton University Press, 1998): 107–26. See also Barry R. Weingast, "Political Stability and Civil War: Institutions, Commitment, and American Democracy," in *Analytic Narratives,* ed. Robert Bates, Avner Greif, Margaret Levi, Jean-Laurent Rosenthal, and Barry R. Weingast (Princeton: Princeton University Press, 1998), 148–93; Rui J. P. de Figueiredo, Jr., and Barry R. Weingast, "The Rationality of Fear: Political Opportunism and Ethnic Conflict," in *Civil Wars, Insecurity, and Intervention,* ed. Jack Snyder and Barbara Walter (New York: Columbia University Press, 1999), 261–302.

34. Fearon, "Commitment Problems," 108.

35. Similarly, the Bougainvilleans and Belarussians advanced separatist claims when their central governments were relatively weak—rather than strong and threatening—as a means of obtaining side payments from the state.

36. I am grateful to Valerie Bunce for this point.

37. Erin Jenne, "Secessionism as a Bargaining Posture: A Data Analysis of Secessionist Minorities in the Postwar Period," paper presented at the American Political Science Association conference, San Francisco, 2001.

38. See especially Doug McAdam, Sidney Tarrow, and Charles Tilly, eds., *Dynamics of Contention* (Cambridge, U.K.: Cambridge University Press), 2001. For more on political opportunity structures, see Doug McAdam, John D. McCarthy, and Meyer N. Zald, eds., *Comparative Perspectives on Social Movements* (New York: Cambridge University Press, 1996), chap. 1; Herbert Kitschelt, "Political Opportunity Structures and Political Protest: Anti-Nuclear Movements in Four Democracies," *British Journal of Political*

Science 16 (1986): 57–85; and Sidney Tarrow, *Power in Movement: Social Movements, Collective Action and Politics* (New York: Cambridge University Press, 1994).

39. Peter Eisinger, "The Conditions of Protest Behavior in American Cities," *American Political Science Review* 67 (March 1973): 11–12.

40. Tarrow, *Power in Movement,* chap. 5.

41. Mark R. Beissinger, *Nationalist Mobilization and the Collapse of the Soviet State* (Cambridge, U.K: Cambridge University Press, 2002), 36.

42. Fiona B. Adamson, "Global Liberalism versus Political Islam," *International Studies Review* 7 (2005): 554.

43. External patronage, in particular, has been shown to promote minority rebellion. In a large-N analysis, James Fearon and David Laitin find that the odds that a state will experience an insurgency increase if either the government or the rebels have access to "third-party support." Fearon and Laitin, "Ethnicity, Insurgency, and Civil War," 86. Another quantitative analysis shows that outside military assistance is a strong predictor of both radical minority claims and violent minority rebellion. See Erin K. Jenne, Stephen M. Saideman, and Will Lowe, "Separatism as a Bargaining Posture: The Role of Leverage in Group Claimmaking," *Journal of Peace Research,* forthcoming.

44. Clifford Bob, *The Marketing of Rebellion: Insurgents, Media, and International Activism* (New York: Cambridge University Press, 2005), 4. See also Margaret E. Keck and Kathryn Sikkink, *Activists beyond Borders: Advocacy Networks in International Politics* (Ithaca: Cornell University Press, 1998).

45. For more on the role of kin states in ethnic conflict, see Brubaker, *Nationalism Reframed;* Van Evera, "Hypotheses on Nationalism and War"; Posen, "Security Dilemma and Ethnic Conflict"; Stephen M. Saideman, *The Ties That Divide: Ethnic Politics, Foreign Policy, and International Conflict* (New York: Columbia University Press, 2001); Stephen M. Saideman, "Inconsistent Irredentism? Political Competition, Ethnic Ties, and the Foreign Policies of Somalia and Serbia," *Security Studies* 7 (1998): 51–93; David R. Davis and Will H. Moore, "Ethnicity Matters: Transnational Ethnic Alliances and Foreign Behavior," *International Studies Quarterly* 41 (1997): 171–84.

46. Timor Kuran, "Ethnic Dissimilation and Its International Diffusion," in *The International Spread of Conflict: Fear, Diffusion, and Escalation,* ed. David A. Lake and Donald Rothchild (Princeton: Princeton University Press, 1998), 48–49.

47. Alvin Rabushka and Kenneth A Shepsle, *Politics in Plural Societies: A Theory of Democratic Instability* (Columbus: Charles E. Merrill, 1972), 60–69.

48. Horowitz, *Ethnic Groups in Conflict,* 291–92.

49. Elise Giuliano, "Who Determines the Self in the Politics of Self-Determination? Identity and Preference Formation in Tatarstan's Nationalist Mobilization," *Comparative Politics* 32 (2000): 300.

50. Kanchan Chandra, *Why Ethnic Parties Succeed: Patronage and Ethnic Head Counts in India* (Cambridge, U.K.: Cambridge University Press, 2004), 12–13.

51. Jóhanna Kristín Birner, *Ethnicity and Electoral Politics* (New York: Cambridge University Press, 2006).

52. Class politics tend to be conducted through peaceful channels and rarely lead to violence. This may be because different classes or sectors (e.g., farming, manufacturing, banking) depend on one another for survival and therefore have an incentive to reach compromises that allow for peaceful coexistence. "Class cleansing" is also far less common

than ethnic cleansing, although it has occurred—as seen in the cases of the Khmer Rouge in Cambodia, Maoist China, and the Soviet Union in the 1930s.

53. Independent International Commission on Kosovo, *The Kosovo Report: Conflict, International Response, Lessons Learned* (Oxford: Oxford University Press, 2000), 2–3, 94.

54. Wesley Clark, "Overview," *New York Times,* 27 March 1999.

55. Alan J. Kuperman, "Provoking Genocide: A Revised History of the Rwandan Patriotic Front," *Journal of Genocide Research* 6 (2004): 61. See also Alan J. Kuperman, *The Limits of Humanitarian Intervention* (Washington, D.C.: Brookings Institution Press); Helen Fein, "Genocide: A Sociological Perspective," *Current Sociology* 38 (1990): 1–126; and Barbara Harff and Ted Robert Gurr, "Toward Empirical Theory of Genocides and Politicides," *International Studies Quarterly* 32 (1988): 359–71.

56. It may be argued that defining or naming ethnic groups colludes with the fiction of primordialism by invoking the notion of a stable and/or unitary being. I am sympathetic to this concern but do not believe that defining a group necessarily reifies it, as long as it is borne in mind that *all* social categories are fluid and contested and therefore subject to change.

57. This definition is drawn partly from Gurr, *Minorities at Risk,* chap. 1. While one or more of these criteria form the basis of ethnic identification in any given case, none is universally important across cases.

58. Zsuzsa Csergő argues that the domestic conditions in the Hungarian minorities' kin and host states were far more important than EU and OSCE conditionality in improving minority protections in the late 1990s. This provides further justification for considering the impact of these organizations only insofar as they changed the preferences of the main principals of ethnic bargaining-host states and lobby actors. See Zsuzsa Csergő, *Language, Division, and Integration: Lessons from Postcommunist Romania and Slovakia* (Ithaca: Cornell University Press, 2007).

59. The extremity of group demands is measured along a continuum, with secession or irredentism as the most extreme and relatively minor claims such as affirmative action as the least extreme. A complete discussion of this variable is given in chapter 2.

60. James Fearon argues that, when two states are in conflict, their respective reservation values—the minimum amount of a divided good that each state will accept in lieu of going to war—determines the bargaining range of possible negotiated settlements. Each side therefore has an incentive to convince the other side that its reservation value is close to its ideal point in order to induce a more generous offer from its opponent. In the context of intercommunal conflict, ethnic radicalization is one means by which groups credibly signal a high reservation value. See James D. Fearon, "Rationalist Explanations for War," *International Organization* 49 (1995): 379–414.

61. Ashutosh Varshney makes a similar point, noting that "[t]he standard research strategy, with some exceptions, has been to seek the commonalities across the many cases of violence. Although this approach will continue to enlighten us, it can give us only the building blocks of a theory, not a full-blown theory of ethnic conflict." Ashutosh Varshney, "Ethnic Conflict and Civil Society: India and Beyond," *World Politics* 53 (2001): 370–71.

62. E. J. Hobsbawm, *Nations and Nationalism since 1780: Programme, Myth, Reality* (Cambridge, U.K.: Cambridge University Press, 1992); Miroslav Hroch, "From National Movement to the Fully-Formed Nation: The Nation-Building Process in Europe," *New Left*

Review 198 (1993): 3–20; Ernest Gellner, "Nationalism," in *Thought and Change* (Chicago: University of Chicago Press, 1964), 147–78; Gellner, *Nations and Nationalism*.

63. Fredrik Barth, Introduction to *Ethnic Groups and Boundaries: The Social Organisation of Culture Difference*, ed. Fredrik Barth (Bergen/Oslo, Norway: Universitetsforlaget, 1969), 9–38.

1. The Origins of Ethnic Bargaining

1. Integrationist versus segregationist rights differ from the more familiar "rights" dichotomies: (1) individual versus group rights and (2) positive versus negative rights. In brief, the integrationist versus segregationist dichotomy refers to the rights of groups to integrate into majority society versus their rights to self-rule (usually on a territorial basis). In contrast, individual versus group rights refer to the rights derogated to individuals versus those that belong to the group as a whole. Meanwhile, negative versus positive rights refer to the rights to nondiscrimination versus the rights to benefits. For more on these two dichotomies, see Hurst Hannum, *Autonomy, Sovereignty, and Self-Determination: The Accommodation of Conflicting Rights* (Philadelphia: University of Pennsylvania Press, 1990); Will Kymlicka, *Multicultural Citizenship: A Liberal Theory of Minority Rights* (Oxford, U.K.: Oxford University Press, 1995).

2. Ann Swidler uses the term "tool kit" to describe the ways in which culture influences individual actions by "shaping a repertoire...of habits, skills, and styles from which people construct 'strategies of action' in pursuit of their material interests." Ann Swidler, "Culture in Action: Symbols and Strategies," *American Sociological Review* 51 (1986): 273. In the present context, minority leaders appropriate symbols and ideas from the global culture of minority politics in the process of bargaining with their respective centers.

3. This periodization is loosely adapted from Natan Lerner, *Group Rights and Discrimination in International Law* (Dordrecht: Martinus Nijhoff, 1991), 7.

4. *Integrationist* rights refer to the rights of minorities to equal standing in the majority-dominated society. These rights have been used to justify demands ranging from nondiscrimination to affirmative action to cultural or linguistic autonomy.

5. Stephen Krasner, a theorist of international relations, sees no real improvement in minority protections over the past 450 years. Indeed, he questions the value of minority rights themselves, arguing that they are effective only insofar as they are "self-reinforcing"— that is, insofar as they coincide with the interests of powerful states. See Stephen D. Krasner, *Sovereignty: Organized Hypocrisy* (Princeton: Princeton University Press, 1999), chap. 3.

6. Minority recognition as *domestic* policy has even earlier roots. In the 1500s, the Ottoman Sultanate divided the empire's non-Muslim population into four millets, which were given considerable local autonomy: Armenians, Catholics, Jews, and Orthodox.

7. Krasner, *Sovereignty*, 83.

8. Fred L. Israel, ed., *Major Peace Treaties of Modern History 1648–1967* (New York: Chelsea House, 1967), 978, Article IV.

9. Lerner, *Group Rights*, 7–8.

10. Nathan Feinberg, "International Protection of Human Rights and the Jewish Question (a historical survey)," *Israel Law Review* 3 (1968): 492.

11. Woodrow Wilson, *U.S. Congressional Record* 54, pt. 2, p. 1742, quoted in A. Rigo Sureda, *The Evolution of the Right of Self-Determination: A Study of United Nations Practice* (Leiden: A. W. Sijthoff, 1973), 20 n. 12.

12. *Segregationist* minority rights hold that groups are entitled to a degree of self-government when they have (1) a distinctive national identity and (2) legitimate grievances against the center due to past or ongoing discrimination. These rights have been used to justify demands ranging from territorial autonomy to irredentism or secession. Because they conflict—to a greater or lesser extent—with the norm of state sovereignty, segregationist rights are more controversial than integrationist rights.

13. Woodrow Wilson, address before the League to Enforce Peace; May 27, 1916; *U.S. Congressional Record* 53, pt. 9, p. 8854, quoted in Sureda, *Evolution of the Right of Self-Determination,* 20 n. 12.

14. Lenin, Critical Remarks on the National Question: *The Right of Nations to Self-Determination* (Westport: Greenwood Press, 1951), 76. This passage is excerpted from a thesis written by Lenin in March 1916 titled *The Socialist Revolution and the Right of Nations to Self-Determination.*

15. Jacob Robinson, Oscar Karbach, Max M. Laserson, Nehemiah Robinson, and Marc Vichniak, *Were the Minorities Treaties a Failure?* (New York: Institute of Jewish Affairs of the American Jewish Congress and the World Jewish Congress, 1943), 35.

16. Wilson made repeated attempts to insert an article on national self-determination into the League Covenant. In the end, however, he was overruled by those who contended that such a provision would be a constant source of political conflict—raising hopes for national independence that could never be fulfilled. The article was consequently omitted from the final draft. See Thomas D. Musgrave, *Self-Determination and National Minorities* (Oxford: Oxford University Press, 1997), 30–31.

17. See Lerner, *Group Rights,* 13; Robinson et al., *Were the Minorities Treaties a Failure?* 36–38. These provisions were generally reserved for territorially concentrated minorities.

18. The procedure for adjudicating minority disputes was laid out in the Tittoni Report of 1920, which provided that petitions, communications, and reports would be accepted from (1) members of the Council, (2) League members not in the Council, and (3) members of the minorities themselves; Robinson et al., *Were the Minorities Treaties a Failure?* 87.

19. *The League of Nations Official Journal,* July 1929, vol. 10, no. 7, p. 1144 n. 1.

20. The individual petitions—including those made by external actors on behalf of minorities—are too numerous to list here. They include complaints by the Ukrainians, the Ruthenians, and other minorities in eastern Galicia; the Germans in Poland and Czechoslovakia; the Albanians in Serbia, Greece, and Macedonia; the Poles in Lithuania; the Hungarians in Transylvania and Czechoslovakia; the Turks and Greeks in the population exchange between Greece and Turkey; the Jews in Hungary; and many others. See Edward A. Reno, Jr., ed., *League of Nations Documents, 1919–1946: A Descriptive Guide and Key to the Microfilm Collection,* 3 vols. (New Haven: Research Publications, 1973–75), 1: 55–91; Robinson et al., *Were the Minorities Treaties a Failure?* 133.

21. Otto Junghann, *National Minorities in Europe* (New York: Covici, Friede, 1932), 86.

22. Sitzungsberichte der Kongresse der organisierten nationalen Gruppen in den Staaten Europas [Records of the Congresses of European Nationalities], Vienna, 3, 49, quoted in Robinson et al., *Were the Minorities Treaties a Failure?* 253. By the early 1930s, the Geneva-based

organization could claim to represent approximately 27 million people in Europe (Junghann, *National Minorities in Europe,* 91).

23. Sitzungsberichte der Kongresse der organisierten nationalen Gruppen in den Staaten Europas 5, 63, quoted in Robinson et al., *Were the Minorities Treaties a Failure?* 256.

24. Robinson et al., *Were the Minorities Treaties a Failure?* 133–34.

25. League of Nations, *Report on the Work of the League, 1938–1939,* General 1939, 2, 29. Comparable figures for the 1920s are not available because the Minorities Section began to record the total number of petitions it received only in 1930.

26. This pattern provides further support for the hypothesis that power considerations play a key role in minority mobilization.

27. Norman M. Naimark, *Fires of Hatred: Ethnic Cleansing in Twentieth Century Europe* (Cambridge, MA: Harvard University Press, 2001), 108–24.

28. Steffen Prauser and Arfon Rees, ed., "The Expulsion of 'German' Communities from Eastern Europe at the end of the Second World War" (European University Institute, Florence: EUI Working Paper, 2004), http://cadmus.iue.it/dspace/bitstream/1814/2599/1/HEC04–01.pdf, 4, accessed May 2006.

29. C. Michael McAdams, "Yalta and the Bleiburg Tragedy," presented at the International Symposium for Investigation of the Bleiburg Tragedy, Zagreb, Croatia, and Bleiburg, Austria, May 17 and 18, 1994, http://www.ess.uwe.ac.uk/genocide/yugoslav-hist1.htm, accessed 18 May 2006.

30. Michael Clodfelter, *Warfare and Armed Conflicts: A Statistical Reference to Casualty and Other Figures, 1618–1991* (Jefferson, N.C.: McFarland, 1992), 2:953–57.

31. Both the UN Charter and the 1948 Universal Declaration of Human Rights give precedence to individual and state rights over group rights. In these and subsequent covenants, minorities were guaranteed protection only as individual members of minorities—groups themselves had no standing in the corpus of international law. Where they did exist, minority rights were generally limited to protection against nondiscrimination.

32. Antonio Cassese, *Self-Determination of Peoples: A Legal Reappraisal* (Cambridge, U.K.: Cambridge University Press, 1995), 37–38.

33. The framers of Article 1(2) did not intend it to give minorities the right to secede from a sovereign country, colonial peoples the right to independence, peoples in sovereign countries the right to choose their own leaders through democratic elections, or two or more nations in one or more sovereign countries the right to form a new state (ibid., 37–47).

34. Eastern Turkistan Republic 1944, UIGHUR-L Archives, http://www.taklamakan.org/uighur-l/archive/etr.html, accessed March 2002.

35. The Jura Independentist [*sic*] Movement website, http://www.multimania.com/mijura/en/history.htm, accessed March 2002, translation by Jonathan Terra.

36. Glenn T. Morris, "Nagaland: Still Fighting after All These Years," *Fourth World Bulletin* (April 1994), http://carbon.cudenver.edu/public/fwc/Issue7/naga-1.html, accessed April 2002.

37. Ibid.

38. Hannum, *Autonomy, Sovereignty, and Self-Determination,* 34.

39. Ibid., 46; W. Ofuatey-Kodjoe, *The Principle of Self-Determination in International Law* (New York: Mellen, 1977), 129–47.

40. Neil Mullan, "Mixed Message from Quebec Poll," *Socialism Today* 35 (February 1999), http://www.socialismtoday.org/35/quebec35.html, accessed March 2002.

41. "Political Aspects of Using the WWW and Technology for Native Hawaiian Self-Determination and Sovereignty," *Hawaiian Language, Literacy, and Technology* (2000), http://english.ohio-state.edu/people/lum.6/hl/political.html, accessed March 2002.

42. International Federation of Tamils, "Tamil Eelam Demand in International Law," paper presented at the Towards a Just Peace Conference, School of Oriental and African Studies, University of London, 1992.

43. Kurdistan Information Bureau, "Nationalism and the Kurdish National Liberation Movement," Cologne, Germany, March 1995, http://www.etext.org/Politics/Arm.The. Spirit/Kurdistan/PKK.ERNK.ARGK/pkk-nationalism.txt, accessed May 2006.

44. Territorially concentrated indigenous groups have sometimes used the discourse of segregationist rights to justify demands for territorial autonomy. In contrast, ethnoclasses—which tend to be territorially dispersed—have generally limited their demands to nondiscrimination or affirmative action.

45. Bain Attwood and Andrew Markus (with Dale Edwards and Kath Schilling), *The 1967 Referendum, or When Aborigines Didn't Get the Right to Vote* (Canberra, Australia: Australian Institute of Aboriginal and Torres Strait Islander Studies, 1997).

46. Pamela Burke, Blacks in Colombia (Afro-Colombians or Black Colombians). Minorities at Risk (MAR) data files, 1995, http://www.bsos.umd.edu/cidcm/mar/blkcol.htm, accessed March 2002.

47. Allison Brysk, *From Tribal Village to Global Village: Indian Rights and International Relations in Latin America* (Stanford: Stanford University Press, 2000), 68.

48. Rodolfo Stavenhagen, "Challenging the Nation-State in Latin America," *Journal of International Affairs* 45 (Winter 1992): 434.

49. Hannum, *Autonomy, Sovereignty, and Self-Determination,* 83.

50. Clifford Bob, The Marketing of Rebellion: Insurgents, Media, and International Activism (New York: Cambridge University Press. 2005), chap. 4.

51. Pamela Burke, Indigenous Groups in Mexico, MAR data files, 1995 (updated by David Quinn, 2000), http://www.cidcm.umd.edu/inscr/mar/, accessed March 2006.

52. Christopher Day, "The Zapatistas' Long March: Indigenous Rights and the Future of Mexico," *Freedom Road Magazine* 2 (Winter 2002), http://www.freedomroad.org/component/option.com, accessed March 2006.

53. See, for example, Robert Kaplan, "The Coming Anarchy," *Atlantic Monthly* 273 (February 1994): 44–76; John Mearsheimer, "Back to the Future: Instability in Europe after the Cold War," *International Security* 15 (Summer 1990): 5–56; Stephen Van Evera, "Hypotheses on Nationalism and War," *International Security* 18 (Spring 1994): 5–39.

54. Hurst Hannum, "International Law," in *Encyclopedia of Nationalism* (New York: Academic Press, 2001), 1:411.

55. Patrick Thornberry, "Introduction: In the Strongroom of Vocabulary," in *Minority Rights in the 'New' Europe,* ed. Peter Cumper and Steven Wheatley (The Hague: Kluwer Law International, 1999), 3. The full title of the covenant is the UN Declaration on the Rights of Persons Belonging to National or Ethnic, Religious and Linguistic Minorities.

56. Hannum, "International Law," 1:415; Gerd Oberleitner, "Monitoring Minority Rights under the Council of Europe's Framework Convention," in *Minority Rights in the 'New' Europe,* ed. *Cumper and Wheatley,* 71–88.

57. Adam Biscoe, "The European Union and Minority Nations," in *Minority Rights in the 'New' Europe,* ed. Cumper and Wheatley, 97.

58. Demetres Christopulos, "Minority Protection: Toward a New European Approach," *Balkan Forum* 2 (1994): 172, quoted by Adam Burgess, "Critical Reflections on the Return of National Minority Rights to East/West European Affairs," in *Ethnicity and Democratisation in the New Europe,* ed., Karl Cordell (London: Routledge, 1999), 49.

59. Maastricht Treaty on the European Union, *Official Journal* C 191, 29 July 1992, Article 128, No. 1, http://www.europa.eu.int/eur-lex/lex/en/treaties/dat/11992M/htm/ 11992M.html#0001000001, accessed April 2006.

60. Copenhagen Document, para. 35, quoted in Javaid Rehman, "The Concept of Autonomy and Minority Rights in Europe," *Minority Rights in the 'New' Europe,* ed. Cumper and Wheatley, 226, emphasis mine.

61. Article 11, Council of Europe Recommendation 1201, 1993, http://www.ciemen.org/ mercator/Ce9-gb.htm, accessed April 2006.

62. Ratko Mladić, quoted in Massimo Calabresi, "We Didn't Begin This War," *Time Magazine* 45 (August 28, 1995). The Krajina region was reincorporated into the Croatian state not long after this interview.

63. Nurdane Oksas, "Chechnya in Brief: Timeline of Significant Events Related to Chechnya," *Chechen Republic Online* (1997), http://www.amina.com/, accessed March 2002.

64. Bob, *The Marketing of Rebellion,* 178–79. See also Fiona B. Adamson, "Globalisation, Transnational Political Mobilization, and Networks of Violence," *Cambridge Review of International Affairs* 18 (April 2005): 31–49.

65. Jeff Delisio, email correspondence, April 26, 1995, quoted in Scott Crawford and Kekula Bray-Crawford, "Self-Determination in the Information Age," paper delivered at the Internet Society 1995 International Networking conference, Honolulu, 1995, http:// www.hawaii-nation.org/sdinfoage.html, accessed April 2002.

66. Ka Lahui Hawai'i, member of the Unrepresented Nations and Peoples Organisation (UNPO), http://www.unpo.org/member.php?arg = 28, accessed April 2002.

67. Richard Griggs, "The Meaning of 'Nation' and 'State' in the Fourth World," Center for World Indigenous Studies, University of Capetown, 1992, http://www.cwis.org/fwj/ index.htm, accessed April 2002.

68. "What Is the UNPO?" Unrepresented Nations and Peoples Organisation, http:// www.unpo.org/maindocs/0201what.htm, accessed April 2002.

69. These virtual countries include the Republic of Jura (for Jurassians in Switzerland); Oromia (for Oromos in Ethiopia); and Shanland (for Shans in Myanmar). Significantly, the flags of some of the UNPO members are also those of their external lobby states. For example, the Hungarians of Romania display the Hungarian national flag, the Greeks of Albania have posted the Greek flag on their site, and the Kosovar Albanians have adopted the Albanian flag.

70. Ron Gluckman, "The Long Wait," *Asiaweek.com* (May 1, 1998), http:// www.asiaweek.com/asiaweek/98/0501/nat7.html, accessed April 2002.

71. Quoted in "East Timor: President-Elect Xanana Gusmao to Lead His People toward Full Independence," UNPO News (February–April 2002), http://www.unpo.org/ news_detail.php?arg = 01&par = 112, accessed March 2002.

72. Jason Burke, *Al-Qaeda: The True Story of Radical Islam* (London, U.K.: Penguin Books, 2003), 15–16.

73. Ibid., 99–100.

74. Using the Phase IV MAR data set, I conducted a descriptive analysis of trends in group protest over the postwar period. Using Quinquennial Protest Scores from 1945 to 1999, I code groups "politically active" if the group engaged in verbal opposition (petitions, posters, agitation), symbolic resistance (sit-ins, blocking traffic), or small to large public demonstrations (*Minorities at Risk Dataset Users Manual.1002,* 169). The data set and manual are available online at http://bsos.umd.edu/cidcm/mar/list.html.

75. These definitions are drawn from Ted Robert Gurr, *Minorities at Risk: A Global View of Ethnopolitical Conflicts* (Washington, D.C.: United States Institute of Peace Press, 1993), 18.

76. See Ted Robert Gurr, *People versus States* (Washington, D.C.: United States Institute of Peace, 2000), chap. 2.

77. Klaus Gantzel found a similar cumulative rise in the number of ongoing civil wars since World War II, suggesting that the mechanisms underlying civil wars and ethnic mobilization in the postwar period are related, if not the same. Klaus Jürgen Gantzel, "War in the Post–World War II World: Some Empirical Trends and a Theoretical Approach," in *War and Ethnicity: Global Connections and Local Violence,* ed. David Turton (Rochester, N.Y.: University of Rochester Press, 1997), 128.

2. The Theory of Ethnic Bargaining

1. Take, for example, minority behavior in Yugoslavia during the late 1990s. Despite numerous reports of official discrimination against the ethnic Hungarians in Vojvodina, the Hungarians did not mobilize against the Serbian authorities. The Roma also failed to radicalize against the Serbs even though they suffered severe discrimination. In contrast, the Montenegrins *did* radicalize against Serbia, in spite of their lack of clear grievances or security concerns.

2. See Rogers Brubaker, *Nationalism Reframed: Nationhood and the National Question in the New Europe* (Cambridge, U.K.: Cambridge University Press, 1996).

3. Ibid., 76.

4. See the introduction for definitions of these terms.

5. Donald Horowitz, "Irredentas and Secessions: Neglected Connections," in *Irredentism and International Politics,* ed. Naomi Chazan (Boulder: Lynne Rienner, 1991), 13.

6. By arguing that group claims serve chiefly as bargaining chips, I do not mean to suggest that members of minorities are not also interested in achieving these goals. However, the fact that group demands often shift radically from one year to the next indicates that demands are used mainly in a strategic capacity.

7. Donald Rothchild, "Collective Demands for Improved Distributions," in *State versus Ethnic Claims: African Policy Dilemmas,* ed. Donald Rothchild and Victor A. Olorunsola (Boulder: Westview, 1983), 172–98. While Rothchild posits a distinction between "negotiable" and "non-negotiable" demands, I would argue that *all* demands are negotiable. This is because demands reflect the group's prevailing bargaining position against the center, which itself is subject to change.

8. Steven Solnick, "Will Russia Survive: Center and Periphery in the Russian Federation," in *Post-Soviet Political Order,* ed. Barnett R. Rubin and Jack Snyder (London: Routledge, 1998), 59.

9. Rupen Cetinyan, "Ethnic Bargaining in the Shadow of Third-Party Intervention," *International Organization* 56 (Summer 2002): 657. Cetinyan's argument is similar to the one presented here in that group leverage is hypothesized to drive up group demands against the center. Strangely, however, Cetinyan's model predicts neither minority rebellion nor external intervention. Because he assumes that all actors perfectly anticipate the result of their actions, the group will ask for only as much as its host state is willing to offer. Therefore, there will be no overt conflict between the minority and majority, and, consequently, no reason for the kin state to intervene on the minority's behalf.

10. It is reasonable to assume that the larger the minority relative to the state, the greater its ability to exit or fundamentally alter the state framework. The minority's absolute size may matter as well—small groups are unlikely to mount extreme demands for political independence due to their inability to defend themselves militarily. For arguments concerning the correlation between group size and secessionism, see Alberto F. Alesina and Enrico Spolaore, "On the Number and Size of Nations," *Quarterly Journal of Economics* 112 (1997): 1027–56; David Friedman, "An Economic Theory of the Size and Shape of Nations," *Journal of Political Economy* 85 (1977): 59–77; Beth V. Yarbrough and Robert M. Yarbrough, "Unification and Secession: Group Size and 'Escape from Lock-In'," *Kyklos—International Review for Social Sciences* 51 (1998): 171–96. Territorial concentration, too, should limit the extremity of group demands. This is because territorially dispersed groups are insufficiently integrated—both economically and politically—for statehood. Monica Toft was the first to use the MAR data to identify a positive correlation between territorial concentration and ethnic rebellion (Monica Toft, *Geography of Ethnic Violence: Identity, Interests, and the Indivisibility of Territory* [Princeton: Princeton University Press, 2003]). See also Stephen Saideman and R. William Ayres, "Determining the Causes of Irredentism: Logit Analyses of Minorities at Risk Data for the 1980s and 1990s," *Journal of Politics* 62 (November 2000): 1126–44.

11. The model assumes that the actions in this game have strategic value as well. Both minority and majority elites have incentives to posture, rally constituents, make demands, and enact nationalist policies in order to attract constituent support and thereby weaken their political competitors. Because of this, both sides have an incentive to move down the game tree rather than reach a settlement at the outset of the game, in contrast to Cetinyan's model (see above).

12. According to Saideman, state leaders formulate their foreign policies largely in response to the interests of their domestic selectorate—those responsible for keeping them in power. If their constituents have strong ethnic ties to a beleaguered minority in a neighboring state, the government may extend support to the group (Stephen M. Saideman, *The Ties That Divide: Ethnic Politics, Foreign Policy and International Conflict* [New York: Columbia University Press, 2001], 22–26).

13. Cetinyan, "Ethnic Bargaining in the Shadow of Third-Party Intervention," 666–68; Will H. Moore and David R. Davis, "Transnational Ethnic Ties and Foreign Policy," in *The International Spread of Ethnic Conflict: Fear, Diffusion, and Escalation,* ed. David A. Lake and Donald S. Rothchild (Princeton: Princeton University Press, 1998), 98–100.

14. Milada Anna Vachudova, *Europe Undivided: Democracy, Leverage, and Integration after Communism* (Oxford, U.K.: Oxford University Press, 2005), 170–75; Judith G. Kelley, *Ethnic Politics in Europe: The Power of Norms and Incentives* (Princeton: Princeton University Press, 2004), chap. 6.

15. Lobby actor support is a joint function of its willingness *and capacity* to intervene on behalf of the minority. If the external patron is unable to intervene effectively, minority members are likely to discount its signals of support. State capacity is particularly important in the Sudeten German case (see chap. 3), which shows that Berlin's signals of nationalist intent were only taken seriously once Germany became relatively powerful vis-à-vis Czechoslovakia.

16. I assume that the minority prefers concessions to a liberal society due to its intrinsic vulnerability and consequent need for protection at the substate level.

17. The logic follows that x is a sign of y if x is evidence for y and y caused x. For example, high fever is a sign of sickness because high fever is in indication of sickness and sickness causes high fever. A person's high fever does not provide definitive evidence that the person is sick. The presence of a high fever does, however, increase the estimated probability that this is the case.

18. See Jack L. Snyder, *From Voting to Violence: Democratization and Nationalist Conflict* (New York: W. W. Norton, 2000), chap. 2.

19. See Arendt Lijphart, "The Comparable-Cases Strategy in Comparative Research," *Comparative Political Studies* 8 (1975): 158–77. Charles Ragin introduces several ingenious techniques to help deal with this dilemma; most of these involve analyzing cases as configurations of variables (see Charles C. Ragin, *The Comparative Method: Moving beyond Qualitative and Quantitative Strategies* [Berkeley: University of California Press, 1987]; *Fuzzy-Set Social Science* [Chicago: University of Chicago Press, 2000]).

3. A Full Cycle of Ethnic Bargaining

1. Named after a mountain range in North Bohemia and Moravia, the term *Sudeten Germans* originally denoted all Germans living in the Czech lands. Since World War II, it has come to mean all Germans residing within the borders of the first Czechoslovak Republic (Nancy Merriwether Wingfield, *Minority Politics in a Multinational State: The German Social Democrats in Czechoslovakia, 1918–1938* [Boulder: East European Monographs, 1989], xiv–xv). I have adopted the latter meaning for the sake of simplicity.

2. The extremity of group demands is measured as the extent to which they constitute a challenge to the existing state framework. See chapter 2 for an in-depth discussion of this variable and for definitions of specific claims.

3. Janusz Bugajski, *Ethnic Politics in Eastern Europe: A Guide to Nationality Policies, Organizations, and Parties* (Armonk: M. E. Sharpe, 1994), 294.

4. Czechoslovak census statistics from 1921, in *Twenty Years of Sudeten German Losses, 1918–1938*, ed. F. W. Easler (Vienna: Friedrich Jasper, 1938), 1.

5. It was thought that the unification of Austria and Germany would facilitate the annexation of the Sudetenland. The Allies ruled out such a union at the Peace Conference to prevent the reemergence of a revanchist German state.

6. Herman Kopeček, "Zusammenarbeit and Spoluprace: Sudeten German-Czech Cooperation in Interwar Czechoslovakia," *Nationalities Papers* 24 (1996): 67; "Němečtí průmyslníci proti Deutschböhmen" [German industrialists against the German Czechs], *Lidové noviny*, 9 Dec. 1918, 1.

7. Wingfield, *Minority Politics in a Multinational State,* 5. Bohemia and Moravia are the two historic lands that make up most of the territory of today's Czech Republic.

8. In the Bohemian Diet, for example, the big landowners (only a few people) elected 70 representatives, the chambers of commerce 15, the towns 72, and the rural districts 79. This meant that the towns (which were mostly German) had one representative per 11,666 people while the rural districts (which were disproportionately Czech) had one deputy per 49,081 people. Elizabeth Wiskemann, *Czechs and Germans: A Study of the Struggle in the Historic Provinces of Bohemia and Moravia* (Oxford: Oxford University Press, 1938), 29. Even after universal suffrage was implemented in 1907, the legislative bodies in the Czech lands were still weighted by property, giving the Germans political power significantly out of proportion with their actual numbers.

9. Ibid., 52.

10. Ibid., 82.

11. "Německý plán národního Shromáždění" [The German plan for a national assembly], *Lidové noviny,* 18 Oct. 1918.

12. "Čeští Němci a český stat" [Czech Germans and the Czech state], *Lidové noviny,* 19 Oct. 1918.

13. Wiskemann, *Czechs and Germans,* 83.

14. "Němci nám berou jižní Moravu" [Germans take south Moravia from us], *Lidové noviny,* 6 Nov. 1918.

15. "Německé zázemí v Čechách se vzdává," [German directorate in the Czech lands concedes], *Lidové noviny.* 8 Nov. 1918.

16. Quoted in Johann Wolfgang Bruegel, *Czechoslovakia before Munich: The German Minority Problem and British Appeasement Policy* (Cambridge, U.K.: Cambridge University Press, 1973), 30. Days later, Seliger recounted this episode in an impassioned speech to a German audience; Rašín's words were repeated throughout the interwar period by German orators seeking to incite nationalist fervor—always to great effect (Gregory F. Campbell, *Confrontation in Central Europe: Weimar Germany and Czechoslovakia* [Chicago: University of Chicago Press, 1975], 51–52). Rašín had actually been quoting the Austrian General Windischgraetz's famous rebuke to the Czechs after the failed Prague Revolution of 1848. That "their" words were now being used against them indicated to them that the Czechs intended to turn the tables.

17. Wingfield, *Minority Politics in a Multinational State,* 10–11. The occupation forces were recruited from Czechoslovakia's foreign *legionnaires,* who had fought on the side of the Entente after having deserted or been taken prisoner of war.

18. Wiskemann, *Czechs and Germans,* 95.

19. "Prohlášení Německo-rakouské republiky," [The declaration of the German-Austrian Republic], *Lidové noviny,* 13 Nov. 1918.

20. "Území československého státu" [The territory of the Czechoslovak state], *Lidové noviny,* 23 Nov. 1918.

21. "Prezident Masaryk armádám československým," [President Masaryk to the Czechoslovak army] *Lidové noviny,* 28 Nov. 1918.

22. Tomáš Garrigue Masaryk, *Cesta demokracie* [The path of democracy] (Prague: Čin, 1933), 20. Calling the Sudeten Germans "immigrants and colonists" was hardly fair given that most Germans had roots in Czechoslovakia going back more than one hundred years. This speech was followed by a New Year's address in which Masaryk pointed out

that self-determination could not feasibly be applied to *both* the Slavs and the Germans and, further, that the Czech lands belonged to the Czechs and Slovaks by right of first settlement. In contrast, the Germans constituted not a nation, but rather a "colonising avant-garde" (50). Although this was meant to persuade the Germans of the justice of the Czechoslovak state and assure them of their rights within it, Masaryk merely succeeded in inciting further ethnic animosity.

23. Wingfield, *Minority Politics in a Multinational State,* xiv.

24. Ordinary Germans, too, stood to lose from annexation because their livelihoods depended on the success of Sudeten German industries, which were integrated into the Czechoslovak market. Second, Czechoslovakia had a far stronger economy than either war-torn Austria or Germany and therefore promised greater job security to its workers.

25. Their underlying ambivalence toward irredentism is evidenced by the fact that, after Czechoslovak forces had occupied the region, German industrialists were among the first to make their peace with the authorities (Campbell, *Confrontation in Central Europe,* 51).

26. "Nazdar Německé vzpoury" [Goodbye German rallies], *Lidové noviny,* 5 March 1919; "Útok na české vojáky" [An attack on the Czech soldiers], *Lidové noviny,* 6 March 1919.

27. Wiskemann, *Czechs and Germans,* 85; Bruegel, *Czechoslovakia before Munich,* 34–35.

28. Bruegel, *Czechoslovakia before Munich,* 31.

29. "Rakousko se nesmí připojit k Německu" [Austria must not be united with Germany], *Lidové noviny,* 5 May 1919.

30. "Přehled volebních výsledků v Čechách a na Moravě" [An overview of election results in Bohemia and Moravia], *Lidové noviny,* 4 July 1919.

31. "Německý stát v československé republice" [A German state in the Czechoslovak Republic], *Lidové noviny,* 1 July 1919.

32. Campbell, *Confrontation in Central Europe,* 72. It is quite likely that Austria's territorial claims on Czechoslovakia were at least partly intended to improve its bargaining position with Prague—Austria could later cede these claims in return for favorable terms of trade with its more industrialized neighbor.

33. Quoted in "Slezští Němci a mírové podmínky Rakouska" [Silesian Germans and Austria's peace conditions], *Lidové noviny,* 11 June 1919. An early agitator for Sudeten irredentism, Rudolf Lodgman fled the country when Czechoslovak forces occupied Reichenberg (Liberec), the seat of his territorial government. Lodgman and his deputies first traveled to Germany (which refused him succor) and finally settled in Vienna, where he continued to campaign in exile for the annexation of the Sudetenland. Despite this setback, Lodgman remained active in Sudeten politics—declaring the Czechoslovak occupation "illegal" and calling on ethnic Germans to resist the Czech government.

34. Minority leaders began to scale back their demands in spring 1919 as it became increasingly obvious that their lobby states were unable to support a movement for Sudeten irredentism. Sudeten German calls for irredentism were abruptly curtailed once the signing of the 1919 peace treaties ruled this out as a possibility.

35. "Nač se Němci v Čechách připravují?" [What are the Germans in the Czech lands preparing for?], *Lidové noviny,* 3 May 1919 (emphasis added).

36. "Naši Němci o rozhodnutí konference" [Our Germans on the conference decision] *Lidové noviny,* 11 May 1919.

37. Bugajski, *Ethnic Politics in Eastern Europe,* 295.

38. Wiskemann, *Czechs and Germans,* 92–93. The Minority Treaty was part of the Treaty of Versailles under which central European countries recognized one another's borders and promised to respect one another's sovereignty. Czechoslovakia's Minority Treaty (later enshrined in the constitution) was actually much broader in scope than what the Allies had required, promising equal treatment of all Czechoslovak citizens without regard to birth, nationality, race, or religion. *Národní shromáždění Republiky československé v prvém desítiletí* [National Assembly of the Czechoslovak Republic in the first ten years] (Prague: Government Printing Press, 1928), 403, 482–86.

39. Wiskemann, *Czechs and Germans,* 118.

40. *Negativism* (as opposed to *activism*) referred to the Sudeten German stance of noncooperation with the Czechoslovak government.

41. Campbell, *Confrontation in Central Europe,* 82–83.

42. Proponents of the reform defended it on the grounds that it would increase the efficiency of land use. A key underlying motive was to destroy the power of the old Austrian nobility and simultaneously create a large class of farmers that would be loyal to the new state (Antonin Pavel, "Land Reform," in *Czechoslovakia: A Survey of Economic and Social Conditions,* ed. Josef Gruber [New York: Macmillan, 1924], 49).

43. F. W. Essler, *Twenty Years of Sudeten German Losses, 1918–1938* (Vienna: Friedrich Jasper, 1938), 18. German nationalists believed that the intent of the reform was to dilute German landholdings in the Sudetenland as a means of consolidating state control over the border regions. Although there may be some truth to this, the government did not redistribute the land on the basis of ethnicity but, rather, according to individual wealth.

44. What a Czechoslovak language meant in practice was not immediately clear because the Czech and Slovak languages were distinct, albeit very similar. At the time, it was thought that some laws and official correspondence would be written in Slovak and others in Czech and that ultimately the two languages would converge. The Czechs defended this reform on the grounds of practicality. However, the Germans believed that it intentionally privileged the language of one minority (Slovaks) over that of another (Germans) as a means of demoting Germans to second-class citizens. This was all the more objectionable because the Germans actually outnumbered the Slovaks. Harry Klepetar, ed., *Der Sprachenkampf in den Sudetenlandern* (Prague: Strache, 1930).

45. Laws on census-taking became highly politicized during this period because population statistics determined the designation of minority districts where members of linguistic minorities would be allowed to use their native language in public life.

46. Largely as a result of this law, almost half of all German civil servants (excluding teachers) lost their jobs between 1921 and 1930 (Campbell, *Confrontation in Central Europe,* 82).

47. *Národní shromáždění,* 482–83.

48. "Poslední zprávy, Němci v Čechách budou 'osvobozeni'" [Latest news: Germans in the Czech lands will be 'liberated'], *Lidové Noviny,* 22 Nov. 1919 (emphasis added).

49. Wingfield, *Minority Politics in a Multinational State,* 14–15.

50. Josef Seliger, a prominent Social Democratic delegate in the *Reichsrat* and architect of the Sudetenland's provisional governments in 1918, was the first chairman of the DSAP party.

51. Wingfield, *Minority Politics in a Multinational State,* 14–15.

52. According to the 1921 census, the ratio of Czech, German, and Slovak deputies corresponded almost exactly to the ethnic ratio in the state as a whole. This shows that

individuals voted in accordance with their ethnic identity (Campbell, *Confrontation in Central Europe*, 84).

53. Oskar Krejčí, *Kniha o volbách* [The book on elections] (Prague: Victoria Publishing, 1994), 135–36.

54. The German and Czech Social Democrats had a history of collaboration in the prewar era. For example, the two parties had worked together in the early part of the century to broaden the empire's electoral franchise to the nonpropertied working class (Wiskemann, *Czechs and Germans*, 37–39).

55. The Social Democrats took the reins of government after their resounding victory in the June 1919 communal elections.

56. The electoral success of the socialists was consistent with the larger pattern of Bolshevization in the region; this was driven in turn by economic hardship as well as the rising influence of revolutionary ideology emanating from Russia.

57. Johann Wolfgang Brügel, *Tschechen und Deutsche, 1918–1938* (Munich: Nymphenburger Verlagshandlung, 1967), 147–48; Ferdinand Peroutka, ed., *Budování státu* (Prague: F. Borový, 1920–1921), 3:1280–83.

58. Charles Hoch, *The Political Parties in Czechoslovakia* (Prague: Orbis, 1936), insert.

59. *Národní shromáždění*, 218–19.

60. Peroutka, *Budování státu*, 3:1109–10. Despite his outspoken hostility, Lodgman had greatly moderated his position toward the Czechoslovak government. Once the leading proponent of Sudeten irredentism and armed resistance, Lodgman had returned from self-imposed exile and was now heading the bloc of German bourgeois parties in parliament. This demonstrates the crucial impact that perceived minority leverage has on the positions of minority elites.

61. *Národní shromáždění*, 207–8; Wingfield, *Minority Politics in a Multinational State*, 19.

62. Wingfield, *Minority Politics in a Multinational State*, 19–20.

63. Infighting in the Social Democratic Party intensified during this period—particularly over whether it should join the communist Third International. In the end, the leftists declared themselves the true leaders of the Social Democratic Party and occupied the party's headquarters in Prague. This led to a party split when the right-wing leadership wrested control of the headquarters away from the Marxists, expelling fifteen members from the organization (ibid., 21).

64. Wingfield, *Minority Politics in a Multinational State*, 25–27; Campbell, *Confrontation in Central Europe*, 85–86.

65. Peroutka, *Budování státu*, 3:1510–11; *Národní Shromáždění*, 254–55.

66. Peroutka, *Budování státu*, 3:1518–20.

67. Ibid., 3:1610.

68. Hans Singule, *Der Staat Masaryks* (Berlin: Freiheitsverlag, 1937), 40; Campbell, *Confrontation in Central Europe*, 156.

69. Peroutka, *Budování státu*, 3:1610.

70. Campbell, *Confrontation in Central Europe*, 157.

71. Ibid., 158; *Národní shromáždění*, 1190–91.

72. Wingfield, *Minority Politics in a Multinational State*, 60–62.

73. Beneš resigned from his position as premier in October 1922 to devote more energy to his role as foreign minister. Antonín Švehla, the Agrarian Party leader, then assumed the premiership, preserving the all-national governing coalition, much to the chagrin of the

German Agrarians and Populists who had hoped to join the new ruling coalition. Despite fresh overtures to Sudeten German leaders and Švehla's conciliatory attitude toward national minorities, the Czechoslovak parties still rejected inter-ethnic government.

74. Campbell, *Confrontation in Central Europe,* 161.

75. Ibid., 142–43.

76. Kopeček, "Zusammenarbeit and Spoluprace," 69.

77. Campbell, *Confrontation in Central Europe,* 186.

78. Ibid., 167.

79. Ibid., 164.

80. Bertold Spuler, ed., *Regenten und Regierungen der Welt* (Bielefeld: A. G. Ploetz, 1953), 512–13.

81. Kopeček, "Zusammenarbeit and Spoluprace," 70.

82. *Národní shromáždění,* 374.

83. Ibid., 1192.

84. Josef Chmelař, *Political Parties in Czechoslovakia* (Prague: Orbis Library, 1926), 70–71.

85. Campbell, *Confrontation in Central Europe,* 204.

86. Ibid., 203–4.

87. Ibid., 202.

88. *Národní Shromáždění,* 1196.

89. Wingfield, *Minority Politics in a Multinational State,* 82–83.

90. The other negativist party, the German Nationals, failed even to gain enough votes to enter parliament.

91. Gustav Beuer, *Berlin or Prague? The Germans of Czechoslovakia at the Cross-Roads* (London: Lofox, 1944), 25–26.

92. See Bruegel, *Czechoslovakia before Munich;* Bohumil Bílek, *Fifth Column at Work* (London: Trinity Press, 1945).

93. Campbell, *Confrontation in Central Europe,* 211–12.

94. Milan Hodža, *Federation in Central Europe* (London: Jarrold's, 1942), 103–7. For a detailed discussion of the 1930s economic crisis and its relative impact on the German and Czech communities, see Wiskemann, *Czechs and Germans,* chap. 13; Campbell, *Confrontation in Central Europe,* 254–64.

95. Richard Freund, *Watch Czechoslovakia!* (London: Thomas Nelson and Sons, 1937), 59.

96. Wiskemann, *Czechs and Germans,* 165.

97. Ibid., 166–67.

98. *Annuaire statistique de la République Tchécoslovaque* (Prague: Orbis, 1935), 125, quoted in Campbell, *Confrontation in Central Europe,* 258. See also Freund, *Watch Czechoslovakia!* 58.

99. Franz Koegler, *Oppressed Minority?* (London: Hutchinson, 1943), 21. See also Beuer, *Berlin or Prague?* 34; Campbell, *Confrontation in Central Europe,* 258–59.

100. The German nationalists also claimed that minority contributions to the state budget exceeded federal outlays to Sudeten areas, a charge Premier Hodža took pains to refute (Hodža, *Federation in Central Europe,* 140–41). Such claims were also made—with less success—by Moravian nationalists in postcommunist Czechoslovakia (see chap. 5).

101. Ibid., 140.

102. Wingfield, *Minority Politics in a Multinational State,* 121.

103 Stripped of their preferential access to central European markets and entangled in Czechoslovakia's financial and export crises, Sudeten capitalists began to view the economic resurgence in the Reich with envy. They therefore set out to finance a parallel fascist movement in the Sudetenland in hopes of annexation by Germany or economic concessions from the government (Beuer, *Berlin or Prague?* 34–35).

104. Freund, *Watch Czechoslovakia!* 61.

105. Rudolf Jahn, *Konrad Henlein spricht: Reden zur politischen Volksbewegung der Sudetendeutschen* (Karlsbad: Karl H. Frank, 1937), 19. (This is a compilation of Konrad Henlein's public addresses.)

106. Ibid., 103.

107. Beuer, *Berlin or Prague?* 35.

108. Some have contended that Henlein plotted with Hitler to destroy Czechoslovakia, citing as evidence Henlein's public statements in which he described how he had duped the Czechoslovak leaders into accepting the *Heimatfront* as a democratic organization (see Bruegel, *Czechoslovakia before Munich*). However, given that Henlein made these statements during and immediately after the Nazi takeover, it is likely that he exaggerated his duplicity in order to assure his constituents—and any Nazi leaders still skeptical about his commitment to the Reich—that he had been an *Anschluss* enthusiast from the beginning.

109. This argument is made by Brügel, *Tschechen und Deutsche 1918–1938* and *Czechoslovakia before Munich;* Campbell, *Confrontation in Central Europe.*

110. Ronald M. Smelser, *The Sudeten German Problem, 1933–1938* (Middletown, Conn.: Wesleyan University Press, 1975), 57.

111. See ibid., chaps. 4–6, for a detailed discussion of the factional strife in the Henlein movement as well as the ways in which the German government intervened to influence the outcome of these struggles.

112. Ibid., 71.

113 Ibid., 72.

114. Bundesarchiv, Koblenz, Schumacher Sammlung, 313, quoted in ibid. Hitler's lack of genuine concern for the German minorities is evidenced by his failure to speak out against the cultural assimilation faced by ethnic Germans in Italy during this time.

115. Jahn, *Konrad Henlein spricht,* 103.

116. Beuer, *Berlin or Prague?* 36. The *Heimatfront* changed its name to the Sudeten German Party after the government reluctantly allowed the organization to run in the 1935 elections. Masaryk made this decision based on Henlein's repeated assurances that he was committed to the Czechoslovak state and disavowed Nazism (Bruegel, *Czechoslovakia before Munich,* 121–22).

117. Oskar Krejčí, *Kniha o volbách* [The book on elections] (Prague: Victoria, 1994), 135.

118. Smelser, *Sudeten German Problem, 1933–1938,* 132.

119. See Jahn, *Konrad Henlein spricht,* 22–41; quotation from Bruegel, *Czechoslovakia before Munich,* 118.

120. Beuer, *Berlin or Prague?* 36.

121. Brügel, *Tschechen und Deutsche,* 266–67.

122. Smelser, *Sudeten German Problem, 1933–1938,* 146.

123. Hitler ultimately rejected the proposal because he did not want to limit Germany's options for future territorial expansion.

124. Smelser, *Sudeten German Problem, 1933–1938,* 154–55.

125. Ibid., 155–56.

126. Ibid., 128–29; see also chap. 8 for an account of *Schutzstaffel* (SS) infiltration of the agencies of the German government.

127. Ibid., 204; Bruegel, *Czechoslovakia before Munich,* 158–59.

128. Bruegel, *Czechoslovakia before Munich,* 159–60.

129. Smelser, *Sudeten German Problem, 1933–1938,* 206.

130. Hodža, *Federation in Central Europe,* 143.

131. Wingfield, *Minority Politics in a Multinational State,* 150–51.

132. The SdP declared that although the memorandum was an inadequate solution to Sudeten German problems, it would not obstruct its implementation (Hodža, *Federation in Central Europe,* 145). In this way, the SdP could take credit for the successes of the German activists while remaining in opposition.

133. Ibid., 144.

134. Freund, *Watch Czechoslovakia!* 75.

135. Alexander Henderson, *Eyewitness in Czecho-slovakia* (London: George G. Harrap, 1939), 82–84; Smelser, *Sudeten German Problem, 1933–1938,* 214. On February 20, Hitler spoke for the first time about the "plight" of Germans abroad. The Sudeten Germans interpreted his speech as a definitive commitment to support the minority against the Czechoslovak government. This complicated Henlein's task of maintaining discipline within the party while continuing to negotiate with the Czechoslovak government (Smelser, *Sudeten German Problem, 1933–1938,* 221).

136. Hodža, *Federation in Central Europe,* 152–53.

137. Smelser, *Sudeten German Problem, 1933–1938,* 222.

138. Hodža, *Federation in Central Europe,* 147.

139. Ibid., 148.

140. For a detailed account of the cat-and-mouse game played by the SdP leadership from 1936 to 1938, see Henderson, *Eyewitness in Czecho-slovakia,* chap. 6.

141. Henlein's meeting with Hitler in March 1938 was his first real communication with the German leader—a fact that seriously undermines the argument that Henlein had worked closely with Hitler throughout the 1930s to facilitate the Nazi invasion (Smelser, *Sudeten German Problem, 1933–1938,* 217–18). Indeed, Hitler only became interested in the Sudeten Germans in 1938 (209), well *after* the formation of the Sudeten movement.

142. Henderson, *Eyewitness in Czecho-slovakia,* 84–85.

143. Ibid., 88.

144. Ibid., 90.

145. Ibid., 85.

146. Freund, *Watch Czechoslovakia!* 76.

147. In the weeks following the *Anschluss,* the German bourgeois parties (including the Christian Socialist and Agrarian parties) left the coalition government to join the SdP, extolling the virtues of National Socialism. The German Social Democrat and Communist parties were the last to join because their political positions were the least compatible with fascism. For a chronology of this stunning turn of events, see Gerhard Fuchs, *Gegen Hitler und Henlein* [Against Hitler and Henlein] (Berlin: Rütten & Loening, 1961), 215–20.

Czechoslovak political elites complained bitterly that this betrayal by their long-time allies demonstrated the duplicity of the Germans, who had proclaimed allegiance to the state while secretly plotting its demise. However, this "betrayal" must be evaluated in light of the growing untenability of German activism in the wake of the *Anschluss*.

148. Beuer, *Berlin or Prague?* 38.

149. Leopold Grünwald argues that only a minority of the Sudeten German population were pro-fascist zealots at the time of the German takeover and that the majority of Henlein's supporters waited hopefully for the tide to turn against Hitler's war machine (see Leopold Grünwald, *Sudetendeutscher Widerstand gegen Hitler* [The Sudeten German resistance against Hitler] [Munich: Fides, 1978], 12–14).

4. Triadic Ethnic Bargaining

1. The issue of Hungarian minorities was not completely dormant during the Cold War. In the 1960s, for example, Hungarian Premier János Kádár suggested that Hungarians in the diaspora could serve as "Bridges of Friendship" between the socialist countries. Indeed, Hungary was concerned about the treatment of its co-ethnics throughout the Cold War period. However, this interest was subordinated to the maintenance of good diplomatic relations with its neighbors. Hungarian minorities reemerged as a major political issue in 1988, when Ceauşescu stepped up his campaign of repression against ethnic Hungarians in Transylvania (see below). I am grateful for Stephen Deets for raising this point.

2. George Schöpflin has argued, for example, that language and education rights enable a minority community to exist and reproduce itself. Insofar as the Hungarian minorities constitute communities whose future in majority-controlled states is under threat, they are unlikely to compromise on demands for cultural or linguistic autonomy. See especially George Schöpflin, "Nationalism and National Minorities in East and Central Europe," *Journal of International Affairs* 45 (Summer 1991): 51–65.

3. Official languages confer material benefits on the native speakers of these languages at the expense of non-native speakers. Each group therefore has an incentive to obtain official status for its language in order to gain advantages in civil service employment, university admissions, and so on. See, for example, David D. Laitin, "Language Policy and Political Strategy in India," *Policy Sciences* 22 (1989): 415–36; Paul M. Sniderman, Joseph F. Fletcher, Peter H. Russell, and Philip E. Tetlock, "Political Culture and the Problem of Double Standards: Mass and Elite Attitudes toward Language Rights in the Canadian Charter of Rights and Freedoms," *Canadian Journal of Political Science* 22(1989): 259–84.

4. Joseph Rothschild, *East Central Europe between the Two World Wars* (Seattle: University of Washington Press, 1974), 155.

5. Edwin Bakker, *Minority Conflicts in Slovakia and Hungary?* (Capelle an den Ijssel, The Netherlands: Labyrint, 1997), 43.

6. There was an implicit agreement among socialist governments to refrain from criticizing one another's domestic policies in order to maintain solidarity within the communist bloc. See Gábor Kardos, "The Culture of Conflict: Hungary's Role in Resolving Ethnic Disputes," *World Policy Journal* 12 (spring 1995): 102; see also Robert J. Patkai, "Hungarian Minorities in Europe: A Case Study," *Ecumenical Review,* 1 April 1995, 218.

7. Zsuzsa Csergő, *Language, Division, and Social Integration: Lessons from Post-Communist Romania and Slovakia* (Ithaca: Cornell University Press, 2007), chap. 3.

8. Interview, Edit Bauer, former deputy chair of the Coexistence Party of Democratic Coalition, Bratislava, Slovakia, June 22, 1998.

9. *Lidové noviny,* 1 August 1990.

10. Interview, Kálmán Petőcz, Deputy Chair of the Hungarian Civic Party, Bratislava, June 23, 1998.

11. Jan Obrman, "Language Law Stirs Controversy in Slovakia," *Report on Eastern Europe,* 16 November 1990, 13–16.

12. The 1990 language law had few practical consequences for the Hungarians. The only other reform that adversely affected the minority during this time was the increased threshold for entering parliament. However, the new 5 percent threshold was intended to limit the number of small parties in parliament rather than discriminate against ethnic Hungarians.

13. Gáspár Miklós Tamás, "Új reformkor vagy új Horthy-korszak," in *Másvilág, Politikai esszék* [Otherworld, Political Essays] (Budapest: Új Mandátum Könyvkiadó, 1994), 156–57, quoted in Ignác Romsics, *Hungary in the Twentieth Century* (Budapest: Corvina Osiris, 1999), 439.

14. Interview, Bauer, June 22, 1998.

15. Martin Bútora Grigorij Mesežnikov et al., eds., *The 1998 Parliamentary Elections and Democratic Rebirth in Slovakia* (Bratislava: Inštitút pre verejné otázky [Institute for Public Affairs], 1999), 246.

16. Zsuzsa Csergő, "Beyond Ethnic Division: Majority-Minority Debate about the Postcommunist State in Romania and Slovakia," *East European Politics and Societies* 16 (2002): 3.

17. The Slovak and Hungarian Christian Democrats, for example, jointly sponsored legislation on religious issues. See Edith Oltay, "Hungarians in Slovakia Organize to Press for Ethnic Rights," *Report on Eastern Europe 22,* 1 June 1990, 24.

18. Interestingly, Vladimír Mečiar was himself a leading member of the PAV and from 1990 served as prime minister of a coalition government that included the IHI. He was ousted from power in spring 1991, at which point he left the PAV to form the Movement for a Democratic Slovakia (MDS).

19. Edith Oltay, "Hungarian Minority in Slovakia Sets Up Independent Organizations," *Report on Eastern Europe 2,* 16 March 1990, 19–20.

20. Interview, Miroslav Kusý, Chair of the Department of Political Science and Human Rights Education, Comenius University, and former PAV Member of Parliament, Bratislava, 19 June 1998.

21. Bakker, *Minority Conflicts in Slovakia and Hungary,* 52–53.

22. SOS Transylvania—Geneva Committee 1994, 7, quoted in ibid., 78.

23. Stefan Wolff, "'Bilateral' Ethnopolitics after the Cold War: The Hungarian Minority in Slovakia, 1989–1999," *Perspectives on European Politics and Society* 2 (summer 2001): 179.

24. Patkai, "Hungarian Minorities in Europe," 218.

25. Kardos, "Culture of Conflict," 103.

26. Quoted in Alfred Reisch, "Hungary's National Security and Its Ethnic Minorities," *OMRI Daily Digest,* 19 February 1992.

27. In 1990, 79 percent of the population favored associate status for Hungary in the European Community (*Magyar Hírlap*, 10 January 1991.) At the same time, 68 percent felt that Hungarian refugees from Romania were poor and "should be helped," while 78 percent of Hungarian citizens believed that the loss of Hungarian territories under the Treaty of Trianon was the "deepest historical trauma of Hungarian history" (György Csepeli and Tibor Závecz, "Conflicting Bonds of Nationality in Hungary: National Identity, Minority Status, and Ethnicity," *European Journal of Social Sciences* 5 [1992]: 77–94).

28. Alfred Reisch, "Hungary's Ties with Slovakia," *OMRI Daily Digest*, 24 July 1992.

29. Bakker, *Minority Conflicts in Slovakia and Hungary*, 64–65.

30. Miklós Duray, Coexistence Party Chair, even campaigned for the MDF in Hungary's elections (Soňa Szomolányi and Grigorij Mesežnikov, eds., *Slovakia: Parliamentary Elections 1994* [Bratislava: Interlingua, 1994], 209).

31. Besides this, the government also set up Duna Televizió, a Hungarian television station broadcast by satellite to Hungarian audiences over the border (Zsuzsa Csergő and James M. Goldgeier, "Virtual Nationalism," *Foreign Policy* 125 [July–August 2001]: 76–77; Ignác Romsics, *Hungary in the Twentieth Century* [Budapest: Osiris Kiadó, 460–61]).

32. Alfred A. Reisch, "The Difficult Search for a Hungarian-Slovak Accord," *RFE/RL Research Report* 1 (23 October 23 1992): 25–26.

33. Lynn M. Tesser, "The Geopolitics of Tolerance: Minority Rights under EU Expansion in East-Central Europe," *East European Politics and Societies* 17 (summer 2003): 509.

34. In late 1993, Hungary suspended treaty talks with Slovakia in protest of Mečiar's policies toward ethnic Hungarians. Even Socialist Leader Gyula Horn said at the time that he would sign the treaty only if the Hungarian minority were given regional autonomy.

35. Alfred A. Reisch, "Slovakia's Minority Policy under International Scrutiny," *RFE/RL Research Report* 2 (10 December 1993): 37.

36. Sharon Fisher, "Slovakia's Ethnic Hungarians Demand Autonomy," *OMRI Daily Digest*, 15 December 1993.

37. The three main Hungarian parties ran together as a coalition in the 1994 elections to ensure that they passed the new threshold for entering parliament (Bakker, *Minority Conflicts in Slovakia and Hungary*, 116).

38. Ibid., 213.

39. The most radical Hungarian party, Coexistence, enjoyed the greatest grass roots support during this time—serving as further evidence that the minority rank and file had radicalized (Soňa Szomolányi and Grigorij Mesežnikov, *Slovakia*, 208–9).

40. Jan Obrman, "Slovak Prime Minister Comments on Slovak-Hungarian Relations," *OMRI Daily Digest*, 29 April 1994.

41. Tesser, "The Geopolitics of Tolerance," 515.

42. Sharon Fisher, "Minorities in Slovakia," *RFE/RL Report*, 22 November 1994, emphasis added.

43. Interview, Kusý, June 19, 1998.

44. Judith Pataki, "Horn on Hungarian-Slovak Treaty," *OMRI Daily Digest*, 5 July 1994. Although pleased with the more liberal Slovak administration, Budapest maintained its original position that the rights of Hungarians must be guaranteed in the bilateral treaty.

45. Jiri Pehe, "Slovak Party Leaders' Pre-election Debate," *OMRI Daily Digest*, 19 September 1994.

46. Interview, Kálmán Petőcz, deputy chair of the Hungarian Civic Party, Bratislava, June 24, 1998.

47. Sándor Bordás, et al., *Counter-Proof: The Examination of the Slovak-Hungarian Relationship with Sociological and Ethnopsychological Methods in Slovakia* (Budapest: Nap Kiadó, 1995), 106.

48. Ibid., 49.

49. With elections in the fall and opinion polls showing Mečiar in the lead, Moravčík's party could ill afford to accede to Csáky's demand at this point for fear of alienating Slovak voters.

50. Martin Bútora and Thomas W. Skladony, eds., *Slovakia 1996–1997: A Global Report on the State of Society* (Bratislava, Slovakia: Institute for Public Affairs/Inštitút pre verejné otázky, 1998), 39–41.

51. Diana Némethová and László Öllös, "Hungarians in the Slovak Government," in *A New Balance: Democracy and Minorities in Postcommunist Europe,* ed. Monica Robotin and Levente Salat (Budapest: Open Society Institute, 2003), 124.

52. "Minorities Complain about Slovak Premier's Suggestion," *OMRI Daily Digest,* 12 September 1997.

53. According to a survey conducted in January 1997, 71 percent of Hungarians agreed that "The Hungarian minority has limited rights and possibilities for its development"—only 47 percent had agreed with this statement in 1994. A poll taken later that year revealed that 80 percent of Hungarians felt their situation had worsened since the 1994 elections. Zora Bútorová, ed., *Democracy and Discontent in Slovakia: A Public Opinion Profile of a Country in Transition* (Bratislava: Institute for Public Affairs, 1998), 152–53.

54. In early 1995, the EU announced that no state could gain admission before first normalizing relations with its neighbors.

55. Kardos, "Culture of Conflict," 105.

56. Interview, Kusý, June 19, 1998.

57. Sharon Fisher, "Ethnic Hungarians Hold Protests in southern Slovakia," *OMRI Daily Digest,* 30 June 1995.

58. Interview, Pál Csáky, Chair of the Coalition of Hungarian Parties, 1994, and Chair of the Hungarian Christian Democratic Party, Bratislava, Slovakia, June 23, 1998.

59. Interview, Kálmán Petőcz, Deputy Chair of the Hungarian Civic Party, Bratislava, June 24, 1998.

60. The three largest Hungarian parties merged to form the SMK for the 1998 elections in order to meet the new threshold requirements for entering parliament.

61. The SMK plan would re-divide the country into thirteen regions, one of which would be majority Hungarian. These regions were to have extensive powers over education, culture, and language. This plan became a point of contention in the post-1998 coalition government.

62. Quoted in Martin Bútora et al., eds., *The 1998 Parliamentary Elections and Democratic Rebirth in Slovakia* (Bratislava: Institute for Public Affairs, 1999), 251.

63. Ibid., 252. With over 9 percent of the popular vote, it appears that nearly the entire Hungarian population had voted for the SMK.

64. The SDK and the SMK had signed a pre-election agreement the previous year that paved the way for the inter-ethnic government. After signing the agreement, SMK Chair

Béla Bugár stated in satisfaction that "90 percent of the Coalition's program priorities have been included in the government program" (Ethan Frome, Hungarian Minorities Monitor, October 28, 1998, http://www.hhrf.org/monitor/).

65. Interview, Zoltán Kántor, László Teleki Institute Research Fellow, Budapest, December 1, 2003.

66. Eugen Tomiuc, "Hungary: Status Law Causing Dispute with Neighbors," *RLE/RL Newsline,* 4 October 2001, http://www.rferl.org/features/2001/10/04102001 123954.asp. The two most likely explanations for the status law are: (1) that Fidesz initiated the law to appeal to its constituents' nationalist preferences and (2) that the government wanted to ensure that Hungarians in the diaspora had no economic incentives to emigrate to Hungary once the country gained EU membership. Although there may be something to both accounts, the first is more plausible because concerns about immigration cannot explain why Hungarians in *Austria* (already an EU country) had been included in the original proposal. Moreover, the fact that Fidesz accelerated its efforts to push the bill through parliament in the run-up to the 2002 elections suggests that the law was more politically motivated.

67. It should be noted that Romania and Slovakia had already enacted their own status laws, which contained many of the same provisions they found objectionable in the Hungarian law.

68. Michael Shafir, "Orbán on Relations with Neighbors," *RFE/RL Newsline,* 21 December 1998.

69. P.B., "Czechs, Hungarians Look to Bring Slovakia Back into the Fold," *RFE/RL Newsline,* 12 October 1998

70. Quoted in Eugen Tomiuc, "Romania/Slovakia: Authorities Highly Critical of Hungarian 'Status Law,'" *RFE/RL Newsline,* 6 March 2003, http://www.rferl.org/features/2003/03/06032003164145.asp.

71. Eugen Tomiuc, "Hungary: Status Law Causing Dispute with Neighbors," *RFE/RL Newsline,* 4 October 2001.

72. In contrast, Zsuzsa Csergő argues that whatever influence outside actors had in this decision, the change in the status law occurred primarily because the more liberal Socialists had come to power in 2002 (Csergő, *Language, Division and Social Integration,* chap.3). While the change in government certain facilitated the amendment to the status law, it must be remembered that the law had been passed in 2001 with the support of almost every party in parliament (*including* the Socialists). The amendment therefore cannot be explained solely by a change in political leadership. Moreover, it is very possible that EU pressures were also responsible for bringing the more liberal government to power, as happened in Slovakia in 1998.

73. "Ditching the Diaspora?" *The Economist,* 4 September 2003.

74. Michael Shafir, "Autonomous University Faculty for Slovak Hungarians," *RFE/RL Newsline,* 18 August 1999.

75. Speech delivered to the SMK Congress in Komárno, November 1999, quoted in Némethová and Öllös, "Hungarians in the Slovak Government," 129.

76. The Hungarians received three other positions in the cabinet as well, including the Agricultural and Regional Development ministerships; these portfolios were especially important to the minority because the Hungarian regions of south Slovakia were predominantly agricultural.

77. Quoted in Michael Shafir, *RFE/RL Newsline,* 14 January 2002.

78. Balázs Jarábik, "Recent Developments in Slovak Political Life," in *A New Balance: Democracy and Minorities in Postcommunist Europe,* ed. Monica Robotin and Levente Salat (Budapest: Open Society Institute, 2003), 147–48.

79. Judith Pataki, "Free Hungarians in a Free Romania: Dream or Reality?" *Report on Eastern Europe,* 23 February 1990, 18–19; "The Timisoara Declaration," *Report on Eastern Europe,* 6 April 1990, 41.

80. "Timisoara Declaration," 41.

81. This represents a significant departure from Ceauşescu's policy of ethnic assimilation through the "systematization of settlements," under which numerous Hungarian villages were destroyed in the 1980s. For a discussion of Ceauşescu's policies toward Hungarians in Transylvania, see Rudolf Joó and Andrew Ludanyi, eds., *The Hungarian Minority's Situation in Ceauşescu's Romania* (Highland Lakes, N.J.: Atlantic Research and Publications, 1994). See also George Schöpflin and Hugh Poulton, *Romania's Ethnic Hungarians* (London: Minority Rights Group, 1990), 12–18.

82. Radio Bucharest, 5 January 1990, 10 p.m., quoted in Pataki, "Free Hungarians in a Free Romania," 21.

83. Wendy Hollis, *Democratic Consolidation in Eastern Europe: The Influence of the Communist Legacy in Hungary, the Czech Republic, and Romania* (Boulder: East European Monographs, 1999), 207.

84. Pataki, "Free Hungarians in a Free Romania," 19.

85. *New York Times,* 2 January 1990, quoted in ibid.

86. Interview, Tibor Szatmári, DAHR adviser on international relations, Bucharest, Romania, May 26, 1998. In the 1990s, the DAHR consistently obtained around 7 percent of the popular vote in national elections. Because ethnic Hungarians made up around 7 percent of the Romanian population, we may infer that the Hungarian minority voted as a bloc for the DAHR. This, together with the fact that its leaders were democratically elected and its platform established at the local level, means that the position of the DAHR should reflect prevailing minority preferences on the ground.

87. Pataki, "Free Hungarians in a Free Romania," 21 (emphasis added).

88. Schöpflin and Poulton, *Romania's Ethnic Hungarians,* 20.

89. Vladimir Socor, "Forces of Old Resurface in Romania: The Ethnic Clashes in Târgu-Mureş," *Report on Eastern Europe,* 13 April 1990, 36. It is quite likely that the *Vatra Românească* played a key role in the clashes, possibly with the support of the Securitate, which was then facing major budget cuts and institutional subordination to the army. According to most accounts, the Securitate bused in Hungarians and Romanians from surrounding villages, armed them with weapons, and provoked them to attack one another. After a few days, the Securitate intervened to restore order, thereby demonstrating the usefulness of an independent, well-funded secret service (interview, György Tokay, Minister for National Minorities, Romanian government, Bucharest, 2 April 1998). Events in Hungary may have also contributed to the conflict. Significantly, the attacks occurred just days after the anniversary of the 1848 Hungarian Revolution. With the borders now open, thousands of Hungarian citizens streamed into Romania to join their relatives in Transylvania for national celebrations. The Hungarian flag was flown in towns across Transylvania, lending credibility to warnings of Hungarian irredentism. To make matters worse, the candidates in Hungary's national elections were campaigning on promises to defend the Hungarian diaspora. The convergence of these events greatly increased the likelihood of conflict.

90. Tom Gallagher, "Vatră Românească and Resurgent Nationalism in Romania," *Ethnic and Racial Studies* 15 (October 1992): 582–83.

91. Carmen Pompey, "Decision on Education Protested by Minorities," *Report on Eastern Europe,* 6 July 1990, 46.

92. Gallagher, "Vatra Românească," 578.

93. Michael Shafir, "The Greater Romania Party," *Report on Eastern Europe,* 15 November 1991, 26.

94. A full text of the Romanian constitution can be found at http://domino.kappa.ro/guvern/constitutia-e.html#a18, accessed May 2006.

95. Quoted in Judith Pataki, "The Hungarian Authorities' Reactions to the Violence in Tărqu-Mureş," *Report on Eastern Europe,* 13 April 1990, 24. Radio Free Europe received a translation of the letter from the Hungarian Mission of the United Nations in New York.

96. Karoly Okolicsanyi, "Prime Minister Presents New Government's Program," *Report on Eastern Europe,* 8 June 1990, 22.

97. Alfred Reisch, "Hungarian Parties Seek to Reassure Romania on Border Issue," *Report on Eastern Europe,* 15 June 1990, 30.

98. See Alfred Reisch, "Primary Foreign Policy Objective to Rejoin Europe, *Report on Eastern Europe,* 28 December 1990; Karoly Okolicsanyi, "Relations with the European Community," *Report on Eastern Europe,* 26 July 1991.

99. Judith Pataki, "Ethnic Hungarians Contest Romanian Elections," *Report on Eastern Europe,* 1 June 1990, 40–43.

100. Romániai Magyar Szó, April 10, and June 7, 11, and 13, 1991, quoted in Edith Oltay, "The Hungarian Democratic Federation of Romania: Structure, Agenda, Alliances," *Report on Eastern Europe,* 19 July 1991, 32.

101. Quoted in Edith Oltay, "The Hungarian Democratic Federation of Romania: Structure, Agenda, Alliances," *Report on Eastern Europe,* 19 July 1991, 30.

102. Michael Shafir and Daniel Ionescu, "The Minorities in 1991: Mutual Distrust, Social Problems and Disillusion," *Report on Eastern Europe,* 31 December 1991, 30.

103. Aurel Zidaru-Barbulescu, "Romania Seeks Admission to the Council of Europe," *RFE/RL Research Report* 2, January 8, 1993.

104. According to a March 1993 poll, 27 percent of Romanians felt their country needed an "authoritarian, iron-handed leadership"; this was reflected in the Greater Romania Party platform (Michael Shafir, *RFE/RL Research Report,* 2 April 1993). In the 1992 elections, the nationalist PDSR and the two ultra-nationalist parties together garnered over one-half of the popular vote.

105. *Új Magyarország,* 20 February 1992, quoted in Edith Oltay, "Minority Rights Still an Issue in Hungarian-Romanian Relations," *Report on Eastern Europe* 20 March 1992, 17.

106. Ibid.

107. Alfred Reisch, "Magyar Ethnic Leaders from Romania Visit Hungary," *OMRI Daily Digest,* 1 March 1993.

108. Karoly Okolicsanyi, "Hungarian Official Says Autonomy Inevitable for Minorities," *OMRI Daily Digest,* 26 October 1994.

109. At this point, a factional split appeared in the DAHR. László Tőkés began to advocate more extreme separatist demands, claiming that "small steps" had yielded nothing but frustration for the Hungarian minority. Tőkés and other radicals asserted that "[b]y sanctifying compromise as part of the [DAHR] credo, . . . the moderates are not displaying realism but accepting the perpetuation of the existing situation" (quoted in Michael Shafir, "The HDFR Congress: Confrontations Postponed," *RFE/RL Research Report* 2, 26 February 1993).

110. The Democratic Convention was the main opposition bloc in the Romanian parliament, consisting of over a dozen parties. The DAHR joined the DC in 1991 but ran on separate candidate lists in the elections, enabling the DC to protect itself against accusations that it was allied with Hungarian revisionists (Hollis, *Democratic Consolidation in Eastern Europe*, 232–34).

111. Dan Ionescu, "Ethnic Tension Rises in Transylvania," *OMRI Daily Digest*, 7 December 1992.

112. Territorial autonomy would grant the designated group a degree of self-rule over a bounded territory, whereas communal autonomy would give the group a degree of self-administration in the areas of education and culture on a *non*-territorial basis. Communal autonomy is therefore more akin to cultural or linguistic autonomy than it is to territorial autonomy. I am grateful to Stephen Deets for this point. See Stephen Deets and Sherrill Stroschein for a discussion on the problems with implementing territorial autonomy (Stephen Deets and Sherrill Stroschein, "Dilemmas of Autonomy and Liberal Pluralism: Examples Involving Hungarians in Central Europe," *Nations and Nationalism* 11 [2005]: 285–305).

113. Shafir, "HDFR Congress," 38

114. Tom Gallagher, "Ethnic Tensions in Cluj," *RFE/RL Research Report* 2 (26 February 1993).

115. Michael Shafir, "Hungarian Minority Claims Stir Angry Romanian Reaction," *OMRI Daily Digest*, 11 August 1994 (emphasis added).

116. Michael Shafir, "Transylvanian Bishop Makes 'Alternative Reconciliation' Proposal," *OMRI Daily Digest*, 1 November 1995.

117. Michael Shafir, "Democratic Convention of Romania to Sever Hungarian Ties," *OMRI Daily Digest*, 10 February 1995.

118. Edith Oltay, " . . . While Hungary, Romania Continue to Disagree," *OMRI Daily Digest*, 17 March 1995.

119. Michael Shafir and Matyas Szabo, "Romanian President Meets with Clinton," *OMRI Daily Digest*, 27 September 1995.

120. Study on NATO Enlargement, 1995, http://www.nato.int/docu/basictxt/enl-9501. htm, chap. 1, para 6, accessed May 2006.

121. Michael Shafir, "Congress of Hungarian Minority Party in Romania," *OMRI Daily Digest*, 29 May 1995. The DAHR objected strongly to resolving the standoff by compromising on minority issues. At a party congress in May, Markó reiterated Hungarian demands for territorial autonomy and criticized Hungary and the U.S. government for undermining the minority's position.

122. Dan Ionescu, "Hammering on NATO's Door," *Transition*, 24 June 1996.

123. Edith Oltay, "Hungarian Debate on Treaties," *OMRI Daily Digest*, 23 February 1995.

124. Adevărul, March 9–10, 1996, in Ionescu, "Hammering on NATO's Door."

125. Michael Jordan, "Hungary and Romania Get an Offer They Can't Refuse: Make Up or Else," *Christian Science Monitor* 4 October 1996.

126. Interview, Tokay, 2 April 1998.

127. For a comparison, see Democratic Alliance of Hungarians in Romania, Documents, Cluj, 1994; Democratic Alliance of Hungarians in Romania, Documents and Brief Presentation, Cluj-Napoca, 1998.

128. Interview, Szatmári, 26 March 1998 (emphasis added).

129. Zsolt-Istvan Mato, "Romanian Coalition Conflict Continues," *RFE/RL Newsline*, 13 October 1998.

130. Micahel, Shafir, "Transylvania's Glass Still Half-Empty," *RFE/RL Newsline,* 15 August 1997.

131. Quoted in Eugen Tomiuc, "Hungary: Status Law Causing Dispute with Neighbors," *RFE/RL Newsline,* 4 October 2001.

132. Ibid.

133. "Viktor Orban, an Assertive Hungarian," *The Economist,* 2 March 2003; Monica Ciobanu, "Problems of Democratic Consolidation in Eastern Europe: The Case of Romania in Comparative Perspective (Part 2)," *RFE/RL East European Perspectives,* 20 August 2003.

134. Csergő, "Beyond Ethnic Division," 23–24.

135. The protocol included a promise to ratify the EU Regional and Minority Languages Charter by 2002, provisions to ensure that police officers in minority regions spoke the minority language, guarantees that national minorities would be represented in local and national governments, and provisions for the creation of new Hungarian faculties and research chairs at the Babeş-Bolyai University and other universities in Transylvania (Ana-Maria Dobre, "EU Conditionality Building and Romanian Minority Rights Policy: Towards the Europeanisation of the Candidate Countries," *Perspectives on European Politics and Society* 4 [2003]: 71, 80 n. 40).

136. Interview, Julius Rostaş, government adviser, Department for the Protection of National Minorities, government of Romania, Bucharest, 22 July 1998.

137. Some of these radicals left the DAHR to form the Székely National Council and the Hungarian National Council of Transylvania in 2003 with the support of nationalist organizations abroad. Their aim was to achieve "internal self-determination" and "self-administration" (territorial autonomy) for ethnic Hungarians—goals no longer championed by the mainstream leadership.

138. Zsolt-Istvan Mato, "Romania's Hungarian Democratic Federation Experiences Turmoil Again," *RFE/RL Newsline,* 11 July 2000.

139. Quoted in Eugen Tomiuc, "Hungary: Status Law Causing Dispute with Neighbors," *RFE/RL Newsline,* 4 October 2001.

140. Michael Shafir, *RFE/RL Newsline,* 22 December 2003.

141. Irinel Popescu, NPCDP, State Secretary to the Minister of Health, quoted in Dan Chiribucă and Tivadar Magyari, "Impact of Minority Participation in Romanian Government," in *A New Balance: Democracy and Minorities in Postcommunist Europe,* ed. Monica Robotin and Levente Salat (Budapest: Open Society Institute, 2003), 94–95.

142. Slovenskej republiky [Statistical Office of the Slovak Republic], in Adrian Smith, "Ethnicity, Economic Polarization and Regional Inequality in Southern Slovakia," *Growth and Change* 31 (spring 2000): Appendix, Table 4.

143. *Anuarul Statistic al României* [Romanian Statistical Yearbook] (Bucharest, Romania: Comisia Naţională pentru Statistică, 1997), 818.

144. Milada Vachudova writes that EU and NATO pressures contributed to ethnic peace in central Europe both directly, by encouraging illiberal governments to adopt more liberal minority policies, and indirectly by strengthening the hand of the liberal opposition, thereby inducing the emergence of more liberal regimes (Milada Anna Vachudova, *Europe Undivided: Democracy, Leverage, and Integration after Communism* [Oxford, U.K.: Oxford University Press, 2005], chap. 6). Judith Kelley, too, argues that the material incentives offered by international organizations induced domestic policy changes in these countries, noting that EU membership conditionality has had a particularly potent effect in this regard (Judith G. Kelley,

Ethnic Politics in Europe: The Power of Norms and Incentives [Princeton: Princeton University Press, 2004], chaps. 6–7).

5. Dyadic Ethnic Bargaining

1. Bohemia, Moravia, and Silesia are the historic lands that make up present-day Czech Republic. In addition to the Slovak and Moravian movements, there was also a very weak autonomy movement in Silesia after 1989. However, because the Moravian movement quickly absorbed Silesian regionalism, I do not deal with the Silesian movement separately here.

2. For accounts that focus on national consciousness and the legacy of conflict between the Czechs and Slovaks, see Carol Skalnik Leff, "Inevitability, Probability, Possibility: The Legacies of the Czech-Slovak Relationship, 1918–1989," in *Irreconcilable Differences? Explaining Czechoslovakia's Dissolution,* ed. Michael Kraus and Allison Stanger (Lanham, Md.: Rowman and Littlefield, 2000), 29–48; Zdeněk Suda, "Slovakia in Czech National Consciousness," in *The End of Czechoslovakia,* ed. Jiří Musil (Budapest: Central European University Press, 1995), 106–27; Jan Rychlík, "National Consciousness and the Common State (A Historical-Ethnological Analysis)," in *The End of Czechoslovakia,* ed. Musil, 97–105.

3. See, for example, Oldřich Dědek, ed., *The Break-Up of Czechoslovakia: An In-Depth Economic Analysis* (Avebury, U.K.: Aldershot, 1996).

4. Shari J. Cohen, *Politics without a Past: The Absence of History in Postcommunist Nationalism* (Durham, N.C.: Duke University Press, 1999), chaps. 5–6; Petr Kopecký, "From 'Velvet Revolution' to 'Velvet Split': Consociational Institutions and the Disintegration of Czechoslovakia," in *Irreconcilable Differences?* ed. Kraus and Stanger, 69–86.

5. See Kopecký, "From 'Velvet Revolution' to 'Velvet Split'"; Sharon Wolchik, "The Impact of Institutional Factors on the Breakup of the Czechoslovak Federation," in *Irreconcilable Differences?* ed. Kraus and Stanger, 87–106; František Turnovec, "Electoral Rules and the Fate of Nations: Czechoslovakia's Last Parliamentary Election," in *Irreconcilable Differences?* ed. Kraus and Stanger, 107–36; Allison Stanger, "The Price of Velvet: Constitutional Politics and the Demise of the Czechoslovak Federation," in *Irreconcilable Differences?* ed. Kraus and Stanger, 137–62; Eric Stein, *Czecho/Slovakia: Ethnic Conflict, Constitutional Fissure, Negotiated Breakup* (Ann Arbor: University of Michigan Press, 1997); Robert A. Young, *The Breakup of Czechoslovakia* (Kingston, Ont., Canada: Institute of Intergovernmental Relations, 1994); Jon Elster, "Consenting Adults or the Sorcerer's Apprentice? Explaining the Breakup of the Czechoslovak Federation," *East European Constitutional Review* (winter 1995): 36–41.

6. It is almost received wisdom that the Moravian movement failed because it was based on a false or contrived identity. However, this is belied by the fact that nearly half of the residents of Moravia declared themselves to be Moravian rather than Czech in the 1991 census. Moreover, the movement *was* taken seriously at the time—not only by the Czechs, who negotiated with Moravian leaders over regional autonomy, but also by scholars of nationalism, including Gurr and Bugajski, who warned of growing Moravian separatism after the revolution (Ted Robert Gurr, *Minorities at Risk: A Global View of Ethnopolitical Conflicts* [Washington, D.C.: United States Institute of Peace Press, 1993]; Janusz Bugajski, *Ethnic Politics in Eastern Europe: A Guide to Nationality Policies, Organizations, and Parties*

[Armonk: M. E. Sharpe, 1994], 298). The puzzle, then, is why the Moravian movement died out so quickly whereas Slovak nationalism continued to grow in strength, ultimately producing the Czechoslovak split.

7. For the purposes of this analysis, *political opportunity structure* is defined as an institutional opening in the state that changes the balance of power between the group and the center; here, opportunity structures include regime change and negotiations over the federal constitution. See Doug McAdam, John McCarthy, and Mayer Zald, eds., *Comparative Perspectives on Social Movements: Political Opportunities, Mobilizing Structures, and Cultural Framings* (New York: Cambridge University Press, 1996), chap. 1.

8. The Hungarian military began to mobilize along the Slovak border with the aim of regaining lost territory. Militarized conflict was averted when the Czechoslovak army made a show of force on the Slovak side of the border. See James Ramon Felak, *At the Price of the Republic: Hlinka's Slovak People's Party, 1929–1938* (Pittsburgh: University of Pittsburgh Press, 1994); Bugajski, *Ethnic Politics in Eastern Europe.*

9. During the interwar period, the interests of the Czechs and Moravians were basically aligned (see below). It undoubtedly helped that Tomáš Masaryk, the foremost proponent of the federation and its first president, was himself a Moravian.

10. Robert A. Kann, *A History of the Habsburg Empire, 1526–1918* (Berkeley: University of California Press, 1974), 464.

11. Carol Skalnik Leff, *National Conflict in Czechoslovakia: The Making and Remaking of a State, 1918–1987* (Princeton: Princeton University Press, 1988), 12–15.

12. Hugh Seton-Watson, *Eastern Europe between the Wars, 1918–1941* (New York: Harper and Row, 1962), 42.

13. Ibid., 20–24; Bugajski, *Ethnic Politics in Eastern Europe.*

14. Felak, *At the Price of the Republic,* 28.

15. In the course of the 1968–1969 federal negotiations, Moravian leaders began to call for a position in the federation as well. (Dr. Boleslav Bárta represented the Moravians in the talks and later played a key role in the post-1989 autonomy movement.) Although the Czechs and Slovaks were sympathetic to Moravian demands, they ultimately judged a separate status unnecessary because Moravian interests were believed to coincide with Czech interests.

16. The 1969 federal structure was the only reform to survive the Prague Spring. After the crackdown, regime hardliners preserved the federal constitution to secure Slovak support against reformers and dissidents (Bugajski, *Ethnic Politics in Eastern Europe,* 323–24).

17. Valerie Bunce, *Subversive Institutions: The Design and the Destruction of Socialism and the State* (Cambridge, U.K.: Cambridge University Press, 1999), 81.

18. See, for example, Leff, "Inevitability, Probability, Possibility"; Leff, *National Conflict in Czechoslovakia;* Rychlík, "National Consciousness and the Common State."

19. Viktor Knapp, "Socialist Federation—A Legal Means to the Solution of the Nationality Problem: A Comparative Study," *Michigan Law Review* 82 (April–May 1984): 1223–25.

20. Jaroslav Bohm, ed., *The Great Moravian Empire* (Prague: Czechoslovak Academy of Sciences, 1963); Lubomír E. Havlík, *Kronika o Velké Moravě* [A Chronicle of Greater Moravia] (Brno: JOTA, 1992).

21. Several books on Moravian history were published in the early 1990s. These consisted of narratives about landmark national events, national heroes who died defending the Moravian nation, Moravian culture and folklore, and so on. These writers (mostly Moravian

nationalists) agree that the Moravian identity was co-opted by Czech national elites in the twentieth century as part of the Czech nation-building project. They therefore set out to reclaim these symbols as a means of rehabilitating the Moravian nation. For examples, see *Za Moravu* [For Moravia] (Brno: Jednota Moravská, 1991); Jiří Pernes, *Pod moravskou orlicí aneb Dějiny moravanství* [Under the Moravian eagle aka the history of Moravianism] (Brno: Barrister and Principal, 1996).

22. Petr Daněk, "Moravian and Silesian Nationalities: A New Phenomenon in the Ethnic Map of the Czech Lands?" *Geojournal* 30.3 (1993): 250.

23. For a description of the Bohemian and Moravian diets under the Austro-Hungarian Empire, see Elizabeth Wiskemann, *Czechs and Germans: A Study of the Struggle in the Historic Provinces of Bohemia and Moravia* (New York: St. Martin's, 1938).

24. Jan Novotný, *O Bratrské družbě Čechů a Slováků za národního obrození* [On the brotherhood of Czechs and Slovaks during the National Revival Movement] (Prague: Státní nakl. politické literatury, 1959), 98.

25. Pernes, *Pod moravskou orlicí aneb Dějiny moravanství*, 225–26.

26. The Civic Forum also existed in Slovakia but did not play a major role in postcommunist Slovak politics.

27. Most state institutions were retained after the transition, including the Slovak veto in the federal assembly on issues of national interest.

28. Jon Elster, "Transition, Constitution-Making and Separation in Czechoslovakia," *Archives Europeenne de Sociologie* 36 (1995): 112.

29. Quoted in Eric Stein, "Post-Communist Constitution-Making: Confessions of a Comparatist (Part I)," *New Europe Law Review* 1 (1993): 446.

30. Ibid.

31. *Programové vyhlásenie občianskej iniciatívy Verejnost' proti násiliu a koordinačného výboru slovenských vysokoškolákov* [Declaration of civic initiatives of the Public Against Violence and the Committee of Slovak Students], document 18, 25 November 1989.

32. H. Gordon Skilling and Paul Wilson, eds., *Civic Freedom in Central Europe: Voices from Czechoslovakia* (Basingstoke, U.K.: Macmillan, 1991), 25, quoted in Abby Innes, *Czechoslovakia: The Short Goodbye* (New Haven: Yale University Press, 2002), 49.

33. For an overview of the Federal Assembly during this period, see Zdeněk Jičínský, "Political and Legislative Conditions for the Creation of a Democratic Political System," in *The 1990 Election to the Czechoslovakian Federal Assembly: Analyses, Documents, and Data,* ed. Ivan Gabal (Berlin: Sigma, 1996), 111–25.

34. The notable exception is the April 1990 "hyphen war" between Czech and Slovak deputies over the name of the new federal republic.

35. Marek Bohuszak, Vladimír Rak, and Ivan Gabal, "Political Climate before the Election—Attitudes, Preferences, and Expectations of the Czechoslovakian Public," in *The 1990 Election to the Czechoslovakian Federal Assembly,* ed. Ivan Gabal (Berlin: Sigma, 1996), 98–99.

36. Young, *Breakup of Czechoslovakia,* 10; "Jak jsme volili" [How we voted], *Lidové noviny,* 11 June 1990. Innes writes that whereas PAV leaders were mainly dissident idealists, SNP leaders were political entrepreneurs who capitalized on the growing nationalism in Slovakia to gain political power (Innes, *Czechoslovakia,* 49). The rising support for the SNP (until mainstream Slovak parties began to coopt their national message) testifies to the rapid change in the Slovak political landscape following the transition.

37. Quoted in Peter Martin, "The Hyphen Controversy," *Report on Eastern Europe*, 20 April 1990.

38. "Vzduchem i po zemi" [Through the air and on the ground], *Lidové noviny*, 5 June 1990. Public reaction to Havel's visit was mixed. In his public address in Komárno, he was continually interrupted by supporters of the SNP, who cried, "End the federation, Slovaks on your feet!"

39. "Aktuální problémy vzájemnosti" [Current problems of mutuality], *Lidové noviny*, 4 April 1990.

40. Peter Martin, "The Governments Present Their Programs, *Report on Eastern Europe*, 27 July 1990.

41. Following the name dispute, negotiations over the federation and other politically sticky issues were postponed until after the elections (Innes, *Czechoslovakia*, 53; interview with Petr Pithart in "První kroky k demokracii" [First steps toward democracy], *Lidové Noviny*, 24 January 1990).

42. Martin, "Hyphen Controversy," 15.

43 Jiri Pehe, "Growing Slovak Demands Seen as a Threat to Federation," *Report on Eastern Europe*, 22 March 1991, 1–6.

44. "Daň za slobodu" [The tax on freedom], *Lidové noviny*, 31 March 1990.

45. "Federální summit" [Federal summit], *Lidové noviny*, 9 August 1990.

46. *Svobodné slovo*, 7 October 1990, quoted in Innes, *Czechoslovakia*, 101.

47. Ján Čarnogurský, interview by Slovak journalist Slávka Jančíková, Bratislava, Slovakia, 22 April 2004. It should be pointed out that Čarnogurský, too, changed his stance in response to increasing nationalism on the ground. When polls showed that popular support for the pro-independence SNP had increased to 18 percent in September 1990, the Slovak Christian Democrats made more extreme demands for Slovak autonomy to compete for the radicalized Slovak vote (Young, *Breakup of Czechoslovakia*, 12).

48. ČTK [Czech news agency], 9 December 1990, quoted in Jiri Pehe, "Power-Sharing Law Approved by Federal Assembly," *Report on Eastern Europe*, 21 December 1990.

49. Quoted in Jan Obrman and Jiri Pehe, "Difficult Power-Sharing Talks," *Report on Eastern Europe*, 7 December 1990, 8.

50. Bernard Wheaton and Zdenek Kavan, *The Velvet Revolution: Czechoslovakia, 1988–1991* (Boulder: Westview, 1992), 164–68.

51. By September 1991, Slovak unemployment had edged up to 10.3 percent—against 3.8 percent in the Czech lands (Martin, "Rising Unemployment in Czechoslovakia," *RFE/RL Research Report* [17 January 1992]: 39). It is important to note, however, that Slovak nationalism had already taken hold in 1990, well *before* people began to experience economic hardship. This casts doubt on relative deprivation accounts of Slovak mobilization.

52. Interview, Fedor Gál, former PAV leader, Prague, 9 July 1998.

53 Institute for Public Opinion Research, cited in Sharon Wolchik, "The Politics of Transition and the Breakup of Czechoslovakia," in *The End of Czechoslovakia*, ed. Musil, 236–37.

54. Peter Martin, "The 1991 Budget: Hard Times Ahead," *Report on Eastern Europe*, 1 March 1991, 15.

55. Jiri Pehe, "Opinion Polls on Economic Reforms," *Report on Eastern Europe*, 25 January 1991, 5.

56. *Aktuálne problémy slovenskej spoločnosti* [Current Problems of Slovak Society], Institute for Public Affairs (IVO), Bratislava, October 1990 and May 1991.

57. Stanger, "Price of Velvet," 146.

58. Jiri Pehe, "The First Weeks of 1991: Problems Solved, Difficulties Ahead," *Report on Eastern Europe,* 8 March 1991, 8.

59. *Aktuálne problémy slovenskej spoločnosti.*

60. Ibid.

61. Ibid., 2–5.

62. ČTK, 10 September 1991 (emphasis added); Jan Rychlík, "The Possibilities for Czech-Slovak Compromise," in *Irreconcilable Differences?* ed. Kraus and Stanger, 56.

63. Sharon Wolchik, *Czechoslovakia in Transition: Politics, Economics and Society* (London: Pinter, 1991), 124–25.

64. Young, *Breakup of Czechoslovakia,* 33.

65. Interview, Jan Kalvoda, Prague, 7 July 1998.

66. Young, *Breakup of Czechoslovakia,* 31; Stanger, "Price of Velvet," 146.

67. Stanger, "Price of Velvet," 148 (emphasis added).

68. *Foreign Broadcast Information Service Daily Report, Eastern Europe* (14 February 1992), 14.

69. Stanger, "Price of Velvet," 150.

70. Carol Skalnik Leff, *The Czech and Slovak Republics: Nation versus State* (Boulder: Westview, 1997), 130–31.

71. Jiri Pehe, "Czechoslovakia's Changing Political Spectrum," *RFE/RL Research Report* (31 January 1992): 6.

72. Jan Obrman, "The Czechoslovak Elections: A Guide to the Parties," *RFE/RL Research Report* (29 May 1992): 12.

73. According to opinion polls conducted in the second half of 1991, support for the PAV had dropped to 3–6 percent (Pehe, "Czechoslovakia's Changing Political Spectrum," 4). The CF disappeared completely following its split in early 1992.

74. *Rudé právo,* 25 June 1991, 3, quoted in Innes, *Czechoslovakia,* 177.

75. Marvin Ott, *Christian Science Monitor,* October 2, 1992, 1.

76. Bárta helped establish the Society for Moravia and Silesia (SMS) in 1968, which survived the 1969 crackdown. Originally a cultural organization, the SMS was registered as a political party in 1990.

77. For a description of efforts to secure Moravian autonomy in the 1968–1969 constitutional negotiations, see H. Gordon Skilling, *Czechoslovakia's Interrupted Revolution* (Princeton: Princeton University Press, 1976), 470–74.

78. Wheaton and Kavan, *Velvet Revolution,* 87–88.

79. Pernes, *Pod moravskou orlicí aneb Dějiny moravanství,* 222.

80. *Provolání Moravského občanského hnutí ze dne 20.11.1989* [Proclamation of the Moravian Civic Movement], Official District Archive, Uherské Hradiště, Collection of Raw Materials, box 7, folder "Letáky a plakáty všeobecně," Czech Republic; translation by author.

81. Interview, Miroslav Mareš, Professor of politics, Masaryk University, Brno, 4 February 1998.

82. Pernes, *Pod moravskou orlicí aneb Dějiny moravanství,* 231–32.

83. Bárta maintained that he had been involved in anti-regime activities in the 1980s. However, this is a dubious claim in light of his probable collaboration with the Státní bezpečnost (StB; the communist secret service) during that time.

84. Miroslav Mareš, ed., *Etnické a regionální strany v ČR po roce 1989* [Ethnic and regional parties in the Czech Republic after 1989] (Brno: Centrum pro studium demokracie a kultury, 2003), 38.

85. Wheaton and Kavan, *Velvet Revolution,* 138–39.

86. *Lidové noviny* ran a series of editorials questioning the need to recognize a separate Moravian identity because there was "no real difference" between the Czechs and Moravians; others feared that the growth of Moravian nationalism would have fatal consequences for the federation ("Daň za slobodu"; "Co se opravdu děje na Moravě?" [What's really going on in Moravia?], *Lidové noviny,* 17 March 1990). One writer asserted that the Moravian identity was no more real than the South or East Bohemian identity and that the Moravian nation was therefore an elite invention ("Dopis Moraváka Moravákům" [A letter from a Moravian to Moravians], *Lidové noviny,* 31 January 1990).

87. "Nejen pro Čechy a Slováky" [Not only for Czechs and Slovaks], *Lidové noviny,* 5 April 1990.

88. Quoted in "Nový Obsah Federace" [A new content of the federation], *Lidové Noviny,* 10 February 1990.

89. An early symbolic concession to the Moravians was the design of the new state seal. The Czech coat of arms depicted two Czech lions, the Moravian eagle, and the Silesian eagle.

90. Interview, Jiří Bílý, Moravian National Party Chairman, Brno, 4 February 1998.

91. Interview, Mareš, 4 February 1998.

92. See, for example, *Informační bulletin* [Information Bulletin], HSD-SMS, 1990 CSFR elections, 11. These claims can be supported only if we use a certain set of indicators (see n. 103); interview, Tomáš Sirovátka, professor of sociology, University of Masaryk, Brno, 18 December 1997.

93. Institut pro výzkum veřejného mínění (IVVM) [Institute for Public Opinion Research], Závěrečná zpráva z výzkumu [Final Research Report] (Prague, 1990), 23.

94. *Informační bulletin,* 9; see also Miroslav Mareš, *Moravské regionální strany* [Moravian regional parties], Masaryk University, unpublished manuscript, Brno, fall 1997.

95. One reason why the HSD-SMS prevailed over the MOH was that it was the only Moravian party to run alone in the 1990 elections; it was therefore an obvious choice for those who wanted to cast a vote for Moravian autonomy (interview, Mareš, 4 February 1998). The party's success was also partly due to Bárta's connections to the local political establishment. Bárta's charisma as well as his historical legacy were also contributing factors in the victory of the HSD-SMS. The MOH won only one seat in the Federal Assembly in 1990—Richter left the political scene soon afterward, fatally weakening the party.

96. Jan Obrman, "The Issue of Autonomy for Moravia and Silesia," *Report on Eastern Europe,* 12 April 1991.

97. Pernes, *Pod moravskou orlicí aneb Dějiny moravanství,* 235.

98. "Na Programu Zákony" [Laws on the program], *Lidové Noviny,* 19 June 1990.

99. Mareš, *Moravské regionalní strany,* 2.

100. After Richter stepped down as chair of the MOH, Ivan Dřímal assumed the leadership of the party, now called the Moravian National Party (MNS).

101. These disputes came into the open at the first HSD-SMS party congress in late 1990. Party delegates quarreled over Bárta's suspected collaboration with the StB as well as the underlying aims of the movement; Dřímal and Bílý openly opposed Bárta's more moderate approach. Despite these differences, the delegates unanimously renounced all forms of separatism as well as any other goal that would "endanger the foundation of our state" (*Moravskoslezská orlice* 2, 2).

102. Interview, Bílý, 4 February 1998. An anonymous reviewer pointed out that this was unlikely to have been a major factor in the movement's demise because Slovak support for Moravian autonomy was never very strong.

103. ČTK and Radio Prague, 26 January 1991, quoted in Martin, "The 1991 Budget," 12.

104. Moravian leaders repeatedly accused the government of regional discrimination in budgetary outlays (*Informační zpravodaj* [Information Bulletin], HSD-SMS Information and Electoral Program [Brno: HSD-SMS Headquarters, February, 1992], 3–7). These claims can only be substantiated with certain indicators. For example, in 1991, Moravia and Silesia received less state funding *per capita* than Prague or the rest of the Czech Republic. However, Moravia and Silesia received more state funding *per square kilometer* (*Mladá fronta Dnes,* 7 February 1991); interview, Sirovátka, 9 February 1998.

105. Obrman, "Issue of Autonomy," 20–21.

106. At a Czech National Council meeting in February 1991, Pithart claimed that of the proposals that had been considered, he was most in favor of a tripartite federation (ibid., 17).

107. The government made these concessions while denying budgetary discrimination against Moravia and Silesia (*Mladá fronta Dnes,* 7 February 1991). Despite the leadership's efforts to accommodate the Moravians, right-wing CF deputies blocked a final parliamentary vote on devolving power to the regions.

108. Associated Press, B-Wire FF147, 15 January 1991.

109. Interview, Mareš, 8 February 1998.

110. Jiri Pehe, "The State Treaty between the Czech and Slovak Republics," *Report on Eastern Europe,* 7 June 1991, 13.

111. ČTK, 26 April 1991; ČTK, 27 April 1991.

112. Pernes, *Pod moravskou orlicí aneb Dějiny moravanství,* 248–49. It is unclear how important Bárta was to the movement at this point because his position had already been undermined by charges that he and another HSD-SMS deputy had been agents for the StB.

113. ČTK, 10 September 1991.

114. The unemployment figures for north Moravia in 1990 and 1991 were 1.18 and 6.17 percent, respectively (compared with the Czech average of 0.73 and 4.13 percent). Unemployment statistics for south Moravia were roughly equivalent to the Czech average (*Czech Statistical Yearbook* [Prague: Czech Statistical Office, 1994]).

115. "Poslední příležitost?" [Last opportunity?] *Svobodné slovo,* 9 March 1992.

116. *Informační zpravodaj,* List of HSD-SMS initiatives in the Czech National Council.

117. Both the Czechs and the Slovaks had courted the Moravian autonomists to gain leverage against one another in the federal talks. They abandoned their support for Moravian autonomy when it came down to cutting a deal.

118. Interview, Jan Kryčer, 4 February 1998.

119. Mareš, *Moravské regionální strany,* 3.

120. Tomáš Kostelecký, *Geografické analýzy volebních výsledků jako součást politické geographie* [Geographic Analysis of Electoral Results as the Contemporary Political Geography] (Institute of Geography, Czech Academy of Sciences, Prague, Unpublished Dissertation, 1992), 110–23.

121. Mareš, *Moravské regionální strany,* 3–4.

122. Interview, Ivan Dřímal, Chair of Moravian National Party, Brno, Czech Republic, 3 February 1998.

123. Although Pithart had promised autonomy for Moravia after the June elections, he joined Klaus in urging the public not to vote for the HSD-SMS in the November elections, arguing that it was unlikely to meet the 5 percent threshold for entering parliament (Pernes, *Pod moravskou orlicí aneb Dějiny moravanství*, 236).

124. Interview, Bílý, 3 February 1998.

125. Interview, Alena Nedomová, Assistant to the Czech Minister without Portfolio, Prague, Czech Republic, 4 February 1998.

126. For accounts of the split that focus on Slovak national identity, see Suda, "Slovakia in Czech National Consciousness"; Rychlík, "National Consciousness."

127. Bugajski, *Ethnic Politics in Eastern Europe*, 293; interview, Dřímal, 3 February 1998.

128. See especially Gurr, *Minorities at Risk*; see also Michael Hechter, *Internal Colonialism* (Berkeley: University of California Press, 1975); Ernest Gellner, *Nations and Nationalism* (Ithaca: Cornell University Press, 1983); Tom Nairn, "Scotland and Europe," *New Left Review* 83 (1974): 57–82.

129. Milica Zarkovic Bookman, "Economic Issues Underlying Secession: The Case of Slovenia and Slovakia," *Communist Economies and Economic Transformation* 4 (1992): 111–34.

130. Peter Martin, "Economic Reform and Slovakia," *Report on Eastern Europe*, 5 July 1991, 9–10.

131. Václav Průcha, "Economic Development and Relations, 1918–89," in *The End of Czechoslovakia*, ed. Musil, 75.

132. *Historická statistická ročenka ČSSR* [Historical Statistical Yearbook of the ČSSR] (Prague, 1985), quoted in Václav Průcha, "Economic Development and Relations, 1918–89," in *The End of Czechoslovakia*, ed. Musil, 62.

133. Bookman, "Economic Issues Underlying Secession," 126 (emphasis added).

134. See, for example, Eva Petrášová, *Prípad Mečiar* [The case of Mečiar] (Prague: Cesty, 1991); Marek Dobrovolný, *Mečiar* (Prague: JPM Tisk, 1998). These books address Mečiar's role in the split, although they focus rather more on his subsequent role in Slovak politics.

135. Innes, *Czechoslovakia*, 172–73; Comisso, "Prediction versus Diagnosis: Comments on a Ken Jowitt Retrospective," *Slavic Review* 53 (spring 1994): 191.

136. Elster, "Transition, Constitution-Making, and Separation in Czechoslovakia," 105–34; Jiří Musil, Introduction to *The End of Czechoslovakia*, ed. Musil.

137. Shari J. Cohen, *Politics without a Past: The Absence of History in Postcommunist Nationalism* (Durham, N.C.: Duke University Press), 1999.

138. Bunce, *Subversive Institutions*, 90.

139. Stanger, "Price of Velvet"; Wolchik, "Impact of Institutional Factors"; Wolchik, "Politics of Transition"; Leff, "Inevitability, Probability, Possibility."

140. Interestingly, the Moravian towns with the highest levels of voter support for the HSD-SMS in 1990 were those that had kept their administrative status in the government until 1960, in contrast to towns that had lost their status before 1949 (Daněk, "Moravian and Silesian Nationalities," 252–53). This suggests that institutions may also account for variation in the level of support for nationalism *within* a group.

141. Interview, Fedor Gál, Founder of Public Against Violence, 9 July 1998, Prague, Czech Republic; interview, Jiří Musil, professor of sociology at Central European University, Prague, Czech Republic, 15 October 1997. Musil believes that the split might have been averted if

Czech and Slovak elites had begun to rebuild the federation through incremental settlements on less inflammatory issues such as federal transportation and communication regimes.

6. Ethnic Bargaining in the Balkans

1. One important difference, of course, is that most of Vojvodina had been part of the Habsburg Empire, whereas Kosovo had the experience of Ottoman rule. A second difference is that the Serbs had historically better relations with the Hungarians than with the Albanians.

2. Tamás Korhecz, "Vojvodina—The Next Stage of the Dismantling Process?—Chances of Conflicts in Vojvodina," *Minorities and Majorities: Vojvodina Case Study Workshop,* course reader, Central European University, winter 2000, 2. Vojvodina was vital to the development of the Serbian nation during the eighteenth and nineteenth centuries. Serbian refugees from the Ottoman Empire flooded Serbian academies, monasteries, and cultural societies that sprang up in the region to nurture the nascent Serbian culture (Francine Friedman, "Kosovo and Vojvodina: One Yugoslav Solution to Autonomy in a Multiethnic State," in *Governing Peoples and Territories,* ed. Daniel J. Elazar [Philadelphia: Institute for the Study of Human Issues, 1982], 62–63).

3. Stephen Borsody, "State- and Nation-Building in Central Europe: The Origins of the Hungarian Problem," in *The Hungarians: A Divided Nation,* ed. Stephen Borsody (New Haven: Yale Center for International and Area Studies, 1988), 19.

4. Friedman, "Kosovo and Vojvodina," 64.

5. Although both regions were permitted to send delegations to the Federal Assembly, they had no real influence over government policy (ibid., 67).

6. Károly Kocsis and Eszter Kocsis-Hodosi, *Hungarian Minorities in the Carpathian Basin* (Toronto: Matthias Corvinus, 1995), 84.

7. According to the 1991 Yugoslav census, roughly 340,000 of Vojvodina's 2 million inhabitants declared themselves Hungarian. However, the actual number of ethnic Hungarians in the region is likely to have been higher because tens of thousands of Hungarians declared themselves to be Yugoslavs in the census (ibid., 97).

8. Tim Judah, *Kosovo: War and Revenge* (New Haven: Yale University Press, 2000), 11.

9. Ibid., 22.

10. Julie A. Mertus, *Kosovo: How Myths and Truths Started a War* (Berkeley: University of California Press, 1999), 19.

11. International Crisis Group, "The View from Tirana: The Albanian Dimension of the Kosovo Conflict," *ICG Balkans 36* (10 July 1998): 2.

12. Janusz Bugajski, *Nations in Turmoil: Conflict and Cooperation in Eastern Europe* (Boulder: Westview, 1993), 136–37, 141.

13. When reports surfaced in January 1991 that Hungary had been providing military aid to the Croatian secessionists, Belgrade launched a media campaign against ethnic Hungarians, accusing them of colluding in the arms sales to promote the collapse of Yugoslavia. Edith Oltay, "Hungarians in Yugoslavia Seek Guarantees for Minority Rights," *Report on Eastern Europe 2,* 20 September 1991, 44.

14. Edith Oltay, "Minorities as Stumbling Block in Relations with Neighbors," *RFE/RL Research Report* (May 8, 1992): 28.

15. MTI [Hungarian news agency], April 20, 1991, quoted in ibid., 27 (emphasis added).

16. "Military Denies Selling Scuds to Croatia," MTI (Hungarian news agency), *Foreign Broadcast Information Service Daily Report, Eastern Europe* [hereafter *FBIS*] 207 (October 25, 1991): 11.

17. Milan Andreyevich, "Vojvodina Hungarian Group to Seek Cultural Autonomy," *Report on Eastern Europe*, 12 October 1990, 44.

18. Interviews with DCHV deputy presidents Sándor Hódi and János Vékás, in István Schlett, "Vojvodina: Increasing Opportunities, Increasing Dangers, or the Paradox of Transformation," *Társadalmi Szemle*, July 1991, 36–48, quoted in Oltay, "Hungarians in Yugoslavia," 40.

19. Edith Oltay, "Hungarians under Political Pressure in Vojvodina," *RFE/RL Research Report*, 3 December 1993, 46.

20. Ibid. Tibor Várady, a former Hungarian representative in Yugoslavia, claimed that Ágoston had confided that the proposal had been made solely for the benefit of the Hungarian rank and file—strikingly, they had not even bothered to translate the proposal into Serbo-Croatian for the government's perusal! (interview, Tibor Várady, Budapest, Hungary, 3 September 2002.) This is an illustration of the ways in which group demands are used for strategic purposes.

21. Jonathan Fox, "Hungarians in the Vojvodina Region of Yugoslavia (Serbia and Montenegro)," *Minorities at Risk Project Files*, 15 January 1996 (updated by Lyubov Mincheva, 1 July 1999), http://www.cidcm.umd.edu/inscr/mar/data/yughung.htm.

22. Helsinki Committee for Human Rights in Serbia, "Report on the Status of Hungarians," *Report on Human Rights in Serbia for 1997* (Belgrade, 1998), 87

23. Fox, "Hungarians in the Vojvodina Region."

24. Carol J. Williams, "Hungarians in Serbian Province Fear They May Be Next," *Los Angeles Times,* 12 October 1993.

25. Quoted in Alfred A. Reisch, "The New Hungarian Government's Foreign Policy," *RFE/RL Research Report* (15 August 1994): 46–47.

26. Edith Oltay, "Hungarian Foreign Minister on Relations with Neighboring Countries," *RFE/RL Newsline, Central and Eastern Europe*, 12 October 1994.

27. Hungary adopted a hands-off policy toward its co-ethnics largely at the behest of NATO and EU leaders, who warned that the country would not gain admission to these organizations until it resolved its outstanding disputes with its neighbors. The new Socialist leadership was also keen to increase trade with its neighbors in order to boost Hungary's flagging economy. Budapest's new stance reflected grassroots sentiment within the country itself. Reisch observed at the time that "[b]ecause of the large number of refugees from Romania and Vojvodina, and because of the mistakes of the previous government, the original feeling of solidarity for and sympathy with the Magyar minorities abroad had diminished in Hungary and been replaced by indifference and even hostility" (Reisch, "The New Hungarian Government's Foreign Policy," 50).

28. Another explanation for Ágoston's declining political fortunes was that Hungary did not want a radical minority leader in Vojvodina who might stir up trouble as Hungary was preparing to enter EU-accession talks. Kasza's party was therefore created as a moderate alternative by the World Alliance of Hungarians with financial backing from the Horn government.

29. Interview, Várady, September 3, 2002.

30. Judith Ingram, "Trying to Save a Symbol of Tolerance," *New York Times,* 14 August 1993.

31. Interview, László Józsa, Deputy Chair of the Democratic Alliance of Hungarians, Subotica, Yugoslavia, November 29, 2002. An analysis of these bombings and how they fit into NATO's overall war strategy is beyond the scope of this chapter. See Ivo Daalder and Michael O'Hanlen, *Winning Ugly: NATO's War to Save Kosovo* (Washington, D.C.: Brookings Institution Press, 2000). See also Greg Campbell, *The Road to Kosovo: A Balkan Diary* (Boulder: Westview, 2000); Independent International Commission on Kosovo, *The Kosovo Report* (Oxford: Oxford University Press, 2000).

32. Justin Brown, "NATO Hits Serbia's Northern Province Hard," *Christian Science Monitor,* 22 April 1999; Carlotta Gall, "No Water, Power, Phone: A Serbian City's Trials," *New York Times,* 4 May 1999.

33. Hungary had actually *supported* the NATO air strikes in Vojvodina, permitting the Alliance to fly bombing missions to the region from Hungary. The new Hungarian premier, Viktor Orbán, even defended the bombing of the bridges in Novi Sad, despite the fact that Hungarian companies suffered losses due to blockages in transportation lines. Note that these events go against primordialist expectations that national homelands will naturally come to the aid of their co-ethnics due to cross-border ethnic ties. By all accounts, Hungary—a new NATO member eager to prove its pro-Western credentials—felt constrained to act against, or even speak out against, these strikes. A minority representative in Vojvodina confirmed that Budapest's "extreme" support for the air strikes would certainly harm ethnic Hungarians in Yugoslavia (Pete Baumgartner, "Moscow and Minsk Virtually Alone in Support of Milosevic," *RFE/RL Research Report* ([2 April 1999]).

34. Quoted in Michael Shafir, "Hungary's Premier on Magyar Minority in Vojvodina," *RFE/RL Research Report,* 8 April 1999; interview, Várady, 3 September 2002.

35. When Fidesz won the elections in Hungary in 1998, Orbán called for establishing autonomy in Vojvodina along the lines of what was being proposed in Kosovo. These and other public statements served to radicalize Vojvodinian Hungarians, who began to revive calls for Hungarian autonomy in 1998–1999. During the Kosovo war, however, Hungary ceased to lobby for the minority due to its constraints as a NATO member. Kasza responded to Hungary's moderation by abandoning his own demands for autonomy. For a chronology of these events, see Fox, "Hungarians in the Vojvodina Region."

36. Patrick G. Moore, "Call for Vojvodina Autonomy," *RFE/RL Research Report* (26 February 2001).

37. Interview, Tamás Korhecz, Novi Sad, Serbia, 28 November 2002.

38. Judah, *Kosovo,* 49.

39. Slavoljub Djukíc, *Između slave i anateme: politicka biografija Slobodana Miloševíca* (Belgrade, 1994), 14, quoted in Judah, *Kosovo,* 53. Speaking before a different audience, Milošević claimed that the memorandum was "nothing else but the darkest nationalism" that would "mean the liquidation of the current socialist system of our country" (50). Milošević's Janus-faced rhetoric demonstrates his willingness to say or do whatever was necessary to achieve and consolidate power, including displacing his mentor and friend, Ivan Stambolić, as president of Serbia in 1987.

40. Bruce Fekrat, *Minorities at Risk Project File for Kosovo,* November 1993 (updated by Jonathan Fox, December 1995; Erica Shauber, April 1998; Lyubov Mincheva, June 1999 and June 2001; Michael Johns, December 2001), http:www.cidcm.umd.edu/inscr/mar/data/yugalban.htm.

41. In one of the first organized protests of this period, the Trepča miners marched fifty-five kilometers in freezing temperatures to the local party headquarters in Priština to protest the removal of Albanian leaders from the League of Communists. They carried Albanian flags and pictures of Tito and chanted in support of the 1974 constitution, shouting Titoist slogans such as "Brotherhood and Unity" (Julie A. Mertus, *Kosovo: How Myths and Truths Started a War* [Berkeley: University of California Press, 1999], 178). As in the Priština University student protests of 1981, the staged quality of the strike suggests that its organizers had received backing and training from outside sources, most likely from within Albania.

42. Ibid.

43. Judah, *Kosovo,* 58. It is significant that Kosovo's first shadow government was based in Ljubljana from October 1991.

44. Chris Hedges, "Kosovo's Next Masters," *Foreign Affairs* 78 (May–June 1999), http://www.kosovo.com/kla4.html.

45. International Crisis Group, "View from Tirana," 2–3. As a Gheg from northern Albania with family ties to Kosovo Albanians over the border, Berisha had a personal interest in the diaspora issue. Many Albanians in Kosovo therefore believed that Berisha's rise to power would lead to the emergence of a Greater Albanian state.

46. Fekrat, *Minorities at Risk Project File for Kosovo.*

47. The demonstration effects of regime change in Eastern Europe may have also contributed to Kosovar Albanian radicalism. In this respect, however, it is important to note that not *all* minorities in the region, or even in Yugoslavia, mobilized in reaction to these events. Those that did so by and large believed that they enjoyed external backing—whether it be from the European Community (as in the cases of Slovenia and Croatia) or external homeland states (as in the cases of the Bosnian Serbs and Croats).

48. Fekrat, *Minorities at Risk Project File for Kosovo.* This phrase was also used to refer to the persecution of Hungarians in Vojvodina, which was occurring at the same time.

49. Ibid.

50. *Rilindja,* 22 February 1995, 5, *FBIS* (24 February 1995): 43; *Neue Zürcher Zeitung,* 6 March 1995, 14, cited in Sabrina Petra Ramet, *Whose Democracy: Nationalism, Religion, and the Doctrine of Collective Rights in Post-1989 Eastern Europe* (Lanham, Md.: Rowman and Littlefield, 1997), 153.

51. International Crisis Group, "View from Tirana," 3; Judah, *Kosovo,* 96–97.

52. Judah, *Kosovo,* 73.

53. Lynn Walsh, "The KLA and the Struggle for Kosovar Self-Determination," *Socialism Today—Kosovo and the KLA* 39 (June 1999), http://www.socialism today.org/39/kla39.html (emphasis added).

54. Judah, *Kosovo,* 132–33.

55. Sam Vaknin, "KLA: The Army of Liberation," in *The Union of Death: Examining Terrorists and Freedom Fighters in the Balkans,* Part 5, 7 June 2000, http://www.kosovo. net/kla4.html, accessed 19 May 2006 (emphasis added). It is widely acknowledged that the sudden influx of arms into Albania enhanced the capacity of the KLA forces. Albanian authorities even assisted the transfer of arms to Kosovo. In one particularly blatant example, Berisha-backed officers of the National Intelligence Agency captured a large number of weapons during the 1997 uprising and shipped them to the Dürres, where they could be transferred to the KLA(International Crisis Group, "View from Tirana," 10).

56. Judah, *Kosovo,* 133–34.

57. International Crisis Group, "View from Tirana," 10.

58. Interview, Owen O'Sullivan, Head of the Department for Security Cooperation, OSCE presence in Albania, Tirana, Albania, 4 April 2003.

59. Interview, Xhemil Shahu, Albanian field officer, United Nations High Commissioner for Refugees, Emergency Management Group Protection Officer, Tirana, Albania, 5 April 2003.

60. Quoted in International Crisis Group, "View from Tirana," 6.

61. Judah, *Kosovo,* 135.

62. International Crisis Group, *Kosovo Spring* (Priština and Sarajevo, 1998), 23, quoted in Judah, *Kosovo,* 136.

63. Hedges, "Kosovo's Next Masters."

64. Tim Judah, "KLA Is Still a Force to Be Reckoned With," *Wall Street Journal,* 7 April 1999; see also Chris Hedges, "Victims Not Quite Innocent," *New York Times,* 28 March 1999.

65. Judah, *Kosovo,* 141.

66. Ibid., 146.

67. Ibid., 150–51.

68. Vaknin, "KLA: The Army of Liberation." The KLA and NATO engaged in joint military planning for a year prior to and during the 1999 NATO air war. Although Jamie Shea, the official NATO spokesperson, denied ever having direct contact with the KLA, NATO is reported to have held regular security and intelligence meetings with KLA commanders. During the war, NATO officials maintained frequent radio contact with the militia in Kosovo and even approved KLA maneuvers on the ground (Robert Fisk, "War in the Balkans: 'It All Went Very Well,' Said the General," *The Independent,* 15 May 1999; see also Robert Fisk, "Comment—NATO Resorts to War by Proxy," *The Independent,* 22 April 1999, http://www.tks.org/kosovo/robert_fisk.htm, accessed May 2006).

69. Vaknin, "KLA: The Army of Liberation," 166 (emphasis added).

70. Nicholas Kralev, "Kostunica Signals a Warming of Ties with US," *Financial Times,* 28 December 2000.

71. Irina Bazhenova, "FRY FM Says Buffer Zone Around Kosovo Can Be Reduced," *Itar—Tass News Wire,* New York, 17 January 2001; Tamara Zamyatina and Nikolai Kalintsev, "Kosovo Status to Be Determined at International Forum—UN Official," *Itar—Tass News Wire,* New York, 14 February 2001.

72. Chris Hedges, "Crisis in the Balkans: The Separatist; Leaders of Kosovo Rebels Tied to Deadly Power Play," *New York Times,* 25 June 1999.

73. Martin McLaughlin, "KLA Seizes Kosovo Positions, Serb Flight Grows," World Socialist Website, 16 June 2001, http://www.wsws.org/articles/1999/jun1999/yug-j16.shtml.

74. Tony Robson, "Elections Confirm Popular Hostility towards Kosovo Liberation Army," World Socialist Website, 17 December 2001, http://www.wsws.org/articles/1999/dec2001/kos-d17.shtml.

75. Peter Beaumont, "Killings Blamed on KLA," *The Observer,* 25 July 1999.

76. Vitali Makarchev, "Situation Worsening on Macedonia-Kosovo Border," *Itar—Tass News Wire,* 27 February 2001.

77. The infamous "freezing weeks" of 1944 were undertaken in revenge for the three "Cold Days," when the Hungarian Army rounded up and executed hundreds of suspected

Serbian partisans in Novi Sad. For one of the few accounts of this episode in English, see Tibor Cseres, *Titoist Atrocities in Vojvodina, 1944–1945: Serbian Vendetta in Bácska* (Buffalo: Hunyadi, 1993).

78. Barry Posen, "The Security Dilemma and Ethnic Conflict," in *Ethnic Conflict and International Security,* edited by Michael Brown (Princeton: Princeton University Press, 1993), 108–9; Stephen van Evera, "Hypotheses on Nationalism and War," *International Security* 18 (spring 1994): 40–41.

79. It is interesting to compare the ethnic geography of Bosnia and Croatia with that of Vojvodina. Ethnic islands existed in all three cases, yet irredentism occurred only in Croatia and Bosnia (see map 6.1).

80. Posen, "The Security Dilemma and Ethnic Conflict."

7. Conclusion and Policy Implications

1. Daniel Posner arrives at much the same conclusion in his comparative analysis of the Chewa-Tumbuka ethnic cleavage in two neighboring African states. As the two-state comparison holds constant preexisting conditions such as economic factors, their colonial experience, and ethnic differences, he concludes that the differing salience of this cleavage in Malawi versus Zambia can only be explained by the *relative mobilizational value* of the cleavage in one political system as opposed to the other. An additional comparison shows that such cleavages might be mobilized even in the *absence* of these preexisting conditions. See Daniel N. Posner, "The Political Salience of Cultural Difference: Why Chewas and Tumbukas Are Allies in Zambia and Adversaries in Malawi," *American Political Science Review* 98 (2004): 529–46.

2. Broad territorial autonomy or federal or confederal arrangements have also been proposed as solutions to the separatist conflicts in Nagorno-Karabakh, Sri Lanka, Abkhazia, and Transdniestria, among other places. The logic follows that autonomous institutions will satisfy aspirations for self-determination by providing groups with a degree of self-government, thereby protecting them against cultural assimilation. See Hurst Hannum, *Autonomy, Sovereignty, and Self-Determination: The Accommodation of Conflicting Rights* (Philadelphia: University of Pennsylvania Press, 1990), chaps. 16–19; Kjell-Åke Nordquist, "Autonomy as a Conflict-Solving Mechanism—An Overview," in *Autonomy: Applications and Implications,* ed. Markku Suksi (The Hague: Kluwer Law International, 1998), 59–77; Ruth Lapidoth, *Autonomy: Flexible Solutions to Ethnic Conflicts* (Washington, D.C.: United States Institute for Peace Press, 1996).

3. Svante Cornell examines secessionist movements in the Caucasus and concludes that the possession of autonomous institutions may actually *increase* the likelihood that a minority will pursue full statehood, sometimes through violence (Svante Cornell, "Autonomy as a Source of Conflict: Caucasian Conflicts in Theoretical Perspective," *World Politics* 54 [2002]: 245–76). Philip Roeder and Henry Hale make similar arguments concerning the effects of national institutions on secessionism in the former Soviet Union. (See Philip G. Roeder, "Soviet Federalism and Ethnic Mobilization," *World Politics* 43 [1991]: 196–232; and Henry E. Hale, "The Parade of Sovereignties: Testing Theories of Secession in the Soviet Setting," *British Journal of Political Science* 30 [2000]: 31–56.) Alexander Downes, too, questions the potential of power-sharing and autonomy arrangements for resolving separatist conflicts,

pointing out that "autonomy provides an institutional base for ethnic groups that increases their ability and motivation to make further demands or launch a rebellion" (Alexander B. Downes, "The Problem with Negotiated Solutions to Ethnic Civil Wars," *Security Studies* 13 [2004]: 244).

4. See especially Ted Robert Gurr, *Minorities at Risk: A Global View of Ethnopolitical Conflicts* (Washington, D.C.: United States Institute of Peace Press, 1993); Donald L. Horowitz, *Ethnic Groups in Conflict* (Berkeley: University of California Press, 1985).

5. For a discussion of the absence of Romani mobilization in Eastern Europe, see Zoltan D. Barany, "Ethnic Mobilization without Prerequisites: The East European Gypsies," *World Politics* 54 (2002): 277–307.

6. David Scheffer argues that international tribunals can be used to prosecute state leaders who engaged in atrocities in the course of civil war, adding that the jurisdiction of such tribunals could also be extended to "officials of separatist movements." The hope is that fears of future prosecution might actually *deter* individuals from undertaking such policies in the first place. See David J. Scheffer, "International Judicial Intervention," *Foreign Policy* 102 (spring 1996): 38–40.

7. Richard Haas asserts that, under certain limited conditions, military intervention might be justified in order to remove a particularly nefarious government from power (Richard N. Haas, "Military Force: A User's Guide," *Foreign Policy* 96 [fall 1993]: 28). The same logic might be applied to the organizers of ethnic insurgencies.

8. Stuart Kaufman, "Spiraling to Ethnic War: Elites, Masses, and Moscow in Moldova's Civil War," *International Security* 21 (1996): 136. For other theories of conflict that focus on elite influence, see Paul Brass, *Ethnicity and Nationalism: Theory and Comparison* (Newbury Park, Calif.: Sage, 1991); V. P. Gagnon, Jr., "Ethnic Nationalism and International Conflict: the Case of Serbia" *International Security* 19 (winter 1994–1995): 130–66; Valery Tishkov, *Ethnicity, Nationalism and Conflict in and after the Soviet Union: The Mind Aflame* (London: Sage, 1997), chap. 10. While emphasizing the role played by elites in sectarian violence, most of this scholarship argues that such processes are driven by a combination of factors.

9. Gagnon, "Ethnic Nationalism and International Conflict," 166–68.

10. Barry Posen, "The Security Dilemma and Ethnic Conflict," *Survival* 35 (1993): 27–47.

11. Barbara F. Walter, "The Critical Barrier to Civil War Settlement," *International Organization* 51 (1997): 335–64.

12. Chaim Kaufmann, "Possible and Impossible Solutions to Ethnic Civil Wars," *International Security* 20 (spring 1996): 137. See also Kaufmann, "When All Else Fails: Ethnic Population Transfers and Partitions in the Twentieth Century," *International Security* 23 (fall 1998): 120–56; John J. Mearsheimer and Stephen Van Evera, "When Peace Means War," *New Republic* (18 December 1995); Downes, "The Problem with Negotiated Solutions to Ethnic Civil Wars." In a recent empirical analysis, Alan Kuperman contends that, although partition is probably not as necessary as Kaufmann believes for resolving entrenched ethnic civil wars, it may sometimes be called for (Alan J. Kuperman, "Is Partition Really the Only Hope? Reconciling Contradictory Findings about Ethnic Civil Wars," *Security Studies* 13 [2004]: 314–49).

13. Horowitz, *Ethnic Groups in Conflict*, 588–91; Radha Kumar, "The Troubled History of Partition," *Foreign Affairs* 76 (1997): 22–34; Robert Schaeffer, *Warpaths: The Politics of Partition* (New York: Hill and Wang, 1990); Amitai Etzioni, "The Evils of Self-Determination," *Foreign Policy* 89 (winter 1992–1993): 21–35; Gidon Gottlieb, "Nations

without States," *Foreign Affairs* 73 (May–June 1994): 100–112; David Carment and Dane Rowlands, "Vengeance and Intervention: Can Third Parties Bring Peace without Separation?" *Security Studies* 13 (2004): 366–93; and James D. Fearon, "Separatist Wars, Partition, and World Order," *Security Studies* 13 (2004): 394–415.

14. Nicholas Sambanis, "Partition as a Solution to Ethnic War: An Empirical Critique of the Theoretical Literature," *World Politics* 52 (July 2000): 437–83. David Laitin corroborates Sambanis' findings in a more recent empirical analysis using the Minorities at Risk (MAR) dataset. David D. Laitin, "Ethnic Unmixing and Civil War," *Security Studies* 13 (2004): 350–65.

15. See James D. Fearon, "Commitment Problems and the Spread of Ethnic Conflict," in *The International Spread of Ethnic Conflict: Fear, Diffusion, and Escalation,* ed. David Lake and Donald Rothchild (Princeton: Princeton University Press, 1998), 107–26; and Barry R. Weingast, "Political Stability and Civil War: Institutions, Commitment, and American Democracy," in *Analytic Narratives,* ed. Robert Bates, Avner Greif, Margaret Levi, Jean-Laurent Rosenthal, and Barry R. Weingast (Princeton: Princeton University Press, 1998), 148–93; Rui J. P. De Figueiredo, Jr., and Barry R. Weingast, "The Rationality of Fear: Political Opportunism and Ethnic Conflict," in *Civil Wars, Insecurity, and Intervention,* ed. Barbara Walter and Jack Snyder (New York: Columbia University Press, 1999), 261–302.

16. Pieter van Houten, "The Role of a Minority's Reference State in Ethnic Relations," *Archives européenes de sociologie* 34 (spring 1998): 110–46. David Laitin observes that the predictions yielded by van Houten's model vary depending on the actions of the minority's homeland state. If the homeland signals non-interventionist intent, the minority will make its decision as though it had no homeland. On the other hand, if the homeland signals bellicose intent, the minority will be emboldened to fight and the majority will have no incentive to make concessions to the minority. Only when the homeland sends *mixed* signals to the minority (as Russia has done with regard to Russian minorities in the Baltics), does this create the requisite uncertainty on both sides to induce a compromise solution. See David D. Laitin, "Secessionist Rebellion in the Former Soviet Union," *Comparative Political Studies* 34 (2001): 855–57.

17. William Durch, "Keeping the Peace: Politics and Lessons of the 1990s," in *UN Peacekeeping, American Policy, and the Uncivil Wars of the 1990s,* ed. William Durch (New York: St. Martin's, 1996), 1–29; Timothy Sisk, "Peacemaking Processes: Forestalling Return to Ethnic Violence," in *Preventive Negotiation: Avoiding Conflict Escalation,* ed. I. William Zartman (Lanham, Md.: Rowman and Littlefield, 2001), 67–89; Charles M. Maynes, "Relearning Intervention," *Foreign Policy* 98 (spring 1995): 96–113.

18. For more on the consociational approach to conflict resolution, see Arendt Lijphart, "The Power-Sharing Approach," in *Conflict and Peacemaking in Multiethnic Societies,* ed. Joseph V. Montville (New York: Lexington Books, 1991), 491–510. See also Donald L. Horowitz, "Making Moderation Pay," in *Conflict and Peacemaking in Multiethnic Societies,* ed. Montville, 451–76; I. William Zartman, "Putting Things Back Together," in *Collapsed States,* ed. Zartman, 267–73.

19. Donald Rothchild and Philip G. Roeder, "Power Sharing as an Impediment to Peace and Democracy," in *Sustainable Peace: Power and Democracy after Civil Wars,* ed. Philip G. Roeder and Donald Rothchild (Ithaca: Cornell University Press, 2005), 29–50.

20. Marie-Joëlle Zahar, "Power Sharing in Lebanon: Foreign Protectors, Domestic Peace, and Democratic Failure," in *Sustainable Peace,* ed. Roeder and Rothchild, 219–40.

21. See, for example, David A. Lake and Donald Rothchild, "Containing Fear: The Origins and Management of Ethnic Conflict," *International Security* 21 (fall 1996): 41–75; Crawford Young, *The Politics of Cultural Pluralism* (Madison: University of Wisconsin Press, 1976).

22. Alan J. Kuperman, "Provoking Genocide: A Revised History of the Rwandan Patriotic Front," *Journal of Genocide Research* 6 (2004): 61–84.

23 Lotta Harbom and Peter Wallensteen, "Armed Conflict and Its International Dimensions, 1946–2004," *Journal of Peace Research* 42 (2005): 627, 629.

24. Ibid., 628.

25. David Carment and Dane Rowlands review the scholarly literature on the role of bias in interventions. While all or most of this scholarship finds that military intervention usually fails to resolve internal conflicts, there appears to be little consensus as to whether bias is helpful or harmful. They conclude that while an impartial intervention is often not possible (and that bias may even be preferable under certain conditions), biased interventions carry the risk of actually *worsening* the conflict—increasing the intensity of attacks by the non-favored side and thereby escalating the violence. See David Carment and Dane Rowlands, "Twisting One Arm: The Effects of Biased Interveners," *International Peacekeeping* 10 (2003): 18.

26. U.S. Department of State, "Erasing History: Ethnic Cleansing in Kosovo," 1 May 1999, http://www.state.gov/www/regions/eur/rpt_9905_ethnic_ksvo_toc.html, accessed 23 May 2006.

27. There is a vast and growing literature on EU conditionality and its impact on EU candidate states in central and Eastern Europe. For useful overviews of this literature, see especially Frank Schimmelfennig and Ulrich Sedelmeier, "Introduction: Conceptualizing the Europeanization of Central and Eastern Europe," in *The Europeanization of Central and Eastern Europe,* ed. Frank Schimmelfennig and Ulrich Sedelmeier (Ithaca: Cornell University Press, 2005), 1–28; Milada Anna Vachudova, *Europe Undivided: Democracy, Leverage, and Integration after Communism* (Oxford: Oxford University Press, 2005), 1–9; Judith G. Kelley, *Ethnic Politics in Europe: The Power of Norms and Incentives* (Princeton: Princeton University Press, 2004), chap. 2. For more on how EU conditionality has been used to promote minority protection at the substate level, see Thomas Diez, "Why the EU Can Nonetheless Be Good for Cyprus," *Journal on Ethnopolitics and Minority Issues in Europe,* Special Focus 2 (2002); Guido Schwellnus, "The Adoption of Nondiscrimination and Minority Protection Rules in Romania, Hungary and Poland," in *The Europeanization of Central and Eastern Europe,* ed. Schimmelfennig and Sedelmeier, 51–70; Peter Vermeersch, "Ethnic Mobilisation and the Political Conditionality of European Union Accession: The Case of the Roma in Slovakia," *Journal of Ethnic and Migration Studies* 28 (January 2002): 83–101.

28. Frank Schimmelfennig and Ulrich Sedelmeier, "Introduction," 10–17; Heather Grabbe, "How Does Europeanization Affect CEE Governance? Conditionality, Diffusion and Diversity," *Journal of European Public Policy* 8(2001): 1013–31. Vachudova shows how negotiations over EU accession with the countries of East Central Europe in the mid- to late 1990s helped catapult moderate political forces into positions of power in Romania, Bulgaria and Slovakia (Vachudova, *Europe Undivided,* chap. 6).

29. Although these protections had yet to be fully implemented when this book went to press, the emergence of an inter-ethnic government in Slovakia did much to alleviate ethnic tensions in that country.

30. For an excellent guide to electoral systems that have been used to manage conflict in divided societies, see Peter Harris and Ben Reilly, eds., *Democracy and Deep-Rooted Conflict: Options for Negotiators* (Stockholm: International Institute for Democracy and Electoral Assistance, 1998).

31. Philip G. Roeder, "Power Dividing as an Alternative to Ethnic Power Sharing," in *Sustainable Peace,* 51–82.

Interviews

Bauer, Edit. Former Deputy Chair of the Coexistence Party of Hungarian Coalition, 22 June 1998, Bratislava, Slovakia.

Bílý, Jiří. Moravian National Party Chairman, 4 February 1998, Brno, Czech Republic.

Bobák, Ján. Director of Slovak Historical Institute, Matice Slovenskej, 24 June 1998, Bratislava, Slovakia.

Čarnogurský, Ján. Chair of Christian Democratic Party, 23 June 1998, Bratislava, Slovakia.

Csáky, Pál. Coalition Chair of Hungarian Parties (1994) and Chair of the Hungarian Christian Democratic Party, 23 June 1998, Bratislava, Slovakia.

Daněk, Petr. Professor of Geography, Masaryk University, 4 February 1998, Brno, Czech Republic.

Dřímal, Ivan. Chair of Moravian National Party, 3 February 1998, Brno, Czech Republic.

Gál, Fedor. Former Chair of Public against Violence, 9 July 1998, Prague, Czech Republic.

Giňa, Ondřej. Roma Representative on the National Council for Minorities, 24 November 1997, Pardubice, Czech Republic.

Holomek, Karel. Minority Representative on the National Council for Minorities, and Co-founder of the Romani Citizen's Initiative, 9 March 1998, Brno, Czech Republic.

Horáková, Monika. Freedom Union Deputy in Czech Parliament, 31 January 1998, Prague, Czech Republic.

Hübschmannová, Milena. Professor of Romani Studies, Philosophy Faculty of Charles University, 24 February 1998, Prague, Czech Republic.

Józsa, László. Deputy Chair of the Democratic Alliance of Hungarians. 29 November 2002, Subotica, Serbia.

Kalvoda, Jan. Former Deputy Prime Minister, Czech government, 7 July 1998, Prague, Czech Republic.

Kántor, Zoltán. Researcher, László Teleki Institute, 1 December 2003, Budapest, Hungary.

Korhecz, Tamás. Representative of Vojvodina Regional Government, 28 November 2002, Novi Sad, Serbia.

Kostelecký, Tomáš. Doctoral Candidate in Political Geography, Czech Academy of Sciences, 30 January 1998, Prague, Czech Republic.

Kryčer, Jan. Chair of Movement for Moravian and Silesian Self-Government-Association for Moravia and Silesia (HSD-SMS), 4 February 1998, Brno, Czech Republic.

Kusý, Miroslav. Chair of Department of Political Science and Human Rights Education, Comenius University, Bratislava, and former PAV Member of Parliament, 19 June 1998, Bratislava, Slovakia.

Mareš, Miroslav. Professor of Politics, Masaryk University, 4 February 1998, Brno, Czech Republic.

Matei, Liviu. Education Ministry of the Romanian Government, 21 June 1997, Bratislava, Slovakia.

Meşca, Sever. Deputy of Greater Romania Party, Romanian Parliament, 6 April 1998, Bucharest, Romania.

Mesežnikov, Grigorij. Director of Institute for Public Opinion Research, Bratislava, 24 June 1998, Bratislava, Slovakia.

Musil, Jiří. Professor of sociology at Central European University, 15 October 1997, Prague, Czech Republic.

Nedomová, Alena. Assistant to the Minister without Portfolio, Czech Government, 4 February 1998, Prague, Czech Republic.

Oprescu, Dan. Roma Representative, Department for Protection of National Minorities, Romanian Government, 8 April 1998, Bucharest, Romania.

O'Sullivan, Owen. Head of Department for Security Cooperation, Organization for Security and Co-operation in Europe (OSCE), Presence in Albania, 4 April 2003, Tirana, Albania.

Pambuccian, Varujan. Member of Romanian Parliament and Head of Parliamentary Club for National Minorities, 8 April 1998, Bucharest, Romania.

Petöcz, Kálmán. Deputy Chair of Hungarian Civic Party, Slovak Parliament, 23 June 1998, Bratislava, Slovakia.

Petrescu, Alexandra-Luminiaţa. Advisor to Romanian President on Nonprofit Organizations, Romanian Government, 7 April 1998, Bucharest, Romania.

Pospiśal, Milan. Secretary of the Council for National Minorities, Czech Government, March 13, 1998, Prague, Czech Republic.

Rostaş, Julius. Government Adviser, Department for the Protection of National Minorities, Romanian Government, 22 July 1998, Bucharest, Romania.

Shahu, Xhemil. Albanian field officer, United Nations High Commissioner for Refugees, Emergency Management Group Protection Officer. 5 April 2003. Tirana, Albania.

Sirovátka, Tomáš. Professor of Economics, University of Masaryk, Brno, 18 December 1997; 9 February 1998, Brno, Czech Republic.

Szatmári, Tibor. UDMR Adviser on International Relations. 26 May 1998. Bucharest, Romania.

Tokay, György. Minister for Ethnic Minorities, Romanian Government, 2 April 1998, Bucharest, Romania.

Várady, Tibor. Former Minister of Justice and Hungarian Minority Representative, Yugoslavia, 3 September 2002, Budapest, Hungary.

Varga, Attila. Democratic Alliance of Hungarians in Romania Deputy, Romanian Parliament, 8 April 1998, Bucharest, Romania.

Veselý, Ivan. Member of the Czech Government Commission on Roma Affairs, 8 July 1998, Prague, Czech Republic.

Voicu, Mădălin. Roma Party Deputy, Romanian Parliament, 7 April 1998, Bucharest, Romania.

Selected Bibliography

Adamson, Fiona B. "Global Liberalism versus Political Islam." *International Studies Review* 7 (2005): 547–69.

——. "Globalisation, Transnational Political Mobilization, and Networks of Violence." *Cambridge Review of International Affairs* 18 (2005): 31–49.

Alesina, Alberto F., and Enrico Spolaore. "On the Number and Size of Nations." *Quarterly Journal of Economics* 112 (1997): 1027–56.

Anderson, Benedict. *Imagined Communities: Reflections on the Origins and Spread of Nationalism.* London: Verso, 1991.

Bakker, Edwin. *Minority Conflicts in Slovakia and Hungary?* Capelle an den Ijssel, The Netherlands: Labyrint, 1997.

Barany, Zoltan D. "Ethnic Mobilization without Prerequisites: The East European Gypsies." *World Politics* 54 (2002): 277–307.

Barth, Fredrik. Introduction to *Ethnic Groups and Boundaries: The Social Organisation of Culture Difference,* edited by Fredrik Barth, 9–38. Bergen/Oslo, Norway: Universitetsforlaget, 1969.

Beissinger, Mark R. *Nationalist Mobilization and the Collapse of the Soviet State.* Cambridge, U.K.: Cambridge University Press, 2002.

Beneš, Eduard. "After Locarno: The Problem of Security Today." *Foreign Affairs* 4 (January 1926): 195–210.

Beuer, Gustav. *Berlin or Prague? The Germans of Czechoslovakia at the Cross-Roads.* London: Lofox, 1944.

Bílek, Bohumil. *Fifth Column at Work.* London: Trinity, 1945.

Birner, Jóhanna Kristín. *Ethnicity and Electoral Politics.* New York: Cambridge University Press, 2006.

Bob, Clifford. *The Marketing of Rebellion: Insurgents, Media, and International Activism.* New York: Cambridge University Press, 2005.

Bohm, Jaroslav, ed. *The Great Moravian Empire.* Prague: Czechoslovak Academy of Sciences, 1963.

Bookman, Milica Zarkovic. "Economic Issues Underlying Secession: The Case of Slovenia and Slovakia." *Communist Economies and Economic Transformation* 4 (1992): 111–34.

Borsody, Stephen. "State- and Nation-building in Central Europe: The Origins of the Hungarian Problem." In *The Hungarians: A Divided Nation,* edited by Borsody. New Haven: Yale Center for International and Area Studies, 1988.

Brass, Paul. *Ethnicity and Nationalism: Theory and Comparison.* Newbury Park, Calif.: Sage, 1991.

———. *Language, Religion and Politics in North India.* Cambridge, U.K.: Cambridge University Press, 1974.

Breuilly, John. *Nationalism and the State.* Chicago: University of Chicago Press, 1994.

Brock, Peter. *The Slovak National Awakening.* Toronto: University of Toronto Press, 1976.

Brown, Michael E. *Ethnic Conflict and International Security.* Princeton: Princeton University Press, 1993.

Brubaker, Rogers. "Nationhood and the National Question in the Soviet Union and Post-Soviet Eurasia: An Institutionalist Account." *Theory and Society* 23 (1994): 47–78.

———. *Nationalism Reframed.* Cambridge, U.K.: Cambridge University Press, 1996.

Brügel, Johann Wolfgang. *Tschechen und Deutsche, 1918–1938.* Munich: Nymphenburger Verlagshandlung, 1967.

———. *Czechoslovakia before Munich: The German Minority Problem and British Appeasement Policy.* Cambridge, U.K.: Cambridge University Press, 1973.

Brysk, Allison. *From Tribal Village to Global Village: Indian Rights and International Relations in Latin America.* Stanford: Stanford University Press, 2000.

Buchanan, Allen. "Self-Determination and the Right to Secede." *Journal of International Affairs* 45 (winter 1992): 347–66.

Bugajski, Janusz. *Ethnic Politics in Eastern Europe: A Guide to Nationality Policies, Organizations, and Parties.* Armonk, N.Y.: M. E. Sharpe, 1994.

Bunce, Valerie. *Subversive Institutions: The Design and the Destruction of Socialism and the State.* Cambridge, U.K.: Cambridge University Press, 1999.

Burgess, Adam. "Critical Reflections on the Return of National Minority Rights to East/West European Affairs." In *Ethnicity and Democratisation in the New Europe,* edited by Karl Cordell, 49–60. London: Routledge, 1999.

Bútora, Martin, and Thomas W. Skladony, eds. *Slovakia 1996–1997: A Global Report on the State of Society.* Bratislava, Slovakia: Institute for Public Affairs/ Inštitút pre verejné otázky, 1998.

Byman, Daniel L. "Divided They Stand: Lessons about Partition from Iraq and Lebanon." *Security Studies* 7 (autumn 1997): 1–29.

Campbell, Gregory F. *Confrontation in Central Europe: Weimar Germany and Czechoslovakia.* Chicago: University of Chicago Press, 1975.

——. *The Road to Kosovo: A Balkan Diary.* Boulder: Westview, 2000.

Capotorti, Francesco. *Study on the Rights of Persons Belonging to Ethnic, Religious and Linguistic Minorities.* New York: United Nations, 1979.

Carment, David, and Dane Rowlands. "Vengeance and Intervention: Can Third Parties Bring Peace without Separation?" *Security Studies* 13 (2004): 366–93.

Cassese, Antonio. *Self-Determination of Peoples: A Legal Reappraisal.* Cambridge, U.K.: Cambridge University Press, 1995.

Cetinyan, Rupen. "Ethnic Bargaining in the Shadow of Third-Party Intervention," *International Organization* 56 (2002): 645–77.

Chandra, Kanchan. *Why Ethnic Parties Succeed: Patronage and Ethnic Head Counts in India.* Cambridge, U.K.: Cambridge University Press, 2004.

Chazan, Naomi, ed. *Irredentism and International Politics.* Boulder: Lynne Rienner, 1991.

Chmelař, Josef. *Political Parties in Czechoslovakia.* Prague: Orbis Library, 1926.

Cohen, Shari J. *Politics without a Past: The Absence of History in Postcommunist Nationalism.* Durham, N.C.: Duke University Press, 1999.

Collier, Paul, and Anke Hoeffler. "Greed and Grievance in Civil War." *Oxford Economic Papers* 56 (2004): 563–95.

Connor, Walker. *Ethnonationalism: The Quest for Understanding.* Princeton: Princeton University Press, 1994.

Cornell, Svante. "Autonomy as a Source of Conflict: Caucasian Conflicts in Theoretical Perspective." *World Politics* 54 (2002): 245–76.

Cseres, Tibor. *Titoist Atrocities in Vojvodina, 1944–1945: Serbian Vendetta in Bácska.* Buffalo: Hunyadi, 1993.

Csergő, Zsuzsa. *Language, Division, and Integration: Lessons from Post-Communist Romania and Slovakia.* Ithaca: Cornell University Press, 2007.

Cumper, Peter, and Steven Wheatley, eds. *Minority Rights in the "New" Europe.* The Hague: Martinus Nijhoff, 1999.

Daalder, Ivo, and Michael O'Hanlen. *Winning Ugly: NATO's War to Save Kosovo.* Washington, D.C.: Brookings Institute, 2000.

Deets, Stephen, and Sherrill Stroschein. "Dilemmas of Autonomy and Liberal Pluralism: Examples Involving Hungarians in Central Europe," *Nations and Nationalism* 11 (2005): 285–305.

De Figueiredo, Rui J. P., Jr., and Barry R. Weingast. "The Rationality of Fear: Political Opportunism and Ethnic Conflict." In *Civil Wars, Insecurity, and Intervention,* edited by Barbara Walter and Jack Snyder, 261–302. New York: Columbia University Press, 1999.

Diez, Thomas. "Why the EU Can Nonetheless Be Good for Cyprus." *Journal on Ethnopolitics and Minority Issues in Europe* (2002), Special Focus 2.

Dobre, Ana-Maria. "EU Conditionality Building and Romanian Minority Rights Policy: Towards the Europeanisation of the Candidate Countries." *Perspectives on European Politics and Society* 4 (2003): 55–83.

Dobrovolný, Marek. *Mečiar.* Prague: JPM Tisk, 1998.

Downes, Alexander B. "The Problem with Negotiated Solutions to Ethnic Civil Wars," *Security Studies* 13 (2004): 230–79.

Durch, William. "Keeping the Peace: Politics and Lessons of the 1990s." In *UN Peacekeeping, American Policy, and the Uncivil Wars of the 1990s,* edited by William Durch, 1–29. New York: St. Martin's Press, 1996.

Eisinger, Peter. "The Conditions of Protest Behavior in American Cities." *American Political Science Review* 67 (March 1973): 11–28.

Elster, Jon. "Consenting Adults or the Sorcerer's Apprentice? Explaining the Breakup of the Czechoslovak Federation." *East European Constitutional Review* (winter 1995): 36–41.

——. "Transition, Constitution-Making and Separation in Czechoslovakia." *European Journal of Sociology/Archives Europeenne de Sociologie* 36 (1995): 105–34.

Essler, F. W. *Twenty Years of Sudeten German Losses, 1918–1938.* Vienna: Friedrich Jasper, 1938.

Etzioni, Amitai. "The Evils of Self-Determination." *Foreign Policy* 89 (1992–1993): 21–35.

Fearon, James D. "Commitment Problems and the Spread of Ethnic Conflict." In *The International Spread of Ethnic Conflict: Fear, Diffusion, and Escalation,* edited by David Lake and Donald Rothchild, 107–26. Princeton: Princeton University Press, 1998.

——. "Rationalist Explanations for War." *International Organization* 49 (1995): 379–414.

——. "Separatist Wars, Partition, and World Order." *Security Studies* 13 (2004): 394–415.

Fearon, James D., and David D. Laitin. "Ethnicity, Insurgency, and Civil War." *American Political Science Review* 97 (2004): 75–90.

Fein, Helen. "Genocide: A Sociological Perspective," *Current Sociology* 38 (1990): 1–126

Feinberg, Nathan. "International Protection of Human Rights and the Jewish Question: (A Historical Survey)." *Israel Law Review* 3, no. 4 (1968).

Felak, James Ramon. *At the Price of the Republic: Hlinka's Slovak People's Party, 1929–1938.* Pittsburgh: University of Pittsburgh Press, 1994.

Friedman, David. "An Economic Theory of the Size and Shape of Nations." *Journal of Political Economy* 85 (1977): 59–77.

Friedman, Francine. "Kosovo and Vojvodina: One Yugoslav Solution to Autonomy in a Multiethnic State." In *Governing Peoples and Territories,* edited by Daniel J. Elazar, 59–87. Philadelphia: Institute for the Study of Human Issues, 1982.

Freund, Richard. *Watch Czechoslovakia!* London: Thomas Nelson & Sons, 1937.

Fuchs, Gerhard. *Gegen Hitler und Henlein.* Berlin: Rütten & Loening, 1961.

Gagnon, V. P., Jr. "Ethnic Nationalism and International Conflict: The Case of Serbia." *International Security* 19 (winter 1994–1995): 130–66.

——. *The Myth of Ethnic War: Serbia and Croatia in the 1990s.* Ithaca: Cornell University Press, 2004.

Gallagher, Tom. "Vatra Românească and Resurgent Nationalism in Romania." *Ethnic and Racial Studies* 15 (1992): 570–98.

Gantzel, Klaus Jürgen. "War in the Post–World War II World: Some Empirical Trends and a Theoretical Approach." In *War and Ethnicity: Global Connections and Local Violence,* edited by David Turton, 123–44. Rochester, N.Y.: University of Rochester Press, 1997.

Geertz, Clifford. "The Integrative Revolution: Primordial Sentiments and Civil Politics in the New States." In *Old Societie and New States: The Quest for Modernity in Asia and Africa,* edited by Clifford Geertz, 105–57. New York: Free Press, 1963.

Gellner, Ernest. *Nations and Nationalism.* Ithaca: Cornell University Press, 1983.

Giuliano, Elise. "Who Determines the Self in the Politics of Self-Determination? Identity and Preference Formation in Tatarstan's Nationalist Mobilization." *Comparative Politics* 32 (2000): 295–316.

Gorenburg, Dmitry P. *Minority Ethnic Mobilization in the Russian Federation.* Cambridge, U.K.: Cambridge University Press, 2003.

Gottlieb, Gidon. "Nations without States." *Foreign Affairs* 73 (1994): 100–112.

Gourevitch, Peter Alexis. "The Reemergence of 'Peripheral Nationalisms': Some Comparative Speculations on the Spatial Distribution of Political Leadership and Economic Growth." *Comparative Studies in Society and History* 21 (1979): 303–23.

Grabbe, Heather. "How Does Europeanization Affect CEE Governance? Conditionality, Diffusion and Diversity." *Journal of European Public Policy* 8 (2001): 1013–31.

Gruber, Josef, ed. *Czechoslovakia: A Survey of Economic and Social Conditions.* New York: Macmillan, 1924.

Grünwald, Leopold. *Sudetendeutscher Widerstand gegen Hitler.* Munich: Fides, 1978.

Gurr, Ted Robert. *Minorities at Risk: A Global View of Ethnopolitical Conflicts.* Washington, D.C.: United States Institute of Peace Press, 1993.

——. *People versus States.* Washington, D.C.: United States Institute of Peace, 2000.

——. *Why Men Rebel.* Princeton: Princeton University Press, 1971.

Gurr, Ted Robert, and Will H. Moore. "Ethnopolitical Rebellion: A Cross-sectional Analysis of the 1980s with Risk Assessments for the 1990s." *American Journal of Political Science* 41 (1997): 1079–1103.

Haas, Richard N. "Military Force: A User's Guide." *Foreign Policy* 96 (1993): 21–37.

Hale, Henry E. "The Parade of Sovereignties: Testing Theories of Secession in the Soviet Setting." *British Journal of Political Science* 30 (2000): 31–56.

Hannum, Hurst. *Autonomy, Sovereignty, and Self-Determination: The Accommodation of Conflicting Rights.* Philadelphia: University of Pennsylvania Press, 1990.

——. "International Law." In *Encyclopedia of Nationalism.* New York: Academic Press, 2001.

Harbom, Lotta, and Peter Wallensteen. "Armed Conflict and Its International Dimensions, 1946–2004." *Journal of Peace Research* 42 (2005): 623–35.

Harff, Barbara, and Ted Robert Gurr. "Toward Empirical Theory of Genocides and Politicides." *International Studies Quarterly* 32 (1988): 359–71.

Harris, Peter, and Ben Reilly, eds. *Democracy and Deep-Rooted Conflict: Options for Negotiators.* Stockholm: International Institute for Democracy and Electoral Assistance, 1998.

Havlík, Lubomír E. *Kronika o Velké Moravě.* Brno: JOTA, 1992.

Hechter, Michael. *Internal Colonialism.* Berkeley: University of California Press, 1975.

Henderson, Alexander. *Eyewitness in Czecho-slovakia.* London: George G. Harrap, 1939.

Heraclides, Alexis. *The Self-Determination of Minorities in International Politics.* London: Frank Cass, 1991.

Herrera, Yoshiko M. *Imagined Economies: The Sources of Russian Regionalism.* Cambridge, U.K.: Cambridge University Press, 2005.

Hobsbawm, E. J. *Nations and Nationalism since 1780: Programme, Myth, Reality.* Cambridge, U.K.: Cambridge University Press, 1992.

Hoch, Charles. *The Political Parties in Czechoslovakia.* Prague: Orbis, 1936.

Hodža, Milan. *Federation in Central Europe: Reflections and Reminiscences.* London: Jarrold's, 1942.

Horowitz, Donald L. *The Deadly Ethnic Riot.* Berkeley: University of California Press, 2001.

——. *Ethnic Groups in Conflict.* Berkeley: University of California Press, 1985.

——. "Making Moderation Pay." In *Conflict and Peacemaking in Multiethnic Societies,* edited by Joseph V. Montville, 451–76. New York: Lexington Books, 1991.

Hroch, Miroslav. "From National Movement to the Fully-Formed Nation: The Nation-Building Process in Europe." *New Left Review* 198 (1993): 3–20.

Innes, Abby. "The Breakup of Czechoslovakia: The Impact of Party Development on the Separation of the State." *East European Politics and Societies* 11 (fall 1997): 393–435.

——. *Czechoslovakia: The Short Goodbye.* New Haven: Yale University Press, 2002.

Israel, Fred L., ed. *Major Peace Treaties of Modern History, 1648–1967.* New York: Chelsea House, 1967.

Jahn, Rudolf, ed. *Konrad Henlein spricht: Reden zur politischen Volksbewegung der Sudetendeutschen* [A compilation of Konrad Henlein's public addresses]. Karlsbad, Czechoslovakia: Karl H. Frank, 1937.

Jenne, Erin. "A Bargaining Theory of Minority Demands: Explaining the Dog That Did Not Bite in 1990s Yugoslavia." *International Studies Quarterly* 48 (2004): 729–54.

Jenne, Erin K., Stephen M. Saideman, and Will Lowe. "Separatism as a Bargaining Posture: The Role of Leverage in Group Claim-making." *Journal of Peace Research,* forthcoming.

Judah, Tim. *Kosovo: War and Revenge.* New Haven: Yale University Press, 2000.

Junghann, Otto. *National Minorities in Europe.* New York: Covici, Friede, 1932.

Kaplan, Robert. "The Coming Anarchy." *Atlantic Monthly* 273 (1998): 44–76.

Kaufman, Stuart. *Modern Hatreds: The Symbolic Politics of Ethnic War.* Ithaca: Cornell University Press, 2001.

———. "Spiraling to Ethnic War: Elites, Masses, and Moscow in Moldova's Civil War." *International Security* 21 (1996): 108–38.

Kaufmann, Chaim. "When All Else Fails: Ethnic Population Transfers and Partitions in the Twentieth Century." *International Security* 23 (fall 1998): 120–56.

———. "Possible and Impossible Solutions to Ethnic Civil Wars." *International Security* 20 (spring 1996): 136–75.

Keck, Margaret E., and Kathryn Sikkink. *Activists beyond Borders: Advocacy Networks in International Politics.* Ithaca: Cornell University Press, 1998.

Kelley, Judith G. *Ethnic Politics in Europe: The Power of Norms and Incentives.* Princeton: Princeton University Press, 2004.

Kitschelt, Herbert. "Political Opportunity Structures and Political Protest: Anti-Nuclear Movements in Four Democracies." *British Journal of Political Science* 16 (1986): 57–85.

Klepetar, Harry. *Der Sprachenkampf in den Sudetenlandern.* Prague: Ed. Strache, 1930.

Knapp, Viktor. "Socialist Federation—A Legal Means to the Solution of the Nationality Problem: A Comparative Study." *Michigan Law Review* 82 (April–May 1984): 1213–28.

Kocsis, Károly, and Eszter Kocsis-Hodosi. *Hungarian Minorities in the Carpathian Basin.* Toronto: Matthias Corvinus, 1995.

Koegler, Franz, and Edward FitzGerald. *Oppressed Minority?* London: Hutchinson, 1943.

Kopeček, Herman. "Zusammenarbeit and Spoluprace: Sudeten German-Czech Co-operation in Interwar Czechoslovakia." *Nationalities Papers* 24 (1996): 63–77.

Kopecký, Petr. "From 'Velvet Revolution' to 'Velvet Split': Consociational Institutions and the Disintegration of Czechoslovakia." In *Irreconcilable Differences? Explaining Czechoslovakia's Dissolution,* edited by Michael Kraus and Allison Stanger, 69–86. Lanham, Md.: Rowman and Littlefield, 2000.

Krasner, Stephen D. *Sovereignty: Organized Hypocrisy.* Princeton: Princeton University Press, 1999.

Kraus, Michael, and Allison Stanger, eds. *Irreconcilable Differences? Explaining Czechoslovakia's Dissolution.* Lanham, Md.: Rowman and Littlefield, 2000.

Krejčí, Oskar. *Kniha o volbách.* Prague: Victoria, 1994.

Kumar, Radha. "The Troubled History of Partition." *Foreign Affairs* 76 (January–February 1997): 22–34.

Kuperman, Alan J. "Is Partition Really the Only Hope? Reconciling Contradictory Findings About Ethnic Civil Wars." *Security Studies* 13 (2004): 314–49.

———. *The Limits of Humanitarian Intervention: Genocide in Rwanda.* Washington, D.C.: Brookings Institution Press, 2001.

———. "Provoking Genocide: A Revised History of the Rwandan Patriotic Front." *Journal of Genocide Research* 6 (2004): 61–84.

Kuran, Timor. "Ethnic Dissimilation and Its International Diffusion." In *The International Spread of Conflict: Fear, Diffusion, and Escalation,* edited by David A. Lake and Donald Rothchild, 35–60. Princeton: Princeton University Press, 1998.

Kymlicka, Will. *Multicultural Citizenship: A Liberal Theory of Minority Rights.* Oxford, U.K.: Oxford University Press, 1995.

Laitin, David D. "Ethnic Unmixing and Civil War." *Security Studies* 13 (2004): 350–65.

———. *Identity in Formation: The Russian-Speaking Populations in the Near Abroad.* Ithaca: Cornell University Press, 1998.

———. "Language Policy and Political Strategy in India." *Policy Sciences* 22 (1989): 415–36.

———. "Secessionist Rebellion in the Former Soviet Union." *Comparative Political Studies* 34 (2001): 839–61.

Lake, David, and Donald Rothchild. "Containing Fear: The Origins and Management of Ethnic Conflict." *International Security* 21 (fall 1996): 41–75.

Lapidoth, Ruth. *Autonomy: Flexible Solutions to Ethnic Conflicts.* Washington, D.C.: United States Institute for Peace Press, 1996.

Leff, Carol Skalnik. *The Czech and Slovak Republics.* Boulder: Westview, 1997.

———. "Inevitability, Probability, Possibility: The Legacies of the Czech-Slovak Relationship, 1918–1989." In *Irreconcilable Differences? Explaining Czechoslovakia's Dissolution,* edited by Michael Kraus and Allison Stanger, 29–48. Lanham: Rowman and Littlefield, 2000.

———. *National Conflict in Czechoslovakia: The Making and Remaking of a State, 1918–1987.* Princeton: Princeton University Press, 1988.

Lenin. *Critical Remarks on the National Question: The Right of Nations to Self-Determination.* Westport: Greenwood, 1951.

Lerner, Natan. *Group Rights and Discrimination in International Law.* Dordrecht: Martinus Nijhoff, 1991.

Licklider, Roy. "The Consequences of Negotiated Settlements in Civil Wars, 1945–1993." *American Political Science Review* 89 (September 1995): 681–90.

Lijphart, Arendt. "The Comparable-Cases Strategy in Comparative Research." *Comparative Political Studies* (1975): 158–77.

———. "The Power-Sharing Approach." In *Conflict and Peacemaking in Multiethnic Societies,* edited by Joseph V. Montville, 491–510. Lexington: Lexington Books, 1991.

Macartney, C. A. *National States and National Minorities.* London: Oxford University Press, 1934.

Mareš, Miroslav, ed. *Etnické a regionální strany v ČR po roce 1989.* Brno: Centrum pro studium demokracie a kultury, 2003.

Masaryk, Tomáš Garrigue. *Cesta Demokracie.* Prague: Čin, 1933.

Maynes, Charles M. "Relearning Intervention." *Foreign Policy* 98 (1995): 96–113.

McAdam, Doug, John McCarthy, and Mayer Zald, eds. *Comparative Perspectives on Social Movements.* New York: Cambridge University Press, 1996.

McAdam, Doug, Sidney Tarrow, and Charles Tilly, eds. *Dynamics of Contention.* New York: Cambridge University Press, 2001.

McAdam, Doug, John D. McCarthy, and Meyer N. Zald, eds. *Comparative Perspectives on Social Movements Political Opportunities, Mobilizing Structures, and Cultural Framings.* New York: Cambridge University Press, 1996.

Mearsheimer, John. "Back to the Future: Instability in Europe after the Cold War." *International Security* 15 (summer 1990): 5–56.

Měřinský, Zdeněk, et al., eds. *Za Moravu.* Brno: Jednota Moravská, 1991.

Mertus, Julie A. *Kosovo: How Myths and Truths Started a War.* Berkeley: University of California Press, 1999.

Minority Rights Group. *World Directory of Minorities.* London: Minority Rights Group International, 1997.

Moore, Will H., and David R. Davis. "Transnational Ethnic Ties and Foreign Policy." In *The International Spread of Ethnic Conflict: Fear, Diffusion, and Escalation,* edited by David A. Lake and Donald S. Rothchild, 89–104. Princeton: Princeton University Press, 1998.

Moore, Will H., and Keith Jaggers. "Deprivation, Mobilization, and the State: A Synthetic Model of Rebellion." *Journal of Developing Societies* 6 (1990): 17–36.

Musgrave, Thomas D. *Self-Determination and National Minorities.* Oxford: Oxford University Press, 1997.

Musil, Jiří, ed. *The End of Czechoslovakia.* Budapest: Central European University Press, 2000.

Naimark, Norman M. *Fires of Hatred: Ethnic Cleansing in Twentieth-Century Europe.* Cambridge: Harvard University Press, 2001.

Nairn, Tom. "Scotland and Europe." *New Left Review* 83 (January– February 1974): 57–82.

Nordquist, Kjell-Åke. "Autonomy as a Conflict-Solving Mechanism—An Overview." In *Autonomy: Applications and Implications,* edited by Markku Suksi, 59–77. The Hague: Kluwer Law International, 1998.

Oberleitner, Gerd. 1999. "Monitoring Minority Rights under the Council of Europe's Framework Convention." In *Minority Rights in the "New" Europe,* edited by Peter Cumper and Steven Wheatley, 71–88. The Hague: Kluwer Law International.

Ofuatey-Kodjoe, W. *The Principle of Self-Determination in International Law.* New York: Mellen, 1977.

Pavel, Antonin. "Land Reform." Chapter 4 in *Czechoslovakia: A Survey of Economic and Social Conditions,* edited by Dr. Josef Gruber. New York: Macmillan, 1924.

Pernes, Jiří. *Pod moravskou orlicí aneb Dejiny moravanství.* Brno: Barrister and Principal, 1996.

Peroutka, Ferdinand, ed. *Budování Státu.* Vols. 3–4. Prague: F. Borovy, 1920–1921.

Petersen, Roger D. *Understanding Ethnic Violence: Fear Hatred, and Resentment in Twentieth-Century Eastern Europe.* Cambridge, U.K.: Cambridge University Press, 2002.

Petrášová, Eva. *Případ Mečiar.* Prague: Cesty, 1991.

Posen, Barry R. "The Security Dilemma and Ethnic Conflict." In *Ethnic Conflict and International Security,* edited by Michael Brown, 103–24. Princeton: Princeton University Press, 1993.

Posner, Daniel N. "The Political Salience of Cultural Difference: Why Chewas and Tumbukas Are Allies in Zambia and Adversaries in Malawi." *American Political Science Review* 98 (2004): 529–46.

Ragin, Charles. *The Comparative Method: Moving beyond Qualitative and Quantitative Strategies.* Berkeley: University of California Press, 1987.

——. *Fuzzy-Set Social Science.* Chicago: University of Chicago Press, 2000.

Ramet, Sabrina Petra. *Whose Democracy? Nationalism, Religion, and the Doctrine of Collective Rights in Post-1989 Eastern Europe.* Lanham, Md.: Rowman and Littlefield, 1997.

Rehman, Javaid. "The Concept of Autonomy and Minority Rights in Europe." In *Minority Rights in the "New" Europe,* edited by Peter Cumper and Steven Wheatley, 217–32. The Hague: Kluwer Law International, 1999.

Robinson, Jacob, Oscar Karbach, Max M. Laserson, Nehemiah Robinson, and Marc Vichniak. *Were the Minorities Treaties a Failure?* New York: Institute of Jewish Affairs of the American Jewish Congress and the World Jewish Congress, 1943.

Roeder, Philip G. "Soviet Federalism and Ethnic Mobilization." *World Politics* 43 (1991): 196–232.

——. *Where Nation-States Come From: Institutional Change in the Age of Nationalism.* Princeton: Princeton University Press, 2007.

Romsics, Ignác. *Hungary in the Twentieth Century.* Budapest: Corvina Osiris Kiadó, 1999.

Rothchild, Donald. "Collective Demands for Improved Distributions." In *State versus Ethnic Claims: African Policy Dilemmas,* edited by Donald Rothchild and Victor A. Olorunsola, 172–98. Boulder: Westview, 1983.

Rothchild, Donald, and Philip G. Roeder. "Power Sharing as an Impediment to Peace and Democracy." In *Sustainable Peace: Power and Democracy after Civil Wars,* edited by Philip G. Roeder and Donald Rothchild, 29–50. Ithaca: Cornell University Press, 2005.

Rothschild, Joseph. *Ethnopolitics: A Conceptual Framework.* New York: Columbia University Press, 1981.

Saideman, Stephen M. "Inconsistent Irredentism? Political Competition, Ethnic Ties, and the Foreign Policies of Somalia and Serbia." *Security Studies* 7 (1998): 51–93.

——. *The Ties That Divide: Ethnic Politics, Foreign Policy and International Conflict.* New York: Columbia University Press, 2001.

Saideman, Stephen, and R. William Ayres. "Determining the Causes of Irredentism: Logit Analyses of Minorities at Risk Data for the 1980s and 1990s." *Journal of Politics* 62 (November 2000): 1126–44.

Sambanis, Nicholas. "Partition as a Solution to Ethnic War: An Empirical Critique of the Theoretical Literature." *World Politics* 52 (July 2000): 437–83.

Schaeffer, Robert. *Warpaths: The Politics of Partition.* New York: Hill and Wang, 1990.

Scheffer, David J. "International Judicial Intervention." *Foreign Policy* 102 (1996): 34–51.

Schimmelfennig, Frank, and Ulrich Sedelmeier, eds. *The Europeanization of Central and Eastern Europe.* Ithaca: Cornell University Press, 2005.

Schöpflin, George. "Nationalism and National Minorities in East and Central Europe." *Journal of International Affairs* 45 (1991): 51–65.

Schöpflin, George, and Hugh Poulton. *Romania's Ethnic Hungarians.* London: Minority Rights Group, 1990.

Schwellnus, Guido. "The Adoption of Nondiscrimination and Minority Protection Rules in Romania, Hungary and Poland." In *The Europeanization of Central and Eastern Europe,* edited by Frank Schimmelfennig and Ulrich Sedelmeier, 51–70. Ithaca: Cornell University Press, 2005.

Seton-Watson, Hugh. *Eastern Europe between the Wars, 1918–1941.* New York: Harper and Row, 1962.

Shepsle, Kenneth, and Rabushka, Alvin. *Politics in Plural Societies: A Theory of Democratic Instability.* Columbus: Charles Merrill, 1972.

Shils, Edward. "Primordial, Personal, and Sacred Ties." *British Journal of Sociology* 8 (1957): 130–45.

Singule, Hans. *Der Staat Masaryks.* Berlin: Freiheitsverlag, 1937.

Sisk, Timothy. "Peacemaking Processes: Forestalling Return to Ethnic Violence." In *Preventive Negotiation: Avoiding Conflict Escalation,* edited by I. William Zartman, 67–89. Lanham, Md.: Rowman and Littlefield, 2001.

Skilling, Gordon H. *Czechoslovakia's Interrupted Revolution.* Princeton: Princeton University Press, 1976.

Slezkine, Yuri. "The USSR as a Communal Apartment, or How a Socialist State Promoted Ethnic Particularism." *Slavic Review* 53 (summer 1994): 414–53.

Smelser, Ronald M. *The Sudeten German Problem, 1933–1938: Volkstumspolitik and the Formulation of Nazi foreign policy.* Middletown, Conn.: Wesleyan University Press, 1975.

Sniderman, Paul M., Joseph F. Fletcher, Peter H. Russell, and Philip E. Tetlock. "Political Culture and the Problem of Double Standards: Mass and Elite Attitudes toward Language Rights in the Canadian Charter of Rights and Freedoms." *Canadian Journal of Political Science/Revue canadienne de science politique* 22 (1989): 259–84.

Snyder, Jack L. *From Voting to Violence: Democratization and Nationalist Conflict.* New York: Norton, 2000.

Solnick, Steven. "Will Russia Survive: Center and Periphery in the Russian Federation." In *Post-Soviet Political Order,* edited by Barnett R. Rubin and Jack Snyder, 58–80. London: Routledge, 1998.

Stanger, Allison. "The Price of Velvet: Constitutional Politics and the Demise of the Czechoslovak Federation." In *Irreconcilable Differences? Explaining Czechoslovakia's Dissolution,* edited by Michael Kraus and Allison Stanger, 137–62. Lanham, Md.: Rowman and Littlefield, 2000.

Stavenhagen, Rodolfo. "Challenging the Nation-State in Latin-America." *Journal of International Affairs* 45 (winter 1992): 421–40.

Stein, Eric. *Czecho/Slovakia: Ethnic Conflict, Constitutional Fissure, Negotiated Breakup.* Ann Arbor: University of Michigan Press, 1997.

———. "Post-Communist Constitution-Making: Confessions of a Comparativist (Part I)." *New Europe Law Review* 1 (spring 1993): 421–88.

Suny, Ronald Grigor. *The Revenge of the Past: Nationalism, Revolution, and the Collapse of the Soviet Union.* Stanford: Stanford University Press, 1993.

Sureda, A. Rigo. *The Evolution of the Right of Self-Determination: A Study of United Nations Practice.* Leiden: A. W. Sijthoff, 1973.

Swidler, Ann. "Culture in Action: Symbols and Strategies." *American Sociological Review* 51 (1986): 273–86.

Tarrow, Sidney. *Power in Movement: Social Movements, Collective Action, and Politics.* New York: Cambridge University Press, 1994.

——. "Social Movements in Contentious Politics: A Review Article." *American Political Science Review* 90 (1996): 874–83.

Tesser, Lynn M. "The Geopolitics of Tolerance: Minority Rights under EU Expansion in East-Central Europe." *East European Politics and Societies* 17 (summer 2003): 483–532.

Tishkov, Valery. *Ethnicity, Nationalism, and Conflict in and after the Soviet Union: The Mind Aflame.* London: Sage, 1997.

Toft, Monica. *The Geography of Ethnic Violence: Identity, Interests, and the Indivisibility of Territory.* Princeton: Princeton University Press, 2003.

Treisman, Daniel S. "Russia's 'Ethnic Revival': The Separatist Activism of Regional Leaders in a Postcommunist Order." *World Politics* 49 (January 1997): 212–49.

Vachudova, Milada Anna. 2005. *Europe Undivided: Democracy, Leverage, and Integration After Communism.* Oxford, U.K.: Oxford University Press.

Van Evera, Stephen. "Hypotheses on Nationalism and War." *International Security* 18 (spring 1994): 5–39.

Van Houten, Pieter. "The Role of a Minority's Reference State in Ethnic Relations." *Archives européenes de sociologie* 34 (spring 1998): 110–46.

Varshney, Ashutosh. "Ethnic Conflict and Civil Society: India and Beyond." *World Politics* 53 (2001): 362–98.

Vermeersch, Peter. "Ethnic Mobilisation and the Political Conditionality of European Union Accession: The Case of the Roma in Slovakia." *Journal of Ethnic and Migration Studies* 28 (2002): 83–101.

Wallensteen, Peter, and Margareta Sollenberg. "Armed Conflict, 1989–99." *Journal of Peace Research* 37 (2000): 635–49.

Walter, Barbara F. "The Critical Barrier to Civil War Settlement." *International Organization* 51 (summer 1997): 335–64.

Weingast, Barry R. "Political Stability and Civil War: Institutions, Commitment, and American Democracy." In *Analytic Narratives,* edited by Robert Bates, Avner Greif, Margaret Levi, Jean-Laurent Rosenthal, and Barry R. Weingast, 148–93. Princeton: Princeton University Press, 1998.

Wheaton, Bernard, and Zdenek Kavan. *The Velvet Revolution: Czechoslovakia, 1988–1991.* Boulder: Westview, 1992.

Wingfield, Nancy Merriwether. *Minority Politics in a Multinational State: The German Social Democrats in Czechoslovakia, 1918–1938.* Boulder: East European Monographs, 1989.

Wiskemann, Elizabeth. *Czechs and Germans: A Study of the Struggle in the Historic Provinces of Bohemia and Moravia.* New York: St. Martin's, 1938.

Wolchik, Sharon L. *Czechoslovakia in Transition: Politics, Economics, and Society.* London: Pinter, 1991.

———. "The Impact of Institutional Factors on the Breakup of the Czechoslovak Federation." In *Irreconcilable Differences? Explaining Czechoslovakia's Dissolution,* edited by Michael Kraus and Allison Stanger, 87–106. Lanham, Md.: Rowman and Littlefield, 2000.

———. "The Politics of Transition and the Break-up of Czechoslovakia." In *The End of Czechoslovakia,* edited by Jiří Musil, 225–44. Budapest: Central European University Press, 1995.

Wolff, Stefan. "'Bilateral' Ethnopolitics after the Cold War: The Hungarian Minority in Slovakia, 1989–1999." *Perspectives on European Politics and Society* 2: 159–95.

Woodward, Susan L. *Balkan Tragedy: Chaos and Dissolution after the Cold War.* Washington D.C.: Brookings Institution Press, 1995.

Yarbrough, Beth V., and Robert M. Yarbrough. "Unification and Secession: Group Size and 'Escape from Lock-In,'", *Kyklos—International Review for Social Sciences* 51 (1998): 171–96.

Young, Crawford. *The Politics of Cultural Pluralism.* Madison: University of Wisconsin Press, 1976.

Young, Robert A. "The Breakup of Czechoslovakia." Research Paper 32. Kingston, Ontario, Canada: Institute of Intergovernmental Relations, Queen's University, 1994.

Zahar, Marie-Joëlle. "Power Sharing in Lebanon: Foreign Protectors, Domestic Peace, and Democratic Failure." In *Sustainable Peace: Power and Democracy after Civil Wars,* edited by Philip G. Roeder and Donald Rothchild, 219–40. Ithaca: Cornell University Press, 2005.

Zartman, William. "Putting Things Back Together." In *Collapsed States: The Disintegration and Restoration of Legitimate Authority,* edited by William Zartman, 267–73. Boulder: Lynne Rienner, 1995.

———, ed. *Preventive Negotiation: Avoiding Conflict Escalation.* Lanham: Rowman and Littlefield, 2001.

Index